Remembering Constantine at the Milvian Bridge

Constantine's victory in 312 at the battle of the Milvian Bridge established his rule as the first Christian emperor. This book examines the creation and dissemination of the legends about that battle and its significance. Christian histories, panegyrics, and an honorific arch at Rome soon commemorated his victory, and the emperor himself contributed to the myth by describing his vision of a cross in the sky before the battle. Through meticulous research into the late Roman narratives and the medieval and Byzantine legends, this book moves beyond a strictly religious perspective by emphasizing the conflicts about the periphery of the Roman empire, the nature of emperorship, and the role of Rome as a capital city. Throughout late antiquity and the medieval period, memories of Constantine's victory served as a powerful paradigm for understanding rulership in a Christian society.

Raymond Van Dam is Professor in the Department of History at the University of Michigan. His most recent books are *Rome and Constantinople: Rewriting Roman History during Late Antiquity* (2010) and *The Roman Revolution of Constantine* (Cambridge, 2007).

REMEMBERING CONSTANTINE AT THE MILVIAN BRIDGE

RAYMOND VAN DAM

UNIVERSITY OF MICHIGAN

CAMBRIDGE
UNIVERSITY PRESS

CAMBRIDGE UNIVERSITY PRESS
Cambridge, New York, Melbourne, Madrid, Cape Town,
Singapore, São Paulo, Delhi, Tokyo, Mexico City

Cambridge University Press
32 Avenue of the Americas, New York, NY 10013-2473, USA

www.cambridge.org
Information on this title: www.cambridge.org/9781107096431

First published 2011

Printed in the United States of America

A catalog record for this publication is available from the British Library.

Library of Congress Cataloging in Publication data

Van Dam, Raymond.
Remembering Constantine at the Milvian Bridge / Raymond Van Dam.
    p.   cm.
Includes bibliographical references and index.
ISBN 978-1-107-09643-1 (hardback)
1. Saxa Rubra, Battle of, Italy, 312.   2. Constantine I, Emperor of Rome, d. 337.   3. Maxentius,
Marcus Aurelius Valerius, Emperor of Rome, d. 312.   I. Title.
DG315.V36   2011
937'.08 – dc22   2010048057

ISBN 978-1-107-09643-1 Hardback

For Anne

CONTENTS

�֍ �֍ ✖

PREFACE

A book about memories of Constantine is also an album of memories for me. Earlier versions of parts of chapters were presented as the Moritz Lecture at Kalamazoo College, a plenary lecture at the annual conference of the North American Patristics Society, and a lecture at Calvin College. The most rewarding moments of those occasions were always the complementary conversations: with Anne Haeckl, John Wickstrom, and their students at Kalamazoo College; with Paul Blowers, Virginia Burrus, Elizabeth Digeser, David Hunter, Adam Schor, and Dennis Trout at NAPS; and with Young Kim, Mark Williams, and their students at Calvin College.

As an undergraduate and a graduate student I was blessed to enjoy the company and learning of wonderful professors. As a professor I continue to learn from the undergraduates in my survey courses and the graduate students in my seminars, who have become my most invigorating teachers. After his victory at the Milvian Bridge, the emperor Constantine relished arguing with bishops at their councils. He would likewise have enjoyed talking about late antiquity with Alex Angelov, Jon Arnold, and Rob Chenault, and with Ian Mladjov, who designed and drew the splendid maps.

Stimulating comments from Mark Humphries and the anonymous Press readers were helpful, encouraging, and much appreciated. Publishing with Cambridge University Press is a high honor; working with Beatrice Rehl, the best editor in academic publishing, is a delightful pleasure.

ABBREVIATIONS

❋ ❋ ❋

ACW   Ancient Christian Writers (Westminster)
Budé   Collection des Universités de France publiée sous le
           patronage de l'Association Guillaume Budé (Paris)
CChr.   Corpus Christianorum (Turnhout)
CIL   *Corpus inscriptionum latinarum* (Berlin)
CSEL   Corpus scriptorum ecclesiasticorum latinorum (Vienna)
FC   Fathers of the Church (Washington, D.C.)
GCS   Die griechischen christlichen Schriftsteller der ersten
           Jahrhunderte (Berlin)
ILS   *Inscriptiones latinae selectae*, ed. H. Dessau (reprint: Berlin,
           1962)
LCL   Loeb Classical Library (Cambridge, Mass.)
MGH   Monumenta Germaniae historica (Berlin, Hannover, and
           Leipzig)
NPNF   A Select Library of Nicene and Post-Nicene Fathers of the
           Christian Church (reprint: Grand Rapids, Mich.)
OCT   Oxford Classical Texts (Oxford)
PG   *Patrologia graeca* (Paris)
PL   *Patrologia latina* (Paris)
PLRE   *The Prosopography of the Later Roman Empire* (Cambridge).
           Vol. 1, A.D. 260–395, ed. A. H. M. Jones, J. R. Martindale,
           and J. Morris (1971). Vol. 2, A.D. 395–527, ed. J. R.
           Martindale (1980). Vol. 3, A.D. 527–641, ed. J. R.
           Martindale (1992)
SChr.   Sources chrétiennes (Paris)
Teubner   Bibliotheca scriptorum graecorum et romanorum
           Teubneriana (Leipzig and Stuttgart)
TTH   Translated Texts for Historians (Liverpool)

TIMELINE

early 21st century: this book

mid-19th century: Jacob Burckhardt's *Die Zeit Constantins des Grossen* (Chap. 1)

late 18th century: Edward Gibbon's *The History of the Decline and Fall of the Roman Empire* (Chap. 1)

mid-17th century: Bernini's statue of Constantine in the Church of St. Peter (Chap. 2)

early 16th century: Raphael's frescoes in papal apartment (Chap. 2)

medieval period: Donation of Constantine (Chap. 2)

late 9th century: Byzantine *Life of Constantine* (Chap. 2)

late 8th or early 9th century: forgery of *Constitution of Constantine* (Chap. 2)

late 6th century: historian Evagrius (Chap. 3)

527–565: emperor Justinian

early 6th century: historian Zosimus (Chap. 3) and historian John Malalas (Chap. 2)

430s–440s: historians Socrates and Sozomen at Constantinople, and bishop Theodoret of Cyrrhus (Chap. 3)

425–455: emperor Valentinian III

early 5th century: historian Rufinus (Chap. 3, 7)

late 4th–early 5th century: Eunapius of Sardis (Chap. 3)

379–395: emperor Theodosius

361–363: emperor Julian

early 350s: revolts of Magnentius and Vetranio; letter of bishop Cyril of Jerusalem (Chap. 3)

after 337: Praxagoras' "History of Constantine the Great" (Chap. 6)

337–361: emperor Constantius II

CONSTANTINE AND EUSEBIUS OF CAESAREA (see next page)

303: visit of Diocletian and Maximian to Rome; Monument of Five Columns (Chap. 6–7, 9)

from 284, Tetrarchic emperors: Diocletian (284–305), Maximian (285–305, 306–310), Constantius I (293–306), Galerius (293–311), Severus (305–307), Maximinus (305–313), Licinius (308–324)

late 3rd century: construction of Aurelian Wall at Rome

161–180: emperor Marcus Aurelius

117–138: emperor Hadrian

98–117: emperor Trajan

31 B.C.–A.D. 14: emperor Augustus

late 3rd century B.C.: construction of Flaminian Way (Chap. 7) and Milvian Bridge (Chap. 10)

late 6th century B.C.: establishment of Republic; defense of Sublician Bridge by Horatius Cocles (Chap. 10)

CONSTANTINE	BOTH [OR NEITHER]	EUSEBIUS OF CAESAREA
		339(?) May 30: death
		after May 337: *Life of Constantine* (Chap. 4)
337 May 22: death		
	336 July 25: celebration at Constantinople of 30th anniversary of Constantine's accession, including banquet for bishops and oration by Eusebius	
330 May 11: dedication of Constantinople		
326 July–August: visit to Rome (Chap. 6)		
	325 July 25: celebration at Nicomedia of 20th anniversary of Constantine's accession, including banquet for bishops and oration by Eusebius	
	325 June–July: council of Nicaea (Chap. 4)	
324–325 winter or 325 spring: visit to Antioch (Chap. 4)		325 March(?): council of Antioch (Chap. 4)
		after September 324: "third edition" of *Ecclesiastical History* 8–10 (Chap. 5)
324 September 18: final victory over Licinius		
	[321 March: Nazarius' panegyric at Rome (Chap. 6)]	
316 October–317 February: conflict with Licinius		
		before autumn 316: "second edition" of *Ecclesiastical History* 8–9 + 10 (Chap. 5)
315 July 21–September 27: visit to Rome; dedication of arch of Constantine (Chap. 6)		315(?): oration at Tyre (Chap. 5, 7)
ca. 314/315: Lactantius' *Deaths of the Persecutors*, at Trier (Chap. 6)		
314 summer: council of Arles (Chap. 7)		
314–335: Silvester, bishop of Rome		
		late 313 or 314: "first edition" of *Ecclesiastical History* 8–9 (Chap. 5)
313 late summer (?): panegyric at Trier (?) (Chap. 6, 7)		
	313 summer: death of Maximinus	
Porfyrius the poet (Chap. 7)		after October 312: anonymous source about Maxentius and Constantine at Rome (Chap. 5, 7)
312 October 29–313 January: visit to Rome; Church of St. John Lateran (Chap. 7)		
312 October 28: battle at the Milvian Bridge; death of Maxentius (Chap. 1, 9)		
311–314: Miltiades, bishop of Rome		
310 summer: death of Maximian; Constantine's vision of Apollo (Chap. 1); panegyric at Trier (Chap. 7)		
306 October 28: Maxentius proclaimed emperor at Rome (Chap. 9)		
306 July 25: Constantine proclaimed emperor at York (Chap. 9)		

CONSTANTINE'S EMPIRE AFTER 312

York

BRITAIN

London

Nijmegen

Cologne • Deutz

Rouen

BELGICA

Rhine

GERMANIA

Reims Trier

Danube

GAUL

Autun

RAETIA

Lyon

ALPS

Bordeaux

Vienne

Milan

Aquileia

Rhone

Po

Arles

Ravenna

Sirmium

ITALY

DALMATIA

Zaragoza

Tiber

SPAIN Tarragona

CORSICA

Ostia Rome

SARDINIA

Naples

Nicopolis
Actium

Iol Caesarea

Carthage

SICILY

MAURETANIA

Cirta

NUMIDIA **AFRICA**

Syracuse

PROCONSULARIS

NORTH AFRICA

Mediterranean Sea

Lepcis Magna

Miles   0   100   200   300

Kilometers 0 100 200 300 400 500

Map by Ian Mladjov

FOREWORD: VISIONS OF CONSTANTINE

CHAPTER ONE

ISTORY REMEMBERS CONSTANTINE'S VICTORY AT THE battle of the Milvian Bridge. In 312 Constantine invaded Italy. Since his accession in 306 at York, the emperor had been residing primarily at Trier and campaigning on the Rhine frontier. He commanded a large army, most of it stationed in northern Gaul and Britain. For his invasion he took only a modest expeditionary force. In Italy the emperor Maxentius commanded another substantial army. To guard against an attack from the east by Licinius, yet another rival emperor who controlled the Balkans, Maxentius had moved troops to garrison Verona at the foot of the eastern Alps in northern Italy. Constantine and his army meanwhile crossed the western Alps at Susa and captured Turin and Milan as they advanced down the Po River valley. After a hard siege, they also captured Verona.[1]

Constantine and his army next marched south on the Flaminian Way through central Italy toward Rome. Although in initial skirmishes Maxentius' troops prevailed, he himself remained inside the

---

[1] For initial orientation to the increasingly voluminous modern bibliography on Constantine, see Van Dam (2007).

capital's massive wall. Constantine's soldiers then approached the Milvian Bridge, which carried the Flaminian Way across the Tiber River about two miles north of the wall. Maxentius' army crossed to meet them, and Maxentius himself joined his troops a bit later. At that point, or perhaps already earlier in anticipation of the invasion, his soldiers cut the permanent bridge and replaced it with a temporary pontoon bridge. But after they were routed in battle, their attempt to isolate the city turned into a bottleneck. While retreating across the makeshift bridge, Maxentius slipped and drowned in the Tiber. On the next day the victorious Constantine entered Rome.[2]

Maxentius had been emperor for exactly six years. He had deliberately chosen to fight on the anniversary of his accession, hoping to add a military victory to future celebrations. Instead, after his humiliating defeat he was dismissed as just another disgraced usurper. Constantine meanwhile went on to a long glorious reign, and after his death he was even proclaimed a divinity. In subsequent years people in Rome celebrated the outcome of the battle on back-to-back holidays as the replacement of a defiled emperor by a deified emperor. October 28, the day of the battle, would become a commemoration of "the expulsion of the tyrant," and October 29, a commemoration of "the arrival of the divine [Constantine]."[3]

THE VISION
In the late third and early fourth century battles between rival emperors and usurpers were common. The emperor Diocletian had instituted the Tetrarchy, a consortium of four concurrent emperors, and considerably increased the overall number of soldiers to deal with increased threats

[2] The details recorded about this battle often conflict: see Kuhoff (1991), for an excellent overview; Nixon and Rodgers (1994) 319n.103, for a concise survey; and Chapters 3–6. Classical Latin authors typically referred to this bridge as *Pons Mulvius*: see Chapter 10. Some authors of late antiquity referred to it as *Pons Milvius*: e.g., Polemius Silvius, *Laterculus* 4, s.v. "Pontes VIIII," ed. Mommsen (1892) 545. In modern Italian the bridge is the Ponte Milvio; hence Milvian Bridge in English.
[3] Celebrations: *Fasti Furii Filocali*, October 28, "evictio tyranni," October 29, "advent(us) divi," ed. Degrassi (1963) 257, with the commentary on p. 527 identifying *divus* as Constantine.

on the frontiers. Multiple emperors, large armies, and insecure frontiers were a recipe for repeated civil wars. Constantius defeated Carausius in northern Gaul and Allectus in Britain during the mid-290s. Diocletian defeated Domitius Domitianus and Aurelius Achilleus in Egypt during the later 290s. Maximian and his son Maxentius defeated Severus in Italy in 307. Maxentius defeated Domitius Alexander in North Africa in 309. Constantine defeated Maximian in southern Gaul in 310. Licinius defeated Maximinus in Thrace in 313. Constantine and Licinius fought an inconclusive war from 316 to 317. Constantine finally emerged as the sole emperor after defeating Licinius in Thrace and again in Bithynia in 324.[4]

In this litany of civil wars the battle of the Milvian Bridge was unremarkable. This was a conflict between sons of former emperors, who had both started out as usurpers and who had been hustling for legitimacy and recognition from other emperors ever since. Instead, already in antiquity the most celebrated feature of the battle would become Constantine's vision. The most important literary source for Constantine's reign is a biography written by Eusebius, bishop of Caesarea in Palestine. His *Life of Constantine* included accounts of the emperor's vision of a cross in the sky and his subsequent dream in which Jesus Christ explained the symbol of the cross. As a result, according to *Life*, the emperor had a military standard constructed in the shape of a cross and decorated with a "christogram," the chi-rho symbol formed from the first two Greek letters of *Christ*. This military standard led him and his troops into battle against Maxentius. After his victory Constantine openly demonstrated his support for Christianity.

Modern historians have often interpreted the vision of Constantine as a transformational moment in the historical trajectories of the Roman empire and early Christianity. This vision seemingly confirmed the emperor's personal conversion to Christianity. It accelerated the conversion of Roman society throughout the empire. It initiated an era in which politics and Christianity were intertwined, for good or ill, and

[4] See Bleckmann (2004), for the frequency of civil wars as a consequence of Tetrarchic emperorship, and Humphries (2008a) 85–87, for Constantine as a usurper.

in which Christianity became a key feature of Western Civilization, for good or ill. The battle of the Milvian Bridge, including Constantine's vision, has become a shorthand reference for momentous change in religion, society, and politics. In this perspective, "nothing counts for more than the year 312."[5]

Yet this revolutionary moment has also raised doubts among modern historians. Several aspects of the vision might seem suspect: the message, the messengers, and the medium. Some skeptics belittle the historical importance, either by claiming that pagan cults were already a spent force and the eventual success of Christianity did not require imperial patronage or by arguing that even after Constantine's reign, Christianity nevertheless long remained a small cult. Others shoot the messenger, whether Constantine or Eusebius. With regard to the emperor, one skeptical approach is to suggest that the vision was irrelevant because he was already a Christian, another that the vision was ineffective because he continued to patronize pagan cults afterward, and another that his advertisement of the vision was merely one more example of his relentless political opportunism. With regard to Eusebius, the typical skepticism concerns whether he misreported the vision, or even whether he fabricated the entire story. It is also possible to critique the medium by claiming that the appearance of the outline of a cross in the sky was merely a consequence of sunlight refracted through ice crystals high in the atmosphere to produce a solar halo. In this case hard natural science supposedly comes to the rescue of fuzzy social science. In modern historiography Constantine's vision is hence simultaneously an epochal moment and an irrelevant event, a deeply spiritual experience and a political gambit, a true divine revelation and a misunderstanding of a spectacular meteorological phenomenon.[6]

---

[5] Personal conversion: Odahl (2004) 106, "At this moment, Constantine converted." Quotation about nothing from MacMullen (1984) 102. Girardet (2006a), concludes his critical overview of the "Constantinian Revolution" by suggesting that the emperor's new religious policies had global consequences: "ohne die Konstantinische Wende . . . hätte die Weltgeschichte einen anderen Verlauf genommen" (p. 155).

[6] Opinions about Constantine's vision are legion. For the prior demise of pagan cults, see Burckhardt (1949) 215, proposing "the twilight of paganism" already before Constantine, as discussed by Leppin (2007); Demandt (2006), insists that Christianity would have expanded

This uneasiness is a symptom of a deeper interpretive anxiety: some-how it seems inappropriate to attribute such a momentous historical impact to a vision. A vision of a cross in the sky seems to encour-age evaluating the moment, and therefore all the subsequent historical consequences, as somehow spiritual and religious. A vision seems to reveal the intrusion of divine guidance into human affairs and to make Roman history appear to have been providential and even teleological all along. A vision complicates any attempt to offer a nonreligious eval-uation, a more secular or perhaps a symbolic analysis, of the moment or of Constantine's reign.

As a result, one antidote for this discomfort is to shift the emphasis from the vision to a proclamation. A few months after the battle, early in 313, Constantine and his fellow emperor Licinius agreed on a joint accord that extended "to Christians and to everyone else the free power to follow whatever religion each person prefers." Such a generous state-ment of religious toleration seems so much more acceptable as a catalyst for the transformation of the Roman world, comparable to other pro-gressive documents such as the Magna Carta and the Declaration of Independence. Such a proclamation of universal pluralism seems to have been a preview of modernity, that is, our enlightened modernity, certainly preferable to a religious vision and its distasteful potential for theocracy and totalitarianism.[7]

MEMORIES, TRADITIONS, NARRATIVES

For historical analysis the availability of so much information and so many opinions is both an opportunity and an obstacle. Constantine has

---

even if Maxentius or Licinius had defeated Constantine. For Constantine as a Christian before 312, see Elliott (1987); for his continued toleration for pagan cults, Clauss (2006); for his limited impact, MacMullen (2009) 111, suggesting that still in 400 less than 7 percent of the population of Rome was Christian: "the evidence from Rome is not at odds with the evidence from cities anywhere else in the empire." For the importance of politics, see Drake (2000) 191: "it is better to situate Constantine's religious development in the context of contemporary power politics and political thought." For the solar halo, see Jones (1972) 99–100 (first published in 1949).

[7] Joint letter (often, but misleadingly, referred to as the Edict of Milan) quoted in Eusebius, *HE* 10.5.1–14, and Lactantius, *De mortibus persecutorum* 48.2–12, with Drake (2000) 194: "a landmark in the evolution of Western thought."

been guaranteed a central place in all discussions of early Christianity and the later Roman empire in particular and of religion and politics in general, from the medieval period to today. As the first Christian emperor Constantine promptly became a standard of comparison for the evaluation of subsequent medieval and Byzantine Christian rulers. Even a pagan orator used Constantine as an exemplar. In 364 Themistius suggested that the emperor Jovian's policy of religious toleration had made him "fully Constantine." Constantine was also a constant topic of analysis for ancient historians, both Christian and pagan. Eusebius ended his *Ecclesiastical History* with Constantine's victory over Licinius; subsequent church historians started their narratives with the vision of the cross or the theological controversies leading up to the normative definition of orthodoxy at the council of Nicaea. Moments in Constantine's reign would become important pivot points of ecclesiastical history and Roman history.[8]

The historians and churchmen of late antiquity also discussed the battle at the Milvian Bridge soon afterward. Within a year or two Eusebius published an initial narrative of the battle in his *Ecclesiastical History*; decades later, after Constantine's death in 337, he repeated that earlier narrative in his *Life of Constantine* even as he added accounts of the vision and the dream. An orator at Trier in 313 and another at Rome in 321 described the invasion and the battle in their panegyrics. The Christian rhetorician Lactantius discussed the activities of both Constantine and Maxentius in an apologetic pamphlet composed within two or three years of the battle. One of the sculpted relief panels on the arch of Constantine at Rome, dedicated in 315, recalled the battle of the Milvian Bridge by depicting combat at the edge of a river. Within a decade the battle was uncommonly widely referenced and described.

Modern scholars often treat these ancient accounts of the battle as documentation, as evidence, as testimony, as "sources" whose information can be filtered and blended into a basic factual framework. Too often, however, this higher criticism has led to oddly speculative and irrelevant outcomes, in particular by disparaging the vision as "a purely

---

[8] Jovian: Themistius, *Orat.* 5.70d.

psychological event" or "the moment of psychological conviction." Freud would be proud. Even in our post-Freudian age a psychological crisis is apparently easier to comprehend than a religious conversion. In the process of evaluation, however, this higher criticism has frequently overlooked the implications of more fundamental questions about the transmission and recording of the accounts. What were the sources for these "sources"? None of these authors was a participant in the battle or even an eyewitness. Where did the authors acquire their information, and how did their personal agendas affect their narratives?[9]

The starting point is in fact Constantine's vision and dream. Constantine was the only participant in the battle whose personal recollections survive, and in *Life* Eusebius pointedly emphasized that he had heard the accounts of the vision and the dream from the emperor himself. The accounts in *Life* were Constantine's stories as subsequently recorded by Eusebius. The timing of the emperor's storytelling is hence vital. Eusebius never met Constantine until the summer of 325 at the council of Nicaea. One possibility is that Constantine first told the stories about his vision and his dream to Eusebius and other churchmen during a banquet celebrating the twentieth anniversary of his accession that he hosted immediately after the council. Another possibility is that he entertained Eusebius and other guests with his stories at Constantinople in 336 during a banquet celebrating the thirtieth anniversary of his accession. In the trajectory of accounts of the battle at the Milvian Bridge, Constantine was a comparatively late contributor. The emperor never told his stories about his vision and his dream, or at least these particular versions of his stories, until long after the battle.

By then Constantine had already heard and seen many other accounts of the battle. He had listened to the panegyric at Trier in 313; he had perhaps heard about the account of Lactantius, who was teaching his son at Trier; and he had attended the dedication of the arch at Rome in 315. Before he told his own stories, he may also have already heard Eusebius' account of his victory at Rome. In 325 Eusebius had "taken

---

[9] Quotation about event from MacMullen (1969) 78, about moment from Barnes (1981) 43. For conversion as a process rather than a moment, see Van Dam (2003c).

the stage at the council of God's ministers" to praise the "gloriously victorious" emperor with "hymns for the twentieth anniversary" of his reign. In 336 he had delivered "garlands of words in honor of the thirtieth anniversary." In this panegyric at Constantinople he had repeated some of his earlier observations on the emperor's actions at Rome after the battle. Perhaps Constantine responded to one of Eusebius' panegyrics by telling his own stories during the anniversary banquet afterward.[10]

Constantine's stories were hence reactions, not catalysts. All of the early accounts of the battle, whether a panegyric, an apologetic pamphlet, a historical narrative, or a decorated monument, had been typically written, orated, or sculpted independently of the emperor's opinions. These accounts had been aimed at Constantine, as recommendations of how he ought to behave as ruler, and were not derived from him. As a result, modern scholars should not string the accounts together as a synopsis of Constantine's views over the years. Instead, the relationship was reversed. These accounts were influences on Constantine. By the time the emperor told his stories, he had been thinking for years not just about the battle but also about subsequent accounts of the battle.[11]

This approach that emphasizes the influences on the stories of the battle, the vision, and the dream draws on important developments in historical and literary studies. One is the significance of individual and

---

[10] Stage, garlands: see Eusebius, *Vita Constantini* 1.1.1, with Chapter 7, for the repetition of passages from Eusebius' *Ecclesiastical History* in his panegyric of 336. Perhaps it is possible to speculate that Constantine had read sections of Eusebius' *History*. Constantine once complimented Eusebius for his "love of learning," and he had certainly read Eusebius' treatise about Easter: see his letter quoted in Eusebius, *Vita Constantini* 4.35.2.

[11] For the mix-up in perspective, note the questionable characterizations of Barnes (1981) 47: "The speech of 313 reveals how Constantine wished the war of 312 to be remembered"; Kuhoff (1991) 138, referring to the reliefs and inscription on the arch at Rome as "die Zeugnisse der konstantinischen Selbstdarstellung"; and Heck (1972) 165, concluding from the invocations to his *Institutes* "daß Lactanz hier constantinische Theologie und Geschichtsauffassung, überhaupt sein Selbstverständnis als christlichen Herrscher reproduziert." For discussions of how these authors and sculptors instead imagined Constantine, see Chapter 6.

community memories in promoting and transmitting versions of earlier events. The past did not generate fixed memories; instead, memories constructed a past. The memories became collective when communities accepted particular versions of what was memorable by designing monuments and celebrating commemorative festivals. Because those memorials and rituals might evoke a range of meanings, both at a specific moment and even more so over time, social memories were powerful political and religious forces. Such "reworking of the past is most pronounced in periods of dramatic social transformation." In the early empire a revived interest in classical Greek culture had allowed provincials in the East to negotiate the disruptive imposition of Roman rule. In the later empire the unexpected appearance of an emperor who openly supported Christianity was equally disruptive. Memories of Constantine's victory, as well as of his vision and dream, helped both Christians and non-Christians cope with the uncertainty and the dislocation. As an event, the battle of the Milvian Bridge was behind them in the past; as a memory, however, it was always with them in the present.[12]

A second development is the formation and transmission of oral traditions. The study of oral traditions is closely allied with memory studies but usually focuses more on the formatting of memories through oral transmission. Oral traditions tend to be episodic, self-contained stories that are typically told in no particular chronological sequence and that often include no specific chronological markers. Because such timeless stories blur the boundaries between narrators and characters, they are highly unstable from one telling to the next. Even oral accounts by eyewitnesses or participants are susceptible to the distortions of selectivity and emotional involvement. Because oral

[12] Quotation about reworking from Alcock (2001) 325, in an excellent discussion of Greek archaism under Roman rule. For the rewriting of the past as a consequence of the rise of Christianity, see Van Dam (2003b) 15–45, on the theological controversy over Eunomius, 82–97, on Christianity in Cappadocia; and Ferguson (2005) 121, on Rufinus' adherence to "the Eusebian pattern of writing history as an apologetic extension of loyalty to a theological tradition."

accounts are public performances, they furthermore respond directly to the needs and interests of the audiences. In turn, members of those audiences can tell their own versions of those accounts to bond with yet other communities of listeners. Some oral stories might, sooner or later, be included in narratives made permanent by writing or by sculpting. In contrast, by constantly responding to changes in communities, pure oral traditions remain flexible enough to be always relevant and contemporary. Constantine fought one battle at the Milvian Bridge; then he and others told many, many stories about it.[13]

A final development is an increased focus on the rhetorical aspects of written narratives. Narratology, the study of literary narratives, has absorbed many of the insights of structuralist analyses of the underlying grammar of myths, and literary scholars are by now accustomed to uncovering the self-conscious enigmas and meanings inherent in the plots of ancient narratives. In constructing their accounts, ancient authors elaborated or condensed similar episodes, they variously claimed to be accurately re-creating actions or merely representing them, they sometimes seemed to know more and sometimes less than their characters, and they perhaps even elided the past time of their characters and their own present time. For modern historians the lessons of narratology challenge the positivist notion of a direct correspondence between the plots of ancient narratives and the sequence of actual events, or between the literary characters and the historical actors. In the ancient narratives about the battle at the Milvian Bridge, Constantine hence performed as an ensemble of one. For his own stories he was both an actor in the past and the narrator in the present. For contemporary panegyrics and a monumental frieze he was both an actor in the past and a listener or a viewer in the present. But for later literary accounts he was only an actor in the past, on his way to

---

[13] For an overview of orality in Roman society, see Thomas (1992) 158–70. The study of oral culture in late antiquity has often highlighted preachers and preaching: see Van Dam (2003b) 101–50, for sermons in Cappadocia, and Maxwell (2006), for John Chrysostom at Antioch. Consideration of oral traditions is especially helpful for understanding stories about saints: see Van Dam (1982) 280–97, (1988).

becoming a historical character, sometimes even a fictional character, whose role could be fashioned to serve authors' objectives.[14]

Memory studies remind us of the ceaseless engagement between past and present that characterizes historical studies in general. Oral traditions and narratology remind us of the shaping of memories in both hearsay accounts and literary narratives. "Memory is . . . a bond tying us to the eternal present; history is a representation of the past." But because oral traditions were so adaptable and literary narratives so constructed, they also raise doubts about the success of any search for a definitive portrait of Constantine.[15]

THAT OTHER VISION

Constantine had a reputation for defining his actions in terms of religious visions and dreams. According to Eusebius, "God often honored him with a vision." Two in particular have become famous. One was a vision of Apollo in 310. After defeating the emperor Maximian in southern Gaul, Constantine stopped at a temple during his march back to the Rhine frontier. There he had a vision of Apollo, or more likely of himself as Apollo. According to a panegyric delivered soon afterward, "Constantine, you saw your Apollo, I believe, accompanied by Victory, offering you wreaths of laurel. . . . You recognized yourself in the appearance of him to whom the poets' divine verses have prophesied that rule over the entire world is owed." Even more consequential, of course, was the emperor's vision of the cross in the sky before the battle at the Milvian Bridge in 312, along with the corresponding dream of his conversation with Jesus Christ.[16]

---

[14] See Prince (1995), for an excellent critical overview of narratology; for the contrast in historical accounts between empathy, the perspective of characters, and hindsight, the perspective of narrators, see Pelling (2009) and Tsitsiou-Chelidoni (2009). Cameron (1997), emphasizes the "apologetic purpose" of Eusebius' *Life*: "If ever there was an author unsuited to a positivist critique, that author is Eusebius" (p. 155).

[15] Quotation from Nora (1989) 8.

[16] Often: Eusebius, *Vita Constantini* 1.47.3. Vision of Apollo: *Panegyrici latini* 6(7).21.4–5, with Woolf (2003), connecting this epiphany with cult images of Apollo in Gaul.

Constantine apparently thought that his visions were routine. Toward the end of his reign, Eusebius acknowledged the emperor's familiarity with visions and dreams. In an oration delivered at the imperial court in 335 he practically invited Constantine himself, "if there were time," to recount "thousands of visions of your Savior and thousands of appearances during sleep." He furthermore claimed that these visions had helped the emperor decide about battles, affairs of state, the army, and legislation.[17]

Eusebius did not know about the early vision of Apollo. In his later years Constantine was not about to share that vision of a pagan god with churchmen, and Eusebius would anyway have been unable to fit such a vision into his perspective on the emperor's career. By then both the emperor and the bishop had entered a future that they could not have anticipated. Early in his reign Constantine had faced repeated threats from rival emperors, while Eusebius had been primarily concerned about the ongoing persecution in the eastern provinces under Maximinus and Licinius. By the time they met, however, the civil wars and the bouts of persecution had ended. Now Constantine had reunified the empire, and Eusebius and other churchmen were his occasional honored guests. Now both emperor and bishop could think that past events had always been leading to this favorable outcome.[18]

Memories are wonderfully malleable and dynamic. Even though memories are ostensibly about the past, they serve as commentaries on the present and perhaps also as hopes for the future. Stories based on

---

[17] Thousands of visions: Eusebius, *De laudibus Constantini* 18.1.

[18] The vision of Apollo has been difficult to accommodate in modern narratives influenced by Eusebius. One unproductive reaction has been attempts to distinguish truth from fiction. Barnes (1981) 36, dismisses the orator's account as "words which betray the fiction." In response, Cameron (1983) 186, quotes Barnes' opinion to dismiss instead . . . the vision of the cross in 312. Harris (2005), concludes that Constantine invented all of his dreams "to improve his soldiers' morale" (p. 494). Another equally problematic reaction is conflation of the two visions. Weiss (2003), identifies only a single vision, the witnessing of a solar halo in 310, which he claims was reinterpreted through "an extension or a shift of its significance" (p. 252) before the battle at Rome in 312; Drake (2009), properly criticizes this emphasis on the halo phenomenon as reductionist.

memories are hence a powerful medium for defining a self, shaping an identity, and bounding a community. Like dreams and visions, memories too function as "a genuine epistemology," "a method that allows for an articulate construction of meaning." Recognizing the constructed nature of these stories and of the accounts derived from them has important implications for modern interpretations of both texts and contexts.[19]

One is that we should not conflate the ancient accounts into a single master narrative. These accounts were not designed to supplement or correct one another; each was instead a unique attempt at constructing meaning. Constantine is an intriguing topic for modern interpretation precisely because of the inherent disagreements among the ancient accounts. We might instinctively consider differences in details as indications of error or invention, but for ancient authors and audiences the small details guaranteed the realism, the authenticity, and therefore the relevance of the accounts. As a result, because the significance was in the details, the discrepancies help us understand the ancient authors' differing agendas. Our goal should be to appreciate and understand each account, not to cancel the divergences among conflicting reports by privileging one or another exclusive option.[20]

Another implication is that on the basis of ancient constructed narratives we cannot pretend to any certainty about the battle, the vision, or the dream. Constantine shaped his memories of the vision of the cross and the dream to correspond to his later circumstances. By then the emperor's memories were interpretations of the original events, stylized stories rather than forensic descriptions. When Eusebius subsequently recorded the emperor's stories in his *Life of Constantine*, he of course reinterpreted them, in part by linking them with a narrative of the battle that he had composed years earlier in his *Ecclesiastical History*. Constantine's interpretation of events in his memories and Eusebius' reinterpretation of those memories in *Life* ought to remind us that the

---

[19] Quotations from Miller (1994) 10.

[20] For a similar analysis of various accounts of the cult of the Forty Martyrs in Asia Minor, see Van Dam (2003b) 132–50.

other ancient accounts of the battle of the Milvian Bridge, whether early or late, were likewise interpretive depictions often derived from oral traditions and reflecting particular agendas. The primary objective of each account was not to reproduce events but to support a point of view. As a result, because the texts we read were already explanatory representations of the events, our goal should be to imagine new interpretive narratives that take advantage of recent advances in scholarship and fresh intellectual paradigms.[21]

Contemporaries quickly began using their accounts of Constantine's reign as a symbolic medium. "Constantine," that is, images of Constantine, became a battleground for articulating political ideas, social concerns, and even religious doctrines. Some of the early orators were scrambling to fit his activities, including the battle at the Milvian Bridge, into classical paradigms structured around pagan deities. At Rome the builders of the arch hoped that he might respect senatorial and Republican traditions. Lactantius, a Christian rhetorician, was amazed to observe an emperor who was open minded about religions. Eusebius, a bishop, was only too ready to claim Constantine as a Christian long before he heard about the emperor's vision of a cross. "Constantine" soon functioned as an epistemology itself, an idiom for evaluating classical culture, pagan cults, ancient traditions, religious tolerance, and the spread of Christianity.

In fact, not only did Constantine coexist with "Constantine" already during his reign, but the emperor himself likewise participated in promoting a mythology. Through the sharing of his memories Constantine too was complicit in the construction of *Constantin imaginaire*, a myth of himself.[22]

---

[21] The fixation on truth and facts is often irresistible: note Alföldi (1948) 17, on Constantine's vision: "Not that Eusebius' account has no kernel of historical fact"; and Lane Fox (1986) 616, on Lactantius and Eusebius: "They should be combined, not contrasted, and their common core of truth can be detached in each case from error." For criticism, see Pietri (1983) 63, on the documents quoted in Eusebius' *Life*: "Les querelles de l'histoire positiviste sont bien encombrantes. Lancées dès le siècle dernier, elles empoisonnent encore la recherche."

[22] *Constantin imaginaire* is the title of Kazhdan (1987), riffing on the title of Dagron (1984).

Imaginary History

In this book the battle of the Milvian Bridge, including the vision of the cross, provides a focal point for investigating some of the numerous representations of Constantine and his reign, both ancient and modern. One outcome is the realization that many modern opinions are not so modern after all. Constantine is a perennial favorite of scholarship on the ancient world, especially during the early decades of each century that mark another series of centennial anniversaries of events in his reign. But each revival of Constantinian studies also seems to require not just reviewing earlier scholarship but replicating it as well.

Edward Gibbon acknowledged that Constantine might well have been a sincere Christian. Gibbon dismissed the rigid criticism that the emperor "used the altars of the church as a convenient footstool to the throne of the empire." Instead, "the specious piety of Constantine, if at first it was only specious, might gradually... be matured into serious faith and fervent devotion." Gibbon published his chapters about Constantine in *The History of the Decline and Fall of the Roman Empire* in 1781. In contrast, Jacob Burckhardt argued that Constantine was motivated only by his "ambition and lust for power": "such a man is essentially unreligious." Burckhardt published the first edition of *Die Zeit Constantins des Grossen* ("The Age of Constantine the Great") in 1853. Eighteenth-century philosophical enlightenment, nineteenth-century rationalist humanism: the modern discussion of no other Roman emperor is so reverential toward the weight of its historiographical tradition, and repeated references to the same Past Masters imply an ongoing concern with their problems. To argue their issues is to concede that these are the important issues to argue. As a result, for more than two centuries scholarship has raised the same threadbare alternatives about Constantine: religion or politics, sincere piety or uninhibited ambition, genuine conversion to Christianity or not.[23]

---

[23] Quotations from Gibbon (1932) 1:650, and Burckhardt (1949) 292, with Schlange-Schöningen (2006), on the abiding influence of Burckhardt, and the overview of Lenski (2006), noting that the emperor's conversion is still "the 'Constantinian question' par excellence" (p. 3).

If interpretations of Constantine often seem to be caught in a continuous time loop, the resources available for studying his reign improved immeasurably during the twentieth century with the publication of new editions of Eusebius and other authors. Eduard Schwartz (d. 1940) devoted the first half of his scholarly career to editing Eusebius' *Ecclesiastical History*. Theodor Mommsen (d. 1903) ended his career with his edition of Rufinus' translation and continuation of Eusebius' *History*. Otto Seeck (d. 1921) reworked Mommsen's edition of the Theodosian Code to calculate a helpful itinerary of Constantine and subsequent emperors. With their additional magnificent commentaries and editions of Latin inscriptions and Latin chronicles, the proceedings of the ecumenical councils, and the letters of Symmachus and Libanius, Mommsen, Schwartz, and Seeck might well be considered the trinity of master builders who laid the bedrock foundations for the modern study of late antiquity. For Constantinian studies another significant contribution has been Friedhelm Winkelmann's outstanding edition of Eusebius' *Life of Constantine*. Our responsibility now is to combine these high standards of meticulous scholarship with the interpretive perspectives of the twenty-first century.[24]

Looking back at the battle of the Milvian Bridge requires excavating many layers of representations of Constantine. Medieval popes participated in arguments over politics and religion by claiming that long ago Constantine had donated secular power directly to the bishop of Rome; Byzantine scholars simply relocated Constantine's vision to Constantinople (Chapter 2). These divergent medieval and Byzantine interpretations followed the lead of the historians of late antiquity, who had already viewed the reign of Constantine as a significant turning point with positive or negative consequences (Chapter 3). Those historians in turn had often relied on the emperor's own later memories, as recorded by Eusebius in his *Life of Constantine* (Chapter 4).

---

[24] For the making of the joint edition of Eusebius' and Rufinus' *HE*, see the prefaces to the three volumes of Schwartz and Mommsen (1903–1909), with Winkelmann (2004), for a generous appreciation of Schwartz's philological achievement. For a critical pietistic reaction to Schwartz's and Seeck's opinions about Constantine, see Baynes (1931).

Years earlier Eusebius had already used another source as the basis for accounts of the battle in his *Ecclesiastical History* (Chapter 5). Other early reactions to the battle likewise each reflected a distinctive agenda. In the years immediately afterward, even though Constantine himself was soon involved in ecclesiastical disputes, many senators at Rome were not thinking about him as a Christian emperor (Chapters 6–7).

The chapters in this book evaluate many of the fundamental texts and monuments about Constantine and the battle. They also discuss some events, texts, and monuments that are often overlooked. The neglected events include subsequent battles linked with visions that predicted success (Chapter 3). The neglected texts include the letters between Constantine and the poet Porfyrius from soon after the battle (Chapter 7). The neglected monuments include a commemorative arch at Malborghetto and a second sculpted right hand almost identical to the right hand of a colossal statue of the emperor at Rome (Chapter 7). Accounts of later battles were interpretive commentaries on the original battle, while the letters and the monuments revealed reactions in the aftermath of the battle.

On the surface this book is about an emperor and a battle. At the same time it is an exercise in adapting the writing and reading of scholarly history to modern media and postmodern interests. Historical analysis is a journey, with many guides but no preordained outcome, no fixed route, and not even a certain destination. In this book the journey is decidedly retro, regressing from now to then, from our present to the Roman past. Such a backward narrative permits us to assess the usual issues from a different angle. Reversing the direction of the narrative allows us to investigate the uncertainties like detectives, to write about the suspense like novelists, and to respond to the surprises like moviegoers (Chapter 8). In the end, after examining the ancient accounts about Constantine it is possible to reconsider the implications of his victory in an alternative analysis that highlights Maxentius, the other emperor who fought at the battle (Chapter 9). Focusing on only one emperor has led to a misleading emphasis on individual psychology and religious conversion; focusing on both emperors stresses instead the competing perspectives on emperorship and empire at stake.

After the battle, memories of the Milvian Bridge were featured in the myth of Constantine; before the battle, however, an ancient myth about defending another bridge at Rome may have influenced Maxentius' tactics (Chapter 10). For both emperors then, subsequently for Christians and their critics, and now for us too, memories of a battle have offered a bridge for linking a mythologized past with present concerns and a coveted future.

THE AFTERLIFE OF
CONSTANTINE

CHAPTER TWO

H IS HORSE IS SPOOKED AND REARS BACK, BUT CONSTANTINE looks up. A radiance brightens his face, and he raises his hands in admiration. Perhaps he is praying.

We visualize the moment of Constantine's vision of the cross in the sky as just such a spectacular epiphany because we have already seen Bernini's luminous marble statue of the emperor astride his horse. During the mid-seventeenth century successive popes hired the gifted sculptor and artist Gian Lorenzo Bernini to complete the new Church of St. Peter in the Vatican. In addition to his grand decoration of the interior, Bernini designed semicircular colonnades to embrace the vast elliptical piazza in front of the church. He also added an oversize statue of Constantine, located in a niche at the juncture between the corridor from the north colonnade and the front portico of the church. In contrast to earlier equestrian statues that had commemorated the generic majesty of emperors, this statue portrayed a precise dramatic moment, "the very turning point of Constantine's life, an instant when the emperor was himself subjected to a superior power." As a result, the installation of the statue in this church seemed to link Constantine's vision with the defense of Christianity and, more specifically, with the enhancement of the power of the popes.[1]

Later historians and churchmen were keen to requisition and exploit the episode of Constantine's vision of the cross. Another episode with obvious potential for reassessment was his baptism. Shortly before his death in May 337, Constantine had been baptized by Eusebius, the bishop of Nicomedia. Even though his baptism was the final confirmation of the emperor's attachment to Christianity, for subsequent narratives some of the historical details were problematic. In particular, both the timing and the officiant were disconcerting. If Constantine had converted to Christianity as a consequence of his vision of the cross before the battle at the Milvian Bridge, then one concern would be the long interval of almost twenty-five years before his baptism on his deathbed. If Constantine had made his reputation as a supporter of the doctrines endorsed by the council of Nicaea in 325, then another concern would be the realization that Eusebius of Nicomedia had been a firm supporter of the heterodox priest Arius, whose doctrines the council had rejected. The responses to these apprehensions were predictable. One was to tighten the chronological nexus of vision, battle, and baptism. Another was to change the identity of the bishop who presided at the baptism. The catalysts for these new legends were frequently associated with medieval Rome and Byzantine Constantinople.[2]

MEDIEVAL POPES

Constantine's victory at the Milvian Bridge marked an important transition for the bishops of Rome. Later traditions claimed that many of

---

[1] Quotation from Lavin (2005) 159, in an excellent overview of Bernini's work at the Church of St. Peter. As counterpoint to this statue of Constantine, in the early eighteenth century the sculptor Agostino Cornacchini added a blandly conventional statue of Charlemagne at the south end of the front portico.

[2] Baptism: Eusebius, *Vita Constantini* 4.60.5–64.2, with Burgess (1999a) 219–32, (1999b), discussing variants in the tradition, and Bleckmann (2006) 28–30, on details in later accounts. Role of Eusebius of Nicomedia: Jerome, *Chronicon* s.a. 337, with Lieu (1998) 136–49, on embarrassment over Constantine's association with Arian churchmen, and Berger (2008), on dealing with problematic aspects of Constantine's reign during the Byzantine period.

the earlier bishops had been martyred during persecutions. In contrast, the tenures of Miltiades, serving in 312, and Silvester, serving in 315 and 326 during Constantine's return visits to Rome, marked the first time since the late second century that two consecutive bishops had not been martyred or exiled. The reigns of Constantine and subsequent Christian emperors considerably enhanced the fortunes of the bishops of Rome, and through gifts and offerings they became wealthier and more powerful. The episcopacy of Rome soon became a prize. In 366 the partisans of two rival deacons fought in the streets, "with a super-human passion," over succession to the see. By the end of the fourth century a distinguished senator who had served as prefect of Rome and had held several pagan priesthoods was thought to have quipped that he would convert to Christianity immediately if he could become bishop of Rome.[3]

The increasing power and pretensions of the papacy form a significant theme of medieval history. To bolster their authority popes and other churchmen eventually deployed a particularly expedient assertion about Constantine's generosity. In the mid-eleventh century pope Leo IX claimed that Constantine himself had once acknowledged his deference and subordination to the bishops of Rome by bestowing powers and possessions on bishop Silvester. According to Leo's treatise, Constantine had granted "power and firm jurisdiction to him [Silvester] and to his successor bishops." At the time, Leo was planning to cite this imperial gift of power in his quarrel with the patriarch of Constantinople over doctrinal and liturgical differences. This dispute culminated in the great schism between the Latin Catholic and Greek Orthodox churches; it also seems to have set a precedent for additional appeals to this so-called Donation of Constantine.

Subsequent popes increasingly resorted to the warranty of this Donation in their conflicts with secular rulers in western Europe, and eventually they even tried to expand their influence by claiming to have

---

[3] Conflict between Damasus and Ursinus: Ammianus Marcellinus, *Res gestae* 27.3.12, passion. Witticism of Vettius Agorius Praetextatus to bishop Damasus: Jerome, *Contra Ioannem Hierosolymitanum* 8 (*PL* 23.361C).

received actual imperial power from Constantine. In the mid-thirteenth century pope Gregory IX confronted the emperor Frederick II, king of Sicily, with the assertion that "Constantine had given to the bishop of Rome the imperial insignia and scepter, the city [of Rome] with its entire duchy, and also the empire with perpetual oversight." In the early fourteenth century pope Boniface VIII was still more explicit: "I am Caesar, I am the emperor." The later medieval bishops of Rome traced their authority over both secular rulers and rival patriarchs to the generosity of Constantine.[4]

In fact, this justification was an imaginative falsehood. The elaborate assertions about the Donation of Constantine were a fiction, developed from earlier legends and documents that were themselves forgeries. One was a legal document known as *Constitution of Constantine*. According to *Constitution*, Constantine had granted to Silvester and his successor bishops of Rome various privileges, including primacy over the other great sees of Antioch, Alexandria, Constantinople, and Jerusalem. Some of the gifts seemed to imply a transfer of imperial provinces and property in the West: "as a return gift to the most blessed bishop, our father Silvester, the universal pope, we decree that our palace . . . as well as the city of Rome and all the provinces, places, and cities of Italy and the western regions must be distributed to his power and the administration of his successor bishops. Through a firm imperial judgment [and] by means of this divine, sacred, and lawful constitution we allow everything to remain under the jurisdiction of the holy Roman church."[5]

A second false legend highlighted the role of bishop Silvester in baptizing Constantine. According to *Constitution*, Constantine was suffering from leprosy when he arrived at Rome. "Priests from the Capitolium," that is, the Temple of Jupiter on the Capitoline Hill,

---

[4] For this survey of medieval popes and the Donation of Constantine, see Fried (2007) 11–33, 42, citing the relevant texts.

[5] *Constitutum Constantini* 12, primacy, 17, Silvester, ed. Fuhrmann (1968) 82–83, 93–94, reprinted in Fried (2007) 134, 136. Fried (2007) 2, clearly distinguishes between the earlier forged document entitled *Constitutum* and its subsequent (mis)readings as the fictional Donation of Constantine. For an excellent survey of the reception of *Constitutum* in medieval juristic exegesis, see Miethke (2008), emphasizing the lack of historical criticism.

suggested that he could be healed by bathing in "the blood of innocent babies." After Constantine declined to initiate this massacre, St. Peter and St. Paul appeared in a dream and encouraged the emperor to find Silvester, bishop of Rome. Silvester first had Constantine perform penance at his "palace on the Lateran" and then presided over his immersion in a "pool of piety." During his baptism the emperor realized that he had been cleansed from his leprosy: "with my own eyes I saw a hand touching me from heaven." Afterward Constantine bestowed gifts and privileges on Silvester.[6]

At Rome this legend about Silvester's influential role was circulating in texts no later than the beginning of the sixth century, and as an oral tradition, already earlier. Originally it seems to have been a distinct story about the emperor's illness and baptism; then it was subverted for other purposes. In *Constitution* the legend that combined healing and baptism provided the rationale for the emperor's gifts to the bishop of Rome. *Constitution* in turn was itself a forgery, produced sometime during the Carolingian period. One possibility is that it was composed during the later eighth century at Rome, perhaps by "a Roman cleric working in the Lateran chancery." In that case *Constitution* would have bolstered the standing of the bishops of Rome in their negotiations with the Byzantine emperors at Constantinople or in their dealings with Pepin and Charlemagne, the new Carolingian kings of the Franks. Another possibility is that it was composed in the Frankish empire during the early 830s by monks at the directive of influential abbots. In that case it may have been an attempt not to expand papal authority but rather to counter the plans of the emperor Louis the Pious to divide the Frankish empire by attributing a unifying jurisdiction to the bishops of Rome. As a result, if composed at Rome during the late eighth century, *Constitution* was a papal forgery useful for clarifying the relationship between the bishops of Rome and Christian rulers such as Frankish kings and Byzantine emperors; if composed at the initiative of Frankish

---

[6] *Constitutum Constantini* 6, leprosy, priests, 7, Peter and Paul, 9, Silvester, 10, baptism, ed. Fuhrmann (1968) 67–80, reprinted in Fried (2007) 131–33, with Fowden (1994b) 153–68, and Pohlkamp (2007), for discussion of the legends of Silvester.

abbots in the early ninth century, it was a monastic forgery meant to mitigate the impact of territorial partitions in the Frankish empire.[7]

Later medieval popes nevertheless read *Constitution* as an authentic gift of secular power from Constantine, and hence as proof of their authority over secular rulers. Forgery had sired fiction: by then "the collective cultural memory had undermined the original meaning of the forgery." This transformation of the forged *Constitution* into the fictitious Donation of Constantine also influenced interpretations of the battle of the Milvian Bridge.[8]

In the early sixteenth century pope Leo X commissioned the famous artist Raphael to decorate a reception room in his Vatican apartment. For this room, now known as the Hall of Constantine, Raphael designed a series of magnificent frescoes displaying scenes from the emperor's career. After Raphael's death in 1520, Giulio Romano and Gianfrancesco Penni, two students in his workshop, modified and completed the paintings. Each of the four large frescoes depicted a consequential moment in Constantine's activities at Rome: the vision of the cross in the sky, the battle at the Milvian Bridge, the baptism of the emperor by the bishop of Rome, and the Donation. The setting for the scene of the Donation in the final fresco was the interior of the Church of St. Peter. In the center the emperor was shown kneeling before the pope to present a statuette of the goddess Roma. In the background a priest was carrying a document, representing perhaps the deed of the Donation, in a procession around the altar. According to this fresco,

---

[7] For the story about Silvester, see *Liber pontificalis* 34.2, 13, with Davis (2000) xlvi–xlvii, arguing that this collection of papal biographies was compiled in the 530s or early 540s; also pseudo-Zachariah of Mitylene, *Historia ecclesiastica* 1.1, tr. Hamilton and Brooks (1899) 16: "the story of his conversion by Silvester is also preserved in writing and in pictures at Rome." Quotation about eighth-century cleric from Brown (1995) 328; also Fuhrmann (1968) 7, dating the composition of *Constitution* between the mid-eighth and the mid-ninth century "wahrscheinlich unter Beteiligung römischer Kleriker," and Noble (1984) 135, "a consensus that the famous forgery was fabricated between the pontificates of Stephen II and Hadrian." For the role of Frankish abbots, see Fried (2007) 88–109: "The forged decree was compiled among the circle of Franks who, late in the reign of Louis the Pious, sought to reform the empire" (p. 111).

[8] Quotation about cultural memory from Fried (2007) 113.

with Constantine's consent St. Peter and his successor bishops at Rome were to become the guardians of imperial power and the old capital.[9]

By then critics of papal power, most notably the humanist scholar Lorenzo Valla in the mid-fifteenth century, had already exposed *Constitution* as a forgery. Seemingly in defiant response, the frescoes designed by Raphael and his students offered instead another partisan narrative that linked the vision and the battle with the emperor's subsequent baptism and Donation. Now the emperor's vision and his victory at the Milvian Bridge were combined with his baptism to buttress the papal account of the Donation of Constantine. In this papal narrative the battle marked only another moment in Constantine's progression as a loyal Christian ruler. As a result, the artistic grandeur of the frescoes has forcefully reinforced the notion that the proper interpretive contexts for the battle are Constantine's personal conversion and the expansion of Christianity.[10]

THE BATTLE AT CONSTANTINOPLE

In the medieval West some of the significant episodes in Constantine's reign, such as his vision, his victory at the Milvian Bridge, and his supposed baptism by bishop Silvester, would be appropriated into the fabricated narrative of the Donation as additional infrastructure for the edifice of papal power. These episodes were also familiar at medieval Constantinople. In the East, however, the same episodes would acquire a much different gloss.

Apparently quite quickly after its appearance at Rome, the legend about Silvester and his role in Constantine's baptism was in circulation at Constantinople. In the eastern capital, however, artists and historians soon detached the legend from its context at Rome to link it instead with distinctly eastern concerns.

---

[9] Fehl (1993), suggests that Raphael modeled the frescoes of the vision and the battle after some of the panels on the arch of Constantine.

[10] For the fresco depicting the Donation of Constantine as a response to critics, see Quednau (2006) 276: "wird hier das durch Lorenzo Valla und andere längst als falsch und unhaltbar Erwiesene letzmalig durch das Bild als historische Wahrheit beschworen."

One was theology. On the Church of St. Polyeuctus, constructed in the early sixth century, Constantine's baptism by Silvester was depicted in a mosaic over the main entrance. According to the epigram inscribed near the mosaic, "it is possible to see... judicious Constantine and how he fled from the idols... and found the light of the trinity by purifying his limbs in the water." The patron who financed the construction of this church was Anicia Juliana, a daughter of the earlier western emperor Anicius Olybrius. As a granddaughter of the emperor Valentinian III, Juliana was also quite probably a direct descendant of Constantine. Because Juliana was a strong supporter of the doctrines endorsed by the council of Chalcedon in 451, the display of this scene of her ancestor's baptism on her church was apparently meant to encourage a rapprochement between the churchmen of Constantinople and Rome over their mutual endorsement of Chalcedonian theology. In this mosaic the legend of Constantine's baptism was a reminder of unity between the two capitals, not an endorsement of one capital's bishop over the other.[11]

A second concern was protecting the eastern frontier. In the edition of his historical narrative completed in the early 530s, John Malalas claimed that Constantine had seen a cross in the sky while he was fighting barbarians somewhere in the West. After his subsequent victory he returned to Rome "carrying the symbol of the cross before himself." He then had bishop Silvester baptize him and his family: "the emperor Constantine became a Christian." Soon afterward the emperor scored another victory in a campaign against the Persians. According to John Malalas' account, Constantine's baptism had led to his success on the eastern frontier.[12]

---

[11] Epigram on church: *Anthologia graeca* 1.10.71–73, with *PLRE* 2:635–36, "Anicia Juliana 3," and Fowden (1994a) 277, on the mosaic: "it seems certain that Juliana... used the Silvester version." Milner (1994), suggests that mosaics depicting Constantine's conversion and his victory over Maxentius accompanied this mosaic depicting his baptism. Juliana's support for the council of Chalcedon: Theophanes, *Chronographia* a.m. 6005. For the ancestry of Valentinian III, see Chapter 3.

[12] John Malalas, *Chronographia* 13.2, vision, baptism, 3, Persians, with Jeffreys et al. (1986) xxiii, on the chronology of composition, and Scott (1994), on John Malalas' image of Constantine.

These two contemporary narratives, the mosaic on the Church of St. Polyeuctus and the history of John Malalas, hence retold the myth about Silvester and the baptism of Constantine but transformed it into a legend with an eastern perspective. In the process the narratives were also indistinct enough to imply that the emperor's baptism had taken place not in Rome, but in "New Rome," Constantinople.

Subsequent Byzantine authors began to write new biographies of Constantine, sometimes drawing on respectable earlier accounts but often inventing new episodes. In these Byzantine biographies the emperor's vision of a cross was a favorite topic.

One format was to retain the connection between the vision and the battle of the Milvian Bridge but to extend the paradigm to include other battles. One *Life* composed in the later ninth century (known now as the Guidi-Vita, named after its editor) drew on Eusebius' *Life* for its general description of Constantine's victory over Maxentius and other accounts for additional details, such as the name of the Milvian Bridge. The narrative in this Byzantine *Life* mentioned the vision, the emperor's subsequent conversation with Jesus Christ in a dream, and the construction of the military standard that led Constantine's army to victory at Rome. As Maxentius and his army had retreated in disarray, "the river and the bridge called 'Mulvian' were filled with horses and riders." In addition, this *Life* described a subsequent battle in similar terms. According to this account, after capturing Licinius, Constantine still had to defeat the "Byzantines," the people of Byzantium. He established his camp "in the spot where the forum is now located." There he saw an encouraging message written in the stars, "just as he had seen earlier [during the campaign] against the tyrant Maxentius." When he looked again, he saw a cross formed from the stars and a caption predicting his victory. "Immediately he recalled the symbol that had appeared to him before, when through the power of the venerated cross he defeated the wicked Maxentius at the Mulvian Bridge over the river of Rome." Constantine's victory at the city that would become Constantinople hence mimicked his victory at Rome, and his new nighttime vision of a cross in the stars imitated his earlier noontime vision of a cross in the sun. To commemorate his victories over Maxentius at Rome, the Byzantines, and the Scythians on the Danube frontier, Constantine later set up three large bronze crosses in Constantinople, which he called Jesus, Christ, and Victory. According to this *Life*, Constantine erected the cross known as Jesus in the forum where he had initially camped. Then everyone could see on display the cross that the emperor had witnessed in his vision.[13]

This Byzantine *Life* used the battle at the Milvian Bridge as a model and invented a similar vision for Constantine before another battle. Another format was to dispense with the battle at Rome and move Constantine's initial vision of the cross in the sky directly to Constantinople during a battle against "Byzantines." An account of the apocryphal martyrdom of Eusignius, for instance, even claimed to include a description of Constantine's battle by a participant. According to its narrative, when Eusignius faced martyrdom under the pagan emperor Julian in the mid-fourth century, he began to recall Constantine's earlier success. Back then when the Byzantines were on the verge of capturing Constantine's soldiers, including Eusignius, the emperor first read a message of encouragement written in the stars and then saw a cross formed from the stars. A description of monuments at Constantinople, composed in the early eighth century, likewise claimed priority for Constantine's vision at the new capital. According to this account, Constantine subsequently commemorated the exact spot of his initial dream by erecting a large gilded cross on top of a square porphyry column: "there he saw the shape of the cross first of all." In these accounts there was no comparison between Constantine's vision at Constantinople and his vision at Rome, or even any reference to Maxentius and the Milvian Bridge. Instead, a battle at Constantinople had replaced the battle at Rome as the site of his famous vision.[14]

[13] *Vita Constantini*, ed. Guidi (1907) 323, bridge, 335–36, camp, Maxentius, 649–50, three crosses; dated to circa 900 by Kazhdan (1987) 201, to mid- to late ninth century by Lieu and Montserrat (1996) 102, and Lieu (1998) 153.

[14] Participant: *Passio Eusignii* 9, ed. Devos (1982) 221–22; dated to the tenth century or earlier by Kazhdan (1987) 203–4. First of all: *Parastaseis syntomoi chronikai* 58; dated to the first half of the eighth century by Cameron and Herrin (1984) 17–29.

Memories of the battle at the Milvian Bridge hence might develop in different directions during the medieval period. In the West the battle was linked with the emperor's vision of the cross, his baptism at Rome, and his gift of possessions and power to the bishops of Rome to become another episode in the legend of the Donation of Constantine. In the medieval West the papacy appropriated memories of the battle as a prop to bolster its claims to sovereignty. In the Byzantine East stories about the emperor's vision of the cross and his baptism were likewise popular and occasionally included references to Maxentius and the battle at the Milvian Bridge. In the East, however, these stories typically appeared in support of theological harmony or military success. They also might be recounted to highlight the foundation of Constantinople. As a result, as Constantinople became more prominent, the Milvian Bridge at Rome was increasingly forgotten in Byzantine accounts of the vision and the battle.

RELICS

Relics of Constantine were thought to have survived at Constantinople throughout the Byzantine period. One was his cloak. In 379 Theodosius supposedly wore Constantine's cloak at his installation as a new emperor. According to a ninth-century account, Theodosius was so tall that "the cloaks of various emperors could not cover his shoulders.... Finally he was clothed with splendor in the purple [cloak] of the most revered emperor Constantine, which fit him perfectly." Another relic was the famous battle standard that Constantine had had constructed in the shape of a cross. In the mid-fifth century a historian claimed that this standard was "in the palace"; in the later ninth century it was supposedly still in storage, "safeguarded as a great gift in the imperial storerooms." The most famous relic was Constantine's body, interred in a mausoleum that became part of the complex surrounding the Church of the Holy Apostles. According to a description from the end of the twelfth century, some of the other emperors buried near this church had been forgotten: "their memories have been buried in their graves." In contrast, Constantine's "purple imperial tomb" was still a conspicuous reminder that he had been the first Christian emperor, the builder of Constantinople, and the successor to the twelve apostles as the "thirteenth herald of the orthodox faith."[15]

Over the centuries Constantine's reputation flourished. In fact, of all the Roman and Byzantine emperors Constantine has had the most influential afterlife. Throughout the medieval and Byzantine period he was invoked "as an imperial prototype, a point of reference, and a symbol of imperial legitimacy and identity." The emperor Marcian was acclaimed as "new Constantine" for presiding over a session of the council of Chalcedon; the Frankish king Clovis seemed to become "new Constantine" at the moment of his baptism in the early sixth century; the emperor Heraclius was hailed as "new Constantine" for his victory over the Persians and his restoration of the relic of the True Cross to Jerusalem in the early seventh century. Councils, baptisms, and military campaigns provided opportunities to associate the religious, personal, and political affairs of Christian leaders with memories of Constantine.[16]

Even in the twentieth century the specter of Constantine influenced contemporary Italian politics. The emperor Augustus was one model for Benito Mussolini's Fascist regime at Rome; Constantine was another. October 28, the day of Constantine's victory at the Milvian Bridge, marked the anniversary of another invasion of Rome from northern Italy, this time Mussolini's march on the capital in 1922. Mussolini's construction projects at Rome included a new bridge known as the Ponte XXVIII Ottobre (now known as the Ponte Flaminio), located just east of the Milvian Bridge. Already during Constantine's reign an orator at Rome had insisted that the emperor's memory was eternal:

---

[15] Cloak: George the Monk, *Chronicon* 9.8, ed. de Boor (1978) 2:563. Battle standard: Socrates, *HE* 1.2.7, and *Vita Constantini*, ed. Guidi (1907) 323. Nicholas Mesarites, *Ecphrasis* 39.3, tomb, herald, 40.10, memories, with Johnson (2009) 119–29, on Constantine's mausoleum, and Wortley (2009), on the fate of Constantine's body.

[16] Quotation about prototype from Magdalino (1994) 3. Marcian: Council of Chalcedon, *Actio* 6.5, 11, ed. Schwartz (1933–1935) 2:140, 155. Clovis: Gregory of Tours, *Historiae* 2.31, with Ewig (1956), for images of Constantine in the early medieval period. Dedications for Heraclius: Grégoire (1922) 21–22, nos. 79–80 (Smyrna), 40, no. 113 (Ephesus), with Whitby (1994) and Haldon (1994).

"the only way to forget Constantine is to destroy the human race." His flattery has been uncommonly clairvoyant.[17]

Those memories were sometimes less than flattering, because Constantine also became a topic for rumors and gossip. He was thought to have invented a hair lotion to compensate for his baldness. He acquired the nickname of "thick-necked," presumably based on his physical appearance but perhaps also as a compliment for his firmness or a critique of his arrogance. A member of his inner circle, one of his own prefects, was thought to have "taken a bite" in a sarcastic couplet that compared Constantine to the disgraced emperor Nero. A later scholar claimed to be embarrassed by all the "drivel" an earlier historian had written about the emperor. In these comments Constantine was treated like a modern-day celebrity, a vacuous embodiment of everything that was admirable or shameful about human experiences. But for keeping his reputation alive, the popular gossip and scandalous allure were as important as grand papal forgeries.[18]

Then there was the fascination with the cross and the christogram. If Constantine could see a cross in the sky, its profile might likewise appear to others almost anywhere. Like modern sightings of silhouettes of Jesus on rust spots, damp stains, and potato chips, in the early sixth century Constantine's cross was thought to have appeared to Christians at Zeugma on the eastern frontier, as if engraved in relief on the shell of a newly hatched goose egg. According to a later Byzantine biography, Constantine himself once recognized "the shape of the precious cross" in the smear on his handkerchief after wiping his bloody nose.[19]

---

[17] For Augustus' influence, see Cooley (2009) 51–55; Mussolini's bridge, Painter (2005) 21–26, 142. Forget: *Panegyrici latini* 4(10).12.4.

[18] Hair gel: Polemius Silvius, *Laterculus* V, "Breviarium temporum," ed. Mommsen (1892) 547. "Trachala" as nickname: *Epitome de Caesaribus* 41.16, with the evaluation of Bruun (1995). Distich of Ablabius: Sidonius, *Ep.* 5.8.2, with Chausson (2002a) 208–9, suggesting possible confusion between Constantine and his son Constantius, and Van Dam (2007) 369–72, for the dating of Ablabius' prefecture during the 330s. Drivel: Eunapius, *Fragmenta historica* 9 = *Suda* K.2285.

[19] Goose egg: *Chronicle of Pseudo-Joshua the Stylite* 68, tr. Trombley and Watt (2000) 86–87, with their note: "The Cross may in fact have been the Chi-Rho." Bloody nose: *Vita Constantini*, ed. Opitz (1934) 545.

Modern historians of antiquity tend to dismiss later traditions about people and events as unreliable, even frivolous legends. The afterlife of Constantine hence seems to have little to contribute to understanding his life and his reign. With regard to factual details, this assessment may be correct. But with regard to the process, the making of myths about Constantine and the battle at the Milvian Bridge had started not after his death but already during his lifetime.

ECCLESIASTICAL HISTORIES

CHAPTER THREE

O NLY TWO GENERATIONS AFTER HIS DEATH, MEMORIES OF the historical Constantine were fading. According to a preacher at Antioch in 387, "he founded many great cities and he conquered many barbarians. We remember none of them." Historians nevertheless continued to read and write about Constantine, either directly as an earlier emperor or indirectly as an influential paradigm. As a social process this shaping of the emperor's legacy was entangled with some of the important trends of late antiquity, including the impact of Constantinople as an eastern capital during the fourth century, the establishment of barbarian kingdoms in the West during the fifth century, and the attempted reconquest of the West by the eastern emperor Justinian during the sixth century.[1]

Thinking about Constantine provided a common denominator for Christians, who usually appreciated him, and for pagans, who typically resented him. For both Christians and pagans Constantine remained meaningful. They could share a discourse even as they disagreed about

---

[1] Remember: John Chrysostom, *Homiliae de statuis* 21.11 (*PG* 49.216), with Van Dam (2008), for the context.

his significance. As a result, both Christians and pagans, both supporters and critics, became, wittingly or not, ecclesiastical historians. Evaluating episodes from Constantine's reign offered an opportunity to assess the place of Christianity in late antique society.

PAGAN CRITICS

At the beginning of the sixth century Zosimus composed a history of the Roman empire that covered the period from the uncertainty over imperial succession in the early third century to the coming of the barbarians in the early fifth century. Constantine's reign was hence at the chronological midpoint of his narrative, and in his discussion of the emperor, Zosimus highlighted civil wars. The first was against Maxentius in 312. According to Zosimus' account, Constantine invaded Italy with an enormous army while Maxentius prepared to defend Rome with an army that was almost twice as large. His defense included the construction of a special breakaway timber bridge over the Tiber. Before the battle Maxentius consulted the Sibylline oracles while Constantine was heartened by seeing a propitious flock of owls on the city's wall. After his troops were overwhelmed, Maxentius was thrown into the river when the bridge collapsed. The residents of Rome rejoiced when they saw Maxentius' head on display at the end of a spear.[2]

The second important civil war was against Licinius in 324. Several years earlier Constantine and Licinius had fought an inconclusive campaign. This time Constantine built a huge fleet in the harbor of Athens while Licinius mobilized ships contributed by regions around the eastern Mediterranean. Constantine's army defeated Licinius' forces in Thrace, and his fleet besieged the fleeing emperor in Byzantium. At his last stand outside Chalcedon, Licinius was again defeated and then

---

[2] Zosimus, *Historia nova* 2.15.1, Constantine's army, 2, Maxentius' army, 3–4, bridge, 16.1, Sibylline oracles, 2, owls, 4, collapse of bridge, 17.1, head, with Paschoud (1979–2000) 1:vii–xx, on the date of composition: "après 498, dans le premier tiers du 6ᵉ s." (p. xvi). Zosimus claimed, quite implausibly, that Constantine invaded Italy with 90,000 soldiers and 8,000 cavalry, and that Maxentius commanded an army of 170,000 soldiers and 18,000 cavalry, including 80,000 Italians and 40,000 Carthaginians.

surrendered. Although initially Constantine exiled his rival to Thessalonica, he soon had him executed.[3]

Zosimus was appalled at Constantine's duplicity in his treatment of Licinius. "He trampled on his oath; this was customary for him." This dismay was simply one outburst of censure in a larger interpretive perspective that was strongly critical of the emperor. Zosimus provided an extensive list of Constantine's mistaken policies. The emperor had founded Constantinople as a counterweight to Rome, encouraged its growth in size "beyond what was required," and subsidized its residents with distributions of free grain. He had impoverished other cities by increasing taxes. He had upset traditional offices by appointing four prefects. He had weakened the frontiers by stationing the troops instead in cities. Zosimus then reinforced his critique of these misguided policies with an exposé of the emperor's character flaws. According to his account, after eliminating his final rival, Constantine had no more restraints on his behavior, and he no longer had to conceal his inherent wickedness.[4]

Perhaps Constantine's worst infraction was his failure to commemorate the Secular Games at Rome. In 17 B.C. the emperor Augustus had celebrated the Secular Games, which included sacrifices and prayers to various gods, in particular Jupiter and Apollo, as well as an extended series of public entertainments presented in Rome. This Augustan version of the games was advertised as a revival of a festival first instituted in the early Republic, and its organizers claimed to have consulted both old archives and an ancient Sibylline oracle. In fact, the festival became a celebration of the emperor himself and his dynasty, "an act of myth-making designed to provide a visually impressive . . . manifestation of the achievements and ideology of the Augustan regime." Subsequent emperors were hence also eager to associate their rule with this traditional festival. The games were supposed to be celebrated after each *saeculum*, an interval interpreted as 110 years. The

---

[3] Zosimus, *Historia nova* 2.22.1–2, fleets, 23.1, Byzantium, 28.2, execution.

[4] Zosimus, *Historia nova* 2.28.2, customary, 29.1, wickedness, 30.1, counterweight, 32.1, grain, 33.1–2, prefects, 34.2, troops, 35.1, beyond, 38, taxes and cities.

emperor Claudius nevertheless celebrated the games in 47, presumably to coincide with the eight hundredth anniversary of the foundation of Rome, and the emperor Domitian in 88, likewise out of sequence. The emperor Septimius Severus celebrated the games in 204, which did correspond to the cycle established by Augustus. These games were hence due to be celebrated again in 314.[5]

Zosimus included an extended digression on the origins of the Secular Games and the details of their festivities. On the first night the emperor himself was to join a college of priests to sacrifice three lambs at three altars on the bank of the Tiber. On the next day he and the priests were to preside at sacrifices on the Capitoline Hill. As confirmation Zosimus quoted at length the Sibylline oracle that had originally recommended the rituals. In his perspective, "as long as all these rituals were celebrated in accordance with custom, the empire of the Romans was protected and they continued to hold our entire world beneath their domination." Even emperors who rarely visited Rome acknowledged the significance of the games. During a joint visit with Diocletian in 303, Maximian apparently began planning to celebrate the games during the next year, clearly out of sequence but nevertheless a full century after the previous games. His plans were abandoned when the emperors decided to retire instead. A decade later Constantine and Licinius could have celebrated the games after the proper interval in 314. Because by then Constantine controlled Rome, he would have had the golden opportunity to preside. Instead, Zosimus lamented his neglect: "because this festival was not maintained, events necessarily evolved into the misfortune that now oppresses us."[6]

---

[5] Quotation from Beacham (2005) 162, with Beard, North, and Price (1998) 1:201–6, and Beacham (1999) 114–19, for excellent overviews of the games.

[6] Zosimus, *Historia nova* 2.5, rituals, 6, oracle, 7.1, empire, 2, Maximian's plans, misfortune. Zosimus attributed the origin of the Secular Games to Valesius, who was later renamed Manius Valerius Tarantinus and considered the founder of the Valerian family: see Zosimus, *Historia nova* 2.1–3. Diocletian, Maximian, and the other Tetrarchic emperors consistently included Valerius in their official names: see Van Dam (2007) 90–102. So perhaps Maximian was interested in celebrating the Secular Games as a reaffirmation of the "Valerian" dynasty of Tetrarchic emperors, in particular at Rome.

Zosimus likewise could find nothing positive to say about Constantine's promotion of Christianity. Even though he did attribute a moment of conversion to the emperor, his version was quite different from accounts that associated it with a vision and a battle. Instead, according to Zosimus, Constantine was simply trying to soothe his guilty conscience. Constantine had already promoted Crispus, his oldest son, as a Caesar, a junior emperor, and during the final campaign against Licinius, Crispus had commanded his father's fleet. Despite his achievements, Crispus was eventually suspected of an improper liaison with Fausta, his stepmother, and Constantine had ordered his son's execution in 326. But when Helena, Constantine's mother, became distraught at "the destruction of the young man," the emperor "remedied that evil deed with a greater evil deed" by ordering the death of Fausta. Now he was complicit in the murders of his son and his wife. Because of his remorse, he asked pagan priests for absolution for his misdeeds. When they demurred, he instead listened to "an Egyptian who had come to Rome from Spain." This adviser informed Constantine that "the teachings of Christians removed every sin and offered this promise, that unbelievers who converted were immediately established beyond their every sin." On the basis of this assurance of forgiveness the emperor accepted the new doctrine and abandoned the traditional rituals. In Zosimus' perspective, what Christians would see as Constantine's rejection of pagan cults had been in fact "the beginning of his impiety."[7]

Zosimus located Constantine's change of mind comparatively late in his reign, and he provided a nonreligious explanation. As a result, his account linking conversion with guilt effectively has become the prototype for modern interpretations that explain the emperor's religiosity in terms of hidden ulterior motives, whether political or personal.

Yet Zosimus was concerned less about the motivations for Constantine's decision and more about the outcome for the state. By failing

[7] Zosimus, *Historia nova* 2.29.2, Crispus and Fausta, 3, priests, Egyptian, 4, beginning. This "Egyptian" (in the sense of *charlatan*) is often identified as bishop Ossius of Corduba: see Paschoud (1979–2000) 1:237.

to celebrate the Secular Games, by discarding traditional religious ceremonies, the emperor had disrupted the continuity between the assistance of the gods in the past and their continued support for the empire in the future. Subsequent emperors had likewise failed to revive traditional rituals. In Zosimus' perspective it was precisely that neglect that had contributed to the current withered condition of the empire, which was now "under the control of barbarians, diminished, destroyed." Zosimus had seen the future. As a resident of the eastern empire he was presumably thinking about the misfortunes of the western provinces and Rome. His historical narrative had concluded most likely with the brief seizure of Rome by the Visigoths in 410, and by the time he started writing, there were no more Roman emperors in Italy. But in contrast to other pagan commentators, Zosimus did not associate the ransacking of Rome or the demise of imperial rule in the West directly with the rise of Christianity. Instead, he criticized Constantine simply as a negligent emperor. His disregard of pagan ceremonies had led to the weakening of the empire. By the time he died, Constantine had "destroyed the state."[8]

Zosimus derived much of the information for his narrative of the fourth century from Eunapius, a sophist who had taught at Sardis during the late fourth and early fifth century. Eunapius had composed an account of Roman history that covered the period from the later third century to the early fifth century. Subsequently his historical account was largely lost, excepting some quotations and allusions in later accounts. During the ninth century Photius, a bishop of Constantinople, was still able to read and compare the complete narratives of both historians. In his estimation, "Zosimus did not write a history, but instead rewrote the [history] of Eunapius." In addition to recycling the information, Zosimus no doubt inherited many of Eunapius' distinctly hostile opinions about Christianity. According to Photius, Eunapius' commitment to pagan cults had tarnished his historical

---

[8] Zosimus, *Historia nova* 1.58.4, barbarians, 2.39.1, the state, with Kaegi (1968) 117, "he [Zosimus] seldom discusses Christian beliefs," and Feeney (2007) 114, on Constantine's failure to celebrate the Secular Games as "a symbolic rupture of great power."

interpretations: "in every way and without restraint he abuses and disparages those [emperors] who ruled the empire with piety, in particular the great Constantine." Eunapius may well have told the story about the squalid circumstances of Constantine's conversion in a critique of the emperor or of Christianity.[9]

This story about Constantine's guilty conversion was certainly already in circulation soon after the emperor's death. The hero of Eunapius' historical narrative was the emperor Julian, a nephew of Constantine. During Julian's short reign in the early 360s Eunapius had been only a young teenager; decades later, however, he still remembered the intoxication of his strong feelings for the emperor. Julian had almost self-consciously fashioned himself as a reverse image of Constantine, right down to living out a religious trajectory that was the opposite of his uncle's. Julian too had "converted." Although he had grown up as a Christian, once he became sole emperor he openly endorsed pagan cults. At the moment of his unsanctioned acclamation as a senior emperor, his transformational experience had included a prayer for the assistance of Zeus and a vision of the guardian spirit of the Roman state. *Julien imaginaire*, the emperor who converted from Christianity through a vision, would become a mirror image of *Constantin imaginaire*, the emperor who converted to Christianity through a vision. To praise one was to criticize the other. Eunapius hence underlined his critique of Constantine by presenting his historical narrative as a "panegyric of Julian."[10]

Julian himself had already been a critic of Constantine. In contrast to his uncle, who had been a professional soldier, Julian was an intellectual. His academic pedigree dominated his thinking as an emperor. Even during his preparations for a campaign against the Persians he

<hr/>

[9] Photius, *Bibliotheca* 77, description of Eunapius' *History*, 98, Zosimus' reliance on Eunapius, with Blockley (1981–1983) 1:5–6, arguing that Eunapius ended his narrative with events of 404.

[10] Strong feelings: Eunapius, *Fragmenta historica* 15. Request: Julian, *Epistula ad Athenienses* 284C. Vision: Ammianus Marcellinus, *Res gestae* 20.5.10, with Athanassiadi (1981) 74–75, on "the moment of Julian's 'conversion' to a theocratical conception of kingship." Panegyric: Photius, *Bibliotheca* 77.

took time out to rank his imperial predecessors in a satirical treatise. Before Julian's imaginary tribunal each emperor was allowed to extol his own accomplishments. After Constantine's presentation, however, the pagan gods who were serving as the panel of judges dismissed his military victories as transient and ridiculed the emperor himself as a chef and a hairdresser. Constantine responded to his dismissal by taking refuge with Jesus, who was preaching about baptism and forgiveness. "Whoever is corrupt, stained with blood, abominable, and disgusting, let him come with no fear. For I will appear and immediately wash him clean with this water. And if he will again be guilty of the same [sins], I will allow him, as he pounds his chest and beats his head, to be clean." According to Julian's scenario, because Constantine had "his family's blood" on his hands, he had been "very happy" to hear Jesus' message of unconditional clemency.[II]

Julian furthermore had a personal grievance, because after Constantine's death, soldiers had murdered various imperial relatives, including one of Constantine's half brothers who was Julian's father. Subsequently Julian had held the emperor Constantius, one of Constantine's sons, responsible for this massacre. He also blamed his cousin Constantius for his own extended exile to an imperial estate in Cappadocia. In his intellectual isolation Julian had read the Christian books in the library of a local churchman, and he had studied the Bible, theological controversies, and early ecclesiastical history. Despite his preference for pagan cults, Julian most likely surpassed all the Christian emperors of the fourth century, including Constantine, in his knowledge of early Christianity. He would certainly have been familiar with more favorable evaluations of Constantine. In fact, because he had studied at least one

---

[II] Julian, *Caesares* 328D–329D, victories, 335A–B, chef and hairdresser, 336A–B, Jesus, blood. The orator Libanius, a supporter of Julian, likewise thought that Constantine had converted to Christianity after his victory over Licinius in 324, but only in order to plunder the pagan temples: see Libanius, *Orat.* 30.6, "After defeating the man [Licinius] who had previously encouraged the cities to flourish, he [Constantine] thought it was useful to classify some other [deity] as God, and he used the sacred resources on the construction of the city [Constantinople] that he was promoting," with Malosse (1997), discussing Libanius' veiled criticism of Constantine already during the 340s.

apologetic treatise by Eusebius of Caesarea, perhaps he had also read Eusebius' historical writings. Even for non-Christian authors Eusebius' writings would become a catalyst.[12]

In reaction to the flattering evaluations of churchmen like Eusebius, pagan critics such as Julian, Eunapius, and subsequently Zosimus preferred to construct Constantine as the object of their criticism. "Constantine" could be both a positive and a negative image. By maligning Constantine each critic found an outlet for articulating his own concerns, including a family feud, anger at the rise of Christianity, and despair over the welfare of the state. For pagans too "Constantine" served as a symbolic medium.

Christian Historians

Zosimus' account of Constantine provoked a strong reaction from a Christian historian. Evagrius, a legal adviser for bishop Gregory of Antioch during the later sixth century, was especially offended. Because his ecclesiastical history covered the period from the council of Ephesus in 431 to the reign of the emperor Maurice at the end of the sixth century, his narrative did not overlap Zosimus' historical narrative at all. But when discussing the abolition of a particular property tax by the emperor Anastasius in 498, Evagrius noted that Constantine had originally introduced the tax. Zosimus' account may have been his source for that information, but suddenly Zosimus himself became the object of Evagrius' scorn.[13]

Zosimus had claimed that Constantine's innovations, including his adoption of Christianity and his neglect of pagan cults, had led to a weakening of the Roman state. Evagrius pointedly disagreed: "on the contrary it has been made perfectly clear that the affairs of the Romans

[12] Books: Julian, *Ep.* 23, 38, with Van Dam (2002) 173–74, on Julian in Cappadocia. Apologetic treatise: Julian, *Contra Galilaeos* 222A, objecting to a claim of Eusebius, *Praeparatio evangelica* 11.5 (*PG* 21.852D), about the literary talents of Moses and David, with Van Dam (2007) 357–62, on Julian's familiarity with Christian theology.

[13] Abolition of the *chrysargyron*, also known as the *collatio lustralis*: Evagrius, *HE* 3.39; imposed by Constantine: Zosimus, *Historia nova* 2.38.2, with Whitby (2000) xxvi–xxvii, for the likelihood that Evagrius had read Zosimus' account.

have been enhanced with our faith." The best example was the contrast between Constantine and Julian. For Zosimus, Julian had been a hero; for Evagrius, he was the true culprit. Although the Christian emperor Constantine had "governed the Roman empire bravely and courageously with the assistance of our religion," the pagan emperor Julian had "dumped so many disasters on the state." Evagrius also rejected Zosimus' claim that Constantine had converted to Christianity to find forgiveness for his guilty conscience after the deaths of his wife and his son. His counterarguments were quotations from Eusebius' *History* implying that Constantine had been a Christian already upon becoming emperor. Evagrius' refutation here was in fact not reliable, because in his *History* Eusebius had most likely misunderstood Constantine's early reign. But Evagrius was certainly convinced enough to slander Zosimus as "a wicked and defiled demon": "you abominable and thoroughly accursed man!" From the perspective of a Christian historian like Evagrius, maligning Constantine was proof that Zosimus had been an irresponsible historian.[14]

At the beginning of his narrative Evagrius carefully located his narrative in the arc of accounts by earlier ecclesiastical historians. Among these predecessors, his canon of four historical evangelists included Eusebius, of course, as well as his historiographical heirs, Socrates, Sozomen, and Theodoret of Cyrrhus. The latter three historians had each continued Eusebius' *History* through the fourth century into the early fifth century. The starting point for each of their narratives had been the reign of Constantine.[15]

Socrates wrote at Constantinople during the later 430s. Although he intended his narrative to start in 324 at the end of Eusebius' *History*, he first included some background on "the way the emperor Constantine came to be a Christian." His narrative included the vision of the cross, the dream of Christ, the construction of the battle standard, and the victory over Maxentius "outside Rome near the so-called Mulvian

---

[14] Critique of Zosimus: Evagrius, *HE* 3.40–41, with Chapters 4–5, 7, for Eusebius' misinterpretations. Sozomen, *HE* 1.5, had already tried to refute the allegation that Constantine's conversion was a consequence of his guilt over Crispus' death: "it seems to me that these [accusations] were fabricated by people who wished to slander the religion of Christians."

[15] Sequence of historians: Evagrius, *HE* 1 preface, 5.24.

bridge." Excepting the detail about the name of the bridge, Socrates had extracted this information from Eusebius' *Life of Constantine*. Using *Life* as a source had nevertheless made him nervous. Socrates thought that Eusebius' *Life* had been too laudatory about the emperor and too partisan about theological controversies. In his estimation, "Eusebius wrote a biography of Constantine in which he offered a partial recollection of the events concerning [the heterodox priest] Arius. He was concerned more about his eulogies of the emperor and the grandiloquence of the words in his panegyric, as if in an encomium, than about an accurate narrative of events." Socrates hence conceded that after his victory at Rome "Constantine acted like a Christian," even as he distanced his account from Eusebius' perspective.[16]

Sozomen wrote his historical narrative a few years later and also at Constantinople. First he composed a separate account of Christian history "from the ascension of Christ into heaven to the elimination of Licinius." This treatise was presumably an epitome of Eusebius' *History*. Even though Sozomen started his own historical narrative in 324, he also included a flashback describing the events that had led Constantine to honor Christianity. The most important was "the sign of God that appeared to him." Sozomen elaborated by describing the vision of the cross, the dream, and the construction of the battle standard, and he explicitly attributed these stories to Eusebius. Then his narrative diverged from Eusebius' *Life*. Sozomen supplemented Eusebius' account by letting the churchmen whom Constantine consulted about his dream add comments about resurrection, salvation, and repentance. He also did not describe a battle against Maxentius. Instead, he claimed that the emperor "always had this symbol [the battle standard] carried in front of his troops." Sozomen too seemed reluctant to follow Eusebius' *Life* too closely.[17]

---

[16] Socrates, *HE* 1.1.2, biography, 4, came to be, 2.7, Mulvian bridge, 3.1, like a Christian, with Van Nuffelen (2004) 10–14, arguing that Socrates published his *History* in 439–440.

[17] Sozomen, *HE* 1.1.12, epitome, 3.1, sign of God, 2, attribution to Eusebius, 4–6, churchmen, 4.3, symbol, with Grillet (1983) 25–31, suggesting that Sozomen completed his *History* between 443 and 448, Leppin (1996) 279–81, in the later 440s, and Van Nuffelen (2004) 59–61, in the mid-440s.

In Syria bishop Theodoret of Cyrrhus wrote another historical nar-rative at the end of the 440s. He also decided to begin his narrative at the end of Eusebius' *History*. But unlike his contemporaries Socrates and Sozomen, Theodoret did not first look back at Constantine's early career. Instead, he plunged forward to describe the theological con-troversies that followed the elimination of the "evil tyrants Maxentius, Maximinus, and Licinius." In his narrative Theodoret quoted many letters about these disputes, including one by Eusebius in which he had tried to explain the harmony between his doctrines and Nicene theology. In his description of the council of Nicaea, Theodoret quoted extracts from "another treatise" by Eusebius, his *Life*. Despite these references, Theodoret seems to have known little about Eusebius and his writings.[18]

These Greek ecclesiastical historians presented their own narratives as continuations of Eusebius' *History*, and they extracted a few episodes from his *Life* in their accounts of Constantine's vision, dream, and victory at Rome and the council at Nicaea. Even though the later historians were suspicious of Eusebius' theology, none challenged his history. In contrast, in the West their older contemporary Rufinus did challenge both Eusebius' theology and his historical account of Constantine's victory at Rome.

Rufinus had lived in Egypt and Palestine before returning to his homeland of Italy. In 401 the bishop of Aquileia asked him to translate Eusebius' *Ecclesiastical History* into Latin. Rufinus' translation was more of a paraphrase than an exact rendition. With regard to the final books of Eusebius' *History* that discussed Constantine, Rufinus retained most of books 8 and 9 in his translation but omitted much of book 10, including, most conspicuously, a long sermon by Eusebius. He then combined "whatever history remained" from book 10 with his translation of book 9. Following the lead of Eusebius' *History*, Rufinus ended his translation

[18] Theodoret, *HE* 1.1.4, beginning and end, 2.1, tyrants, 12.1–18, Eusebius' letter, 13.1–4, another treatise (quoting Eusebius, *Vita Constantini* 3.13–14, 21.4–22.1); for the date of composition of Theodoret's *History*, see Parmentier and Scheidweiler (1954) XXVI, in late 449 and early 450, and Martin (2006) 29–37, before 448.

with Constantine's victory over Licinius in 324. But he then went on to add two new books as a sequel that covered the period "from the era of Constantine after the [ending of] persecution to the death of the Augustus Theodosius" in 395. Rufinus' translation both modified and extended Eusebius' *History*.[19]

Adaptation and elaboration were already apparent in Rufinus' version of Constantine's march on Rome. His account was notably different from Eusebius' account, which he was nominally translating. First, Rufinus added information that he may have based on reading Eusebius' *Life of Constantine*. In particular, he added a description of the emperor's dream. According to Rufinus, while advancing against Maxentius, Constantine often looked to the sky and prayed for divine assistance. "While sleeping he saw toward the east the symbol of a cross gleaming with a fiery glow in the sky." In Eusebius' *History* Constantine had prayed to God and Jesus Christ before his military campaign, but there had been no mention of a vision or a dream. In Eusebius' *Life* Constantine had witnessed the cross in a daytime vision. In his translation of Eusebius' *History* Rufinus had Constantine witness the cross during a nighttime dream.[20]

Second, Rufinus added details that were not in Eusebius' *Life*. Rufinus claimed that Constantine was already "a supporter of the Christian religion and a worshipper of the true God," although he had not yet accepted "the symbol of the Lord's suffering," that is, he had not yet been baptized with the sign of the cross. When the emperor witnessed the symbol of the cross in his dream, Rufinus added that he also saw angels standing nearby who reassured him with an acclamation: "Constantine, conquer in this." Although Eusebius had not mentioned angels, Rufinus may nevertheless have derived their chant from the slogan that Eusebius claimed had accompanied the vision of the cross in the sky. In fact, Rufinus even quoted the angels' acclamation in Greek. These were some of the few Greek words he included in his translation, and the only ones not copied or directly derived from Eusebius' *History*.

[19] Rufinus, *HE* prologus.
[20] Prayer: Eusebius, *HE* 9.9.2.

Constantine subsequently constructed a military standard in the shape of a cross. He also, according to Rufinus, carried "in his right hand a symbol of the cross fabricated from gold." Another detail Rufinus added was a reference to the Milvian Bridge by name.

Rufinus hence amended Eusebius' account in *History* by mentioning a dream of the cross, which he may have derived from Eusebius' *Life*, and by adding the new details about the emperor's prior commitment to Christianity, the angels, and the gold cross. The most notable of his additions, however, was his interpretive perspective. Rufinus explicitly compared Constantine's dream with the legendary vision of the apostle Paul. Long ago Paul too, then still known as Saul, had seen a light from heaven. "Constantine was invited to the faith from heaven. To me he is no less significant than the man to whom likewise a voice was heard from heaven: 'Saul, Saul, why are you persecuting me? I am Jesus of Nazareth.' [The difference is that] this [emperor] was invited not while he was still a persecutor, but while he was already a follower." After his vision Paul had been baptized. Likewise after his dream Constantine had "marked the symbol of the cross on his forehead." In Eusebius' *Life* Constantine was not baptized until the very end of his life. In Rufinus' account, however, there was no mention at all of a baptism by churchmen. Instead, immediately after witnessing the cross Constantine had essentially baptized himself.

Rufinus' narrative of the subsequent battle was not just anticlimactic; there was nothing to describe. According to Rufinus, as Constantine approached Rome he was distressed that he could "restore liberty to the fatherland" only through bloodshed. He was rescued from his anguish by his rival. As a stratagem Maxentius had ordered the construction of a bridge floating on boats. But when he rode out to confront Constantine, he "forgot his own artifice," capsized the boats, and drowned. "Maxentius preserved the pure right hand of the religious emperor from civil bloodshed." In Rufinus' version Maxentius drowned before engaging Constantine, and there was no battle at the Milvian Bridge.[21]

---

[21] Rufinus, *HE* 9.9.1–8, with Chapter 7, for discussion of Rufinus' subsequent account of Constantine at Rome, and Christensen (1989) 292–97, downplaying Rufinus' familiarity

Rufinus' comparison of Constantine with the apostle Paul has been very influential, although in a roundabout way. Modern historians are understandably hesitant about most of his additional details, including, of course, the disappearance of the battle. Simultaneously, however, it is often difficult for modern scholars to avoid interpreting the emperor's experience as another unexpected conversion, similar to Paul's moment of redemption. Rufinus' interpretive gloss has reinforced the perception of Constantine's career as a sequence of abrupt moments, including military victories, rather than as an extended process of hesitations and ambiguities. The most abrupt of those moments seems to have been a sudden conversion to Christianity.

NEW VISIONS

Toward the end of his reign Constantine arranged to be succeeded by his three surviving sons and a nephew. After his death in May 337, however, troops at Constantinople killed the nephew as well as other imperial relatives. During the massacre the soldiers supposedly shouted that they "would support no other ruler than the sons of Constantine." This initial bloodshed seems to have set the tone for subsequent interactions among the brothers. Constantine II was killed in 340 after invading Constans' territory, and Constantius and Constans almost went to war over a disagreement about Christian doctrines. Not only were the brothers eliminating, or trying to eliminate, each other, but their confrontations also jeopardized the long-term continuation of the Constantinian dynasty. Constantine had had (at least) six children, including four sons, and he had slowly purged his imperial rivals in a series of civil wars to ensure the succession of his sons. In contrast, none of the three sons who had succeeded him had yet produced

---

with Eusebius' *Life*: "Rufinus relied on a tradition here, which despite all the similarities, is independent of Eusebius's account in *Vita Constantini*" (p. 295n.301). Heim (2001), suggests that Rufinus modified the account of the battle at the Milvian Bridge to recall the recent victory of the emperor Honorius' troops over the Visigoths in north Italy on Easter 402: "Dieu sera aux côtés des Romains.... La bataille de Pollentia... répète celle du Pont Milvius" (p. 209); note also Humphries (2008b) 157, suggesting that Rufinus' translation would reassure "the nervous Christians of Aquileia."

any children, and now they were engaging in their own fraternal conflicts.[22]

In January 350 army officers and imperial magistrates hailed the commander Magnentius as emperor in Gaul. After his agents assassinated Constans, Magnentius crossed into northern Italy and marched toward the Balkan frontier. At about the same time, troops in Pannonia had proclaimed their commander Vetranio as emperor. Magnentius settled for control of the western empire, including Italy and North Africa, while Vetranio controlled the Balkans. Constantius was meanwhile still campaigning against the Persians on the eastern frontier.

Both usurpers were career soldiers from simple provincial backgrounds. Because his father had been from Brittany and his mother had been a Frank, Magnentius was belittled as a "barbarian." Vetranio hailed from Moesia, along the middle Danube, and was supposedly illiterate. To compensate for these deficiencies in their pedigrees, both tried to associate themselves with the legacy of Constantine. Vetranio had been proclaimed as Caesar, a junior emperor, by Constantina, one of Constantine's daughters. Magnentius suggested that Constantius marry his daughter, and after his offer to marry Constantina was rebuffed, he instead married Justina, who was probably a young great-granddaughter of Constantine.[23]

These emperors also publicized their new Constantinian affiliation through the images and legends on their coins. One issue of coins from Trier and Lyon depicted Magnentius holding a military standard

---

[22] Support: Zosimus, *Historia nova* 2.40.3.

[23] Magnentius' pedigree: Aurelius Victor, *De Caesaribus* 41.25, *Epitome de Caesaribus* 42.7, Zosimus, *Historia nova* 2.54.1, with Paschoud (1979–2000) 1:281 and Drinkwater (2000) 138–45. Vetranio's pedigree: Aurelius Victor, *De Caesaribus* 41.26. Constantina and Vetranio: Philostorgius, *HE* 3.22. According to Peter the Patrician, *Frag.* 16, ed. Müller (1851) 190, Magnentius offered to marry "Constantia, a sister of Constantius." *PLRE* 1:222, "Constantina 2," identifies this "Constantia" as Constantina; Chausson (2007) 115–16, suggests that she was Constantius' half sister, another daughter of Constantine with an anonymous wife whom he married after Fausta's death in 326. Justina's pedigree: see *PLRE* 1:488–89, "Iustina," and Van Dam (2007) 121n.49, for various conjectures, with Woods (2004), arguing that she was a granddaughter of Crispus, and Chausson (2007) 105, 161, suggesting that she was a granddaughter of Julius Constantius, a half brother of Constantine.

decorated with the chi-rho symbol, the christogram formed from the first two Greek letters of *Christ*. Another issue from various mints in Gaul depicted the christogram flanked by an alpha and an omega, the first and last letters of the Greek alphabet, referring to God's eternal power. Coins minted in Pannonia meanwhile depicted Vetranio likewise holding a military standard decorated with the christogram, surrounded by an encouraging legend: "in this sign you will be a victor." By quoting the caption that had reportedly accompanied the sighting of the cross in the sky, this legend was a "manifest evocation of the vision of Constantine." Through their associations with relatives of Constantine, through their use of symbols that recalled the original vision of the cross, both Magnentius and Vetranio hoped to edge into the limelight of the Constantinian dynasty.[24]

These two usurping emperors had hence revived memories of Constantine in a similar fashion, in particular by deploying symbols associated with Constantine's vision of the cross, but for opposite reasons. Magnentius hoped to claim the heritage of Constantine to pose as a viable alternative to Constantius, while Vetranio publicized his devotion to Constantine as a sign of his loyalty to Constantius. Vetranio apparently saw himself as a temporary emperor holding the Balkans on behalf of Constantius. Once Constantius arrived in late 350, Vetranio was divested of his emperorship and his troops joined Constantius' army.[25]

Constantius' campaign against Magnentius quickly became a conflict over "the succession of Constantine." In 337 Constantius may well have initiated the massacre of his relatives to safeguard the succession of himself and his brothers as the only true heirs to Constantine's imperial

---

[24] Magnentius' coins depicting military standard: Kent (1981) 157, nos. 259–60, Trier, 184–85, nos. 108–14, Lyon; depicting christogram: Kent (1981) 123, nos. 34–45, Amiens, 163–65, nos. 318–27, 332–37, Trier, 217, nos. 188–202, Arles. Vetranio's coins from Siscia: Kent (1981) 369, nos. 272, 275, 278–79, 282–83, 286–88, 291–92, "hoc signo victor eris." Quotation about evocation from Kent (1981) 344.

[25] Note Dearn (2003), suggesting that Vetranio's coinage demonstrated his loyalty to Constantius, not opposition, and Drinkwater (2000) 156: "Vetranio was an unwilling emperor and in his heart remained loyal to Constantius."

rule. Now, as the last surviving son of Constantine, he had to protect his imperial authority against a usurper who was trying to marry into the Constantinian dynasty. This time the dispute over dynastic succession also included dueling claims to the legacy of Constantine's vision of the cross.[26]

In 351 one eastern bishop made his preference very clear by using the symbolism of the cross to link father and son. In a letter to Constantius, bishop Cyril of Jerusalem first declared that "the wood of salvation belonging to the cross" had been found at Jerusalem during the reign of Constantine, "your father." This assertion about the early discovery of the True Cross on which Jesus Christ had been crucified was dubious at best. But it allowed Cyril to note that an apparition even more impressive than the relic of the True Cross had recently appeared in the sky: "the trophy of victory over death belonging to our Lord and Savior Jesus Christ, the only-begotten Son of God – I am speaking of the blessed cross – appeared at Jerusalem, twinkling with sparkles of light." This luminous cross of light, which "surpassed the beams of the sun," had stretched across the sky from Golgotha to the Mount of Olives and lasted for many hours. Motivated by fear or by joy, everyone went to the church and praised Jesus Christ. Cyril then wrote to reassure Constantius that he would have God as his ally if he displayed "the trophy of the cross, . . . the sign revealed in the sky." The appearance of this new apparition of a cross in the sky was proof that God would reward the emperor's support for the churches and his defense of the Roman empire. In his letter Cyril had connected Constantius to his father's vision of a cross in the sky while also hinting that the son would surpass his father's achievements.[27]

---

[26] Succession: Themistius, *Orat.* 3.43a. For the probability that Constantius had been the mastermind behind the massacre of Constantine's half brothers and some of their sons in 337, see Burgess (2008), with Van Dam (2007) 104–11, 118, 302, on the competing factions.

[27] Cyril of Jerusalem, *Epistula ad Constantium* 3.12, wood, father, 15–16, trophy, 4.18, Golgotha, 20, sun, 21, church, 5.32, trophy, 8.44, churches, empire, with Drijvers (1992) 79–145, on legends about the role of Helena in the discovery of the True Cross, (2004) 162, suggesting that Cyril knew about Constantine's vision, (2009) 241–45, suggesting that Cyril was promoting his own see of Jerusalem. Cyril's letter was apparently soon available in general circulation:

Constantius' army fought a series of battles against Magnentius. During this extended campaign Constantius explicitly promoted the memory of his father. To remind soldiers of their loyalty to the imperial dynasty, his supporters denigrated Magnentius as a "murderer of a son of Constantine" while praising Constantius as the last "son of Constantine." The images and legends on his coins also strengthened his dynastic claim. On coins minted at Sirmium and Thessalonica the images depicted Constantius holding a military standard decorated with a christogram, while the legends again explicitly recalled Constantine's vision: "in this sign you will be a victor." In this case the legends on the coins offered a correct forecast, as Constantius' forces won a final victory over Magnentius in the summer of 353. His victory seemed to confirm that only a true Constantinian emperor could claim the military assistance of Constantine's cross.[28]

Constantius was the last son of Constantine to reign as emperor. There were no grandsons. Subsequent emperors nevertheless continued to emphasize their connections to the Constantinian dynasty. The emperor Gallus, Constantine's nephew, married Constantina, Constantine's daughter, and Julian, another nephew, married Helena, another daughter. As his second wife the emperor Valentinian I married Justina, probably Constantine's great-granddaughter and by then the widow of Magnentius; his son Gratian married Constantia, the daughter of Constantius. Thereafter Gratian claimed Constantius as "my ancestor." As his second wife the emperor Theodosius married Galla, the sister of the emperor Valentinian II. Through their mother, Justina, both Galla and Valentinian II were probably direct descendants of Constantine. As a

---

see Socrates, *HE* 2.28.22, Sozomen, *HE* 4.5, Philostorgius, *HE* 3.26. One tradition even claimed that Constantius and his army, although far away in Pannonia, had witnessed the same vision of the heavenly cross before a battle: see *Chronicon Paschale* s.a. 351.

[28] Zosimus, *Historia nova* 2.44.3, murderer, 46.3, son. Constantius' coins: Kent (1981) 386, nos. 23–24, Sirmium, 416, no. 146, Thessalonica. In their polemic over theological controversies, however, churchmen typically contrasted Constantius and his father: see Humphries (1997) 464, "To establish Constantine as a paradigmatic Christian emperor it was necessary . . . to condemn his son's ecclesiastical policies as excessive and aggressive."

result of this marriage the new Theodosian dynasty of emperors could also claim to be the heirs of Constantine.[29]

In 394 Theodosius marched west from Constantinople to confront the usurper Eugenius at the Frigidus River (modern Vipava River) near Aquileia. Eugenius went into battle with the support of Jupiter and Hercules. He set up statues of Jupiter in the foothills of the Alps overlooking the battlefield, and an image of Hercules led his army. Theodosius meanwhile prayed with clerics at the shrines of martyrs and apostles. He also claimed to have had a vision of two men riding white horses, who identified themselves as the evangelist John and the apostle Philip and offered their assistance. Theodosius' army then went into battle led by a military standard in the shape of a cross. A river, a vision, a cross used as a battle standard: Theodosius' victory was represented as a reminder of Constantine's victory at the Milvian Bridge. Theodosius was another new Constantine. Less than a year later in a funeral oration for the emperor a bishop described a family reunion in heaven. Among those imagined to have gathered to welcome Theodosius was his putative "ancestor" Constantine.[30]

Eusebius' account linking a vision with Constantine's victory at the Milvian Bridge had established a model for subsequent historiography. New Constantines needed new visions, and it is not surprising that later historians attributed visions to Christian rulers before important battles. In fact, in the twelfth century one Byzantine historian allocated even more visions to Constantine himself by claiming that during his campaign against Licinius the emperor had witnessed a horseman carrying an image of the cross, two young men slicing through enemy units, and a light that illuminated his camp during the night. Like the story about the original vision of the cross in the sky, this tendency to multiply visions may have derived from Constantine himself. According

---

[29] My ancestor: Ausonius, *Gratiarum actio* 11, with Lenski (2002) 97–104, on connections with Constantine in the family of Valentinian I. For the possibility that Theodosius was himself descended from a collateral branch of the Constantinian dynasty, see Chausson (2002a) 220–23, (2002b) 150.

[30] Statues of Jupiter: Augustine, *De civitate Dei* 5.26. Praying with clerics: Rufinus, *HE* 11.33. Theodoret, *HE* 5.24.4, image of Hercules, cross, 5–6, vision. Reunion: Ambrose, *De obitu Theodosii* 40.

to Eusebius' *Life of Constantine*, before battles the emperor would pray to "his God" until "he certainly received a vision." Then, "as if motivated by divine inspiration," he would mobilize his army. In his subsequent campaigns Constantine too seems to have hoped to revitalize the memory of his own original vision of the cross by praying for new visions.[31]

MEMORIES OF CONSTANTINE

The emperor Valentinian III was a grandson of Theodosius and Galla. If Justina, Galla's mother, had in fact been a granddaughter of Constantine's son Crispus, then Valentinian was the final direct descendant of Constantine to reign as an emperor. Because dynastic inheritance was a sign of an emperor's success, Constantine would have been gratified at this extended succession, which lasted almost 150 years. But he would most likely also have been surprised by this particular successor. Unlike his distant ancestor, Valentinian was neither a frontier emperor nor an emperor at Constantinople. Instead, he was proclaimed a senior emperor at Rome in 425, and he spent most of his reign at Ravenna before relocating to Rome. In 455 he was murdered in the Campus Martius.

One of Valentinian's daughters married a son of Geiseric, the king of the Vandals in North Africa who had once briefly captured Rome. Their son, Hilderic, later himself became king of the Vandals. Valentinian's other daughter married Anicius Olybrius, a distinguished senator at Rome who became emperor briefly in 472. In the later fifth century the contrasting marriages of Constantine's direct descendants, as the wives of an emperor at Rome and a Vandal king, succinctly symbolized the great transformation of the West from the illustrious past of a Roman empire to a future defined by barbarian successor states.[32]

The final fates of the daughters of Valentinian also neatly reflected the significant changes in the political and religious dynamics of the East

---

[31] Divine inspiration: Eusebius, *Vita Constantini* 2.12.2. Additional visions: Zonaras, *Annales* 13.1.27–28, with Bleckmann (1992), speculating about Zonaras' source.

[32] Eudocia, wife of Huneric, and Placidia, wife of Olybrius: see *PLRE* 2:407–8, "Eudocia 1," 572–73, "Hunericus," 796–98, "Anicius Olybrius 6," 887, "Placidia 1."

initiated long ago by Constantine. One daughter died in Constantinople, Constantine's new capital for the eastern empire, and the other in Jerusalem, the focus of the Christian Holy Land once patronized by Constantine. Thereafter the Constantinian pedigree seems to have lost its luster, and subsequent descendants were traced back instead to their more recent imperial ancestors. After the emperor Justinian's army defeated the Vandals in North Africa, the children and grandchildren of Hilderic arrived at Constantinople in 534 as captives. Justinian decided to support these "descendants of the emperor Valentinian" with financial subsidies. One of Olybrius' remote descendants may have been married to a relative of Theodora, Justinian's wife, at Constantinople. Even though some later Byzantine emperors claimed to be direct descendants of Constantine, by the mid-sixth century Constantine's legacy was no longer the glow of a ruling imperial dynasty but only memories of a distant emperor.[33]

Other casualties of the fading of Constantine's legacy were Eusebius' *Ecclesiastical History* and *Life of Constantine*. During the fourth century the emperor Julian had read some of Eusebius' writings, and Eusebius' account in *Life* of Constantine's vision of a cross had established a rhetorical paradigm for thinking about other Christian emperors and their battles. During the fifth century Rufinus had translated Eusebius' *History*, and Socrates, Sozomen, and Theodoret had written historical narratives that continued Eusebius' *History* and referenced his *Life*. In the later sixth century Evagrius had cited Eusebius' *History*. Historians long continued to use Eusebius' writings for information about early Christian history and the reign of Constantine.

At the same time they had deep misgivings about his theology. Even as Evagrius complimented Eusebius for his ability to persuade readers about Christianity, he noted that his predecessor's arguments had been "very mistaken." Despite the condemnation of the doctrines of the

---

[33] Justinian's subsidies: Procopius, *Bella* 4.9.13. For Georgius Areobindus, husband of Proba, who was a great-great-great-granddaughter of Olybrius, see Nicephorus, *Chronographikon*, ed. Dindorf (1829) 756 (correcting the reference in *PLRE* 3:515, "Georgius 7"). For the claims that the emperors Basil I, Constantine VII, and Nicephorus Phocas were descendants of Constantine, see Brubaker (1994) and Markopoulos (1994).

priest Arius at the council of Nicaea, Eusebius was remembered as "the most outspoken advocate of Arius' impiety." Eusebius' theology threatened to undermine his history.[34]

One reaction was editing for religious correctness. In his translation of Eusebius' *History* Rufinus revised or omitted passages that were theologically suspect. As a result, in the Latin West Eusebius' *History* was known mostly through the sanitized version of Rufinus.[35]

Another reaction, especially in the Greek East, was uncertainty and extreme caution. In one manuscript of Eusebius' *History* a copyist added a note of warning. "Reader, watch out lest you are seduced by the heretical outlook of this author. Although this present book is especially useful regarding history, . . . he is an Arian and he reveals his thinking in disguise." Germanus, bishop of Constantinople in the early eighth century, was unsure where to store Eusebius' books in the patriarchal library. Even as he admired Eusebius' historical narrative for its "recollection of ancient affairs," he was uneasy about his doctrines. "Because of these opinions expressed by him [Eusebius], even the staff in our library never shelve his books with the works of the orthodox writers; instead they put them separately in their own crate next to the stack of those among the most prominent of the heretical books." As a result, Photius, bishop of Constantinople during the later ninth century, worried that heterodox doctrines had tainted Eusebius' *Life of Constantine*: "the narrative is neither accurate nor clear."[36]

These later readers had concluded that Eusebius' *History* and *Life* offered valuable history but suspect theology. The most important sources for the reign of Constantine seemed to be radioactive.

[34] Mistaken: Evagrius, *HE* 1 praef. Advocate: Jerome, *Ep.* 84.2.
[35] For discussion of Rufinus' Nicene translation, see Van Dam (2007) 329–34, and Humphries (2008b).
[36] Marginal note: ed. Schwartz and Mommsen (1903–1909) 1:4. Recollection, library: Germanus of Constantinople, *De haeresibus et synodis* 14 (*PG* 98.52D–53A), with Lemerle (1971) 96n.81, discussing the patriarchal library, and Winkelmann (1991) xxviii: "rechnete die VC mehr zu den Schriften, die die falschen theologischen Ansichten des Euseb enthalten." Narrative: Photius, *Bibliotheca* 127, with Amerise (2008), distinguishing Photius' praise of Constantine from his criticism of Eusebius.

CONSTANTINE'S
MEMORIES

CHAPTER FOUR

USEBIUS' ACCOUNT OF CONSTANTINE'S VISION AND DREAM
before the battle at Rome in his *Life of Constantine* has become
powerfully influential among modern historians. This is an
odd outcome. Eusebius was still revising *Life* when he died
probably in May 339, more than twenty-five years after the battle. He
was the bishop at Caesarea in Palestine and hence knew little about
events at distant Rome. He clearly used his biography of the emperor
to promote a theological and political agenda about the nature of
Christian emperorship. Late, far away, sectarian, partisan: Eusebius'
account should have struggled to become so significant.

The redeeming factor of his account of the vision and the dream was
the declaration that he had heard it directly from Constantine himself.
Eusebius claimed to be recording the memories of an eyewitness. But
this assertion in turn raises another set of issues about the dating of
Constantine's recollections, the reliability of Eusebius' reporting, and
the accuracy of his interpretations. Constantine recalled his memories
for Eusebius and other bishops for specific reasons at a specific moment
long after the battle; Eusebius subsequently recorded the emperor's
stories for different reasons at a different moment after the emperor's

death. The account of the emperor's vision and dream in *Life* hence represented three distinct layers of particular circumstances: Eusebius' remembrance of Constantine's memories of events from long ago.

EUSEBIUS AND CONSTANTINE

Eusebius of Caesarea first met Constantine at the council of Nicaea, which the emperor convened during June and July 325. Subsequently he noted that he had in fact once glimpsed Constantine decades earlier as Diocletian and the imperial entourage passed through Palestine on their way to Egypt during the winter of 301–302. Back then Constantine had been a junior military officer serving at the court of an emperor who was soon to initiate persecutions against the Christians. In 305 Constantine had joined his father, Constantius, in northern Gaul. Thereafter his primary concern had been military campaigns along the northern frontiers, first in Britain with his father, then, after he had become an emperor himself in July 306, along the Rhine. Constantine had also fought against two rival emperors, Maxentius in Italy and Licinius in the Balkans and northern Asia Minor. During the first two decades of his reign Constantine had been, above all, a soldier and a military commander in the West.[1]

    After his final victory over Licinius in September 324, Constantine had reunified the empire under his sole rule. Soon afterward he sent letters to the provincials in the eastern regions that were then under his rule. In a general letter to the people in the East he described himself as a "servant of God" and claimed that his military success had been a direct outcome of his humility. Although other emperors who had failed to acknowledge "the power of the great God" had suffered defeats, "the divinity" had approved Constantine himself as the agent of their overthrow. With that endorsement the emperor had marched from "the ocean next to the British people" all the way to "the regions in the East" to enhance "the most blessed faith." In another letter to the eastern provincials he explained that although previous emperors, that is, his rivals, had been "very harsh" as persecutors, he had instead

[1] Eusebius, *Vita Constantini* 1.19.1, earlier sighting.

championed "the greatest God." "Everywhere I displayed your seal as I led a victorious army."[2]

In these letters Constantine represented himself as a patron of Christianity and a successful military commander. But with regard to both concerns, his religious beliefs and his wars, he did not mention any specific battles or particular turning points. Instead, he recalled his preference for Christianity and his previous military campaigns in a longer, unbroken trajectory of predictable success. Even though he looked back as far as his campaigns in Britain, he did not note any particular episode of discontinuity. In fact, because in one letter he went back even earlier by recounting a story he had heard when he was "still a boy" at Diocletian's court, he seemed to want to lengthen even farther the uninterrupted arc of his life and the continuity of his religious beliefs. Despite the interlude of almost twenty years in western provinces, from his last service in the East under Diocletian until his return in 324, there had been no moment of disjunction or of a sudden conversion.[3]

Constantine also introduced himself to the bishops in the East in a circular letter that instructed them to attend to the repairs of their churches or the construction of new churches. The bishops now had the emperor's permission to request supplies from the provincial governors or the department of the prefect. One of the bishops who received a copy of the letter was Eusebius of Caesarea. Eusebius was ecstatic, and when he included a copy of the letter in his *Life of Constantine*, he carefully noted that it had been "the first letter addressed to me by name." Almost fifteen years later Eusebius seemed to want to leave the impression that already in late 324 he had been known personally to the emperor.[4]

If indeed Constantine had already heard of Eusebius, it would most likely have been in the context of disputes over theology. When Eusebius

---

[2] Eusebius, *Vita Constantini* 2.24.2, great God, 28.1, divinity, 28.2, British people, faith, 29.1, East, 29.3, servant of God, 49.1, very harsh, 55.1, God, army.

[3] Eusebius, *Vita Constantini* 2.51.1, still a boy.

[4] Eusebius, *Vita Constantini* 2.45.2, first letter.

received the emperor's letter, he was preparing to defend his doctrines yet again. During the winter of 324–325, or perhaps in the spring, Constantine traveled across Asia Minor twice, to and from Antioch. During his visit he may have attended a council at Antioch in early spring of 325. Eusebius was certainly present. This council formulated a doctrinal creed that opposed the teachings of Arius, a priest from Egypt. All but three of the bishops in attendance accepted the creed. Eusebius was one of the dissenters.[5]

The council of Nicaea was Eusebius' next opportunity to defend himself and his doctrines, and he arrived prepared to make his case. First he presented his own creed to the members of the council, and then he solicited the emperor's support. According to his own account, the council did not object, and Constantine was enthusiastic: "he was the first to admit that this creed included the most correct statements." Nor did the emperor stop with an endorsement. "He confessed that he thought the same, and he urged everyone there to agree and subscribe to these doctrines." Although Constantine did suggest that *homoousios*, "of the same essence," should be included as the appropriate adjective to characterize Jesus Christ in his relationship with God the Father, Eusebius could now argue that this vital term was a logical extension of his own theology. After discussing these issues "in the presence of the emperor himself, who was most beloved of God," everyone agreed with the new terminology, including Eusebius. Through the emperor's intervention he too could now accept the Nicene creed. Constantine first met Eusebius in the process of embracing him in the fold of Nicene orthodoxy.[6]

After the council of Nicaea, Constantine and Eusebius met again occasionally. Consistently it was the bishop who went to the emperor. Eusebius was among the bishops who attended the banquet, most likely

---

[5] Council of Antioch: Urkunde 18. For the uncertainty about the dating of Constantine's trip, see Van Dam (2007) 150n.1.

[6] Eusebius' letter to his congregation at Caesarea: Urkunde 22.7, the first, *homoousios*, 14, presence, quoted in Athanasius, *De decretis Nicaenae synodi* 33.7, 14, and Socrates, *HE* 1.8.41, 52.

at Nicomedia, that the emperor hosted immediately after the council to celebrate the beginning of the twentieth year of his reign in July 325. He probably attended a council that Constantine convened at Nicomedia in December 327 to decide on the readmission of the heterodox priest Arius and some of his supporters. In late 335 he was one of the envoys sent to the court by the bishops who had been meeting in a council at Tyre. At Constantinople he and the other bishops in the delegation accused their detested rival Athanasius, bishop of Alexandria, of meddling with the grain supply from Egypt. In November Constantine sent Athanasius into exile in Gaul. Eusebius, however, was honored to deliver a panegyric about the Church of the Holy Sepulcher, which had only recently been dedicated in Jerusalem. He delivered his oration in the palace at Constantinople before a large crowd. The emperor stood with the other listeners, and repeatedly declined Eusebius' suggestions that he sit and rest on the imperial throne: "it is pious to listen to divine matters while standing." Instead, he offered a careful critique of Eusebius' argument and "asserted the truth of his theological doctrines." After this oration Eusebius noted that "I went home and resumed my customary activities." In the next year he was back in the eastern capital to attend another council convened by Constantine. After this council he stayed to help celebrate the thirtieth anniversary of the emperor's reign in July by delivering another panegyric in the palace, and he attended another banquet hosted by the emperor. He may also have remained in Constantinople into the spring of 337 to collect information for the biography of the emperor that he was already planning to write. During these visits to the capital Eusebius either witnessed or heard about aspects of the emperor's personal piety, including his regimen of intense prayers in the palace.[7]

Eusebius also received more letters from Constantine. In one sent during the later 320s the emperor mentioned his intention to construct

---

[7] Participation in embassy of 335: Athanasius, *Apologia contra Arianos* 87.1. Eusebius, *Vita Constantini* 4.22.1, prayers, 33, oration at Constantinople on Church of the Holy Sepulcher, 46, banquet in 336. For the possibility that Eusebius remained in Constantinople until the spring of 337, see Drake (1988).

a new church commemorating the appearance of the Savior and two angels to the patriarch Abraham at the site of Mamre, south of Jerusalem. Eusebius implied that the emperor had sent this letter directly to him alone: "he sent these reasonable instructions to me, the writer of this history." In fact, Constantine had addressed the letter "to Macarius and the other bishops of Palestine." In this case Eusebius was downplaying a slight. Even though he was the metropolitan bishop of the province, he was being overshadowed by Macarius, a subordinate bishop whose prestige was increasing along with the growing reputation of his see of Jerusalem. At about the same time Eusebius sent a letter to Constantine declining an invitation to become bishop of Antioch. Constantine replied in a letter flattering Eusebius for his respect for the traditions of church order. Later in his reign the emperor wrote once to thank Eusebius for a copy of his treatise about Easter, and again to request him to have his scribes prepare fifty copies of the Bible for the churches in the capital. Despite Eusebius' occasional hints at an intimate friendship, this was a strictly professional relationship between the emperor and a provincial bishop, limited to infrequent meetings and intermittent letters.[8]

CONSTANTINE'S STORIES

At the council of Nicaea and during subsequent years Constantine began to spend more time talking and corresponding with eastern churchmen, including Eusebius of Caesarea. He still, of course, continued to lead military campaigns in the Balkans and even again on the Rhine frontier, and at the end of his life he was planning a major campaign against the Persian empire. But with churchmen he discussed primarily ecclesiastical and, sometimes, civil affairs, as well as theology. The anniversary banquet of 325 had become the model for balancing military and ecclesiastical concerns. At that banquet soldiers and bodyguards, "with the blades of their swords drawn," had ringed the

---

[8] Eusebius, *Vita Constantini* 3.51.2, instructions, 52, letter to Macarius, 61, Constantine's letter about Antioch, mentioning that "I have read with much pleasure the letter that your intelligence has composed," 4.35, letter about treatise, 36, letter about Bibles.

entrances to the imperial palace. But the bishops, "the men of God," had proceeded inside, where they had reclined on couches with the emperor. Likewise in the empire, having now eliminated his rivals, Constantine could restrict his military campaigns to the outer frontiers and chat about religious concerns with civilian bishops in the inner provinces.[9]

Yet military affairs nevertheless came up in his conversations with bishops. In his oration delivered in 335 Eusebius even encouraged the emperor to tell "us about the conspicuous assistance in battles from God, your champion and protector, and about the destruction of enemies and traitors." At some point Constantine did describe his military campaigns, including his victories over both Maxentius and Licinius, for Eusebius and other bishops. The earliest Eusebius could have heard the emperor's memories was in 325, most likely not during the council of Nicaea, when he and the other participants were arguing over theology, but perhaps during a more informal conversation at the subsequent anniversary banquet. He and the other bishops might also have listened to the emperor reminiscing during the mid-330s, perhaps after being invited by Eusebius to talk about his victory, or perhaps during the celebration of the thirtieth anniversary of his accession at Constantinople in 336. But whenever in the later years of his reign Constantine became a raconteur, it was substantially after the original events, and in the case of the battle of the Milvian Bridge, long after. By then his memories had expanded to include stories about a vision of a cross in the sky and a dream of Jesus Christ.[10]

The catalyst for the emperor's stories was, apparently, an opportunity to explain the circumstances behind the construction of his famous military standard and its effectiveness in battles. Eusebius noted that

[9] Eusebius, *Vita Constantini* 3.15, banquet.
[10] Eusebius, *De laudibus Constantini* 18.3, assistance. Barnes (1981) 266, suggests the council of Nicaea as the setting for these stories; Bleckmann (2007) 55–56, suggests that Eusebius heard Constantine's account during the celebration of the emperor's thirtieth anniversary at Constantinople in 336: "In diesem Fall kann der Visionsbericht nicht als intimer Bericht über eine persönliche Bekehrung gelten, sondern es handelt sich um die offizielle Version der spätkonstantinischen Zeit."

he himself had seen the military standard: "the emperor himself once allowed me to observe this standard with my own eyes." The standard resembled a *vexillum*, a conventional military standard consisting of a flag or a banner hanging from a crossbar attached to an upright shaft (or spear). The novelty of Constantine's standard, however, was the addition of a Christian emblem. According to Eusebius' description, the new standard had been designed in the shape of a cross that supported a decorated tapestry banner, displayed a portrait of the emperor and his family, and was topped with a bejeweled wreath encircling a chi and a rho, the initial Greek letters of *Christ*. Eusebius hence interpreted the entire military standard as a Christian symbol.[11]

The version of the military standard that Eusebius observed and described was certainly not one constructed in 312. The inclusion of Greek letters would seem out of place for a military standard designed by a Latin-speaking emperor in the western provinces. In addition, Eusebius mentioned that the imperial icon on the standard depicted Constantine and his sons; but Constantine's second son, Constantine II, was not born until 316 and not proclaimed a Caesar until 317. Even though in *Life* he inserted his depiction of the military standard in the middle of an account of the invasion and battle in 312, Eusebius was obviously describing a later version that he had seen only sometime after Constantine began spending more time in the East. But perhaps he and the other bishops had been curious about the symbols on the standard and their meanings, and one of them had asked for an explanation. As is common in the transmission of oral traditions, an object served as a cue for the background story. The military standard was a memento, a relic of an earlier moment: "storytelling is a little like fingering a

[11] Eusebius, *Vita Constantini* 1.30, own eyes. Although Eusebius himself did not call Constantine's military standard a *labarum*, subsequently an editor or copyist added an explanation in the heading to *Vita Constantini* 1.31: "a description of the symbol in the shape of a cross, which the Romans now call a *labarum*." For the *vexillum*, see Bruun (1966) 56, "The vexillum as an emblem of power is no doubt a Constantinian innovation." Note that the *labarum*, a *vexillum* with Christian symbols, apparently did not appear on coins until after Constantine's reign: see Bruun (1966) 62–64, with Singor (2003), summarizing scholarly speculation about the *labarum*.

holy medal that is both a symbol and a source of power." And the emperor was presumably happy to oblige the request. Eusebius noted that Constantine supplemented this viewing of the military standard with stories about its origins and effectiveness: "a long time afterward the victorious emperor himself narrated [this story] to me, the author of this account, when I was honored with his acquaintance and his conversations." Constantine's memories about his battles were now included in his polite conversation with bishops.[12]

Constantine's recollections about the military standard covered two imperial rivals and several separate episodes. One set of stories was associated with the prelude to the victory over Maxentius in 312. One episode described the famous vision of the cross in the sky before the battle at Rome, and another the emperor's subsequent dream of Christ, who had urged him to make a copy of the "sign that he had seen in the sky" and use it against enemy attacks. This set of stories most likely also included the emperor's consultation with the churchmen who explained their theology of God and the meaning of the symbol. A second set of stories focused on the victory over Licinius in 324. This battle too had been preceded by a vision, this time among Licinius' soldiers, who seemed to see units loyal to Constantine marching through cities, as if they were already victorious: "through a divine and higher power this obvious vision prophesied what the future would be." Another episode described the success of Constantine's soldiers in repelling successive attacks, with "the trophy of salvation" leading the way. Eusebius stated that he had heard this story too directly from Constantine: "the emperor himself narrated these events to me, the author of this account, at a time of relaxation long after the events." Yet another episode described the miraculous protection offered by the military standard to nearby soldiers. Once more Constantine was the source. "This story is not

---

[12] Eusebius, *Vita Constantini* 1.28.1, long time, 31.2, sons. Quotation about storytelling from Slater (1986) 74. While describing the Greek letters on this military standard, Eusebius clearly contrasted past and present by claiming that "in times after these events the emperor was accustomed to display these letters on his helmet": Eusebius, *Vita Constantini* 1.30.1.

mine, but again belongs to the emperor himself, who recalled it for my ears in the presence of companions."[13]

Constantine supplemented the stories about battles with additional stories about his army. He had taught his soldiers to observe "the day of salvation," that is, Sunday. In another edict he had instructed them to recite a prayer to "the Emperor in heaven" as their "giver of victory, savior, protector, and helper." Because the prayer had been in Latin, Eusebius provided a Greek translation. Constantine furthermore had had his soldiers depict "the symbol of the trophy of salvation" on their shields, and he directed their processions to follow only "the trophy of salvation." Because the trophy was presumably the cross that had been incorporated in the military standard, these stories about the military prayer and the military symbols were perhaps also episodes in the larger collection of memories about the military standard.[14]

Constantine told his stories to Eusebius and the other bishops to explain the origin of his military standard and its subsequent success in defeating his two most important imperial rivals. Two aspects are important to note. First, the episodes all seem to have been part of a single extended recollection, an anthology of collected memories. Although Constantine claimed that he had first used this military standard at the battle against Maxentius, it had also proved its effectiveness in the battle against Licinius. Constantine's continuous sequence of episodes highlighted the value of the standard in all of his campaigns, and he did not prioritize one or the other victory. Second, his primary concern in those campaigns had been the loyalty and confidence of his soldiers. In his story of the vision in the sky Constantine insisted that the "trophy

[13] Eusebius, *Vita Constantini* 1.29, sign, 2.6.2, trophy, 8.2, relaxation, 9.3, not mine. Bleckmann (2007) 57, also distinguishes separate episodes by suggesting that the spectacle in the sky was "das älteste und ursprüngliche Element der komplexen Visionserzählung." If Constantine himself designed the military standard, then the omission of an image of Jesus Christ might reflect his preference: see Grigg (1977), suggesting that the emperor wanted "to preserve the traditional aniconic worship of the Christian Church" (p. 32).

[14] Eusebius, *Vita Constantini* 4.18.3, day of salvation, 19.1, "second edict," 20.1, prayer, 21, shields.

of the cross" had appeared after midday, above the sun and formed from light, and that it had been accompanied by a slogan, "conquer by this." One guarantee of this story came from Constantine himself: "he said that he saw it with his own eyes." An additional warranty for the details of this vision came from his soldiers. "Amazement at this spectacle overwhelmed both him and his entire army, which . . . observed this marvel." Whatever reassurance the emperor had received from this vision had been shared by his troops.[15]

Constantine hence told these stories to bishops to explain the subsequent deployment of religious symbols on his military standard. But as he remembered the use of the cross in the military standard, his stories were primarily about the loyalty of his soldiers and their success in battles, not about his own religious beliefs and the role of churchmen. In his memories Constantine did not highlight specifically the victory over Maxentius, but he did emphasize the military aspects of the cross, first in the vision that he had shared with his soldiers and subsequently as a military standard.

EUSEBIUS' MEMORIES

Constantine obviously liked to talk, and he often summoned his courtiers to hear his "philosophy." During a visit to Constantinople, Eusebius presumably watched and listened to one of the emperor's performances. According to his description, Constantine wrote his own discourses without the assistance of speechwriters and delivered them in Latin. Interpreters then translated them into Greek on the spot. In his discourses he sometimes talked about moral behavior by denouncing theft and greed, and sometimes about religion by condemning pagan cults and encouraging worship of "the God who rules alone." Whenever

---

[15] Eusebius, *Vita Constantini* 1.28.2, trophy, entire army. Note that later images may have shaped the details of these stories. In the imperial palace at Constantinople the ceiling of one room was decorated with an ornate cross: see Eusebius, *Vita Constantini* 3.49: "the symbol of the Savior's suffering was attached to the middle of a large open panel, made from many valuable gems and set in thick gold." Perhaps the splendor of this dazzling cross influenced Constantine's memory of his vision or Eusebius' recollection of the emperor's story about his vision.

he talked about God, "he stood up straight, with a serious face and a low voice." If his audience murmured in approval, he indicated that they should not applaud him but instead "look up to heaven" and worship "only the Emperor over all." All he would claim for himself was that "the God over all had presented him with an empire over everything on earth." Constantine must have truly enjoyed talking about himself as God's impresario.[16]

Perhaps the emperor shared his memories about his military standard in the same way, talking earnestly to a captive audience of churchmen about his divine entitlement. He also insisted on the accuracy of his memories: "Constantine confirmed this story with oaths." Eusebius had no reason to doubt Constantine's account of the origin and effectiveness of the military standard, especially because it seemed to corroborate his own impressions about the overall direction of the emperor's reign. But after hearing the emperor's stories, he nevertheless shaped them for his own purposes in his *Life of Constantine*.[17]

As an ecclesiastical historian Eusebius was an innovator and a pioneer in terms of coverage, research techniques, and the citation of sources. In the late third century there were still few precedents for writing a continuous narrative of early Christianity from the life of Jesus to his own time. Eusebius himself thought that he was setting off as an explorer on an unknown trail, completely undisturbed even by "the bare footprints of earlier travelers." Most of that exploration consisted of sitting in his library at Caesarea in Palestine and studying the many books that first his mentor Pamphilus and then he himself had collected. After he had completed his research and excerpted information from the books, he had to decide how to present his findings. Although earlier historians had of course relied on sources, both written and oral, they had conventionally not quoted documents and cited informants, or even acknowledged their dependence on earlier texts. In contrast, Eusebius quoted verbatim extracts from documents, some

---

[16] Eusebius, *Vita Constantini* 4.29.1, speechwriters, 2, stood up, look up, 3, ruled alone, 4, God over all, 32, Latin.

[17] Eusebius, *Vita Constantini* 1.28.1, oaths.

quite lengthy. In *Ecclesiastical History* he quoted letters and edicts issued by the Tetrarchic emperors and their heirs, including Constantine from the early years of his reign. In *Life of Constantine* he would continue this practice by quoting more of Constantine's letters from the later years of his reign. Eusebius' treatises, whether theological, apologetic, or historical, were literary mosaics, collages of excerpts and quotations.[18]

During the early twentieth century the authenticity of the documents quoted in *Life* was challenged. Then a few lines from a letter of Constantine sent in 324 were identified on an almost-contemporary papyrus from Egypt that predated the publication of *Life*. The existence of this independent copy of Constantine's letter implied that the other documents that Eusebius cited were also genuine. Scholars could then shift their concern to the problems posed by the commentaries in which Eusebius had embedded the documents. Because his commentaries did not always correspond to the contents of these documents, his interpretive readings were sometimes suspect, if not outright misleading. One example is Constantine's letter to the provincials in the East, sent in the autumn of 324. Although the emperor indicated his preference for Christianity in this letter, he also extended toleration to supporters of pagan cults. "Those who persist in their errors are to receive a similar gift of peace and tranquility as the believers." In contrast, Eusebius' commentary on this letter was more absolute, claiming that the emperor was trying to "block his subjects from demonic error" while "urging them to pursue the true worship of God." The policy of religious toleration in Constantine's letter had become a firm mandate against pagan cults in Eusebius' commentary.[19]

---

[18] Eusebius, *HE* 1.1.3, footprints. On the innovation of Eusebius' historiography, see Momigliano (1963) 91, "a new type of historical exposition which was characterized . . . by the lavish use of documents." For an excellent discussion of Eusebius' literary techniques, see Grafton and Williams (2006) 200–215: "one long adventure in systematic quotation" (p. 202).

[19] Papyrus fragment: ed. Jones (1954), "a contemporary copy of the Letter of A.D. 324" (p. 200); cited in Eusebius, *Vita Constantini* 2.26.1–29.1; and beautifully illustrated in Hartley et al. (2006) 97, figure 39. Eusebius, *Vita Constantini* 2.56.1, persist, 61.1, subjects, with Cameron

Eusebius seems to have followed some of the same techniques of excerpting episodes and quotations and enveloping them in personal interpretations when citing Constantine's memories in *Life*. He first divided the emperor's account into discrete episodes that he clustered around the battle against Maxentius and a battle twelve years later against Licinius. Constantine had apparently narrated a continuous recollection about the origin and value of the military standard; Eusebius instead linked specific episodes with particular battles. Eusebius furthermore surrounded the episodes with additional contextual information that he had derived from various sources. One source for his supplementary commentary was biblical models. Another was probably the extra knowledge of the early years of Constantine's life and reign that he had picked up from stray conversations. Yet another source was himself, as he repeated or recast material from an earlier account in his own *Ecclesiastical History*. In *Life* Eusebius recorded the emperor's oral memories, but he also divided them into episodic fragments and embedded them in his own distinctive commentary.

In *Life* Eusebius located the battle against Maxentius within an extended narrative that stretched from Constantine's service as a young man at imperial courts to his victory over Licinius in 324. He constructed the backstory of the battle in terms of two important role models, the emperor's father and an Old Testament lawgiver. Eusebius included a few stories about the reign of Constantius as a prelude to the emergence of his son as an emperor. Of the four original Tetrarchic emperors, only Constantius had refrained from participating in the persecution of Christians. Instead, he was thought to have stood up to Diocletian, "the emperor who at the time held the top rank in the empire," by demonstrating that he could accumulate a financial surplus without acting harshly, and by retaining the Christians who were serving at his palace while dismissing those court attendants who decided to perform pagan sacrifices. From this perspective Constantius

and Hall (1999) 18, "in several cases it is clear that Eusebius is using a document which does not precisely fit the interpretation which he puts on it."

had differed from his fellow emperors because of his kindness and goodness.[20]

Eusebius noted that he had selected these particular examples about Constantius from the "extensive oral tradition in circulation about this emperor." Because Constantius had reigned as emperor in Gaul and Britain and had never even traveled farther east than his native province of Dacia in the Balkans, Eusebius certainly had no firsthand experiences of his rule. Instead, he had deduced Constantius' piety from the succession of his son. According to this reverse logic, because Constantius had transformed his court into a "church of God" through his celebration of the liturgy, God arranged for his oldest son to inherit his imperial rule. Even though Eusebius presented this moment of succession as unproblematic, others would subsequently wonder why Constantius' other sons had not also become emperors. According to Eusebius, "the father of Constantine is remembered in this way." But it is not obvious whether these memories were the claims of Constantine, defending his succession by primogeniture at the expense of his brothers, or the presumptions of Eusebius, as he constructed a pedigree of Christian piety for the emperor.[21]

The other model that Eusebius highlighted for Constantine's early career was Moses. Just as Moses had grown up among the "tyrants" who oppressed the "Hebrew people," so Constantine had grown up among the "tyrants" who persecuted the church. Eventually he fled the plots at the court of Galerius, "preserving his imitation of the great prophet Moses." Eusebius then foreshortened the chronology to have Constantine show up at Constantius' deathbed just in time to receive his father's blessing and inherit his father's purple cloak. He further condensed the chronology by having the new emperor almost immediately begin to contemplate liberating Rome from "slavery to a

[20] Eusebius, *Vita Constantini* 1.13.1, four emperors, 14.1, kindness, goodness, top rank, 16.1, sacrifices, with M. D. Smith (1997), (2000), arguing that Constantius had in fact been a traditional pagan who worshipped Jupiter and Hercules.
[21] Eusebius, *Vita Constantini* 1.14.1, oral tradition, 17.1, father, 17.3, church of God, 18.2, oldest son. For Constantine's brothers, see Van Dam (2007) 108–9; Hall (1993) 244, suggests that Constantine himself was a source for this oral tradition.

tyrant." The year between Constantine's arrival and his father's death and the six years between his acclamation in 306 and the battle at Rome simply vanished from Eusebius' narrative.[22]

In addition, at that point in his narrative the model of Moses intersected with the model of Constantius. According to Eusebius, while Constantine "looked for a god as his helper" in this campaign against Maxentius in Italy, he decided "to honor only his father's god." As confirmation of this choice he received his vision of the cross. When Moses had been unsure about his calling, he had heard God's voice in a burning bush; Constantine saw his destiny in the sky. According to Eusebius, the emperor decided "to honor with all rituals the god who had appeared." By adding this additional commentary about Constantius and Moses, Eusebius had transformed the emperor's memory about the inspiration for and the construction of a military standard into a story about personal religious conversion. He had also turned it into a story about conversion to the Christian God. Constantine's father's god had become his own God, and like Moses, Constantine had received his reassurance directly from God. Now he would set out with confidence to extinguish "the threat of the tyrant's fire."[23]

Eusebius then highlighted the misbehavior of Maxentius at Rome. His alleged evil deeds included adultery, murder, confiscation, magic, and a deliberate food shortage "such that the people of our time do not remember ever happening at Rome at any other time." In this account Eusebius was repeating his earlier description of Maxentius' actions at Rome in *History*. But in the context of a more extended analogy between Constantine and Moses, he now seemed to be suggesting

---

[22] Eusebius, *Vita Constantini* 1.12.1, Moses, 12.2, Constantine and tyrants, 20.2, great prophet, 22.1, purple cloak, 26.1, slavery. For Eusebius' use of Moses as a model for Constantine, see Wilson (1998), Rapp (2005) 129–31, and Williams (2008) 36–42, stressing his "biblicising" outlook (p. 23).

[23] Eusebius, *Vita Constantini* 1.27.1, helper, 27.3, father's god, 32.3, rituals, 32.3, fire; with Cameron and Hall (1999) 31: "Just as Moses was granted the sign of the burning bush, so Constantine receives his vision," and Price (2005) 4–5, on Eusebius' account of Constantine's vision: "Eusebius' additions conflict with the emperor's own story. . . . [T]he connection of the vision to Constantine's conversion is Eusebius' own invention."

that Maxentius' misbehavior was the equivalent of a series of plagues at Rome. Constantine's subsequent victory was hence comparable to Moses' destruction of the pharaoh and his chariots at the Red Sea. In his account of this battle Eusebius quoted and paraphrased extensively from his earlier account in *History* that had already employed that comparison, but with a few additional comments. In *History* Eusebius had noted that Constantine, when attacking Rome, had relied on the assistance of "God in heaven and his Word, the Savior of all, Jesus Christ himself." In *Life*, however, Eusebius claimed that the emperor, in addition to invoking "the God over all and Christ, Savior and Helper," had trusted "his trophy of victory, the sign of salvation." Without missing a beat, Eusebius had simply blended Constantine's stories about the military standard into both his earlier account of the battle outside Rome and his extended analogy between the emperor and Moses. In his earlier account in *History* Eusebius had also claimed that soon after entering Rome Constantine had ordered the construction of a statue of himself holding a cross. Eusebius may well have misinterpreted his source's description of this statue. But in *Life* he nevertheless repeated his earlier version, this time with the added warranty that Constantine had owed his victory in part to a military standard in the shape of a cross. Constantine's later memories had seemingly validated both Eusebius' earlier analogy with Moses and his earlier interpretation of the emperor's actions.[24]

After his victory over Maxentius, Constantine formed an alliance with Licinius, who married one of his half sisters. In the East Licinius soon defeated his rival Maximinus; but within a few years he and Constantine were themselves rivals. In his account of the wars between these two emperors in *Life*, Eusebius no longer mentioned Constantius or Moses. Instead, his narrative of this new civil war followed the structure of his previous narrative of the war between Constantine and Maxentius, with the hint that Licinius might be another pharaoh.

---

[24] Eusebius, *Vita Constantini* 1.36.2, people of our time, 37.1, trophy, 38.2, Moses and Red Sea, 40.2, statue; *HE* 9.9.2, God and Jesus Christ, 10–11, statue, with Grant (1980) 39, on Eusebius' "self-plagiarization," and Hall (1993) 249, on the changes from *History* to *Life*: "drawing truth from the Scripture rather than from further information." For additional discussion of Eusebius' account in *History* and the statue at Rome, see Chapters 5, 7.

Eusebius first denigrated Licinius as a "wild beast" and a "twisted snake" who threatened churches and provincials. His account here in *Life* repeated and extended the critical evaluation with which he had earlier concluded the final edition of his *History*. According to this account in *Life*, Licinius imposed restrictions on bishops and meetings in churches, he dismissed court officials and army officers who were Christians, and he finally initiated another persecution of Christians. Unlike Constantine, who had eventually imitated his father's piety, Licinius failed to learn a lesson from the miserably painful deaths of previous emperors who had persecuted Christians: "he darkened his mind, as if on a moonless night."[25]

The confrontation between Constantine and Licinius dragged on for years and included an inconclusive series of battles in 316–317 before the final battles in 324. In *Life* Eusebius nevertheless foreshortened the chronology to make the victory over Licinius follow quickly after the victory over Maxentius. Constantine prepared for war and put his hope in his military standard; Licinius supposedly mocked his opponent's reliance on this "symbol of the suffering of salvation." Instead, like a pharaoh, he consulted "Egyptian seers." He also delivered a speech in which he framed the coming battle as a direct conflict between "the one God of Constantine" and "my gods," the "ancestral gods." Eusebius claimed that his sources for information about Licinius' speech were people from the crowd. But by casting Licinius as another pharaoh and Constantine as a liberator, he was able to provide a larger context for Constantine's stories about the success of his military standard in the final battle. Licinius' army trusted in "a multitude of gods," "dead bodies," while Constantine's army advanced behind "the sign of salvation that brought life." Eusebius had interpreted this battle as a more comprehensive confrontation between paganism and Christianity.[26]

In his later account in *Life* Eusebius had repeatedly manipulated Constantine's memories about the success of the military standard.

[25] Eusebius, *Vita Constantini* 1.49.1, wild beast, 59.2, moonless night, 2.1.2, wild beast and twisted snake.
[26] Eusebius, *Vita Constantini* 2.4.2, symbol, seers, 5.2, ancestral gods, 5.3, my gods, one God, 5.5, listeners in crowd, 16.2, multitude, sign.

The victory over Maxentius in 312 became an account of the emperor's personal religious conversion, while the victory over Licinius in 324 became an account of the triumph of Christianity in a reunified empire. In Eusebius' earlier narrative in *Ecclesiastical History* the victory over Licinius had been the conclusion of Constantine's singular rise as a Christian emperor. In *Life*, however, each victory became a transitional moment in longer historical arcs, one of Constantine's own religious growth, the other of the expansion of Christianity in the empire.

As he concluded this extended account of civil wars, Eusebius seemed to concede that his narrative included a bit of misdirection. By then people were celebrating "the forgetting of ancient evils and the oblivion of every impiety." To remind them of what they had forgotten, however, Eusebius had composed this narrative that integrated and contextualized Constantine's memories. But because he had refashioned those memories within his own particular interpretive viewpoint, the original intent of Constantine's stories was forgotten. "Forgetting is an active agent in the formation of memories." Eusebius' narrative hence served two purposes, to remind provincials of the horrors they were now glad to overlook, and to modify the original purpose of Constantine's memories by embedding them in his own commentary. Because of the demands of his own interpretive perspective, Eusebius misrepresented the very memories that he was claiming to remember.[27]

THEOLOGY BECOMES HISTORY

Both Constantine's memories and Eusebius' commentary in *Life* were retrospective interpretations of the emperor's early battles.

---

[27] Eusebius, *Vita Constantini* 1.19.3, forgetting; quotation about forgetting from Whitehead (2009) 121. Deliberate forgetting is to be distinguished from amnesia: see Flower (2006), discussing the erasure of dedications, the disfigurement of statues of delinquent emperors, and the imposition of sanctions against disgraced aristocrats in the late Republic and early empire. To be effective, such condemnation required both lingering memories of the dishonor and constant reminders. As a result, forgetting could readily again become remembrance. For a stimulating discussion of the rehabilitation of the memory of a Roman senator in the early fifth century, see Hedrick (2000) 114, on the paradox of forgetting: "the continuance of memory is essential to the success of the repression."

Constantine's goal in his stories had been to explain the construction of the military standard and its use; Eusebius reinterpreted those stories as accounts of a personal religious conversion before the battle against Maxentius and of the ultimate victory of Christianity over paganism after the battle against Licinius. Eusebius was obviously thinking not only *about* Constantine and his early career but also *with* Constantine as a symbolic medium to articulate his own ideas about spiritual development and the place of Christianity in society. He preferred to narrate Constantine's early career in terms of charged moments and precise turning points rather than as an untidy process of featureless actions.

As he looked back on the later years of the emperor's reign, Eusebius likewise continued to think both about Constantine the Christian emperor and with Constantine as a paradigmatic Christian emperor. In particular, he manipulated his representation of the emperor to advance his own theology and to diminish the role of the army in the making of a Christian emperor. As his own concerns had developed over the years, so had his constructions of Constantine. Eusebius used Constantine, including the emperor's memories, to promote his own personal and theological interests.

Eusebius was not alone in already using images of Constantine as a symbolic idiom. Constantine himself often seemed to be thinking about his own concerns by constructing images of himself. One of those new concerns was his relationship with bishops and other churchmen. Perhaps he could define that relationship in a particular way by telling the history of his reign in a complementary way. The episodic memories that he recalled about his military standard, for instance, might also serve the purpose of promoting his standing among the bishops with whom he was spending increasingly more time.

Within a year of his victory over Licinius, the emperor convened the bishops who attended the council of Nicaea. Constantine had summoned the bishops with "respectful letters." Once they assembled, he delivered an opening oration, participated in the debates, and encouraged them to find agreement. The oddity, however, is that although the bishops were consecrated "ministers of God," Constantine was still only a layman who had not yet even been baptized. Like great senators and local notables, bishops too had a keen sense of rank and status. Some would subsequently be upset by being described as followers of the theology taught by Arius, a mere priest; they would be even more sensitive about taking theological direction from a layman. Constantine's story about his dream of Jesus Christ was hence most useful in helping establish his spiritual authority. In that dream Christ had encouraged the emperor to construct a military standard modeled on the cross that he had seen in the sky. At the same time, the dream confirmed that Constantine had enjoyed a direct access to Christ that was not available even to bishops. As a result, the emperor could joke that he too was an *episkopos*, a "bishop" or "overseer," "appointed by God" to look after everyone outside the church. Eusebius heard this quip "with my own ears" while the emperor was entertaining bishops at a banquet. This pun would have fit nicely with Constantine's memories about the origin of the military standard. His dream of Christ had both assisted his success as a military commander and confirmed his credentials as a "bishop."[28]

Eusebius seems to have agreed with Constantine's elevated assessment of his spiritual standing. After the victory over Maxentius at Rome he claimed that Constantine would convene councils of bishops "like some common bishop appointed by God." These flattering remarks have made Eusebius vulnerable to complaints from modern scholars that his *Life* was simply a tendentious apology that offered a political theory of a Christian emperor who ruled in the image of God. In fact, Eusebius was more concerned about offering a rationale for his own theology. Nicene Christianity, as defined in the creed issued by the council of Nicaea, had highlighted the sameness and the coordination between Father and Son, whereas Arian theology insisted that Jesus Christ the Son was fundamentally subordinate and inferior to God

---

[28] Eusebius, *Vita Constantini* 1.29, dream, 3.6.1, letters, 12.1–5, oration, 12.5, ministers, 13.2, agreement, 4.24, bishop. For Constantine's familiarity with jokes, note that for thirty years he was accompanied by a jester, "who distracted the emperor from his boredom": see Ambrosiaster, *Quaestiones veteris et novi testamenti* 115.75. For the complaints of the bishops at the council of Antioch in 341 about the teachings of the priest Arius, see Athanasius, *De synodis* 22.3.

the Father. Despite his momentary endorsement of the Nicene creed, Eusebius' doctrines about the subordination of the Son to the Father were similar to Arius' teachings.[29]

At some point Eusebius seems to have realized that he could defend his doctrines in *Life* by presenting an emperor who would make sense only in the context of an Arian subordinationist theology that allowed him to be seen as an analogue of Jesus Christ. In true postmodern fashion, Eusebius subverted the conventional literary genres of biography and panegyric for an entirely different purpose. Both biography and panegyric could become theology. In real life the emperor had generously patronized Eusebius; in *Life* the emperor would become the embodiment of Eusebius' distinctive theology. The more closely Constantine resembled Jesus Christ, the more Jesus seemed to be clearly distinct from and subordinate to God the Father.

Eusebius defended his own theology in different ways in the commentary he added to Constantine's memories. One instance specifically focused on the vision and the dream before the battle at Rome. According to the account in *Life*, Constantine had been so stunned at "the marvelous sight" that he decided to worship "no other God than the one he had seen." He then summoned "initiates in his [God's] words," that is, presumably churchmen, and asked about the identity of this God and "the meaning of the sight he had seen of the sign." According to Eusebius, the consultants offered an explanation in terms of Jesus Christ, and in particular his incarnation and crucifixion. They claimed that the "sign" was "a symbol of immortality and a trophy of victory over death, which he had earned while living on earth." They also claimed that "the God was the only-begotten Son of the one and only God."[30]

In his narrative Eusebius located this doctrinal instruction before the battle in 312. At that time the theology of the relationship between God the Father and Jesus Christ his Son was in flux, and there had certainly been no consensus, or even a standard of nominal consensus,

[29] Eusebius, *Vita Constantini* 1.44.2, common bishop.
[30] Eusebius, *Vita Constantini* 1.32.1, sight, no other God, initiates, meaning, 2, symbol, Son.

among eastern churchmen. But by the time Eusebius wrote *Life*, he had attended the council at Nicaea in 325 and his own theology had been criticized severely. After the council at Nicaea, Eusebius had written a letter to his congregation at Caesarea in which he had tried to explain the harmony between the Nicene creed and his own subordinationist theology. Now in *Life* Eusebius used this summary of Constantine's theological lesson in 312 as an implicit confirmation of his own later apology for his own doctrines. Both Eusebius' own creed and the Nicene creed had confessed one God the Father, and they had agreed that Jesus Christ was his only begotten Son. But the point of difference had been the term *homoousios* adopted by the Nicene creed, which emphasized the claim that the Son had been "of the same essence" as God the Father. Not surprisingly, in their exposition to the emperor these consultants in 312 now failed to describe the Son as *homoousios*. Their omission seemed to be a tacit confirmation of Eusebius' theology. Because Constantine, according to Eusebius' narrative, "decided to accept these inspired teachings," he also appeared, at the moment of his conversion, to have endorsed Eusebius' doctrines. Theology became history, and Constantine's vision could be considered a warranty for Eusebius' theology. Through sleight of hand Eusebius had passed off his own later theological apology as a catechism lesson for Constantine in 312.[31]

Eusebius furthermore promoted his theology by stressing the resemblance between Constantine and Jesus Christ. In his panegyric celebrating the thirtieth anniversary of Constantine's reign in 336 Eusebius argued that the Logos, the "Word," who commanded God's heavenly army, and the emperor, who led his army against enemies, were each acting "like a prefect of the Great Emperor," that is, of God. This similarity with a Christian emperor entailed that the Logos was "distinguished with second place in his Father's kingdom." In *Life* Eusebius again seemed to enhance Constantine's standing. He compared the emperor to "a very loud herald of God" and "a heavenly angel of God."

---

[31] Eusebius, *Vita Constantini* 1.32.3, inspired teachings. For Eusebius' letter to Caesarea, see Urkunde 22, quoted in Athanasius, *De decretis Nicaenae synodi* 33.1–17, and Socrates, *HE* 1.8.35–54, who himself cited the Nicene creed when quoting Eusebius' letter.

In his panegyric he had likewise described the Logos as an "angel of great guidance." If both Constantine and Jesus Christ were angels, "messengers" of God, then Constantine's story of his conversation with Christ only reinforced their fundamental similarity and the consequent subordination of the Son to the Father. Eusebius would hence have appreciated Constantine's memory of his dream about Christ, but for a personal theological reason. Constantine had told that story to explain the appearance of his military standard and to enhance his spiritual authority when dealing with bishops. Eusebius retold the story in support of his subordinationist doctrines.[32]

Eusebius had one more objective in recounting Constantine's memories in *Life*. Soldiers and churchmen were fundamentally incompatible, and Eusebius still remembered with horror the participation of soldiers in the persecutions under the Tetrarchs. In early 303 Diocletian had initiated his persecution of Christians by sending officers and soldiers to loot and destroy the church at Nicomedia. Constantine had been a military officer, and he would subsequently admit that he had been at Diocletian's court at the time. After he became a Christian emperor, however, he seems to have sensed that he had to minimize his military demeanor when dealing with churchmen. As a result, although Constantine was eager to present himself as a "bishop" appointed by God, Eusebius was equally eager to represent him as a civilian emperor appointed by God. The same memories of his civil wars that Constantine had recounted to indicate his divine consecration now offered Eusebius an opportunity to create an alternative perspective that downplayed the importance of military support. In *History*, before he had heard those memories, Eusebius had conceded the role of the army in the proclamation of Constantine as emperor. But in *Life*, after describing Constantine's emergence as the sole successor to his father, he completely ignored the involvement of the army: "on his own God,

---

[32] Eusebius, *Vita Constantini* 2.61, herald, 3.10.3, heavenly angel, *De laudibus Constantini* 1.6, second place, 3.5, Logos as prefect, 6, angel of great guidance, 7.13, emperor as prefect. For *Life* as a theological treatise, see Van Dam (2007) 283–85, 310–13; also Adler (2008) 595–96: "When Eusebius later describes the fall of Licinius and the reunification of the Empire under Constantine, his language verges on the messianic."

the ruler of the entire universe, selected Constantine . . . as ruler and governor over all."[33]

From Eusebius' perspective, the emperor's memories about the vision of the cross and his dream of Christ certainly reinforced this notion of divine selection. Constantine had framed his memories in such a way as to ensure his military support: the entire army had seen the vision and then followed the military standard. In contrast, Eusebius retold the stories to demonstrate that Constantine's imperial rule was independent of military support: only the emperor had conversed with Christ. Constantine never forgot that an emperor, even a Christian emperor, needed a military reputation to guarantee support in the army. But while recording and interpreting the emperor's memories, Eusebius seemed to be hoping that a Christian emperor, God's chosen ruler, could be a civilian, like bishops and other churchmen.

FROM MOSES TO JESUS

For understanding the early years of Constantine's reign Eusebius had consistently used a comparison with Moses. He had deployed this comparison first in his early accounts in *History* long before he had met the emperor, and again later in *Life* even after he had heard the emperor's own stories. This comparison with Moses had been especially useful to explain Constantine's victory outside Rome, because he could then also compare Maxentius to the Egyptian pharaoh, swept away in the current. But once Constantine entered Rome, Eusebius no longer compared him explicitly to Moses. Crossing the Tiber seemed to mark a transition from an Old Testament perspective on Constantine to a New Testament perspective. For the remainder of his reign another analogy was more useful for both Eusebius' narrative and Constantine's presentation of himself.[34]

---

[33] Tribunes and church at Nicomedia: Lactantius, *De mortibus persecutorum* 12.2–5, with Chapter 6, for additional discussion of Lactantius. Constantine at Nicomedia: Constantine, *Oratio ad sanctorum coetum* 25.2. God and Constantine: Eusebius, *Vita Constantini* 1.24, with Chapter 5, for Eusebius' earlier accounts of the role of the army.

[34] For this transition in Eusebius' narrative of Constantine's life from reenactment of the Old Testament to reenactment of the New Testament, see Williams (2008) 42.

Eusebius instead highlighted the analogy between Jesus Christ and a Christian emperor to emphasize that both were subordinate to God the Father. In *Life* Eusebius appropriated Constantine's life to support his own particular theology. In part he was following Constantine's own lead, because during the later years of his reign the emperor had already been advertising his resemblance to Jesus Christ, in particular in his new capital at Constantinople. Most notably, the shrine that Constantine constructed as a funerary memorial included a niche for his sarcophagus surrounded by twelve cenotaphs that represented the twelve apostles. Even as the emperor was subsidizing the construction of new churches at Jerusalem and Bethlehem that celebrated the birth, death, and ascension of Jesus Christ, at Constantinople he seemed to be appropriating some of Jesus' divine roles. As a result, if Constantine was to be imagined as an analogue of Jesus Christ, then Constantinople could be thought of as both "Constantine's city" and "Christ's city."[35]

At the end of his life Constantine admitted that he had always hoped to imitate Jesus by being baptized in the Jordan River. Because he was then preparing for an invasion of the Persian empire, he presumably planned to detour to Palestine during his march through the eastern provinces. Such a baptism would not only have publicized his similarity to Jesus in the Holy Land. It would also have distinguished him yet again from Moses, who had been allowed to view the Promised Land from a mountaintop but not to cross the Jordan River. Unlike Eusebius, Constantine had not promoted Moses as a biblical paradigm for his imperial rule. As a Christian ruler he seemed to think that the only proper exemplar was Jesus Christ. After all, even late in his reign when he recalled that battle at Rome, he still remembered that before the combat he had talked directly with Jesus in a dream.[36]

---

[35] Eusebius, *Vita Constantini* 4.58–60, shrine, with Chapter 9, for the implications about emperorship. Constantinople as Christ's city: Sozomen, *HE* 2.3.8.

[36] Eusebius, *Vita Constantini* 4.62.2, Jordan River.

EUSEBIUS' COMMENTARY

CHAPTER FIVE

THE STORIES ABOUT THE EMPEROR'S VISION AND DREAM before the battle outside Rome were Constantine's own memories. Distinguishing those stories from the commentary in which Eusebius subsequently embedded them in *Life of Constantine* has interesting implications. One is that it is possible to detect some of the influences that independently shaped Constantine's memories and Eusebius' commentary. Although the memories and the commentary converged in Eusebius' *Life*, until that moment they had followed separate tracks. The emperor's memories and the bishop's commentary each had a distinct backstory.

After the battle and his return to Gaul early in the following year, Constantine remained in the western provinces. He continued to campaign along the Rhine frontier; he returned to Rome in 315; and after seizing the Balkans from Licinius, he campaigned along the Danube frontier. The backstory for his memories hence included his subsequent experiences in the West, as well as various accounts of the battle that he heard, read, or viewed (Chapters 6–7). In contrast, the backstory for Eusebius' commentary in *Life* consisted largely of his own earlier accounts. For modern historical analysis, disentangling these earlier accounts becomes an opportunity to see Eusebius at work as a historian and an apologist. His narrative in *Life* of Constantine's victory at Rome was not his first account of the battle. Nor was it his second account. In fact, it was not even his third account.

Eusebius had written his *Ecclesiastical History* in a series of revised and enlarged drafts (or so-called editions) over an extended period of decades, ending with some substantial revisions shortly after the defeat of Licinius in 324. In the last three books of *History*, books 8–10, he described Constantine's victories over Maxentius and Licinius. But as he constantly revised those books, he also modified his interpretation of the battle outside Rome. Years later his narrative of the first two decades of Constantine's reign in *Life* overlapped with his earlier narrative of the same period in these final books of *History*. But because he had acquired more information during the years after the final rewriting of *History*, in *Life* he yet again modified his narrative of the battle in 312. Eusebius produced four versions of this battle, three in the sequential revisions of *History* and one more in *Life*. Even as he quoted extensively from version to version, he kept on adjusting his interpretations.[1]

CHANGING THE STORY . . . REPEATEDLY

Eusebius presented his *History* as a straightforward, unitary narrative from beginning to end, covering "the period from our Savior and concluding in our times." In fact, his narrative was a pastiche of segments that included numerous additions and modifications from different moments in his life. In the first seven books he covered the period from Jesus Christ to the late third century. He had been collecting historical

---

[1] Note also the reference to the battle in Jerome's Latin translation of Eusebius' *Chronicle*: see Jerome, *Chronicon* s.a. 312, "Maxentius iuxta pontem Mulvium a Constantino superatus occiditur." Eusebius extended the entries in his *Chronicle* to the twentieth anniversary of Constantine's accession in 325. Although one of his entries did mention Maxentius' defeat and death in 312, it did *not* include the reference to the Milvian Bridge. That information was added by Jerome in his translation: see Burgess (1999a) 55, 97, suggesting that Jerome's source was the list of consuls in *Descriptio consulum* (or *Consularia Constantinopolitana*), ed. Burgess (1993) 235, or the so-called Kaisergeschichte, a lost account used as a source by other fourth-century historians. Burgess (1999a) 62, proposes a reconstruction of Eusebius' original entry: Μαξέντιος ὑπὸ Κωνσταντίνου ἡττηθεὶς ἀνῃρέθη.

material for some time, having started already perhaps before the commencement of the persecutions in 303 under Diocletian, and certainly well before hearing about Constantine's victory in 312. In the first seven books Eusebius firmly insisted "that church and empire were quite distinct." He seems not to have anticipated that the culmination of his narrative would eventually become the reign of a Christian emperor.[2]

Eusebius then added two more books that highlighted the persecutions under Diocletian, Galerius, and Maximinus in the eastern provinces. The eighth book consisted largely of a shortened version of an earlier treatise entitled *Martyrs of Palestine*, and the ninth book concluded with an account of Licinius' victory over Maximinus. Eusebius published this "first edition" of *History* in nine books in late 313 or 314, after Maximinus' death in the summer of 313. Soon afterward, however, he discarded the shortened version of *Martyrs of Palestine* and rewrote the eighth book to widen its focus on persecution, retained the existing ninth book, and added a tenth book that included his own oration on the dedication of a church as well as six imperial documents issued by Constantine and Licinius or by Constantine alone in favor of Christianity. He published this "second edition" of *History* in ten books before the outbreak of hostilities between Constantine and Licinius in the autumn of 316. After Constantine finally defeated Licinius in 324, in a "third edition" Eusebius altered his favorable evaluation of Licinius, in particular by omitting the dossier of imperial documents in the tenth book and instead adding an account of Constantine's most recent victory.[3]

---

[2] Eusebius, *HE* 1.1.1, the period, with the characterization of *History* in Christensen (1989) 9: "It is a mess, both from a compositional and a literary point of view." For the possibility of an early draft of books 1–7 already before the end of the third century, see Barnes (1980), (1981) 128, 145–46. Quotation about church and empire from Tabbernee (1997) 325, in one of the few discussions that carefully tracks the changes in Eusebius' thinking (in this case, about persecution) across the editions of his *History*.

[3] For the detailed arguments that Eusebius published three editions of *History*, the first in 313 or 314, see Louth (1990) and Burgess (1997) 483–86. Modern critical editions of *History* compound the difficulty of examining the changes in Eusebius' ideas, because none exactly reproduces any of Eusebius' own published editions.

FIRST EDITION

In *History* Eusebius first published a reference to Constantine in the new eighth book of the first edition. For most of this eighth book he used an abridged version of his *Martyrs of Palestine*. Eusebius had composed the initial, long version of *Martyrs* already in 311. The long version had highlighted martyrdoms in Palestine; the shortened version still focused on Palestine. But when he recycled the shortened version of *Martyrs* as the core of the eighth book of *History*, he concluded with a short retrospective on the aftermath of the persecutions. In particular, he added an "Appendix" (as it is now known), which described the deaths of the four original Tetrarchs. The three whom Eusebius associated with persecutions, Diocletian, Maximian, and Galerius, had died badly. The fourth was Constantius, whom he characterized as "the most kind and most gentle" of emperors. According to this account, Constantius had not participated in "the war against us." As a result, he had been succeeded by his "legitimate son," Constantine, who "was proclaimed immediately at the beginning as greatest emperor and Augustus by the soldiers." Because Constantine in turn was "most wise and most pious," he imitated "his father's piety toward our teaching." In these concluding remarks Eusebius demonstrated that persecuting emperors died in pain, while the reward for an emperor who had been favorable toward Christianity was the succession of his son.[4]

In the new ninth book Eusebius continued with his narrative of the persecutions in the East. His primary focus remained the hostile activities of Maximinus, and he was presumably pleased to conclude the book with an account of the emperor's agonizingly painful death after his defeat by Licinius in 313. Toward the end of his narrative about eastern persecutions, however, he returned to Constantine by inserting a report of his victory over Maxentius at Rome. This account

---

[4] For the editions of *Martyrs of Palestine*, see Barnes (1981) 149–50. Eusebius, *HE* 8, Appendix 4, Constantius, son, 5, soldiers, piety, with Tabbernee (1997) 327–28, for the novelty of this theme about "the deaths of the persecutors." On the source(s) for the information in the Appendix, see Christensen (1983) 182, "the religiously neutral character of the original account," 203, "an official 'Kaisergeschichte' aimed at justifying Constantine's claim to be *Maximus Augustus*."

of a western battle dramatically interrupted the flow of his narrative of eastern events.

How did Eusebius acquire this information? Because he composed this initial account within about a year of the battle in October 312, he presumably used a written source. This anonymous source seems to have highlighted the military aspects of the battle. It was furthermore apparently already favorable to Constantine and hostile to Maxentius. Eusebius obviously retained the evaluations of the emperors in the source, but by adding his own interpretive glosses, he superimposed a Christian perspective on the battle. In his account Eusebius claimed that Constantine had initiated his campaign to liberate Rome by praying to "God in heaven and his Word, the Savior of all, Jesus Christ himself." Maxentius in contrast had trusted in "the artifices of magic." Constantine nevertheless defeated Maxentius' troops in Italy and advanced on Rome, where "God himself" drew "the tyrant" outside the city's wall. Eusebius then compared the drowning of Maxentius to the loss of the Egyptian pharaoh and his army in the Red Sea; he also compared Constantine to Moses.[5]

Eusebius had reinterpreted the battle as a reenactment of a great moment of liberation in the Old Testament that had previewed Christian salvation. He may have been attracted to this biblical parallel because of the superficial similarity between a battle near a river at Rome

[5] Eusebius, *HE* 9.9.2, God in heaven, 3, magic, 4, tyrant, 5, pharaoh, 8, Moses. For discussion of the source for the battle, see the excellent account of Eusebius' modifications in Christensen (1989) 291, "little hope of identifying this source," 292, a "politically inspired account of pagan origin." This anonymous source was most likely in Latin: see Chapter 7.

Christensen's close reading of *History* followed the techniques pioneered by Schwartz (1909) XLVII–LXI, and Laqueur (1929), described by Christensen (1989) 8, as a detailed critique to reveal "the existence of possible uncertainties, contradictory repetitions and interruptions of the continuity in Eusebius's text." Laqueur in particular tended to explain discrepancies in Eusebius' text by postulating the influence of multiple sources. For the account of Maxentius and Constantine in *History*, Laqueur (1929) 150–60, 180–82, 201, argued that Eusebius added his Christian interpretation to a source with a pagan perspective about the relationship between Constantine and Licinius and a "national Roman" perspective about Maxentius at Rome, and that he also used both a Christian source and a pagan source about Constantine.

and the drowning of the Egyptian army. If Maxentius had suffered the fate of the pharaoh, then Constantine could be represented as a new Moses. Eusebius may also have been inclined to interpret Constantine as a supporter of Christianity because of the emperor's apparent opposition to Maximinus and his policy of persecution. After his victory in October 312, Constantine drafted "a most perfect law on behalf of the Christians" and informed Maximinus of his "victory over the liberated city." In December, Maximinus seems to have responded by announcing his decision to extend religious toleration to all provincials in the East. Eusebius had acquired a copy of Maximinus' letter, and he also knew about Maximinus' subsequent backtracking and defeat by Licinius. By the time he published this first edition of his *History* in late 313 or 314, he had apparently already concluded that opponents of Maximinus, both Constantine and Licinius, might well be supporters of Christianity. If so, then Constantine's victory at Rome could in addition be imagined in biblical terms.[6]

In the eighth and ninth books of the first published edition Eusebius still knew almost nothing about Constantius and the early years of Constantine's reign. He had been motivated to extend his narrative in *History* to describe the persecutions in the eastern provinces, and any information he added about events and emperors in the West was incidental and fortuitous. Even though he had somehow acquired a source describing events at Rome in 312, he had shaped his interpretation of that information with regard to events in the East. In this first edition of *History* Eusebius interpreted Constantine in terms of his concern about Maximinus and his persecutions. In particular, his own hostility to Maximinus had led him to think that an emperor

---

[6] Eusebius, *HE* 9.9.12, most perfect law, 9a.1–9, Maximinus' letter to Sabinus, 9a.12, letter to Maximinus from "the advocates of peace and piety," i.e., Constantine and Licinius. Lactantius, *De mortibus persecutorum* 37.1, Constantine's letter to Maximinus, 44.11, "when the victory of the liberated city was announced to him." Barnes (1982) 67–68, identifies the "most perfect law" with the announcement of victory. Although Eusebius, *HE* 9.9.12, 9a.12, claimed that Licinius joined with Constantine in sending this letter to Maximinus, Barnes (1981) 49, insists that the letter was "the work of Constantine alone."

like Constantine who had seemingly chided Maximinus might well have been favorable to Christianity. This Christianizing interpretation became more apparent in the second edition of *History*.

SECOND EDITION

Shortly after publishing this first edition Eusebius seems to have acquired more information about events in the West. He soon revised the eighth book by replacing the condensed version of *Martyrs* with a more comprehensive narrative of persecutions throughout the eastern provinces to 311. This general narrative included additional information about western emperors and their activities. Although he also discarded the original "Appendix," in this revised eighth book Eusebius repeated his positive assessments of Constantius at the moment of his death and of Constantine at the moment of his accession. In addition, he inserted two distinctive supplementary comments. One was the observation that after his death Constantius had been "hailed among the gods." The other was a revision that downplayed the army's role in the accession of Constantine by emphasizing instead his prior selection by God. In this case all Eusebius had to do was add a new phrase (noted here in italics) to his original sentence: "Constantine . . . was proclaimed immediately at the beginning as greatest emperor and Augustus by the soldiers *and long before them by God himself, the Emperor over all.*"[7]

These supplementary opinions presumably represented both the acquisition of additional information and a major rethinking of Constantine and his father. One opinion was distinctly odd. Eusebius again presented Constantius as a pro-Christian emperor by praising his friendliness toward "the divine Word," Jesus Christ. Presumably he had inferred Constantius' piety from his son's later behavior, and he had wanted to underscore Constantine's pedigree by praising his father. But at the same time, Eusebius noted that as a result Constantius had been the first of the four original Tetrarchic emperors to be hailed as divine. Because Constantius' new standing as *divus* was publicized primarily

---

[7] Eusebius, *HE* 8.13.12, gods, 14, God himself.

in the western provinces controlled by Constantine, it is not obvious how Eusebius had acquired this information. It furthermore remains mysterious why a Christian historian like Eusebius would compliment the divine apotheosis of Constantius as a reward for his support of Christianity.[8]

In contrast, the other new opinion that highlighted God's role in Constantine's succession was quite predictable for a Christian historian. Eusebius preferred to transform the initiative of the army during a military coup into passive acquiescence to a choice made by God. He included these supplementary opinions in the revised eighth book published before the autumn of 316 in the second edition of *History*. The culmination of this second edition was a new tenth book that included some of Constantine's letters, in which he had indicated his support for Christians. Eusebius had presumably concluded that the content of the letters confirmed his earlier inference about Constantine's Christianity, and he now decided to enhance Constantine's pedigree as an emperor by extolling his father and to demote the role of the army by emphasizing instead his preordained selection as emperor by God.

In this revised eighth book Eusebius also included more information about Maxentius. His account was very critical of Maxentius' activities and accused him of sexual misbehavior, a massacre, and sorcery. In particular, this expanded account elaborated on the emperor's scandalous behavior toward the most eminent members of the senate at Rome. One Christian matron, the wife of a prefect of Rome, was even thought to have committed suicide to avoid abduction by Maxentius' associates. Because Eusebius knew of Maxentius' eventual defeat by Constantine,

---

[8] Eusebius, *HE* 8.13.12, divine Word. For the consecration of Constantius as *divus*, see *Panegyrici latini* 7(6).3.3, 14.3, with Christensen (1983) 198, suggesting that Eusebius "made use of a source with a distinctly pagan outlook" for information about Constantius' apotheosis, and Gradel (2002) 365, claiming that *divus* was no longer "an indication of true divinity," but merely "an honorary title." After their deaths Maximian and Galerius had also been consecrated as *divi*, presumably at the initiative of Maxentius: see *ILS* 1:153, no. 671, a dedication to Maxentius at Iol Caesarea in Mauretania Caesariensis, no. 673, a dedication to Romulus, Maxentius' son, on Maxentius' estate (see Chapter 9).

he was probably all too willing to repeat these lurid accusations. But his source for this additional information is not obvious.[9]

One possibility is that the accusations had been included in the same anonymous source that Eusebius had already used for his description of the battle outside Rome in 312 in his original ninth book. If so, then the outlook of that source might help explain one of Eusebius' comments about Maxentius' religious beliefs. Eusebius noted that in an attempt to win over the people of Rome, Maxentius had "impersonated our faith" and ordered an end to the persecution of Christians. Eusebius of course objected to this characterization, and his strong denial might suggest that his source had in fact claimed exactly the opposite, that Maxentius had ended persecution because he had truly been a Christian (or a sympathizer of Christianity) and that his support for Christianity had led to his other shameful misbehavior at Rome.[10]

The accusations of immorality resembled the standard rhetorical charges against despotic tyrants and disgraced emperors. But the source may well have been correct about Maxentius' toleration for Christianity. Toward the end of his reign Maxentius and his praetorian prefect had apparently sent letters to Miltiades, the bishop of Rome, authorizing him to approach the prefect of Rome: "the aforementioned emperor ordered that those [possessions] confiscated during the time of persecution be restored to the Christians." In North Africa "freedom was restored to the Christians when Maxentius extended toleration." In this case, if Eusebius' source had blamed Maxentius' misbehavior on his adherence to Christianity, it was probably hostile to Christianity in general. In contrast, Eusebius wanted to retain the stories of Maxentius' bad behavior but distance his actions from Christianity. As a result, he simply dismissed as pretense any hint in the source of the emperor's sympathy for Christianity. Eusebius instead cast Maxentius, the "tyrant

---

[9] Eusebius, *HE* 8.14.1–6, activities at Rome, 16–17, matron. Chastagnol (1962) 59, suggests that this virtuous woman may have been the wife of Junius Flavianus, prefect of Rome from 311 to 312.
[10] Eusebius, *HE* 8.14.1, impersonated.

at Rome," as similar to his ally Maximinus, the "tyrant in the East" who had persecuted Christians.[11]

This recasting of Maxentius in the revised eighth book influenced Eusebius' interpretation of Constantine's victory at Rome. Now Constantine had an evil opponent similar to the reviled Maximinus; now it was more apparent why Constantine had decided that he had to liberate Rome and its inhabitants from their "enslavement" to this tyrant. As a result, the extended denigration of Maxentius in the revised eighth book considerably enhanced Eusebius' account of Constantine's victory in the ninth book, even though he had retained this ninth book apparently unchanged in this new edition of *History*. According to Eusebius, after the battle the victorious emperor's supporters hailed him with biblical verses from the Israelites' song of triumph celebrating the destruction of the pharaoh and his chariots. The senators and people of Rome welcomed him as "redeemer, savior, and benefactor." In return, in a public dedication Constantine commemorated his liberation of the city from the yoke of the tyrant. The supplementary information about the tyrant Maxentius in the revised eighth book had helped to underscore Eusebius' presentation of Constantine's victory as a form of liberation of Rome.[12]

---

[11] Eusebius, *HE* 8.14.7, tyrant in East and tyrant at Rome. On Eusebius' source for this information about Maxentius, see Christensen (1989) 139–40, "an official piece of propaganda which . . . utilized the criticism of Maxentius's rule which had gradually grown amongst the leading senators in Rome," 141n.99, "a piece of propaganda for Constantine," with Scheidel (2009) 299–301, for the conventional Roman rhetoric linking the abuse of imperial power with promiscuity. Letters of Maxentius and his prefect: Augustine, *Breviculus collationis cum Donatistis* 3.18.34 (CSEL 53:84); also *Ad Donatistas post collationem* 13.17 (CSEL 53:113–14), with De Decker (1968), arguing that Constantine subsequently imitated Maxentius' policy of tolerating Christianity. Toleration in North Africa: Optatus, *Contra Donatistas* 1.18.1.

Maximinus had previously sent envoys to Maxentius at Rome to negotiate an alliance; after his victory Constantine found their letters: Lactantius, *De mortibus persecutorum* 43.3, 44.10. Grant (1980) 156, suggests that Constantine himself may have circulated these documents in a "successful propaganda campaign against the memory of Maxentius and the waning power of Maximin."

[12] Eusebius, *HE* 8.14.6, enslavement, 9.9.8, Israelites' song, citing verses from Exodus 15, 9, senators, 11, dedication, with De Decker (1968) 480, "la personnalité de Maxence, telle qu'elle nous est représentée par Eusèbe, se distingue peu de celle de Maximin Daïa."

For the new tenth book that concluded this second edition of *History* Eusebius had certainly acquired a new source of information about Constantine. In the tenth book he cited a dossier of imperial documents. One was an accord drafted by Constantine and Licinius in early 313 that guaranteed toleration for all religions. Eusebius would presumably have acquired or read a copy of this proclamation after Licinius defeated Maximinus and promulgated it to the governors in his new provinces in the East during the summer of 313. The other documents included two letters from Constantine to the governor of Africa Proconsularis and another to the bishop of Carthage, all three sent during the winter of 312–313, another letter to the bishop of Rome sent in late spring of 313, and yet another summoning the bishop of Syracuse to a council at Arles in August 314. It is again not obvious how Eusebius might have obtained copies of these five letters concerning Constantine's western affairs so quickly. But they seemed to reinforce his earlier interpretation of Constantine as a Christian emperor, and they provided a fitting conclusion to this second edition of *History* published before autumn of 316.[13]

The last three books of Eusebius' *History* have hence preserved traces of a sequence of accounts and interpretations of Constantine's victory over Maxentius that appeared in the four years between autumn of 312 and autumn of 316. Quite quickly after the victory a written source that highlighted political and military aspects of the battle was being circulated in the East. This source was apparently favorable to Constantine, hostile to Maxentius, and most likely hostile to Christianity. Because this source had included examples of Maxentius' antagonism toward the senatorial aristocracy at Rome, it had apparently also criticized him as a Christian or a sympathizer of Christianity. If so, then it presumably would have welcomed Constantine not as a Christian but for restoring traditional values at Rome.

---

[13] Accord: Eusebius, *HE* 10.5.1–14, Lactantius, *De mortibus persecutorum* 48.2–12. For the letters, see Chapter 7. As Eusebius' source for the letters, see the survey of opinions in Carriker (2003) 285, suggesting perhaps a bishop involved in the Donatist controversy.

In contrast, at the same time Eusebius was himself still primarily concerned with dealing with the persecutions in the East. He hence read and interpreted this source through the lens of his eastern pre-occupations. Once he decided to add two more books to his earlier draft of *History*, he also included an account of Constantine's victory over Maxentius. In his initial short account Eusebius recast the information from his source by imposing a biblical interpretation that saw Constantine as a new Moses. Soon after publishing the first edition of his *History* he seems to have acquired more information about western affairs, including copies of Constantine's letters, and he quickly rewrote the eighth book of *History*. In this second edition he highlighted God's role in selecting Constantine as emperor and castigated Maxentius' behavior. Eusebius' source had criticized Maxentius as a Christian and presumably praised Constantine as a restorer of old values; in contrast, Eusebius criticized Maxentius as an ally of the persecutor Maximinus and praised Constantine as a Christian. In each case, the account in the source and then Eusebius' versions, the author was interested less in Constantine himself and more in another emperor, either Maxentius or Maximinus. Constantine was represented simply as the opposite of the other emperor.

THIRD EDITION

In Eusebius' second edition Constantine's greatest military success was still his victory over Maxentius in 312. But after Constantine defeated Licinius in September 324, Eusebius revised his *History* yet again. Because one primary objective in this revision was to denigrate Licinius by obscuring or removing his earlier association with Constantine and by including an account of his final defeat, Eusebius may well have wanted to publish the third edition before meeting Constantine at the council of Nicaea that was to convene in mid-325. Earlier in 325 Eusebius and his theology had been condemned at a council at Antioch. The council at Nicaea would provide a fresh opportunity to defend his doctrines, this time in the presence of the emperor. As he faced renewed scrutiny of his theology, Eusebius may have thought that he could help his cause by flattering Constantine in a new edition of *History*.

The culmination of this revised version of *History* was Constantine's victory over Licinius, which had given him control over the eastern provinces, including the provinces of Palestine. From Eusebius' perspective in Palestine the most recent victory had immediately become the most important of Constantine's reign. In the third edition Eusebius replaced the dossier of imperial documents included in the earlier version of the tenth book with an overview of Licinius' reign. Those imperial documents, consisting of the proclamation of Constantine and Licinius and the five letters of Constantine, had demonstrated Constantine's and Licinius' initial support for Christianity soon after the victory over Maxentius. This new narrative, however, emphasized Licinius' increasing hostility toward Christians in the East during the subsequent years, until finally Constantine had intervened and defeated his rival. Through overt excisions and judicious rewriting Eusebius had transformed Licinius from a supporter of Christianity into a new persecutor.

Even though in this revised edition Eusebius did not rewrite his earlier account of Constantine's victory over Maxentius in the eighth and ninth books, his new emphasis on the war with Licinius was an implicit reinterpretation of the earlier battle. By now Eusebius was focused more on the significance of Constantine's victory over Licinius and less on his earlier victory over Maxentius. The victory over Licinius marked "another beginning." At the end of this revised tenth book of *History* Eusebius celebrated the reunification of the Roman empire and the establishment of a dynasty of Christian emperors in Constantine and his oldest son, Crispus. Because those two joyful outcomes were recent consequences, Constantine's victory over Licinius seemed to mark the most important turning point in his reign. Highlighting the victory over Licinius hence provided a new understanding of the victory over Maxentius by demoting its significance.[14]

---

[14] Eusebius, *HE* 10.9.6, Roman empire, 7–9, dynasty. After excising the dossier of six early imperial documents from the original tenth book, Eusebius may have planned instead to append Constantine's letters and legislation from after his victory over Licinius. Three manuscripts of *History* included as an appendix a copy of a letter of Constantine written in

Modern historians must hence be much more discriminating when citing Eusebius' account in *History* of the battle outside Rome, in particular by clarifying which edition they have in mind. In the first edition Eusebius interpreted his anonymous source in biblical terminology by casting Constantine as a Christian emperor, the new Moses. In the second edition he inserted the battle into a longer continuum of victories over persecuting emperors, both Constantine's victory over Maxentius and Licinius' victory over Maximinus, and he emphasized the support of both victorious emperors for Christianity. In the third edition he downplayed the victory over Maxentius to highlight instead Constantine's victory over Licinius. Even though the words of the basic narrative remained almost the same from edition to edition, the meanings and implications of the battle changed considerably.

Then Eusebius met Constantine at the council of Nicaea and subsequently heard the emperor's own memories. At that moment Constantine was no longer the distant subject of an anonymous literary account that Eusebius reinterpreted in his own narrative or the remote author of imperial letters. Now the emperor could become Eusebius' immediate source, in person.

CHANGING THE BACKSTORY

The defeat of Licinius was a relief for Eusebius. As the tension between Constantine and Licinius had tightened, Licinius had become more intolerant toward the Christians in his eastern provinces. Just as Diocletian and Galerius had consulted the oracle of Apollo at Didyma before they initiated their persecutions of Christians, so Licinius now consulted the same oracle and resorted to pagan sacrifices. By the early 320s he had ordered imperial magistrates and soldiers to offer sacrifices during pagan festivals, and he had imposed restrictions on bishops and their communities. The triumph of Constantine had nipped that possibility

October 324 (subsequently inserted in *Vita Constantini* 2.24–42), as well as an exhortation to collect "all the laws and letters" of Constantine. If Eusebius was planning to attach a new dossier of imperial documents, then according to the exhortation, he intended the victory over Licinius to mark "another beginning": see Schwartz and Mommsen (1903–1909) 2:904, for the text of the exhortation.

of revived persecution: "the great victor Constantine... regained the East that belonged to him, and as in the past he established a single unified empire of the Romans." Eusebius could exhale again.[15]

He also could have revised and extended his *History* by again adding more books. Initially his *History* had focused on the slow expansion of Christianity in the Roman empire; then he had added three more books about persecution, martyrdom, and the rise of Constantine and Licinius as Christian emperors; then he had revised the final book to highlight Constantine's defeat of Licinius. Now he had the opportunity to continue his *History* by extending the arc of ecclesiastical history from Jesus Christ well into the reign of a Christian emperor.

Instead, after he completed his revisions to the final book, his *History* was closed. Eusebius justified stopping after ten books by claiming that ten was the "number of fulfillment." Perhaps he also realized that to continue his *History* would require including more information about himself and his own theology. In the spring of 325 Constantine may have attended the council at Antioch that condemned Eusebius and his doctrines. During the summer Eusebius attended the council at Nicaea, where the emperor himself helped integrate his theology with Nicene theology. But thereafter the theology of the church in the eastern provinces was developing in directions that Eusebius himself could not always support. Ending *History* with Constantine's victory over Licinius in autumn of 324 hence saved Eusebius from personal embarrassment and from having to engage in overt theological polemic.[16]

---

[15] Diocletian and oracle: Lactantius, *De mortibus persecutorum* 11.7. Licinius and oracle of Apollo: Sozomen, *HE* 1.7.2–3. Eusebius, *HE* 10.8.10–19, Licinius' hostilities, 9.6, great victor.

[16] Eusebius, *HE* 10.1.3, number of fulfillment. The disgrace of Crispus' execution in 326 might have initiated subsequent editing. Eusebius had mentioned Crispus favorably in *HE* 10.9.4, 6. Because he ignored Crispus when he repeated these passages from *History* in *Vita Constantini* 2.3.2, 19.2, Schwartz (1909) L, suggested that Eusebius had excised the references. But because the excisions are not found in any of the Greek manuscripts of *History*, it is likely that Eusebius left the references to Crispus in *History*, where they were in fact read and quoted by later Greek historians, such as [Gelasius of Cyzicus], *HE* 1.11.16, 2.1.4, and

Eusebius nevertheless continued to refer to Constantine's victory at Rome in other texts. In an oration at Tyre he alluded to the dedication that the emperor had erected at Rome after the battle. Because he had delivered this oration most likely shortly after the publication of the first edition of *History*, perhaps in 315, he presumably developed this information too from the anonymous source he had used for his account of the battle in that first edition, and he subsequently included the oration in the tenth book of the second edition of *History* published before autumn of 316. Decades later he again mentioned Constantine's construction of a statue and its accompanying dedication at Rome in a panegyric delivered at Constantinople in July 336 to celebrate the thirtieth anniversary of the emperor's reign. In this case too his comments about monuments at Rome may well have been incorrect, based on faulty interpretations of his source. The oddity, however, is that he had continued to rely on his initial inferences about Constantine's activities at Rome even in a panegyric delivered more than a decade after he had first met the emperor. This repetition might imply that he had not yet heard Constantine's own memories of the battle at Rome. In this panegyric of 336 Eusebius was still repeating and elaborating his own initial interpretation of the battle, developed more than two decades earlier for the first edition of his *History*.[17]

Eusebius essentially did the same in his *Life of Constantine*. Eventually of course he did hear Constantine's memories about his vision, his dream, and the construction of the military standard before the battle against Maxentius. As a result, his account of the battle in *Life* was both a bit more elaborate and a bit more condensed than the account in *History*. First, Eusebius provided a different backstory for the invasion, in which Constantine initially hesitated before marching into Italy.

Evagrius, *HE* 3.41. The Syriac translation of *History*, composed perhaps circa 400, omitted the references to Crispus: see Schwartz (1909) XLII. In that case the translator was responsible for the excisions, as implied by Winkelmann (2004) 72.

[17] For discussion of Eusebius' faulty inferences about Constantine's statue and dedication at Rome, see Chapter 7.

In *History* Constantine had been upset that people at Rome were ruled by a tyrant; in *Life*, although he was similarly dismayed to see Rome subject to "the slavery of a tyrant," he at first deferred to "those ruling in other regions because they were older." But after the invasions of Severus and Galerius failed against Maxentius, he set out to liberate the "imperial city" himself.[18]

Second, Eusebius inserted in *Life* some episodes not included in *History*. One described the emperor's dilemma about which god to adopt for assistance against the magic of the tyrant. Severus and Galerius had trusted in "a multitude of gods" and failed. In contrast, Constantine's father, Constantius, had honored one god, "the savior and guardian of the empire and the provider of everything good." So Constantine decided that he too should honor "only his father's god." It is not clear whether this internal debate about the relative merits of polytheism and monotheism derived from the emperor himself or whether it represented Eusebius' own gloss. It certainly provided Eusebius with an opportunity to contrast the power of the Christian God with the futility of the pantheon of deities promoted by Tetrarchic emperors. It also provided a segue to Constantine's memories.[19]

Eusebius then included three episodes from Constantine's memories: the story about the vision of the cross in the sky; the story about the emperor's dream of Christ, who encouraged him to construct a military standard; and the story about his consultation with experts, the "priests of God," who explained the theology of "the God who had been seen" and the cross. Between the second episode of the dream and the third episode of the consultation Eusebius furthermore included a lengthy description of the military standard.[20]

---

[18] Eusebius, *HE* 9.9.2, tyrant, *Vita Constantini* 1.26, slavery, deference. The source for this story about Constantine's hesitation is unknown: see Winkelmann (1991) 28, "Aus anderen Quellen nicht bekannt," and Cameron and Hall (1999) 202, suggesting it was Eusebius' own defense of Constantine's delay in invading Italy.

[19] Eusebius, *Vita Constantini* 1.27, Constantine's dilemma.

[20] For discussion of Constantine's memories, see Chapter 4. Other additions: Eusebius, *Vita Constantini* 1.38.4, the bridge now breaks "by the command of God" (cf. *HE* 9.9.7), 39.1, "Rome" replaced by "ruling city" (cf. *HE* 9.9.9).

Third, Eusebius also omitted a few comments. In *Life*, once the emperor began to plan his campaign Eusebius reverted to his earlier account in the eighth and ninth books of the second edition of *History*. Because he reproduced that earlier account almost verbatim, the small omissions were significant. In *Life* Eusebius did not repeat his earlier dismissal of the possibility that Maxentius had once supported Christians, and he no longer associated Constantine with Licinius as the "two [emperors] beloved by God." Instead, Eusebius classified Maxentius as the western equivalent of the persecuting emperor Maximinus, and he even transferred derogatory comments about Maximinus in *History* to Maxentius in *Life*.[21]

Eusebius' account in *Life* of Constantine's battle against Maxentius relied on two important sources. One was comparatively recent: Constantine and his memories of a vision, a dream, the construction of his military standard, and his consultation with churchmen. The other was comparatively old: Eusebius himself, and in particular his own earlier account in *History*. Eventually Eusebius did decide to continue his narrative of Constantine's reign past 324, the ending date of *History*. But to do so he made two more, rather odd decisions. One was not to expand *History* with additional books; the other was to recycle much of his earlier narrative about Constantine in *History* almost verbatim into *Life*. Even though he now had occasional access to the imperial court, he seems not to have interrogated the emperor and his advisers about earlier events, with the express intention of modifying or at least expanding his earlier narrative. Nor, excepting a few additions and omissions, did he rewrite his earlier narrative in response to hearing Constantine's memories. Instead, he simply included those memories as a new backstory, and he shaped his account of those memories to supplement and confirm his earlier narrative.

---

[21] Eusebius, *HE* 8.14.1, Maxentius and Christianity, 14, comments about Maximinus (transferred to Maxentius in *Vita Constantini* 1.33.2), 9.9.1, Constantine and Licinius. Although Drijvers (2007), properly stresses that Eusebius' description of Maxentius in *Life* was a "literary construct," it was repeated from the description in *History*, which in turn was derived from Eusebius' source.

Modern historians hence must cope with interesting paradoxes when thinking about the account of the battle of 312 in *Life*. On the one hand, Constantine recounted his memories long *after* the events. On the other hand, Eusebius had composed most of the narrative in which he later embedded those memories long *before* he met the emperor and heard his stories. Modern historians take pride in using new data to modify older interpretations. In contrast, Eusebius preferred to mold new information to conform to his own earlier narrative.

SHAPING MEMORIES IN THE WEST

CHAPTER SIX

KNOWLEDGE ABOUT EVENTS IN WESTERN PROVINCES WAS NOT common in eastern provinces. At Athens, Praxagoras composed his "History of Constantine the Great" in two volumes, apparently soon after the emperor's death. Because Praxagoras wrote his history as a young man while only in his early twenties, he had been born after the battle at the Milvian Bridge. According to a short summary of his now-lost history, Constantine had once lived at Diocletian's court at Nicomedia, and the emperor Galerius had plotted against him. After Constantine fled to his father in Britain, he became an emperor and organized an army of "Celts and Germans." According to Praxagoras, Constantine was upset on hearing that Maxentius was mistreating the people of Rome. In the subsequent military campaign "Constantine was victorious in battle and turned [Maxentius] to flight. While he was fleeing, Maxentius experienced a reversal in his life [and the] treachery that he had contrived for his enemies: he fell into a trench he had himself dug. Some of the Romans cut off his head, hung it on a pole, and walked around in the city."

Praxagoras next described Constantine's victory over Licinius at Nicomedia, his consolidation of imperial rule, and his foundation of a new capital at Byzantium. He was clearly quite impressed by the emperor's "virtue, excellence, and total good fortune." But by highlighting these activities in the East, he imposed an overall eastern perspective on the significance of Constantine's reign. In terms of both culture and religion, Praxagoras was a "Greek," an educated gentleman and a pagan. Not only did he know little about the emperor's activities in the West, including the battle outside Rome, but his other historical works discussed the ancient kings of Athens and Alexander the Great. Praxagoras apparently classified Constantine as the most recent in a long continuum of distinguished Greek rulers. He furthermore seems to have ignored the emperor's Christianity entirely. After the battle outside Rome, his Constantine entered the capital not behind a military standard in the shape of a cross but rather behind a pike carrying the head of his defeated rival. Praxagoras' Constantine represented Greekness, not Christianity.[1]

At about the same time Eusebius was composing his *Life of Constantine*, which he based on entirely different ideals and a different viewpoint. That viewpoint was a continuation of the perspective already presented in his earlier narrative in *Ecclesiastical History*. Somehow Eusebius had acquired an anonymous source that described Constantine's victory in 312 and subsequent events at Rome in time to include his own interpretive description in the edition of his *History* published in late 313 or 314. In the next edition of his *History*, published before autumn of 316, he included more information about Maxentius' scandalous behavior at Rome that he had learned from that same anonymous source or another source, and he cited a few of Constantine's letters from 313 and 314. Even though he was in Palestine, during the first few years after the battle of 312 Eusebius was remarkably

---

[1] Summary of Praxagoras' narrative in Photius, *Bibliotheca* 62. More might be deduced about Praxagoras' narrative if it could be considered a source for Libanius, *Orat.* 59: see Wiemer (1994a), and Malosse (2000). For another eastern account of Constantine's reign, note that in the mid-fourth century Bemarchius, a sophist from Caesarea in Cappadocia who taught at Constantinople, composed a history in ten books entitled "Deeds of the Emperor Constantine": see *Suda* B.259, and Libanius, *Orat.* 1.31, 39–44.

well informed about some of Constantine's activities in western provinces.

Even Eusebius, however, appeared to be knowledgeable only in comparison with other eastern Greek historians. During these same years other early accounts of the battle at Rome were composed in the West. One was included in a panegyric delivered most likely at Trier in 313, another in a pamphlet about the recent persecutions composed in 314 or 315 probably at Trier, and yet another in a series of marble panels displayed on a memorial arch dedicated at Rome in 315. The panegyric interpreted Constantine's Italian campaigns from the perspective of the northern Gallic frontier, the pamphlet offered an explicitly Christian point of view, and the arch portrayed the viewpoint of the people and senate at Rome.

Eusebius did not know about these other accounts in the West. But Constantine had been present at the delivery of the panegyric, the author of the pamphlet was a teacher of his oldest son, and the arch had been dedicated during his return visit to Rome. As a result, it is possible to imagine how the panegyric, the pamphlet, and the panels on this arch might have contributed to the shaping of the emperor's own memories of this battle. Because Constantine never told his stories to Eusebius and the other bishops until at least thirteen years after the battle, and possibly more than twenty years later, he had been constructing his memories for a long time during his years in western provinces.

A PANEGYRIC AT TRIER

After his victory Constantine had remained in Rome for a few months. During the winter he had traveled first to Milan in northern Italy to attend the wedding of a half sister to Licinius and to consult with his fellow emperor, and then back to the Rhine frontier, where he campaigned again against the Franks in northern Gaul. In one year, from spring to spring, Constantine and his army had marched more than 1,700 miles round-trip from Trier to Rome and back, and his rule now stretched "from the Tiber to the Rhine." In honor of his recent accomplishments an anonymous orator delivered a panegyric most likely at Trier and most likely in 313. Constantine was in attendance.[2]

This orator highlighted the events of the previous year. He first praised Constantine for his initiative in invading Italy to "liberate the city," that is, Rome. To justify the invasion he listed Maxentius' shameful activities and other shortcomings (including his "most despicable small size"!). During this march Constantine had been received at several cities in northern Italy, including Susa, Turin, Milan, Verona, and Aquileia, although in some cases only after sieges. The orator then noted his rapid advance on Rome from the north. Although Maxentius had survived earlier invasions by remaining inside the city's wall, this time he ventured out to face Constantine "with the Tiber River at his rear." The confrontation quickly became a rout, compounded when Maxentius' troops tried to retreat over the narrow Milvian Bridge. Because Maxentius and many of his soldiers had drowned in the Tiber, the orator was grateful to the river: "Constantine drove the enemy into you, but you killed him." After this victory the orator described the emperor's enthusiastic reception at Rome. During his stay in the capital Constantine presided over games and attended meetings of the senate. But soon he returned to "your [provinces in] Gaul." There his victory over the Franks was similar to his victory over Maxentius: once the barbarians finally dared to cross the Rhine, they were slaughtered. And just as at Rome, so Constantine again celebrated triumphal games.[3]

The source of this information about Constantine's invasion of Italy and his activities at Rome is guesswork. Constantine had led a small army from Gaul, and on his return he had brought back some of the praetorian guards who had supported Maxentius at Rome. The orator may have learned about the military campaigns from officials with

---

[2] Residence of "almost two months": *Panegyrici latini* 4(10).33.6; departure for Milan "during the next winter": Lactantius, *De mortibus persecutorum* 45.1; still in Rome on January 6, 313: *CTh* 15.14.3. Tiber to Rhine: *Panegyrici latini* 12(9).21.5, with Nixon and Rodgers (1994) 289–90, for the date and location of this panegyric.

[3] *Panegyrici latini* 12(9).2.4, city, 4.3, small size, 16.3, Tiber, 17.1, Milvian Bridge, 18.1, the enemy, 21.5, "in Gallias tuas," 23.3, games, with Christie (2006) 326–30, on the fortifications at Susa. This is the earliest literary reference linking the battle with the Milvian Bridge by name.

firsthand familiarity, such as members of the emperor's court, or, more likely, from some of the soldiers who had accompanied Constantine. In particular, the orator's account of the battle at Verona reflected the perspective of participants: "initially, I hear, you arranged your army in two lines." His description of Constantine's entry into Rome may also have been derived from an eyewitness: "the houses themselves, I hear, seemed to be shaken."[4]

In his later stories Constantine would of course claim that a vision of the cross in the sky had appeared to him and to all his soldiers before the battle. In 313, however, such a vision was apparently not among the memories of the battle passed on to this orator by his informants. The orator nevertheless glossed his account of the invasion and Constantine's success by emphasizing the role of divine guidance. He claimed that a god had encouraged the emperor to liberate Rome, and that the "divine mind" had revealed itself to him alone. In his opinion, Constantine had been guided by a "divine divinity," "divine advice," and "divine inspiration." By the time the emperor entered Rome after his victory, the orator was even referring to him as "your divinity." These comments were too vague to be identified as the orator's own interpretations or as the opinions of his informants. They were also not distinct enough to be classified as either cryptically pagan or politely Christian. Instead, the orator had simply associated the emperor's success with divine favor, and he had hinted that Constantine himself had shared in divinity. These were ideas that the emperor might absorb and subsequently revise for use in a more explicitly Christian context.[5]

The orator had described Constantine's invasion of Italy, his battles, including the battle at the Milvian Bridge, and his activities in

---

[4] *Panegyrici latini* 12(9).3.3, less than a quarter of his army accompanied him, 5.1–2, fewer than forty thousand soldiers, 9.1, two lines, 19.1, houses, 21.2–3, defeated soldiers stationed along Rhine and Danube. For tombstones of Constantine's soldiers in northern Italy, see Mennella (2004), suggesting that Constantine's expeditionary army in fact included only four thousand to five thousand soldiers (p. 359).

[5] *Panegyrici latini* 12(9).2.4, "deus," 2.5, "illa mente divina," 4.1, "divinum numen," 4.5, "divino consilio," 11.4, "divino . . . instinctu," 19.1, "numen tuum."

Rome. Even though he had acquired his information most likely from participants in the campaign, he could then interpret their memories to highlight his own concerns. In particular, his comments reflected a Gallic retrospective on the invasion, a view from the northern frontier. In that perspective Constantine's departure from the Rhine frontier, even if to liberate Rome, had caused anxiety, while his homecoming had been a moment to express gratitude. The orator may have been impressed by the success of Constantine's invasion of Italy, but he was more delighted by the emperor's defense of the Rhine immediately on his return. "Although you were weary from your battles and satisfied with your victories,... you did not allow yourself leisure and relaxation. Instead..., you marched to the lower frontier of Germany." In his opinion, protecting the northern frontier was more valuable than liberating Rome. For the people of Gaul, Constantine's victory at the Rhine had been more important than his victory at the Tiber.[6]

Lactantius at Trier

Approximately one year after the battle at Rome this Gallic orator was praising Constantine at Trier for having returned to Gaul to defend the Rhine frontier. At about the same time in Palestine, Eusebius was reading an anonymous source in preparation for writing the first version of his account of the battle in *History*. Both associated Constantine's victory with divine assistance, and Eusebius had concluded that the emperor was already a Christian. Neither, however, mentioned a vision of a cross in the sky, a dream about Jesus Christ, or the construction of a military standard.

At about the same time, Lactantius was preparing to write yet another account of the battle in a pamphlet about the recent persecutions under the Tetrarchic emperors. Lactantius had started his teaching career in

---

[6] *Panegyrici latini* 12(9).2.6–3.3, concern for security of Rhine, 21.5, new campaigns along lower Rhine. For the perspective from Gaul, see *Panegyrici latini* 12(9).14.2, "all Italy this side of the Po [River] having been recovered," referring to northern Italy, which from the perspective of Rome was considered to be Transpadane Italy, "Italy across the Po" (as mentioned in 12(9).7.7).

his native North Africa. Eventually, perhaps toward the end of the third century, he was appointed as a Latin rhetorician at Nicomedia in Bithynia. Nicomedia was a favorite residence of Diocletian. In his desire to make Nicomedia "the equal of Rome," the emperor initiated many construction projects, including basilicas, a circus for horse races, a mint, a weapons factory, and mansions for his wife and daughter. He may also have recruited teachers of Greek rhetoric and culture to move to Nicomedia, including a sophist from Athens. Diocletian himself, however, was a native Latin speaker, and he preferred to use Latin as the language of imperial administration, even in the eastern provinces. With his patronage Nicomedia was to become a "Latin capital." The appointment of Lactantius, as well as of a Latin grammarian, was meant to contribute to the transformation of this "obviously Greek city" into a new center of Latin studies in the Greek East.[7]

DIOCLETIAN'S COURT

Although teachers of Latin rhetoric and grammar were appreciated at Diocletian's Nicomedia, Christians were eventually no longer welcome. In February 303, military officers and soldiers ransacked a church at Nicomedia. In one of his treatises Lactantius admitted that he had been there at the time. "While I was teaching... the culture of oratory in Bithynia, it happened that at the same time a temple of God was demolished." On the next day Diocletian published an edict that imposed penalties on Christians. A subsequent edict ordered the arrest and imprisonment of clerics. The bishop of Nicomedia was beheaded, and other Christians were burned or drowned. When the palace subsequently caught fire, Christians were blamed, and court officials were purged and executed. Although Lactantius himself seems to

---

[7] For Andromachus, a sophist who taught at Nicomedia under Diocletian, see *Suda* A.2185, and Eunapius, *Vitae sophistarum* 457, with Millar (1969) 18, and *PLRE* 1:63, "Andromachus 2." Lactantius' appointment: Jerome, *De viris illustribus* 80, "ob Graecam videlicet civitatem," also mentioning the grammarian Flavius, who wrote a poem about medical practices. Lactantius, *Institutiones divinae* 5.2.2, "ego... accitus," *De mortibus persecutorum* 7.10, construction projects, with Van Dam (2007) 185–88, on the Tetrarchic preference for Latin.

have survived the hysteria untouched, his friend Donatus was tortured in turn by a prefect and two provincial governors.[8]

Lactantius apparently remained in residence at Nicomedia for at least the following two years. If so, then he perhaps witnessed Diocletian when the emperor returned in 304 from an extended trip to Italy and the Danube frontier. Even though Diocletian was gravely ill, he insisted on presiding at the dedication of his new circus. The emperor next appeared in public in March 305, still so enfeebled from his long illness that he was "hardly recognizable." Two months later Diocletian finally abdicated. After the ceremony Lactantius perhaps watched as the former emperor rode back through Nicomedia in a carriage on his way to retirement in a palace in Dalmatia.[9]

In addition to his teaching, Lactantius wrote a long book about Christian philosophy, entitled *Divine Institutes*, most likely already during the years after the outbreak of persecution while he was still at Nicomedia or soon after his departure. One important catalyst had been learning about the remarks of "two men there [in Bithynia] who, whether from arrogance or from rudeness, were insulting the truth that was in ruins and overthrown." One of these critics was a philosopher who had written three volumes attacking "the Christian religion and the Christian name." This philosopher had argued in support of "the cult of the gods by whose divinity and majesty the world was governed" and had praised the emperors for "defending the religions of the gods." He had hence provided a justification for the persecution of Christianity by suggesting that once this "impious and decrepit superstition had been repressed," "everyone . . . might experience the gods and their goodwill

---

[8] Lactantius, *Institutiones divinae* 5.2.2, temple of God, *De mortibus persecutorum* 12, burning of church, 13, first edict, 14.2, palace, 14–15, purge, 16, torture of Donatus. Eusebius, *HE* 8.2.5, second edict, 6.6, bishop, others; with Clarke (2005) 647–65, and Humphries (2009), for excellent overviews of the persecutions under the Tetrarchs.

[9] Lactantius, *De mortibus persecutorum* 17.4, circus, 17.8, recognizable, 19.1–6, abdication, carriage. For Lactantius' hint that he had remained at Nicomedia for at least two years after the outbreak of persecution, see Lactantius, *Institutiones divinae* 5.11.15, "I saw a governor in Bithynia who was wonderfully elated with joy . . . because a man who had resisted with great strength for two years finally seemed to yield."

to men." The other critic, "an important instigator in leading the persecution," can be identified as Sossianus Hierocles, the governor of Bithynia. Hierocles had written two volumes in which he had tried to expose the internal contradictions and falsehoods of the Bible.[10]

In response, Lactantius' *Institutes* provided an extended defense of Christianity. Lactantius promoted justice as a Christian virtue, critiqued pagan philosophers, and criticized the worship of traditional gods as false. In particular, he attacked Jupiter and Hercules, the two gods adopted as patron deities by Diocletian and his fellow Tetrarchic emperors. He claimed that the deceit and hatred that had characterized Jupiter's rule in heaven had now reappeared among the emperors, who were persecuting "those who are just and faithful to God." He also argued in favor of religious toleration: "there is no need for force and insult, because religion cannot be compelled. The experience must be achieved by words rather than by wounds." In this first edition of *Institutes* Lactantius censured the intolerance of pagan cults and strongly endorsed Christianity, but he did not promote the rule of a Christian emperor or even imagine the possibility. He was writing still under the cloud of ongoing persecution and not the sunrise of a Christian emperor.[11]

During his years at Nicomedia, Lactantius had no doubt seen Constantine, who was serving as a tribune, a military officer, at Diocletian's court. Constantine himself subsequently conceded that he had been at Nicomedia when the imperial palace had been burned in 303. In addition, at the moment of Diocletian's abdication in 305, Constantine was standing on the tribunal. Apparently the soldiers in attendance anticipated that he would be announced as one of the new replacement junior emperors. Then Galerius, a senior emperor, sprang

[10] Lactantius, *Institutiones divinae* 5.2.2, two men, 3, philosopher, 4, three volumes, 5, cult of gods, 7, emperors, 12, instigator, 13, contradictions, with Barnes (1981) 291n.96, arguing that Lactantius completed the first edition of *Institutes* in Africa in 308/309, and Digeser (1994) 43–44, between 305 and 310. On Hierocles, see Digeser (2002) 486–95. The identity of the philosopher is contested; for arguments that he was Porphyry of Tyre, see Digeser (1998), and Schott (2008) 177–85.
[11] Lactantius, *Institutiones divinae* 5.5.10–11, deceit and hatred, 19.11, religion.

his surprise. Lactantius may have been watching in the audience as Galerius "stretched his hand backward" and instead introduced Maximinus: "Constantine was pushed aside." Soon afterward Constantine left Nicomedia to join his father, Constantius, in Gaul.[12]

Lactantius' later pamphlet about the persecutions is the best account of details about the personalities of Diocletian and his fellow Tetrarchic emperors. His presence at Nicomedia helps explain how he had acquired much of this information. Not only did he refer to imperial edicts and letters. He also claimed to know about the motives of emperors, perhaps through contacts at court, and he noted personal details about the emperors, most likely from direct observation. Galerius especially, and in particular his repulsive appearance and cruel behavior, seemed to fascinate Lactantius. In his youth Galerius had tended livestock and been known as "cowboy." As emperor he acquired a reputation for arrogance and disruptive behavior. Lactantius assigned the outbreak of persecution to Galerius' initiative: "I have learned that this was the reason for his rage." He attributed Diocletian's abdication to Galerius' threats. He claimed that Galerius was amused by pet bears, "which very closely resembled him in size and meanness." Lactantius concluded that Galerius was himself a "beast" and not a "Roman" at all: his "savagery was alien to Roman descent."[13]

In his pamphlet about the persecutions Lactantius extended his narrative beyond Diocletian's abdication in 305, in particular by highlighting the oppressive behavior of Galerius and Maximinus, the new

[12] At Nicomedia: Constantine, *Oratio ad sanctorum coetum* 25.2. Constantine on tribunal: Lactantius, *De mortibus persecutorum* 19. The historian Praxagoras would claim that Constantius had sent Constantine to Diocletian's court at Nicomedia to be educated: see Photius, *Bibliotheca* 62. Although Praxagoras was presumably thinking of an education in Greek culture, it would be intriguing to imagine that Constantine also had listened to some of Lactantius' lectures at Nicomedia: see Foss (1995) 182, suggesting that Constantine had been a student of Lactantius at Nicomedia.

[13] Lactantius, *De mortibus persecutorum* 9.2, beast, savagery, 10.6, rage, 18, threats, 21.5–6, bears, with Van Dam (2007) 243–44, for Galerius' personality, and Davies (1989) 89, on Lactantius' motive for emphasizing Galerius' hostility: "apologetical convention, not . . . empirical evidence." Galerius as Armentarius: Aurelius Victor, *De Caesaribus* 39.24, 40.1, 6; also *Epitome de Caesaribus* 40.15, "pastor armentorum."

emperors in the East. The continuation of his narrative about eastern affairs hence raises questions concerning his sources and his own whereabouts. One possibility is that he had remained as a rhetorician in Nicomedia for several more years. In 311, as he lay dying, Galerius issued an edict that extended toleration to Christians. Lactantius noted that the edict was published at Nicomedia on April 30 and that immediately afterward his friend Donatus was freed after six years of imprisonment. This detail might imply that Lactantius had been there to greet his friend's release. In June 313 the emperor Licinius posted on public display in Nicomedia an official accord that he and Constantine had negotiated earlier that year. Because Lactantius quoted the declaration at length, perhaps he was himself still residing in Nicomedia.[14]

But it is more likely that he had already left Nicomedia years earlier. The threat from the persecutions was presumably one incentive for departing; another may have been the scarcity of students from the eastern provinces interested in studying Latin. Instead, Lactantius became a teacher in the West when Constantine selected him as a tutor for his oldest son, Crispus. "Lactantius, the most eloquent of all men in his time, instructed Crispus in Latin culture." "During his extreme old age he was the teacher of the Caesar Crispus, a son of Constantine, in Gaul." Constantine would have Crispus proclaimed as a Caesar, a junior emperor, in March 317. By then Crispus was most likely in his early twenties, and one possibility is that he studied with Lactantius after his promotion. But because during the next several years he was conducting military campaigns on the Rhine frontier, it is much more feasible that he would have studied with Lactantius before becoming a

---

[14] Lactantius, *De mortibus persecutorum* 1.1, dedication, 34–35, accord, Donatus' release, 48.1, posting of Licinius' declaration, with Nicholson (1989) 48n.4, suggesting that Lactantius' apology for flight in the face of persecution might have reflected his own behavior, and Digeser (2000) 171, "It is very unlikely that he was in the East in these years, let alone in Nicomedia." In contrast, Odahl (2004) 123–26, suggests that both Lactantius and Crispus left Nicomedia and arrived at Trier in 313, Wlosok (1989) 377, that Constantine invited Lactantius to Trier in 314/315, and Moreau (1954) 1:15n.1, that Lactantius was Crispus' teacher only after 317.

Caesar, during his earlier teen years while growing up most likely at his father's court.[15]

Constantine spent most of the first decade of his reign in northern Gaul, close to the Rhine frontier. His most important residence was Trier, where he initiated many construction projects, including basilicas, a forum, and an impressive circus. Just as Diocletian had enhanced the skyline of Nicomedia, so Constantine now improved Trier. And just as Lactantius' teaching of Latin rhetoric had complemented Diocletian's construction projects, so Constantine invited the same distinguished rhetorician to teach his son. After leaving Nicomedia, Lactantius moved, eventually or more likely soon, to Trier.[16]

CONSTANTINE'S COURT

As a teacher for Crispus, Lactantius would have had close contacts at the court, and he now started soaking up an outlook on events that was favorable to Constantine. This new outlook clearly affected the interpretive perspectives in his writings. At some point he revised *Institutes*, his earlier book about Christian philosophy that he had written in response to his experiences at Nicomedia. Back then Lactantius had focused on countering paganism and the persecution of Christians by refuting the underlying religious and philosophical justification for such intolerance. Subsequently he learned about the nature of Constantine's rule. According to Lactantius, immediately on becoming emperor in 306 Constantine had decided "to restore Christians to their worship and their God": "this was his first directive for the restoration of the holy

---

[15] Most eloquent: Jerome, *Chronicon* s.a. 317, with Burgess (1999a) 97, "derives from an unknown source that provided Jerome with biographical notices on a number of men well-known for their literary endeavours during the reign of Constantine." Scarcity of students, old age: Jerome, *De viris illustribus* 80, with Barnes (1982) 44, Crispus' age, 83, his campaigns. For Lactantius' arrival at Trier, see Digeser (1994) 51, suggesting that Lactantius was in Constantine's entourage from 310 to 313, (1997) 295, "after 310 Lactantius is more apt to have been in Trier than anywhere else," (2000) 135, "probably arrived at Constantine's western court between 306 and 310." Lactantius might also have left Nicomedia because of Galerius' hostility toward eloquence and culture after 305: see Lactantius, *De mortibus persecutorum* 22.4.

[16] Building projects at Trier: *Panegyrici latini* 6(7).22.5–6.

religion." Teaching at Constantine's court at Trier would have given him a firsthand look at this unusual world of open religious toleration. As a result, he inserted new invocations of Constantine at the beginning and the end of his *Institutes*. In the introduction to this revised edition he praised Constantine for his religious beliefs: "after rejecting errors, you are the first of the Roman emperors to acknowledge and honor the majesty of the singular and true God." In the conclusion he claimed that "the highest God has promoted you to restore the dwelling of justice and to govern the human race." "The powerful right hand of God protects you from all dangers." Lactantius now rewrapped his *Institutes* in a dust jacket of invocations to Constantine.[17]

Between 314 and 315 Lactantius furthermore composed a new pamphlet entitled *Deaths of the Persecutors*. Having seen the future, he responded in *Deaths* to the earlier persecutions by highlighting the painful consequences for the persecuting emperors. Diocletian had died supposedly by starving himself, Maximian by hanging himself, Galerius by wasting away, and Maximinus by poisoning himself. Sometimes the stately philosopher of *Institutes* seemed to be enjoying a bit too much the opportunity to describe at length the gruesome deaths of the persecutors.[18]

---

[17] Lactantius, *De mortibus persecutorum* 24.9, restore Christians, first directive, *Institutiones divinae* 1.1.13, the first, 7.26.11, highest God, 14, right hand. Dating the new invocations in *Institutes* is contested. In the introductory invocation Lactantius hoped that Constantine would be able to pass his "rule of the Roman name" to "your children": see *Institutiones divinae* 1.1.14. Constantine married Fausta in 307, but Constantine II, their first surviving child (and Constantine's second), was not born until 316. Digeser (1994) 44–50, (2000) 134, suggests that Lactantius was anticipating dynastic succession and that he added the introductory invocation in 310 and the concluding invocation in 313 at about the same time that he was writing or preparing to write *Deaths*. In contrast, Heck (1972) 150, argues that Lactantius added the introductory invocation in 321/324 and the concluding invocation in 324/325, Wlosok (1989) 378, that both invocations seem to refer to events of 324.

[18] Lactantius, *De mortibus persecutorum* 30.5–6, Maximian, 35.3, Galerius, 42.3, Diocletian, 49, Maximinus. For the date of composition, note that Lactantius mentioned Maximinus' death in summer of 313 and the death of Valeria, Diocletian's daughter, in late summer of 314 (*De mortibus persecutorum* 51.1): see Barnes (1973) 31–32, suggesting "before or during winter 314/315," accepted by Creed (1984) xxxiii–xxxv; also Wlosok (1989) 397, "zwischen Herbst 313 oder spätestens Winter 313/314 und Sommer 316."

In addition, Lactantius highlighted the emergence of Constantine and Licinius as emperors who supported Christianity. According to his narrative, Constantine too had been a victim of the persecuting emperors. After Diocletian's abdication, Galerius had supposedly been reluctant to allow Constantine to travel to his father in northern Gaul, because he worried about Constantine's support among soldiers, and he feared the exposure of his earlier attempts to make Constantine suffer harm. Constantine nevertheless escaped and reached his father, who on his deathbed commended him to the troops. Lactantius commented that "the hand of God always protected the man." In this telling of the story of the rise of Constantine, his acclamation as emperor seemed to have been a response to Lactantius' own invocation in *Institutes*.[19]

In his account in *Deaths* Lactantius foreshortened the interval between Constantine's reunion with his father and his acclamation about a year later, in July 306. He then included stories about Constantine's claim for recognition of the legitimacy of his imperial rule from Galerius; his negotiation with Maximian; Maximian's first plot against Constantine, who nevertheless forgave him; and Maximian's second plot, after which he killed himself. Lactantius' telling of these stories was consistently favorable to Constantine, who, he claimed, had been completely innocent as he negotiated with his devious rivals. Although Maximian's behavior in the plots had been "detestable," Constantine had been quite "unsuspecting." Despite this praise for Constantine, however, Lactantius significantly did not identify him as a Christian during the initial years of his reign. As emperor he had immediately extended toleration, and he had been the opposite of a noted persecutor like Galerius. But according to this account, Constantine had apparently not yet presented himself as a Christian. Lactantius' narrative reflected the concerns of his own preoccupations, not Constantine's later agenda.[20]

---

[19] Lactantius, *De mortibus persecutorum* 24.5, hand of God.

[20] Lactantius, *De mortibus persecutorum* 25, Galerius, 27.1, negotiation, 29.3–8, first plot, 29.4, unsuspecting, 30, second plot, 30.6, detestable life. For the unwarranted characterization of Lactantius as Constantine's mouthpiece, note Creed (1984) 105, on the story of Constantine's escape: "here more than almost anywhere in the work Lact. is the vehicle of Constantinian propaganda," 110, on the plots: "all the marks of official propaganda."

In *Deaths* Lactantius also included an account of Constantine's victory outside Rome in 312. Maxentius' troops seemed to be winning, until Constantine moved his own forces closer to Rome, "in the region of the Milvian Bridge." The emperor then "received advice in his sleep" "that he mark the heavenly sign of God on the shields." After the battle started, Maxentius consulted the Sibylline books and accepted a prophecy that he considered favorable. As he marched out across the Tiber, he had the bridge demolished behind him. But when "the hand of God" turned the battle against him, Maxentius retreated to the broken bridge and was pushed into the Tiber by the press of his fleeing soldiers.[21]

What was the source for Lactantius' account of this battle and other recent events at Rome? Because he was most likely now teaching Constantine's son at Trier, he may have had informants at the court. In his account Lactantius noted some aspects of imperial politics and diplomacy, including the envoys and letters that Maximinus had sent to Maxentius to request an alliance before the battle, the discovery of those letters by Constantine after the battle, the senate's decree to confer the "title of the first name" on Constantine, and Maximinus' mocking response on hearing that Constantine was to be hailed as "Maximus," "greatest" emperor. Lactantius might have talked with someone in Constantine's imperial entourage about this sort of official business.[22]

One of the oddities of Lactantius' account, however, is that its perspective was more attuned to Maxentius than to Constantine. In *Deaths* he had already characterized Maxentius as "arrogant and stubborn," and he had already mentioned the unrest at Rome that had led to the proclamation of Maxentius as emperor in 306; Maxentius' reinvestment of his father, Maximian, who was then living in Campania; Severus' attack on Rome and the desertion of his troops; Galerius' attack on

---

[21] Lactantius, *De mortibus persecutorum* 44.1–9, battle.

[22] Lactantius, *De mortibus persecutorum* 43.3, envoys and letters, 10, discovery of letters, 11, senate's decree, 12, mockery. Lactantius certainly did not accompany Constantine's expedition, and he probably never visited Rome at all: see Nicholson (1999) 14. As the source for his account of the battle at the Milvian Bridge, Creed (1984) 119, speculates "that it came at least from someone in his [Constantine's] entourage." Note that Lactantius may also have listened to the panegyric at Trier in 313.

Rome and his subsequent retreat; and Maxentius' angry expulsion of Maximian from Rome. For the years before the battle Lactantius seemed to know more about Maxentius and his challenges at Rome than about Constantine and his campaigns in Gaul.[23]

His account of the battle at Rome likewise was better informed about Maxentius than about Constantine. Lactantius mentioned Maxentius' initial reluctance to go outside the wall of Rome, because of a fear that he would be killed. He described the different units that made up Maxentius' army and its initial success. He noted that Maxentius was about to celebrate the anniversary of his accession. As the emperor was hosting games in the circus, however, the people had shouted in mockery that he was a "deserter" for not engaging in battle and that Constantine could not be conquered. Lactantius mentioned that Maxentius and some senators consulted the Sibylline books and discovered a prophecy that "on that day an enemy of the Romans would perish." Finally, he reported the end of the battle from the perspective of Maxentius: his army had been terrified, and he himself had fled back to the broken bridge. When Constantine returned to Gaul in the next year, he brought back some of Maxentius' troops. Lactantius' account of the battle makes better sense if it were acquired from talking with Maxentius' former soldiers, first about the preliminary events in the besieged city, then about the fighting. Although researched in Trier at Constantine's court, his account seems to have reflected a perspective on the battle derived from Maxentius' Rome.[24]

A second oddity is the brief description of Constantine's decision to mark his soldiers' shields. Lactantius claimed that before the battle

---

[23] Lactantius, *De mortibus persecutorum* 18.9, arrogant, 26.1–3, proclamation, 7, Campania, 8–11, Severus' invasion, 27.1–8, Galerius' invasion, 28.3–4, expulsion.

[24] Lactantius, *De mortibus persecutorum* 44.1, reluctance, 2, units, 4, anniversary, 7, deserter, circus, 8, Sibylline books, 9, end of battle. For information about another of Constantine's opponents, note that Eusebius would later receive a report about a speech Licinius had delivered to "chosen members of the soldiers in his entourage and his honored friends" from "men who had heard the oration": see Eusebius, *Vita Constantini* 2.5.1, 5. It is not clear where Maxentius was celebrating his anniversary, in a circus inside Rome or in the circus he had constructed on his estate south of Rome: see Chapter 9.

the emperor had "marked Christ on the shields" by using a particular emblem, "a slanted letter X, with the top of its head twisted around." Because his description of this emblem was notably imprecise, the text of this particular passage has been susceptible to modern emendations. Presumably Lactantius had actually seen some emblem that he was trying to describe and interpret. One peculiarity is that he explained the emblem in terms of a Greek word. If, as he claimed, the emblem represented the name *Christ*, then he had presumably interpreted the X as a chi and the bar with a round head as a rho (P), the first and second Greek letters of *Christ*. Even though he was currently teaching as a Latin rhetorician, most likely at Trier, Lactantius nevertheless interpreted the emblem in terms of letters of the Greek alphabet. Because he had previously been teaching at Nicomedia, he certainly knew enough Greek to make this visual association. But among people in the Latin West, including the soldiers in Constantine's army, it is unlikely that this was an obvious connection.[25]

Language was one peculiarity of Lactantius' interpretation of this emblem. Another was that the chi-rho symbol, the christogram, was not yet in common usage when he composed *Deaths*. Stars that might be interpreted as crosses first appeared on coins minted for Constantine sometime after the battle in 312 but before early 317, although the Christian significance of these symbols was dubious, because the coins also celebrated the pagan deities Sol (the sun god) and Mars. In 315 and 316 coins and medallions depicting Constantine wearing a bowl-shaped, high-crested helmet were minted to celebrate the tenth anniversary of his reign. On bronze coins minted at Siscia and silver medallions minted at Ticinum a monogram resembling a christogram appeared as a badge on the crest of the emperor's helmet. Even though this badge may well have been a reminder of the victory in 312, it was not necessarily a christogram, and it did not appear on similar coins produced at the mints in Gaul at Trier, Lyon, and Arles. It also soon disappeared from

---

[25] For textual emendations to the description of the emblem in *De mortibus persecutorum* 44.5, see Moreau (1954) 2:434–36, and Creed (1984) 119; for the possibility that the description should be excised as a gloss, see Rougé (1978) 21–22.

coins. The first coins depicting a christogram as the design on a shield were minted at Trier in honor of Crispus in the early 320s.[26]

Perhaps Lactantius had indeed noticed a new emblem (whether Greek letters or something else) on the shields of the soldiers after their return to Trier from the Italian campaign. In that case the derivation of his story about Constantine's dream was similar to the origin of some of the stories included in Eusebius' *Life*. Eusebius would hear Constantine's memories about his earlier campaigns after he asked the emperor about the military standard; Lactantius heard the story about the battle when he inquired about this battle emblem. The stories they heard were about military successes, not about a religious conversion. But both Lactantius and, decades later, Eusebius glossed the stories and the military emblems in terms of Christianity.

A final oddity is that Lactantius did not make this battle the culmination of his narrative. In his early account in *History* Eusebius compared Constantine to Moses and his victory at Rome to the salvation of the Israelites. Writing at almost the same time as Eusebius, Lactantius might have made a similar comparison in *Deaths*. He was certainly familiar with the significance of Moses' triumph. At the end of *Institutes* he had already offered a description of the last times leading up to the end of the world. As a preview for the inevitable fall of Rome he had highlighted the downfall of the kingdom of the pharaohs in Egypt. God's people had been freed from their slavery by walking safely through the Red Sea, while the pharaoh and his army had been drowned. In *Deaths* Lactantius might hence have suggested that Constantine's victory likewise "would liberate his people from their burdensome slavery to the

---

[26] For the coins and medallions, see Alföldi (1932), modified by Bruun (1962) 5–19: "the christogram was a Greek monogram in Latin territory. . . . It is possible, even probable, that the christogram in 315 was known as the miraculous sign connected with the victory at Ponte Molle, but the general public lacked the pre-requisites to draw further conclusions" (p. 32); also Bruun (1966) 37, "After 320 the new helmet [with the christogram] disappears from the obverses," 64, "Christian symbolism has no place on the coins of Constantine," 197 no. 372, christogram as shield design, and Bruun (1997), arguing that the monogram was initially a Constantinian emblem but later reinterpreted as a Christian symbol.

world." After the ending of persecutions Constantine's victory could have been represented as initiating a new era for Christians.[27]

Instead, while Eusebius, a bishop, used a biblical analogy for Constantine's battle, Lactantius, a rhetorician, thought in terms of classical Latin poetry. In his account he glossed the combat with a line from Virgil's *Aeneid* about a pointless battle between Trojans and Italians, before they blended together to become Romans. This citation from Virgil helped explain Maxentius' futility in consulting the Sibylline books before the battle. Maxentius had indeed misunderstood his prophecy: with his own death an "enemy of the Romans" had in fact been killed. Lactantius represented Constantine's battle as a Roman victory rather than a Christian victory.[28]

LICINIUS' DREAM

The climax of Lactantius' narrative in *Deaths* was instead the outcome of the civil war between Maximinus and Licinius in 313. In anticipation of their confrontation Maximinus remained true to his Tetrarchic background by making a vow to Jupiter. In contrast, Licinius had a dream in which an "angel of God" taught him a prayer for his troops to recite. Before the deciding battle in Thrace his troops recited this prayer three times; then they were victorious with the assistance of the "highest God." After the battle Maximinus fled to Tarsus, where he killed himself during the summer, and Licinius tracked down and killed the relatives of previous emperors, including Diocletian and Galerius. As a persecutor in the eastern provinces Maximinus had been the true successor of Diocletian and Galerius. In the estimation of one eastern churchman in the late fourth century, Diocletian had been the first to discredit Christians, Galerius had been worse, but Maximinus had surpassed

---

[27] Lactantius, *Institutiones divinae* 7.15.2–3, God's people, 4, liberate.

[28] Lactantius, *De mortibus persecutorum* 44.6, citing Virgil, *Aeneis* 10.757. Literary allusions certainly shaped Lactantius' account of the dream and the battle: see Moreau (1954) 2:433, suggesting that Lactantius modeled Constantine's dream on the dream of Judas Maccabaeus in 2 Maccabees 15:11–16, and Nicholson (2000), that Lactantius linked eschatology and history by thinking about the Second Coming of the Son of Man.

both. Maximinus would become the hobgoblin of eastern Christian paranoia, the personification of "the time of the persecutions." After his death Christians smashed his statues and slashed his portraits. In a pamphlet about the horrible fates of persecuting emperors, the death of Maximinus and the annihilation of the other emperors' families hence offered a much more satisfying conclusion than the death of Maxentius at Rome.[29]

Despite his departure from Nicomedia and move to Trier, Lactantius had always remained more interested in events in the East than in the West. Even when he quoted the joint proclamation by Constantine and Licinius that extended toleration to Christianity, he located its publication at Nicomedia, where it had been posted by Licinius, rather than at Constantine's court. Lactantius furthermore dedicated his pamphlet to Donatus, his friend who had suffered during the Tetrarchic persecutions in the East. Donatus too would have been more pleased to hear about events in the East. It is hence not surprising that Lactantius had more to say about Licinius' dream before his victory over Maximinus than about Constantine's dream before his victory over Maxentius. Constantine may have initiated religious toleration, but at the time when Lactantius was writing *Deaths*, Licinius could be credited with a still-greater accomplishment. For both Lactantius and Donatus, Licinius, as the victorious emperor who had ended the threat of persecution in the eastern provinces, would have been more significant than Constantine.[30]

Lactantius' source for events in the East after his departure from Nicomedia, in particular for the details of the war between Licinius and

[29] Lactantius, *De mortibus persecutorum* 46.2, Jupiter, 3, angel, 11, three times, 47.3, highest God. Gregory of Nazianzus, *Orat.* 4.96 (*PG* 35.630B), evaluation of three emperors, disfigurement of portraits; Gregory of Nyssa, *Vita Macrinae* 2, time of persecutions, with Van Dam (2003a) 15–18, 34–39, for memories of persecution in the family of Basil of Caesarea and Gregory of Nyssa. Maximinus' statues: Eusebius, *HE* 9.11.2.

[30] Lactantius, *De mortibus persecutorum* 48.1, proclamation at Nicomedia, 52.5, Donatus, with Moreau (1954) 2:442, "Lactance n'a pas insisté sur le caractère atroce de la fin de Maxence. C'est la preuve qu'il ne considérait pas ce dernier comme un persécuteur," and Christensen (1980) 24, "The centre of gravity of the work is . . . the East."

Maximinus, is not obvious. One possibility is that he had returned to his teaching position at Nicomedia after the proclamation of toleration for Christians in 313. In that case he could have talked again with his friends about events in the East as he composed *Deaths*. Another, more viable possibility, however, is that Lactantius wrote this pamphlet at Trier. In that case he would have had to rely on a written account (or accounts) acquired quite quickly after the events. Like other notable teachers, Lactantius too maintained an extensive correspondence. One of his correspondents was a former student to whom he had already dedicated a treatise composed during his stay at Nicomedia. This former student (and similar correspondents) may well have been providing updates on events in the East.[31]

As a result, Lactantius' sources, oral and written, were exactly the opposite of Eusebius' sources. Eusebius could rely on oral traditions, even eyewitness accounts, for events in the East under Diocletian, Galerius, Maximinus, and Licinius, but he needed a written source for events in the West under Constantine, in particular the battle at Rome. Lactantius would have had access to oral memories at Constantine's court at Trier for contemporary events in the West, but he needed to rely on written accounts for events in the East after his departure from Nicomedia.

Lactantius presumably acquired information about the early years of Constantine's reign, including the battle at the Milvian Bridge,

---

[31] Contrast Barnes (1973) 40, suggesting that Lactantius might have received copies of eastern documents from friends, with Barnes (1981) 14, arguing that Lactantius wrote *Deaths* "in Nicomedia as a subject of Licinius, not of Constantine." For Lactantius' continuing contacts with friends in the East, note that the list of his writings in Jerome, *De viris illustribus* 80, included collections of letters, among them two books of letters exchanged with Demetrianus, "his student"; also Jerome, *Ep.* 84.7, "letters to Demetrianus," with Wlosok (1989) 402, suggesting that the collection of letters to Demetrianus was compiled in Gaul. In the dedication of an early treatise to Demetrianus, Lactantius described himself as "your teacher": see Lactantius, *De opificio Dei* 1.1.

In contrast, if Lactantius did write *Deaths* back in Nicomedia, then he would have needed a source for events in the West. Christensen (1980) 62–64, 72–76, hence speculates that he used the now-lost "Kaisergeschichte," also postulated to be a source for other fourth-century historians writing in Latin; for discussion of the "Kaisergeschichte," see Schmidt (1989b).

from talking with soldiers and officials at the emperor's court at Trier. Most likely Constantine himself had not been a source for Lactantius' description of the battle, the emperor's dream, or other events from the emperor's life. Instead, the relationship may have been reversed, and Lactantius' books, both *Institutes* and *Deaths*, may have influenced Constantine and his later memories of these events. In fact, Lactantius himself might have been a direct source for Constantine's later memories.

Already early in his reign Constantine had shown an interest in philosophical and theological arguments. Studying Lactantius' treatises was perhaps a difficult project, however. Even a learned bishop of Rome subsequently grumbled about reading them. In his estimation, the books were far too long, "thousands of lines," and there were too many erudite digressions about metrics, geography, and philosophy that were suited only for other scholars. But perhaps Lactantius had used his *Institutes* as the basis for a series of public lectures at Constantine's court at Trier. Crispus would have listened as a student, and the emperor perhaps as an interested auditor. As a result, in a letter to bishops in North Africa written in the late summer of 314, Constantine seems to have recycled some of the ideas that Lactantius had highlighted in *Institutes* about disobedience to God. If Lactantius were still at Trier while he was writing *Deaths*, then through reading or through listening to orations, Constantine may likewise have become familiar with his account of events in both East and West, including the battle at the Milvian Bridge and the civil war between Maximinus and Licinius.[32]

---

[32] Complaints of Damasus: Jerome, *Ep.* 35.2. After a friend asked him to compose a condensed version of *Institutes*, even Lactantius conceded that he should "compress the digressions and abbreviate the verbosity": see Lactantius, *Epitome divinarum institutionum* praef. 1. Constantine's letter: *apud* Optatus, Appendix 5, with Digeser (1994), (2000) 170–71, for an excellent argument that Lactantius' philosophy had influenced this letter, and Chapter 7, discussing the context after the council at Arles. Lactantius' ideas may also have influenced Constantine's *Oration to the Saints*, in particular the emperor's interest in Virgil and the Sibylline oracles: see De Decker (1978) 80–81, Guillaumin (1978) 197, "Ce *Discours* aura été rédigé par l'empereur à partir d'un canevas fourni par Lactance," and Lane Fox (1986) 658–62. Schott (2008) 116–17, suggests that Constantine's discussion of divine retribution on wicked emperors (in his *Oratio ad sanctorum coetum* 24–25) "almost certainly owes something to Lactantius's *On the Deaths of the Persecutors*."

Eventually, of course, Constantine had to explain his own victory over Licinius, who at the end of Lactantius' *Deaths* had still been his nominal ally. In Lactantius' account, Licinius had had an elaborate dream experience before his decisive battle against Maximinus, and he had subsequently dictated a prayer for his troops to recite. Constantine may well have appropriated some of these details into his later memories. When he eventually recounted his memories to Eusebius, his account of the effectiveness of his battle standard had expanded to include victories over both Maxentius in 312 and Licinius in 324. His dream was now also more impressive than his rival's dream. Although Licinius had seen an "angel of God," Constantine would claim to have seen Jesus Christ in person in his own dream before the battle in 312. He would furthermore mention a prayer he had composed for his troops, which was similar to Licinius' prayer. Licinius had addressed his prayer to "Highest God," Constantine (perhaps with a better sensitivity for current doctrinal controversies) to "Only God," but each had his soldiers thank God for their victories. The most significant difference between the prayers was the addition of an entreaty for the safety of "our emperor Constantine and his sons, God's friends." As usual, even in a prayer Constantine was already thinking ahead to the establishment of a new imperial dynasty.[33]

Constantine had a gift for consigning his defeated opponents to oblivion by appropriating their accomplishments. After defeating Maxentius, he had purloined credit for his rival's monuments at Rome. After defeating Licinius, he would trump his rival's dream and despoil his rival's prayer to turn it into a victory ode and an endorsement of dynastic succession. Lactantius' account of Licinius' victory over

---

[33] Prayer of Licinius: Lactantius, *De mortibus persecutorum* 46.6; of Constantine: Eusebius, *Vita Constantini* 4.20. Barnes (1981) 48, reverses the sequence by suggesting that Licinius "may have modeled his prayer on one which Constantine originally devised for his own army to recite before the Battle of the Milvian Bridge." If so, it would be odd for Lactantius to know about an imitation prayer at a distant battle in the East but not about the original prayer at a battle that he had discussed with its participants. For an argument that Constantine was familiar with *Deaths*, see Digeser (1997) 292–93. Even though Davies (1989) 81–82, argues that Lactantius became Crispus' tutor only after writing *Deaths* in 314–315, he also suggests that familiarity with *Deaths* motivated Constantine to invite Lactantius.

Maximinus, recorded in *Deaths* but also perhaps publicized in orations, may well have helped shape not only Constantine's subsequent actions but also his later memories about the battle at the Milvian Bridge. In his memories Constantine was perhaps reacting to Lactantius' account by claiming that his own experiences had been much more impressive.

THE ARCH IN ROME

Constantine spent the winters of 313–314 and 314–315 at Trier, precisely the period when Lactantius was collecting information, writing *Deaths*, and perhaps delivering public lectures about the end of persecution, the deaths of the persecutors, and, possibly, the emperor's own expedition into Italy. In the late spring of 315 Constantine started to march south again into Italy. He entered Rome in mid-July and stayed for slightly more than two months. This excursion was not another invasion. Instead, he was returning to Rome to celebrate the tenth anniversary of his accession. He also came to pay his respects to the capital, its residents, and its senate.

During this visit Constantine joined in celebrating the dedication of a large commemorative arch located on the street between the Palatine and Caelian Hills, just south of the junction with Sacred Street, which led west into the Forum. The Colosseum loomed nearby to the northeast of the arch; a colossal bronze statue of the sun god Sol was directly north of the arch; and to the northwest the Temple of Venus and Roma presided on the Velian ridge. This imposing triple arch was almost eighty-five feet wide, almost twenty-five feet deep, and almost seventy feet high, and it consisted of a large central passageway flanked by a smaller archway on each side. The elaborate decorations included many panels and sculptures, of which some had been recycled from earlier imperial monuments and others were new for this arch.

At the top the prominent dedicatory inscription was displayed in the center of each long side of the hulking attic, flanked by panels depicting the emperor performing various traditional activities. Large statues of Dacian prisoners stood next to these top panels. Over the side archways roundels depicted the emperor in scenes of hunting and sacrifice. A frieze of six long panels encircled the arch and depicted episodes from Constantine's earlier invasion of Italy and visit to Rome. Panels with scenes of warfare were placed inside the central passageway and at the ends of the attic, and roundels of Sol, the sun god, and Luna, the moon goddess, stared out from the short sides of the arch. Tall columns framed the three passageways, along with reliefs of winged Victories and other deities in the spandrels. On the bases of the columns reliefs depicted more winged Victories as well as Roman soldiers and barbarian captives. With its inscriptions, relief panels, roundels, and statues the arch was an especially eloquent text about Constantine, a "panegyric of sculptures" as expressive as the panegyric at Trier.[34]

As an overtly honorific monument, the arch commemorated different moments in Constantine's reign. One was his earlier battle outside Rome. Inside the central passageway, short inscriptions accompanied the panels depicting the emperor as a soldier in or after battle. By honoring him as "liberator of the city" and "founder of tranquility," the inscriptions recalled the consequences of his earlier victory. Another moment was the beginning of the tenth anniversary year of Constantine's accession, celebrated on July 25 concurrently with the dedication of the arch. Yet another was the next decennial anniversary. Short inscriptions over the side passageways linked best wishes for the current anniversary with high hopes for the next: "so the tenth, likewise the twentieth," and "with vows for the tenth, with vows for the twentieth." The inscriptions and the iconography hence offered a succinct overview of Constantine's relationship with Rome, from his first appearance as a victorious general in 312 to the current celebration of his tenth anniversary in 315, and on to expectation of the next celebration in ten years. To affirm the bond between Constantine and Rome the arch remembered

---

[34] The analysis and detailed photographs in L'Orange and von Gerkan (1939), remain fundamental for interpreting the iconography of the arch; for additional photographs, see Giuliano (1955). Perhaps there were also sculptures on top of the arch. During his visit to Rome at the beginning of the fifth century, the poet Prudentius had observed honorific arches: see Prudentius, *Contra orationem Symmachi* 2.556–57, "we marvel at the four-horse chariots on the very top of an arch and at the commanders standing in the lofty chariots." Quotation about panegyric translated from Ruysschaert (1962–1963) 92.

a near past, commemorated a joyful present, and anticipated a blessed future.[35]

As a more subtle didactic text, however, the arch was designed to define the relationship between Constantine and Rome and to shape the emperor's behavior at the capital. The preferred interpretive medium was the reframing of history, for which the decoration on the arch provided, first, a representation of Constantine that located him in a longer context of comparisons with emperors from the early empire and, second, a precisely calibrated reading of recent events, including the invasion of Italy and the battle of 312. The message was hence simultaneously generic, about all emperors in general, and specific, aimed directly at Constantine himself. By stressing both earlier Roman imperial history and current events, the arch was trying to mediate any tensions between the expectations of the residents of a very old capital and the intentions of a new emperor.

MEMORIES OF THE PAST

The imperial past depicted on the arch was in fact older, much older, than the battle of 312, and through comparisons with predecessors the inscriptions and iconography represented Constantine as a particular type of emperor. The first concern was to insert him into the longer narrative of good emperors who had honored Rome. Many of the panels and roundels had been recycled from earlier imperial monuments. The eight panels on the long sides of the attic had originally depicted Marcus Aurelius, the eight roundels over the side archways had depicted Hadrian, and the four panels inside the central passageway and at the ends of the attic had originally formed one long panel depicting Trajan. The Trajanic panels showed the emperor in battle and being crowned by Victory afterward. The Hadrianic roundels showed the emperor hunting a bear, a boar, and a lion or sacrificing to Apollo, Silvanus, Diana, and Hercules. The Aurelian panels showed the emperor in scenes of war, including his reception of prisoners, his address to soldiers, and his preparations for a sacrifice, and scenes of peace, including his arrival

[35] Inscriptions: *ILS* 1:156, no. 694 = Grünewald (1990) 217, no. 239.

at Rome, his distribution of coins to the people, and his departure from Rome.

The designers of the iconography on the arch had many earlier panels, sculptures, and architectural marbles available for reuse, because the construction of the massive Aurelian Wall around Rome starting in the 270s had required the systematic demolition of older buildings and monuments in its path. From this stockpile of salvaged building materials the designers decided to highlight specific imperial predecessors. In late antiquity these particular second-century emperors were still highly regarded as successful rulers. Trajan was noted for his victories in wars on the northern and eastern frontiers, and Hadrian for his love of culture; for his virtue and his desire to imitate the gods, Marcus Aurelius was ranked as the best emperor. Constantine was now put in their place. On the recycled panels and roundels most of the emperors' heads were recut as Constantine. This replacement was hence not a condemnation of memories of bad emperors but a revival of memories of good emperors. As a result, enough background features had to remain for viewers to know which emperors were being replaced and renewed. By representing Constantine as the new Trajan, the new Hadrian, and the new Marcus Aurelius, the designers of the arch were also expecting him to behave like them.[36]

A second objective was to associate Constantine with Augustus, the first emperor, and the ideals of an emperorship that respected the traditions of the old Republic. Augustus' massive mausoleum was located in the north end of the Campus Martius, in the narrows between the Tiber and Wide Street (*Via Lata*), which was a continuation of the

---

[36] See De Maria (1988) 303–5, discussing a now-lost arch of Marcus Aurelius that may have been the source of the Aurelian panels, and Coates-Stephens (2001) 232–35, for the availability of building materials recycled from old monuments as a consequence of the construction of the Aurelian Wall. Reputation of emperors: Julian, *Caesares* 311C–D, Trajan and Hadrian, 312B, Marcus Aurelius, 317B, Trajan, 327A–328B, Trajan, 333C, Marcus Aurelius, with Eutropius, *Breviarium* 10.16.3, for Julian's own desire to imitate Marcus Aurelius. Evers (1991) 793, stresses the limited recutting of the heads of Hadrian and Trajan: "le sculpteur du Bas-Empire n'a retouché les portraits impériaux du IIᵉ siècle que de manière tres partielle."

Flaminian Way from the Milvian Bridge into downtown Rome. In his will Augustus had instructed that a copy of *Res gestae*, his own catalog of his "achievements," was to be inscribed on bronze tablets in front of his mausoleum. In *Res gestae* he had stressed his role in restoring the Republic by ending wars, establishing peace, and returning power to the senate and people of Rome. Because Augustus had presented himself as a "Republican" emperor, his paradigm served as a check on the behavior of subsequent emperors, who were likewise expected to demonstrate their reverence for the old Republic: "the tombs of deified emperors encouraged proclamations about history and identity." Constantine would have passed by Augustus' mausoleum as he entered Rome through the Flaminian Gate and then traveled south on Wide Street, first in 312, again in 315. Another reminder of Augustus' achievements would have been the large dedicatory inscription of the new arch, because it likewise honored Constantine for having "avenged the Republic with just arms at one time from both a tyrant and his entire faction." The dedication cast Constantine as another "Republican" emperor, like Augustus, who had equally restored the senate and people of Rome.[37]

This dedication was a message to Constantine from the senate and people about the sort of emperor he should be at Rome. Because the

---

[37] Restoration of Republic: Augustus, *Res gestae* 34.1. Bronze tablets: Suetonius, *Augustus* 101.4, with Favro (2005) 258, for Wide Street as a "carefully choreographed narrative pathway" about Augustus' achievements. Quotation about tombs from Trout (2003) 524. For the possibility that learned Christians were likewise promoting the paradigm of Augustus, note Digeser (1998) 143: "Lactantius showed how Christians could support – not the new fangled worship of Diocletian as *dominus et deus* – but the sort of honours conferred upon the first emperor, Augustus, the *princeps Senatus*."

Note that Constantine himself was thought to have joked about the accomplishments of his imperial predecessors, presumably to enhance his own achievements. See Anonymus post Dionem (= Dio Continuatus), *Frag.* 15.2, ed. Müller (1851) 199: "Since Constantine wished to diminish the accomplishments of earlier emperors, he was eager to belittle their merits with some [disparaging] nicknames. He called Octavian Augustus a 'plaything of fortune,' Trajan 'wall ivy,' Hadrian a 'paintbrush,' Marcus [Aurelius] a 'buffoon,' and [Septimius] Severus . . ."

senate had presumably taken the initiative in designing and constructing the arch and its decorations, the supervisors of the project had most
likely been the prefects of the city. After his victory in 312 Constantine had allowed Maxentius' current prefect, Gaius Annius Anullinus,
to serve for another month. He subsequently appointed first Aradius
Rufinus, who served until late 313, and then Gaius Ceionius Rufius
Volusianus, who in addition held a consulship in 314 and was still serving as prefect when Constantine returned in 315. Both had previously
held high offices under Maxentius, Rufinus as consul and prefect of the
city, Volusianus as praetorian prefect, prefect of the city, and consul.
Constantine was clearly trying to win the loyalty of senators at Rome
by demonstrating continuity of officeholding. Rather than indulging
in reprisals, he reappointed some of the senators who had previously
supported Maxentius.[38]

In return, the prefects presided over the construction and dedication
of the commemorative arch for Constantine. Their ideas of proper
emperorship had presumably been formed while serving Maxentius,
their former patron who had emphasized his respect for the old traditions of the Republic. In fact, Volusianus had already previewed some
of these ideas when setting up a dedication and statue of Constantine in
the Forum of Trajan, probably in anticipation of the emperor's return.
In the dedication he praised Constantine as "the restorer of the human
race, the enlarger of the empire and Roman authority, and the founder
of eternal security." Similar sentiments appeared in the inscriptions on
the arch. Under the leadership of the prefects of the city, the senators
could suggest to Constantine their expectations about proper imperial
behavior at Rome.[39]

---

[38] For the careers of these prefects of Rome, see *PLRE* 1:79, "C. Annius Anullinus 3," 775,
"Aradius Rufinus 10," 976–78, "C. Ceionius Rufius Volusianus 4," with Chapter 7, for
Volusianus' possible exile.

[39] For Maxentius at Rome, see Chapter 9. Volusianus' dedication: *ILS* 1:156, no. 692 =
Grünewald (1990) 217, no. 241. For the didactic message, note Lenski (2008) 247: "By
fashioning the arch and its inscription as they did, Rome and its Senate no doubt hoped to
nudge Constantine toward a similar interpretation of events."

The inscriptions joined with the recycled panels and roundels to represent Constantine as a Republican emperor who deferred to ancestral traditions and their guardians, the senators at Rome. Custom and expectations about the proper behavior of emperors provided senators with a symbolic idiom both for imagining a community of shared expectations and for integrating a new emperor into that community. Another symbolic idiom with the potential for defining a joint community and integrating a new emperor at Rome was the celebration of traditional religious cults. From the perspective of senators at Rome, the Tetrarchic emperors had all been outsiders, undereducated military men who had been born in remote provinces and had served on the frontiers. Despite that boorish background, however, some of the Tetrarchic emperors had wanted to present themselves as champions of traditional cults. The philosopher at Nicomedia who had so offended Lactantius, for instance, had praised the emperors for "defending the religions of the gods" by initiating a persecution of Christians. At Rome, when Diocletian and Maximian had visited in late 303, they had met in the Temple of Jupiter on the Capitoline Hill, and they had erected the Monument of Five Columns in the Forum. This new monument included reliefs depicting scenes of sacrifice, with both an emperor and senators participating. Maximian had furthermore considered reviving the antiquarian festivals of the Secular Games. To establish their credentials as guardians of Romanness, Diocletian and the other Tetrarchic emperors had persecuted Christians, and they had participated in traditional cults at Rome.[40]

The priesthoods at Rome provided additional continuity from one imperial reign to the next. During the visit by Diocletian and Maximian in 303, quite likely Titus Flavius Postumius Titianus was already serving as a priest of the sun god Sol and an augur, Betitius Perpetuus as a *flamen Dialis* (priest of Jupiter), Gaius Ceionius Rufius Volusianus as one of the experts responsible for consulting the Sibylline books, and Gaius Vettius Cossinius Rufinus as a Palatine priest. These aristocrats

[40] For bibliography on the Monument of Five Columns, see Van Dam (2007) 42n.9. For the Secular Games, see Chapter 3; the philosopher, above in this Chapter.

continued to hold their priesthoods under Maxentius; they also served as priests under Constantine after 312.[41]

But despite this continuity, the iconography on the arch did not emphasize the celebration of traditional cults. Constantine had already announced his toleration for Christians, and he may have used Christian symbols during the battle of 312. Because of this uncertainty about his religious preferences, an explicit appeal to traditional religious cults now might smudge the glow of harmony between a new emperor and the senate and people of Rome. The iconography on the arch hence seemed to be rather circumspect about religion. Some of the appropriated roundels and panels did depict earlier emperors, with their heads recut as Constantine, offering sacrifice. But the architects of the arch also had the good sense to omit a depiction of one particular sacrifice. On the attic of the arch the architects had recycled eight large panels from an earlier monument dedicated to Marcus Aurelius. More panels from the same series had nevertheless been available. Among the panels they did not use was one depicting Marcus Aurelius performing a sacrifice in front of the Temple of Jupiter on the Capitoline Hill. During one of his visits to Rome, Constantine himself would decline to participate in a pagan festival on the Capitoline Hill. The architects seem to have anticipated his reluctance and discreetly omitted incorporating this particular panel in the decoration on the arch.[42]

In addition, the large dedicatory inscription was carefully bland about religion, attributing Constantine's victory merely to "the inspiration of divinity and greatness of mind." This religious terminology was not obviously pagan or Christian. It conjured up ideas about divination from the old Republic; it resembled the equally vague language of the panegyric at Trier in 313; it was similar to Constantine's own

[41] Priesthoods: Rüpke (2008) 574, no. 941, "Betitius Perpetuus," 605, no. 1129, "C. Ceionius Rufius Volusianus (1)," 691, no. 1705, "T. Flavius Postumius Titianus," 949, no. 3470, "C. Vettius Cossinius Rufinus," and the list of priests on pp. 395–402.

[42] For discussion and a photo of the unused panel, see Koeppel (1986) 52–56; photo also in De Maria (1988) Tavola 81.3. The iconography on the arch might hence be an early example of an attempt to classify a traditional monument "in a new and neutral category of the secular, defined as neither pagan nor Christian": see Lim (1999) 268.

indeterminate expressions in some of his recent letters. The terminology in the inscription would probably have been acceptable even to both sides of Lactantius' dual identity, as a Christian and as a rhetorician who taught classical Latin literature.[43]

To situate Constantine in the generic context of ancient Roman traditions, the dedicatory inscription and the iconography on the arch highlighted not the mutual celebration of religious cults but the imposing precedent of earlier emperors. The architects apparently wanted the arch to emphasize the proper conduct of emperors at the capital rather than to promote specific religious traditions. At Rome a shared history was more important than a shared religion, and the correct behavior of emperors was more important than their particular beliefs.

MEMORIES OF THE FUTURE

The arch furthermore offered an interpretive narrative of specific contemporary events, including Constantine's invasion of Italy, his victory in 312, and his earlier visit to the capital, that likewise promoted a distinctive perspective about Rome. Locating Constantine in a longer historical context had involved the use of panels and roundels recycled from earlier imperial monuments. In contrast, this narrative about recent events consisted of six long panels that were new for the arch. These panels were apparently meant to be read as a sequence, starting with a scene of a departure on the west end, then scenes of a siege of a city and a battle over water, that is, at the Milvian Bridge, on the south face, then a scene of a ceremonial arrival on the east end, and ending with scenes of a speech on the Rostra in the Forum and the distribution of gifts on the north face.

This new iconographical narrative joined the panegyric of 313, Lactantius' *Deaths*, and Eusebius' first edition of *History* in offering one

---

[43] Dedication: *ILS* 1:156, no. 694 = Grünewald (1990) 217, no. 239, "instinctu divinitatis mentis | magnitudine." For possible influences on the dedicatory inscription, see Grünewald (1990) 78–86, discussing similarities with the terminology of contemporary panegyrics, Hall (1998), stressing Cicero's treatise on divination, and Lenski (2008) 231, "*instinctu divinitatis* was a noticeably pagan way of referring to Constantine's divine inspiration." For Constantine's letters, see Chapter 7.

of the earliest interpretive accounts of Constantine's invasion and the battle of 312. Like those literary accounts, this iconographical narrative commented on the transformation of the emperor himself, the nature of his emperorship, and even, discreetly, on religion. But in contrast to those accounts, the uniquely distinguishing characteristic of this particular narrative was its intense focus on "Romeness," the importance of Rome.[44]

The iconography first correlated the stages of Constantine's invasion and visit with the transformation of the emperor. Constantine appeared in five of the panels. On the panel depicting the siege the emperor was shown standing among his troops, wearing full battle armor and Gallic trousers. On the panel depicting the battle at the Milvian Bridge he was again wearing armor and a sword on his left hip. After the battle he entered the city. On the panel depicting the parade of his troops into Rome he was shown wearing a long military cloak. Constantine was still wearing that long cloak on the panel depicting his speech to the people in the Forum. Standing on the Rostra with him was a crowd of senators wearing togas. Long ago Augustus himself had ordered that only men wearing a toga could enter the Forum. During the past century, however, the number of soldiers stationed in or near Rome had been increased considerably, and the city had been surrounded by a great wall. Increasingly Rome had become "no different from a military camp." Now the iconography of the arch was suggesting that Constantine could restore the capital as "the city of the toga." On the next panel the emperor himself was finally shown wearing a traditional toga as he distributed coins to senators and people.[45]

This sequence of panels had hence demonstrated how Constantine was expected to appear, and behave, as an emperor at Rome, not like

---

[44] For discussion of "Romeness" during the fourth century, see Chenault (2008).

[45] For Constantine's clothing as depicted on the frieze, see L'Orange and von Gerkan (1939) 61–62 (siege), 67 (bridge), 74 (procession), 86 (Forum), 96 (distribution) + Tafeln 6–17, with Van Dam (2007) 47. Augustus' directive: Suetonius, *Augustus* 40.5; Rome as military camp: Dio, *Historiae Romanae* 74.16.2; city of the toga: Prudentius, *Peristephanon* 12.56; with Busch (2007), on the large number of soldiers, possibly more than thirty-five thousand, stationed in or near Rome during the third century.

a provincial warlord but instead like a respectable civilian. A change of clothes could transform a man of war from the frontiers into a man of peace at the capital. The panels had hence inserted the battle at the Milvian Bridge into a longer arc of the "conversion" of Constantine, not a religious conversion, but a social and cultural makeover as the emperor came to acknowledge the traditions and expectations of proper imperial deportment at Rome.

Second, the narrative in the panels also quietly linked Constantine's military campaign with traditional deities. On the panel depicting the departure of the troops one soldier was carrying a small statue of winged Victory, which may well have been a replica of the statue of Victory in the senate house. Another soldier was carrying a small statue of Sol Invictus, "Unconquered Sun." Already in Gaul, Constantine had associated himself with Sol, sometimes in the guise of Apollo. Dedications to and depictions of Sol were common on his coins, and in 310 he had had a vision at a temple in Gaul in which he had seen Apollo, or more likely himself as Apollo, accompanied by Victory, who was offering him laurel wreaths. On the panel depicting the siege Victory hovered over Constantine's soldiers, offering a laurel wreath to the emperor. On the panel depicting the river battle Constantine was shown standing in the midst of deities. The goddess Roma appeared on one side, wearing a helmet and outfitted in full battle gear, similar to an Amazon; Victory stood on the other side, apparently extending a garland to the emperor; and at the emperor's feet was a river god. These panels depicting the soldiers and the battles seemed to suggest that Sol (or Apollo) had inspired and led Constantine's campaign from the beginning; that Victory had always assisted him during the battles; and that Roma, the divine personification of the capital, had likewise helped at the moment of his victory at the Milvian Bridge. Missing in this narrative was any hint of the assistance of the Christian God. The iconography instead discreetly associated Constantine and his military success with the pagan gods of Rome.[46]

---

[46] L'Orange and von Gerkan (1939) 55, statues of Victory ("eine Wiederholung der Victoria in der Curia") and Sol Invictus, 62, Victory and wreath, 66–67, Roma, Victory, river god. The

The next panel depicted the entry of Constantine and his troops into Rome. At the rear of the procession Constantine was shown sitting in his four-horse carriage, having just passed through the Flaminian Gate. Although in theory emperors did not celebrate formal triumphs for victories over rival emperors, in this case the emperor and his soldiers were shown marching or riding on the traditional Triumphal Street. The Triumphal Street eventually passed through the old wall by way of the Triumphal Gate, which was also known as the arch of Domitian. In honor of a successful campaign in the late first century the emperor Domitian had rebuilt this gateway, in particular by placing on its crown statues of a pair of chariots drawn by elephants. At the end of this panel on the arch a small extension around the corner displayed the two lead soldiers in the procession riding through this gateway, with the elephants overhead. Over this panel was a large roundel that depicted Sol, rising from the ocean on his four-horse chariot. This roundel of Sol was, appropriately, on the east end of the arch. But the correlation between the rising of the sun god and the arrival of the emperor seemed to suggest that Constantine was entering Rome as a new Sol or a new Apollo. His procession was not so much to celebrate a victory over a rival emperor as to commemorate a victory for the traditional gods.[47]

The next two panels depicted Constantine in Rome. In combination these panels offered a representation of the proper form of emperor-ship at Rome. At the heart of civic life in the capital was the Rostra, a platform for orators at the west end of the old Forum that had become a renowned symbol of "ancient power." When Constantius, Constantine's son, would visit Rome in 357, he stood on the Rostra and marveled

---

reliefs on the bases of the columns depicted more deities, including several images of Victory and two of Sol Invictus: see L'Orange and von Gerkan (1939) 103–36. Sol on coins: Bruun (1958) 36, "the religious policy of Constantine, at least as mirrored in the bronze coinage of Treveri, appears unaltered ... from A.D. 308 to 318," (1966) 48–50. Vision of Apollo: *Panegyrici latini* 6(7).21.4, with Chapter 1.

[47] Chariots and elephants: Martial, *Epigrammata* 8.65.9, with L'Orange and von Gerkan (1939) 74, 79–80 + Tafeln 12a, Flaminian Gate, 18d, Triumphal Gate, 38a, Sol roundel. The Triumphal Gate and its elephants also appeared on one of the Aurelian panels reused in the attic of the arch: see Koeppel (1986) 56–58, and De Maria (1988) Tavola 79.2.

at "the large concentration of spectacular sights" spread out before him in the Forum. One panel on the arch depicted Constantine delivering an oration on the Rostra. To facilitate his transformation into an emperor who would be more acceptable at Rome, the panel reminded Constantine of various models for imperial rule that he should now abandon.[48]

One was his lingering association with the ideals of Tetrarchic emperorship. At the back of the Rostra was the Monument of Five Columns erected by Diocletian and Maximian during their visit to Rome in late 303. A statue of Jupiter was perched on top of the middle column and a statue of the guardian spirit of each emperor on top of the four flanking columns. This Monument of Five Columns had commemorated the twentieth anniversary of the emperors in the Tetrarchy and their allegiance to its most important patron deity. It also memorialized the failure of Tetrarchic emperors to connect with the people of Rome. Despite their generosity for the capital, Tetrarchic emperors had not been well received at Rome. During their visit Diocletian and Maximian had celebrated a joint triumph before meeting in the Temple of Jupiter on the Capitoline Hill, and Diocletian had intended to assume a consulship in the capital. But when he was unable to endure the outspoken candor of the people at Rome, he was so eager to leave that he did not even wait out a frigid rainstorm. To be received favorably at Rome, Constantine would have to become a different sort of emperor.[49]

Another aspect of imperial rule for Constantine to minimize in the capital was his close association with military force. The large dedicatory inscription was prepared to concede that the emperor had taken up "just arms" and had been victorious "with his own army." Initially the emperor had arrived in Rome as a general with his soldiers. On the panel depicting his oration Constantine stood at the center of the Rostra, still wearing his military cloak, with his sword hanging at his left side under the cloak. Seven young soldiers stood in back, beneath

---

[48] Constantius on the Rostra: Ammianus Marcellinus, *Res gestae* 16.10.13.
[49] Depiction of Monument of Five Columns: L'Orange and von Gerkan (1939) 84–85 + Tafeln 14b–15a. Diocletian's departure: Lactantius, *De mortibus persecutorum* 17.2–3.

two military standards. The military standards were quite conventional, each with an upright shaft and a crossbar supporting a hanging banner. Although each of the standards hence resembled a cross, they were certainly not meant as references to Christianity. Instead, because they neatly framed the statue of Jupiter atop the middle column of the Tetrarchic monument on the back of the Rostra, the military standards underlined again the connection between soldiers and the pagan deities whom Tetrarchic emperors had venerated.[50]

But because the Tetrarchic monument and the soldiers were in the background, the layout of the scene in this panel implied that both the Tetrarchic associations and Constantine's reliance on military force were now behind him. The panel instead emphasized a different model for emperorship. Flanking the emperor at the front of the Rostra was a row of senators, each wearing a toga, all listening intently to the emperor's speech, some lifting their right hands in a gesture of acclamation. These senators were to serve as paradigms for imperial rule. At one end of the Rostra was a life-size statue of Hadrian, seated and holding a scepter in his left hand and a globe in his right. At the other end was a life-size statue of Marcus Aurelius, also seated, holding apparently a book roll in his left hand and gesturing with his right. Like the senators standing on the Rostra around the emperor, these revered emperors were each wearing a toga. The good emperors of the past had looked and acted like senators; by implication, Constantine should do the same.[51]

In the final panel Constantine was depicted as having taken the hint. Here he presided over the distribution of gifts to the people of Rome, perhaps to celebrate the assumption of his consulship for 313 on New

---

[50] Soldiers: L'Orange and von Gerkan (1939) 86 + Tafeln 14b–15a. For depictions of similar military standards in the Aurelian panels, see Koeppel (1986) 57, 61, 64, 69, and De Maria (1988) Tavole 79.2, 80.2, 4.

[51] For the identification of the statues on the Rostra, see L'Orange and von Gerkan (1939) 82–84. In 310 an orator in Gaul claimed that Constantine was descended from Claudius Gothicus, emperor during the later 260s: see Chapter 7. According to SHA, *Divus Claudius* 3.5, a silver statue of Claudius Gothicus had been erected on the Rostra after his death. Bruggisser (2002) 86–91, hence argues that this panel depicting Constantine on the Rostra reinforced his new imperial pedigree.

Year's Day. The emperor was sitting high on a tribunal in the middle of a group of senators, wearing a toga. Now he resembled not only the senators but also the seated statues of Hadrian and Marcus Aurelius depicted in the previous panel. Other senators and ordinary citizens stood below the tribunal, with their right hands outstretched as a sign of acclamation or of petition. Usually magistrates distributed the actual payments, but in this scene the emperor himself was the gift giver, the direct source of the "golden rain." In his right hand he was tilting a tray full of the coins he was about to pour into the front fold of a senator's toga, and to his left another senator was handing him more coins. The scene on the panel obviously highlighted the emperor's generosity to the senators and people of Rome. It is also most striking that in this scene there were no soldiers or bodyguards. Constantine was now a civilian emperor, sitting alone among senators as he performed a traditional imperial obligation to the people of Rome.[52]

Like the accounts by the panegyrist of 313, bishop Eusebius, and the rhetorician Lactantius, the six panels of the new frieze were early interpretations of Constantine's battles and visit to Rome, designed to promote a specific agenda. The scenes on the six panels were so stylized that they cannot be read as accurate descriptions of actual events. Because the scenes were idealized representations of the emperor's departure, military victories, entry into the city, and public appearances in the Forum, they were instead meant to serve as prescriptive images about the sort of emperor Constantine should be at Rome. The designers of the arch wanted the emperor to step away from the military force that had earned his victory in 312 and to move beyond his earlier association with Tetrarchic emperorship and its ideals. As a replacement model they did not even hint at the possibility of a Christian emperorship. Instead, they wanted Constantine to act like a civilian emperor who

[52] L'Orange and von Gerkan (1939) 90–102, suggesting that the depicted donation might be dated to January 1, 313: "Konstantin tritt als Senatskaiser vor die Römer, als Schützer der altrömischen Libertas" (p. 102). For the usual role of *dispensatores* in distributing imperial gifts, see Millar (1977) 135–39. Corippus, *In laudem Iustini* 4.73, "aureus imber," referring to the scattering of coins at the assumption of a consulship by the emperor Justin II in January 566.

would be mindful of the ancient heritage of the old Republic, reverent toward traditional pagan cults, respectful of the senators and their expectations, and prepared to follow the lead of earlier emperors like Trajan, Hadrian, and Marcus Aurelius. The people and senate were implying that Constantine should become a conventional Republican emperor at Rome. The scenes on the arch were less recollections of past events and more "memories of the future."[53]

The iconography of the arch was hence deeply encoded with various messages. The obvious question is whether the medium was adequate for the messages. How effective could this iconographic text have been for Constantine and other spectators? The first concern is the legibility of the details of the sculptures. The Aurelian panels displayed on the attic at the top were each slightly more than ten feet high, and the emperors depicted in them were about life size. The Hadrianic roundels were each almost eight feet in diameter, and the emperors depicted in them were a bit smaller than life size. The six panels in the frieze depicting events from Constantine's invasion and visit in 312 were lower but also smaller and extremely crowded. Each of the panels was less than four feet high; the four panels on the north and south faces were each between seventeen and eighteen feet long, and the two panels on the ends each about four feet longer. The scenes on the panels were filled with soldiers in close combat, senators in groups, and citizens in crowds. The panel depicting the emperor's distribution of gifts, for instance, included more than fifty people. Although the emperor was typically slightly taller than the other people, even he was comparatively small. On the panel depicting the siege the emperor was about three feet tall.[54]

---

[53] A good example of the generic representation of the scenes is the uncertainty over identifying the besieged city depicted in one of the panels. Nixon and Rodgers (1994) 303n.34, suggest the siege of Susa, as described in *Panegyrici latini* 4(10).21, 12(9).5.4–6, L'Orange and von Gerkan (1939) 64–65, Kuhoff (1991) 145–46, and Cameron (2005) 92, the siege of Verona, as described in *Panegyrici latini* 4(10).25–26, 12(9).8–10.

[54] L'Orange and von Gerkan (1939) 61, for "die übergroße Gestalt des Kaisers" at the siege, .92 meter tall, with the line drawings (Abbildungen 1–2, 10–12) for the dimensions of the panels and roundels.

Today modern scholars can rely on telephoto lenses and close-up photos taken when the arch has been surrounded in scaffolding for restoration. Back then, even though they may have had to squint, ancient viewers could still distinguish many of the small details. The Aurelian panels at the top had been carved in exceptionally high relief, and the newly carved figures on the Constantinian panels would have been quite sharp. Despite the height of the monument and the clutter of the Constantinian panels, the details of the sculptures were nevertheless remarkably evident.

The second concern, however, is the intelligibility of the sculptures. How could Constantine and other spectators have deciphered the messages? To supplement the visual iconography people needed a verbal commentary. The meaning of this "panegyric of sculptures" would have benefited from a corresponding panegyric in words.

A Panegyric at Rome

The iconography of the arch was not the only medium employed by senators at Rome. When Constantine had entered the city on the day after the battle in 312, a delegation of senators escorted his carriage. The senate quickly designated him as the senior emperor in the imperial college, and it furthermore dedicated in his honor a gold statue of a goddess, probably Victory or Roma. Statues of Constantine himself, many constructed from gold and silver, were set up "in the most renowned sites." In return, the emperor completed another bath complex, renovated the Circus Maximus, and presided at "days of spectacles and eternal games." In the senate house he delivered a speech in which he reinstated the senate's "traditional authority" and apparently promised clemency to supporters of Maxentius. He also issued a formal constitution that restored privileges to the senate. After his departure the senate and people erected a dedication to him and his fellow emperor Licinius as "liberators" and "restorers of public security." In addition the prefect of the city and other magistrates erected various dedications to Constantine. During his first visit, and afterward during the interlude before his return, Constantine participated in a dialogue of dedications, speeches, and edicts with the senate at Rome. This relationship followed the traditional pattern of reciprocity that balanced requests and the conferral of honors from the senate, magistrates, and people of Rome against favorable responses and benefactions from the emperor. Despite his absence, Constantine still seemed to be behaving like a respectful Republican emperor with regard to Rome.[55]

During his return visit in 315 Constantine again would have interacted with senators. Because he remained at Rome for about two months, from late July to late September, he may have done some sightseeing. When his son Constantius would visit in 357, senators escorted his junkets: "he followed the happy senate through all the streets of the eternal city." According to one account, Constantius visited some of the famous buildings and monuments, including the Temple of Jupiter on the Capitoline Hill, the Colosseum, the Pantheon, the imperial baths, and the Forum of Trajan. He also revealed his interest in historical traditions. While sightseeing with senators, "he read the names of the gods inscribed on the pediments, he inquired about the origins of temples, and he admired the founders." As they showed off the city's monuments, senators would have had an opportunity to reiterate their traditions and prerogatives to the emperor.[56]

Constantine too might have read the primary dedication and the other short inscriptions on the arch. But for learning about the details of the iconography, he would have relied more on listening than on viewing. Another opportunity for representatives of the senate to address the emperor was the dedication ceremony for this arch during the visit in 315. More than likely an orator (or orators) celebrated Constantine's achievements by describing the arch and its decoration. By providing

[55] *Panegyrici latini* 12(9).19.1, delegation of senators, 19.6, games, 20.1–2, speech, 25.4, gold statue, with the discussion of Nixon and Rodgers (1994) 331n.157, on whether the manuscript reading of *dee* should be emended to *dei* or (more likely) *deae*. Senior emperor: Lactantius, *De mortibus persecutorum* 44.11. Aurelius Victor, *De Caesaribus* 40.27, Circus Maximus, baths, 28, statues of gold and silver. Privileges of senate: *CTh* 15.14.4, with Seeck (1919) 64–65, dating the edict to January 313. Dedications to Constantine and Licinius: Grünewald (1990) 98–100, 217, no. 240; from magistrates: Grünewald (1990) 217–20, nos. 241, 245, 247, 258.

[56] Constantius' visit: Symmachus, *Relationes* 3.7, happy senate, names of gods; Ammianus Marcellinus, *Res gestae* 16.10.14–15, tour of buildings.

a commentary on the details of the iconography and articulating some of its messages, the panegyrics would have compensated for the difficulty in trying to understand the arch by sight alone. The words of the panegyrics would have supplemented, if not clarified, the images on the arch. But because no oration has survived from this occasion, a panegyric from a few years later might serve as a substitute exemplar of this sort of expository description.

In 321 the rhetorician Nazarius delivered a panegyric at Rome in honor of Constantine and his two oldest sons, Crispus and Constantine II. His panegyric celebrated the beginning of the fifth anniversary year of the sons' promotion as Caesars, junior emperors, on March 1, and he addressed his panegyric directly to Constantine. In fact, none of the emperors was present, as Constantine, Crispus, and most likely Constantine II were all in the Balkans. Nazarius hence had to imagine the presence of Constantine: "I seem to address you [as if you were] present to my eyes. Even though you are far from our sight, you cannot be snatched from our minds."[57]

The audience in attendance included senators, and Nazarius may have been speaking in the senate house. The senators had not seen Constantine since the visit in 315 that had celebrated the tenth anniversary of his accession with the dedication of the arch. Subsequently Constantine had continued to campaign on the frontiers, and he had also fought a recent war against Licinius in the Balkans. That war had furthermore signaled a shift in the dynamics within Constantine's own family. Since his oldest son, Crispus, had been only a teenager, in the buildup to that confrontation Constantine had still relied on the support of his half siblings and a brother-in-law. Then two more sons were born, Constantine II in 316 and Constantius II a year later. Now Constantine could shift from dependence on half siblings and in-laws to sponsoring his direct descendants. In March 317 he had promoted his two oldest sons as junior emperors.[58]

---

[57] Present: *Panegyrici latini* 4(10).3.1. For the date and location of Nazarius' panegyric, see Nixon and Rodgers (1994) 338.

[58] Senate house: *Panegyrici latini* 4(10).1.1, "in a gathering of happy rejoicing," with Van Dam (2007) 108–11, for the dynastic politics.

The senators at Rome certainly knew about the promotion of Constantine's sons. Already in spring of 317 the prefect of the city had set up a dedication in honor of Crispus, "a son of our lord Constantine, the greatest, unconquered, always Augustus, and a grandson of divine Constantius." The prefect made sure to describe Constantine as *Maximus*, the title bestowed on him earlier by the senate.[59]

In contrast, in his panegyric Nazarius simply ignored Constantine's recent activities, including the frontier campaigns, the war with Licinius, and the dynastic politics. Instead, he looked back almost exclusively to the emperor's accomplishments of 312. One of the important consequences of the emperor's earlier victory had been the enhancement of the senate, which now included in its membership "the best men from all the provinces." Because of the emperor's patronage, "the prestige of the senate was not more illustrious in name than in fact." During his previous visits Constantine had engaged in a dialogue of mutual flattery with the senate. He had honored and rewarded senators at Rome, and they in turn had represented him as a traditional emperor in the scenes on the arch. Nazarius likewise offered a retrospective on Constantine's victory in 312 that would have appealed to, perhaps even reflected, a senatorial perspective.[60]

In his narrative of Constantine's Italian campaign Nazarius seemed to be replicating the sentiments already expressed in the dedicatory inscription and the narrative recorded in the panels on the arch. In fact, because his perspective was both senatorial and focused on the importance of Rome, the scenes on the arch may well have been a primary source. According to Nazarius' account, after crossing into Italy, Constantine had captured Susa, Turin, Brescia, and Verona. As he had approached Rome, Maxentius decided to lead his troops outside the city, where they were slaughtered. Maxentius himself had drowned in the "bloody waves" of the Tiber. Nazarius' description of the battles

[59] Dedication by Ovinius Gallicanus: *ILS* 1:161, no. 716, with *PLRE* 1:383, "Ovinius Gallicanus."

[60] Prestige of senate: *Panegyrici latini* 4(10).35.2. For the mismatch between the date of the oration and its content, see Nixon and Rodgers (1994) 338, "the oration might as well have been given in the same year as *Panegyric* 12" (i.e., in 313), 346n.13, "This oration covers most of the same events as *Pan.* 12, and not much else."

was colorful but did not offer many precise details. In particular, his "account of the battle of the Milvian Bridge is as empty of substance as it is full of descriptive elements." Rather than providing an independent account based on new details, Nazarius seemed to be describing and elaborating on the initial panels in the narrative sequence on the arch. Although he certainly had some exact information about Constantine's battles in northern Italy, he often seemed to be merely expanding the basic iconographical narrative with stock scenes and his own imagination. Many of his comments were the equivalent of captions for the panels.[61]

The next panel in the narrative sequence depicted Constantine's arrival in Rome. Nazarius described the same scene. "The emperor's entrance into the city must be mentioned, and for expressing the great joy of the senate and Roman people an oration is inadequate unless it is itself extravagant." He continued by mentioning Constantine's generosity, which a panel on the arch had also highlighted. The emperor's gifts for the city had included his patronage for construction projects. "The most celebrated [monuments] of the city shine with new efforts." These projects included the renovation of the Circus Maximus with new porticoes and columns.[62]

Nazarius furthermore deployed the terminology of the dedicatory inscription on the arch and provided a commentary in his remarks. On the arch the primary dedication praised Constantine for having avenged the Republic "from both a tyrant and his entire faction." In his panegyric Nazarius consistently called Maxentius a "tyrant." Until Constantine arrived, Rome had been "submerged in the evils of an impious tyranny." After his victory Constantine sent "the most disgusting head

---

[61] Waves: *Panegyrici latini* 4(10).30.1. Quotation about substance from Nixon and Rodgers (1994) 374n.124. Note that Nazarius declined to elaborate on the events of the battle "because they were discussed by me in more detail already yesterday": see *Panegyrici latini* 4(10).30.2. Perhaps he had just recently delivered another oration to celebrate Constantine's birthday on February 27: for the festival at Rome during the mid-fourth century, see *Fasti Furii Filocali*, February 27, "N(atalis) d(ivi) Constantini," ed. Degrassi (1963) 241.

[62] *Panegyrici latini* 4(10).30.4, entrance, 33.4, generosity, 35.4, most celebrated, 35.5, Circus Maximus.

of the tyrant" to Africa. In addition, just as the dedication on the arch had attributed the emperor's success to "the inspiration of divinity," so Nazarius stressed the role of "divinity" in the military campaign. He claimed that even before Constantine's departure from Gaul "armies appeared, which announced that they had been sent ahead by divine influence." The leader of these heavenly armies was Constantius, Constantine's father, who was now "divine" himself. According to Nazarius, Constantine had indeed invaded Italy with the assistance of a "god."[63]

Nazarius' use of religious terms was as neutral as the outlook expressed in the dedication on the arch. His stories about divine assistance, including the appearance of "heavenly armies" from Gaul, might well have been an elaboration of the vague reference to "divinity" in the dedication on the arch. But even though Nazarius emphasized the importance of divine leadership for Constantine's success, he did not associate that guidance with any particular religion. There was certainly no hint of a vision before the battle at the Milvian Bridge or of a subsequent dream about Jesus Christ. In fact, the only deity whom Nazarius mentioned by name as having assisted Constantine was his father, Constantius. In his oration, "Constantius replaces Christ"; as a result, Nazarius remembered Constantine as an imperial scion and a military commander who was also a divine offspring. Like the iconographical narrative on the arch, his panegyric praised Constantine for liberating Rome, not for converting to Christianity.[64]

With his Gallic perspective the orator of 313 had highlighted Constantine's return to the Rhine after his Italian campaign. In contrast, when speaking to an audience of senators at Rome, Nazarius hoped for Constantine's return to the capital. "There is only one event that could make Rome more happy . . . , that it see its defender Constantine and the most blessed Caesars [that is, his sons]." The orator

[63] *Panegyrici latini* 4(10).6.2, tyranny, 7.3, divinity, 14.2, armies, 14.6, Constantius, 16.2, god, 31.4, head. Note that elsewhere in Italy, Maxentius' reign was likewise now classified as a "tyranny": see *ILS* 1:267, no. 1217, a dedication at Atina in Campania to C. Vettius Cossinius Rufinus, erected after 316: ". . . in correctura | eius, quae sevissimam tyran|nidem incurrerat."

[64] Quotation about Constantius from Nixon and Rodgers (1994) 359n.63.

in Gaul had been relieved when Constantine had returned from Italy to the northern frontier. As an orator at Rome, Nazarius hoped that the emperor or his sons would leave the frontiers to visit the capital again.[65]

Much of Nazarius' panegyric hence seems to have been a commentary on the iconographical narrative on the arch, in which he articulated the sentiments of the senators and people about the blessings of an emperor's presence at Rome. If an emperor had actually listened to this sort of oration, there would have been no doubt about the meaning of the iconographical scenes on the arch. In fact, at the end of his panegyric Nazarius was following the lead of the short votive inscriptions on the arch by announcing his expectation that the emperors would indeed return. Even though Constantine and his sons had not attended the imperial anniversary at Rome in 321, Nazarius anticipated that they would return to celebrate the twentieth anniversary of the emperor's reign.

ABSENCE

Each of these narratives in the West offered a distinctively unique perspective on Constantine's victory at the Milvian Bridge. At Trier the orator of 313 thought of it as a model for subsequent military successes on the Rhine frontier. Also at Trier Lactantius contextualized the battle in the longer historical arc of the end of persecution of Christians in the eastern provinces. At Rome the frieze of panels on the arch dedicated in 315 illustrated the transformation of Constantine into a proper Republican emperor who imitated the best of his predecessors and respected the senate. Also at Rome the orator Nazarius essentially read the frieze panels on the arch as his source and verbalized some of the messages inherent in its iconography. His oration may be taken as representative of the sort of panegyric that Constantine might have heard at Rome during his visit in 315. Excepting Lactantius, who located Constantine in the sweep of Christian concerns, the other accounts highlighted the consequences of the emperor's presence. The people of

[65] One event: *Panegyrici latini* 4(10).38.6.

Trier were happy that Constantine had returned, and they wanted him to stay and protect the northern frontiers. The people of Rome were happy that Constantine had visited, and they wanted him to return and restore their ancient traditions and privileges.

During his absence on the frontiers Constantine continued to think about Rome. In late 320, for instance, he replied from Serdica to a report from the prefect of the city about a lightning strike on the Colosseum by allowing the traditional consultation of a diviner. In 322 he instructed the prefect of the city to pardon criminals in honor of the birth of Crispus' child, his own first grandchild. In spring of 324, even as he was preparing for another war against Licinius at Thessalonica, he responded again to the prefect to ensure the supply of pigs to Rome: pork barrel politics at its most literal![66]

In return, the senate and people continued to honor him with dedications. In one erected after Constantine had defeated Licinius, they praised him as "the conserver of the Roman name, the enlarger of his world, the destroyer of tyrannical factions, and the conqueror of barbarian peoples." Once Constantine had defeated his final rival, the citizens of Rome could expand the traditional language of the arch to link Licinius with Maxentius. When the arch had been first dedicated, Constantine had recently defeated the "tyrant" Maxentius, and the senate and people of Rome had praised both Constantine and Licinius, still nominal allies at the time, for their victories over "the most hideous tyrants." After Licinius' inglorious demise, however, he too was maligned in this new dedication as just another "tyrant." Now only Constantine was worthy of traditional Republican terminology at Rome.[67]

In July 326 Constantine did return to Rome for a third visit, this time to celebrate the end of the twentieth-anniversary year of his imperial

---

[66] *CTh* 9.38.1, pardon, 14.4.2, pork, 16.10.1, lightning strike, with Jones (1964) 702–4, on the supply of pork at Rome.

[67] Dedication to Constantine and Licinius: Grünewald (1990) 98–100, 217, no. 240, dated between 313 and 316. Dedication to Constantine: *CIL* 6.8.2:4551, no. 40768a, "factionum | [ty]rannicarum extinctori," dated to 324.

tenure. In the previous summer he had been busy with attending a council of bishops at Nicaea, and he had celebrated the beginning of this twentieth-anniversary year in Nicomedia. Because emperors typically marked only the beginnings of their decennial anniversaries, this celebration at Rome was an exceptional distinction. During his visit Constantine seemed to follow the recommendations of both the iconography of the arch and the hints of an orator like Nazarius, in particular by minting at Rome a large gold medallion that paired a bust of himself on one side with a representation of the senate on the other. Nazarius' comment about the significance of the emperor's presence would have been applicable to this visit too: "Rome, you finally felt that you were the garrison of all peoples and the queen of all regions." In the ancient capital Constantine again was behaving like an ideal emperor of old, respectful of the traditions of the Republic and its guardians in the senate.[68]

Recent events nevertheless cast a shadow over this visit to Rome. First, earlier in 326 Constantine had ordered the execution of his oldest son, Crispus, in murky circumstances. At Rome he was informed about the possible role of his own wife, Fausta, in plotting against Crispus, and he compelled her to commit suicide. These dismal losses motivated Constantine to think again about his plans for dynastic succession. In part he reverted to earlier arrangements, because during his visit to Rome he may have been accompanied by two of his half brothers. The influence of the half brothers was again on the rise, and by the mid-330s each would hold a consulship, and the son of one would join Constantine's three remaining sons as designated successors. During this visit to Rome dynastic succession had become an overriding concern.[69]

---

[68] Gold medallion: Bruun (1966) 326, no. 272, with the suggestion of Alföldi (1947) 12–15, that the image on the reverse was not the emperor but, in accordance with the legend (SENATUS), a personification of the senate, wearing a toga and holding a globe and a scepter: "the Emperor acknowledges once more the high aspirations of the old Capital" (p. 13). Rome: *Panegyrici latini* 4(10).35.2.

[69] Plotting at Rome: Zosimus, *Historia nova* 2.29.1–2. Half brothers: Libanius, *Orat.* 19.19, with Wiemer (1994a) 517.

Second, even at Rome not everyone was thinking of Constantine as a Republican emperor. Other images of emperorship were also in circulation. At Saepinum in south-central Italy a dedication erected in honor of Constantine shortly after the battle at Rome in 312 had hailed him as "the restorer of public liberty, begotten of the gods." This dedication continued to represent the emperor in Tetrarchic terms as a descendant of the traditional gods. In 325 Constantine had celebrated his twentieth anniversary in Nicomedia. Because Nicomedia had once been the favored city of Diocletian, Constantine might have seemed to be reviving aspects of Tetrarchic-style emperorship, in particular its identification of emperors as gods. During the celebration Constantine had hosted a banquet for churchmen. At least one of the bishops who attended that banquet, Eusebius of Caesarea, was prepared to compare the festivities to "an image of Christ's kingdom." Even though Eusebius was of course grateful that Constantine was a Christian emperor, he was nevertheless still imagining him within an old Tetrarchic framework that had linked emperors with deities. Although the Tetrarchy was defunct, images of Tetrarchic emperorship long continued to shape notions of Christian emperorship.[70]

At Rome too the top magistrate would have been thinking about Constantine as some sort of Christian emperor. During the emperor's visit in 326 the prefect of the city was Acilius Severus. Because Severus was a correspondent of Lactantius, he was most likely a Christian himself. Despite holding this traditional office, he may hence have preferred to highlight Constantine's support for Christianity over his connections with Roman traditions. An older Tetrarchic framework, a new Christian perspective: during this visit other models of emperorship may have competed with Constantine's previous tendency to behave like a Republican emperor at Rome. Constantine himself, as well as the citizens of an Italian town, bishop Eusebius in Palestine,

---

[70] Dedication at Saepinum: *L'année épigraphique 1984* (1987) 94, no. 367 = Grünewald (1990) 222, no. 272, dated between the battle at Rome and circa 315. Banquet: Eusebius, *Vita Constantini* 3.15.2.

and a prefect of Rome, was searching for a new way to think about his emperorship.[71]

As a result, the visit in 326 apparently did not go well. This may have been the visit during which Constantine declined to participate in an "ancestral festival" on the Capitoline Hill, the religious center of the city. His refusal deeply upset the senate and the people of Rome. This visit may also have been the occasion when "the people mocked him with shouts of ridicule," and they may have pelted an image of the emperor with stones. Something had gone awry in Constantine's relationship with the old capital. He himself apparently tried to shrug it off by insisting that emperors were supposed to tolerate being "the butt of laughter": "he is noted for enduring the boorish behavior of the Roman people." But during this visit Constantine somehow lost his reputation for acting like a proper Republican emperor. His stay at Rome was hence short, most likely only a few weeks. By the time he departed, "he had made the senate and people hate him."[72]

Constantine might have returned to make amends during the celebration of the thirtieth anniversary of his reign, either in July 335 for the beginning of the anniversary year or July 336 for the end. In 334, presumably in anticipation of such a visit, the prefect of the city set up dedications that revived the traditional terminology by thanking the emperor for having expanded the Republic and the city of Rome. One of the dedications most likely accompanied a new equestrian statue of Constantine in the Forum. In the mid-330s cities in Umbria sent a petition to Constantine requesting that they be allowed to construct a new temple at Hispellum (modern Spello) in honor of the emperor's dynasty. Because they noted that Hispellum was next to the Flaminian Way, the main highway connecting northern Italy to Rome, they too were clearly anticipating that Constantine might stop and view the new

---

[71] Correspondence with Lactantius: Jerome, De viris illustribus 111, with PLRE 1:834, "Acilius Severus 16."

[72] Libanius, Orat. 19.19, laughter, shouts, 20.24, boorish behavior, with Wiemer (1994a) 517–18, (1994b) 475–79, dating this discontent during Constantine's visit in 326. Stones: John Chrysostom, Homiliae de statuis 21.11 (PG 49.216), although not locating the episode in a particular city. Festival, hatred: Zosimus, Historia nova 2.29.5.

temple when he next returned to the capital. In the last year of his reign Constantine and his sons commended the new prefect of Rome in a gracious letter addressed to "the consuls, the praetors, the tribunes of the people, and their senate." In their correspondence the emperor, the magistrates and senate of Rome, and the people of central Italy all still maintained the pretense of proper Republican language.[73]

But Constantine never returned to Rome, or even to central Italy. After his departure in 326 he conducted more campaigns on the Rhine frontier and in the Balkans. Despite the disapproval inherent in the panels on the arch at Rome, Constantine remained closely linked to his troops. In fact, in the letter to the magistrates and senate at Rome he and his sons politely introduced themselves by noting that "we and our armies are well." Constantine also spent increasingly more time in the East. One favored residence was Constantinople, which was formally dedicated in 330. Constantine celebrated both the beginning and the end of the thirtieth-anniversary year of his reign at Constantinople. After his death in 337 he was buried in the new capital. At Rome the senate and people had already anticipated performing the usual ritual of consecration for a dead emperor by dedicating a portrait that depicted Constantine "enjoying an ethereal repose above the arches of heaven." But when they heard that he was not going to be buried in Rome, the people were frustrated and angry.[74]

Constantine's relationship with Rome had started with high hopes, had peaked with the dedication of the arch, and had declined in mockery and resentment. In the end, he had always been more concerned about the support of the army and more interested in campaigns on

---

[73] Dedications by Anicius Paulinus: *ILS* 1:157, no. 698, *CIL* 6.1.237, no. 1142 = Grünewald (1990) 218, nos. 242–43, with Verduchi (1995), on the equestrian statue. Petition from Umbria: *ILS* 1:158–59, no. 705, and Gascou (1967) 610–12, with the discussion in Van Dam (2007) 19–34, 53–57, 363–67. Letter from Constantine and his sons: *CIL* 6.8.2:4555, no. 40776.

[74] Portrait: Eusebius, *Vita Constantini* 4.69.2. Reaction of people: Aurelius Victor, *De Caesaribus* 41.17, with Price (1987), on the traditional role of the senate in passing posthumous judgment on emperors. The senate nevertheless recognized Constantine's apotheosis by granting him the title of *divus*: see Bruun (1954), for the coins, and Amici (2000), for the inscriptions.

the northern frontiers. His failure to be buried at Rome seemed to memorialize a final snub to the old capital.

TWILIGHT

The iconography on the arch at Rome had recalled ancient imperial history, in particular the idealized emperors of the second century, even as it had memorialized current events, in particular Constantine's invasion of Italy and visit to the capital in 312. At the moment of its dedication the arch had been a reassertion of the preeminence of Rome, as contemporary circumstances seemed to intersect with a living past. The arch seemed to imply that Rome could be again in the fourth century the same important capital and imperial residence it had been in the early empire.

Then, over time, the arch became a relic of a lost past that no longer corresponded with present circumstances. As the memories of Constantine's visits faded, he became just another of those ancient emperors, and the once-current events associated with his initial visits lost their specific references and assumed a more timeless significance. Like the other panels on the arch, the series of panels in the new Constantinian frieze could also be read as a depiction of an idealized relationship between emperors and the old capital.

The significant characteristic of this relationship was the oscillation between extended campaigns on the frontiers and occasional visits to Rome. In this perspective the panels in the frieze on the arch were to be read no longer as a onetime linear sequence with a clear beginning on the frontiers and a clear end at Rome but as a continuous timeless cycle of battles on the south side, an arrival at Rome on the east side, activities at Rome on the north side, and a departure on the west side, followed by more battles before another return to Rome and so forth. The circularity of the frieze was intended as a reminder for all emperors that, even though they might depart, they were still expected to keep on returning.

Of course, leaving Rome implied that emperors had first arrived. Soon, however, emperors no longer maintained this cycle, and intermittent stopovers were the best Rome could hope for. During the fourth century Maxentius was the last significant emperor to choose Rome as his primary residence. Constantine did visit Rome three times, but those visits added up to a residence of only five total months in a reign of more than thirty years. After his visit in 326 he did not return during the final eleven years of his reign. The next emperor to visit Rome was one of his sons. Even then that son was not one of the two sons whom Nazarius had hoped for in 321. Crispus campaigned primarily on the northern frontiers, both in northern Gaul and in the Balkans, and Constantine II eventually resided at Trier. Neither ever visited Rome. Nor did Constans, even though Italy was a part of his portion of the empire after Constantine's death. Instead, Constantius would celebrate the next imperial visit to Rome. As a young boy Constantius had accompanied his father to Rome in 326. But he too would then disappear from the capital for decades until returning in 357. By then he had already been reigning as a senior emperor, a successor to his father, for twenty years. Visiting Rome had clearly not been high on his list of priorities.[75]

In 312 Constantine had departed from a frontier city in Gaul to fight his way through Italy to Rome. On the arch at Rome a panel in the new frieze commemorated that departure, because it had implied that the emperor would soon be arriving in Rome. At the time that panel of departure had marked the beginning of Constantine's progress toward Rome. In the long run, however, the panel depicting a departure seemed to mark the end of any emperor's visit to the capital, no longer a departure for Rome but now a departure from Rome. By previewing the diminishing significance of the capital for emperors, the panel had become a statement about Rome itself. Now the sadness of departure overwhelmed the joy of arrival, and the arch seemed to be

---

[75] For the possibility that Constantius was already with Constantine's court in 321, see *Panegyrici latini* 4(10).36.1, mentioning "the most noble Caesars and their brothers"; for his visit to Rome in 326, Barnes (1982) 85. For Constans and Rome, see Van Dam (2007) 73, 116–17. Note that in the mid-fourth century the people of Rome were still celebrating the anniversary of Constantine's departure from Rome in 315: see *Fasti Furii Filocali*, September 27, "Profectio divi," ed. Degrassi (1963) 255.

more poignant than hopeful, a remembrance of a lost past rather than an anticipation of a glorious future.[76]

The panel depicting the emperor's departure was displayed on the west end of the arch. Over it was a large roundel that depicted Luna, the moon goddess, and Hesperus, the evening star. The rising sun associated with Constantine's arrival on the other end of the arch was now setting, and after his reign absence was the common characteristic of the relationship between emperors and the capital. Now twilight seemed never to end at Rome.[77]

---

[76] For the suggestion that the artist Raphael understood the panel on the west side of the arch as a depiction of a departure from Rome, see Fehl (1993) 39, with Chapter 2.

[77] L'Orange and von Gerkan (1939) 164–65 + Tafel 38b, roundel of Luna.

ROME AFTER THE BATTLE

CHAPTER SEVEN

D URING THE EARLY YEARS OF HIS REIGN CONSTANTINE HAD campaigned in Gaul and Britain and resided primarily in Trier. In 310, in the emperor's presence at Trier, an orator celebrated the successful outcome of his recent confrontation with Maximian, one of the original Tetrarchs. Despite his abdication in 305, Maximian had returned to imperial rule to help his son, Maxentius, who had become an emperor at Rome in 306. That assistance had included an alliance with Constantine, who was himself looking for support. Because he had been proclaimed as an emperor by his father's troops in Britain, his accession had defied the wishes of Galerius, the current dominant senior emperor in the Tetrarchy. Even after Galerius had begrudgingly recognized him as a Caesar, a junior emperor, in the Tetrarchy, Constantine's position was still shaky. In 307 he married a daughter of Maximian, who then sanctioned his new son-in-law's rank as an Augustus, a senior emperor.[1]

This alliance with the dissident dynasty of Maximian and Maxentius soon became a liability, however. After a confrontation with his son

---

[1] Acceptance by Galerius in 306: Lactantius, *De mortibus persecutorum* 25.

at Rome, Maximian fled to his son-in-law in Gaul. But at a summit meeting in 308 Maximian had to retire again as emperor, and Galerius again accepted Constantine as a Caesar. In 310 Maximian challenged his host son-in-law and tried to buy the loyalty of troops in southern Gaul. Although Constantine soon suppressed this uprising at Marseille, the threat remained until Maximian's shameful death.

In his panegyric this orator hence had to discuss these recent political events very carefully. Not only did he want to disguise the seriousness of Maximian's challenge to Constantine's imperial rule. He also had to downplay Constantine's own earlier defiance toward his fellow Tetrarchic emperors. Despite his eventual inclusion among the four acknowledged emperors in the official Tetrarchy, one characteristic of Constantine's early years had been a series of apparent affronts to the principles of harmony and hierarchy that defined Tetrarchic emperorship.[2]

Even as the orator conceded some innovations, he nevertheless presented Constantine as loyal to Tetrarchic expectations. Tetrarchic emperors had identified themselves with traditional gods, in particular Jupiter and Hercules. The orator reiterated that pattern but emphasized that Constantine's patron deities were his own ancestors. One such "divinity" was "divine Claudius." The revelation that Claudius Gothicus, a rather nondescript emperor of the later 260s, had been an ancestor provided Constantine with a claim on imperial rule that predated Diocletian and the establishment of the Tetrarchy. Another divine supporter was his father, Constantius, "an emperor on earth but a god in heaven." After his death Constantius had been welcomed to heaven by Jupiter himself, "who extended his right hand," and in the council of the gods he had voted for his son to succeed as emperor. After Constantine's victory over Maximian the god Apollo had emerged as another of his patrons. During his return to northern Gaul, Constantine had stopped at a temple, where in a vision he had seen Apollo essentially identified

---

[2] On the changes in Constantine's rank, see Grünewald (1990) 13–61, and Humphries (2008a).

with himself. According to this panegyrist, Constantine's patron deities included a distant imperial ancestor, his own father, and Apollo.[3]

The emphasis on hereditary succession challenged the Tetrarchic preference for selecting the best men as new emperors, and Apollo had not been one of the most prominent gods associated with Tetrarchic emperors. Yet in 310 this Gallic orator had understated the novelties to present Constantine as a Tetrarchic-style emperor. The institutions and values of the Tetrarchy still defined a dominant style of imperial rule.

Three years later, however, a Gallic orator at Trier omitted even any hints of Tetrarchic imperial rule. Because Constantine had recently returned from his invasion of Italy, the orator instead highlighted his liberation of Rome and his restoration of the Republic: *res publica restituta*. In his panegyric the orator included many references to key figures from the old Republic as either admirable or shameful exemplars, such as Horatius, a heroic defender of Rome; Scipio and his reputation for speedy military actions; the warlords Cinna, Marius, and Sulla; Pompeius Strabo, who had founded a colony in northern Italy; Cicero and his devotion to Italy; and Julius Caesar, who had destroyed a Greek city. Even if in an unflattering reference, the orator also mentioned the naval victory at Actium that Augustus would highlight as the beginning of his own restoration of the Republic.[4]

In the representations offered by these orations, between 310 and 313 Constantine had been converted – or rather, his style of emperorship had been converted from Tetrarchic to Republican. The transforming event was of course the emperor's invasion of Italy and his first visit to Rome. While at the capital, Constantine too could not escape the gravitational pull of traditional notions of Republican emperorship.

---

[3] *Panegyrici latini* 6(7).2.1–2, divinity, divine Claudius, 4.2, emperor on earth, 7.3, right hand, 21.3–4, vision of Apollo, with Van Dam (2007) 84–85, 98–100, and Chausson (2007) 25–95, on the new pedigree.

[4] *Panegyrici latini* 12(9).1.1, Republic, 6.1, Caesar, 8.1, Pompeius, 10.1, Augustus, 15.3, Scipio, 18.2, Horatius, 19.5, Cicero, 20.3–21.1, Cinna, Marius, Sulla, with additional discussion in Chapter 6, and Nixon and Rodgers (1994) 291, on the viewpoint of this panegyric: "Constantine is less of a Tetrarch."

The sheer magnificence of Rome was still a powerful influence to behave like a Republican emperor.

During his residence at Rome, Constantine also acknowledged other influences. One was Christianity. He corresponded with churchmen, intervened in ecclesiastical affairs in Africa, and funded the construction of new churches at the capital. Another important influence was classical culture. The letters that Constantine exchanged with a senator at Rome highlighted literary allusions but not religion. Perhaps the most important influence was his relationship with the army. He had entered the city in the company of his troops, and he soon constructed a large commemorative arch north of the city to celebrate their victory.

In the aftermath of the battle at the Milvian Bridge, Constantine's top priority was not necessarily the promotion of Christianity, or even a declaration of his own Christianity. Instead, he was also pondering the traditions of the capital, the value of classical culture, and, especially, the role of the army and military affairs. Previously he had been strictly a frontier emperor; now he was emperor at Rome. An empire that included Rome compelled Constantine and others to think differently about his emperorship.

PORFYRIUS THE POET

Constantine entered Rome on October 29, the day after the battle, and stayed for more than two months until January. During this visit he exchanged letters with Publilius Optatianus Porfyrius, an aristocrat at the capital. Porfyrius was probably already a senator, and he had perhaps already composed some learned poems at the request of a consul. He served as proconsular governor of Achaea, the province that corresponded to the southern part of the Greek peninsula. He may also have been a supporter of Maxentius at Rome. But once Constantine was victorious, Porfyrius seems immediately to have switched his allegiance.[5]

---

[5] Most of the details about Porfyrius' life are speculative. He wrote *Carm.* 21 at the request of Bassus, who might be identified with Caesonius Bassus, consul in 317, or with Junius Bassus, consul in 331: see *PLRE* 1:154–55, "Caesonius Bassus 12," "Iunius Bassus 14," with Barnes (1975a) 183. In verses woven into an intertextual pattern in this poem Porfyrius identified

Porfyrius apparently initiated contact by sending Constantine a panegyrical poem, to which the emperor replied in a complimentary letter. Constantine noted that even though Homer had been the greatest of the Greek poets and Virgil the best of the Latin poets, it was still possible for poets from a "later age" to enjoy "the reward of favor." In fact, the emperor then emphasized his more general support for intellectual pursuits: "in my age a sympathetic hearing, similar to a gentle breeze, honors writers and orators." Constantine was especially pleased that Porfyrius had preserved the old traditions of versifying while still introducing some innovations. In particular, he admired the poet's skill at inserting additional lines of verse in patterns of letters woven vertically and diagonally through the other lines. In the panegyrical poem

himself: "I, Publilius Optatianus Porfyrius, played with these [verses] by composing every type of meter for you, most honorable Bassus." As a result, Polara (1973) 2:136–37, suggests that *Carm.* 21 may have been Porfyrius' first poem. The recipient of *Carm.* 22 was a consul: see *Carm.* 22.33, "te consule." Seeck (1908) 270, suggests that *Carm.* 22 was one of Porfyrius' earliest poems and that this anonymous consul might also have been Bassus; in contrast, Polara (1973) 1:XXIX–XXX, argues that *Carm.* 22 was spurious, composed instead during the Middle Ages.

The city of Sparta commemorated Porfyrius' proconsulship of Achaea by erecting a statue, paid for by a local patron: see Feissel (1985) 284, no. 22, for the text of the dedication. The date of his proconsulship is quite uncertain, however. The wide spectrum of possibilities includes perhaps before 306 under an eastern Tetrarchic emperor, or perhaps under Constantine after the emperor acquired control over Greece and the Balkans in 317, or perhaps after Porfyrius' return from exile in 324 or 325 but before his first tenure as prefect of Rome in 329: for arguments, see Barnes (1975a) 175–76.

Porfyrius' association with Maxentius is equally provisional. Maxentius once compelled senators to make contributions "under the guise of gifts": see Aurelius Victor, *De Caesaribus* 40.24. The name of Publilius Optatianus was included in a list of seven senators inscribed on a fragment found at Rome: ed. Groag (1926) 102 = *CIL* 6.8.3:5049, no. 41314. This list is perhaps to be linked with another list of senators and their contributions: ed. Groag (1926) 105 = *CIL* 6.4.3:3815, no. 37118. The dating of the lists and their significance for Porfyrius' career are contested. Groag (1926), identifies the senators as priests who had funded the construction of a temple under Maxentius, *PLRE* 1:976–78, "C. Ceionius Rufius Volusianus 4," specifically as *septemviri epulonum*, members of the college of priests responsible for arranging meals in honor of Jupiter and other gods, Cullhed (1994) 72, as contributors to the state under Maxentius, and Rüpke (2008) 605, no. 1129, "C. Ceionius Rufius Volusianus (1)," 862, no. 2859, "Publilius Optatianus Porfyrius," as members of a prestigious college of priests who had shared a common dedication.

presented to the emperor, Porfyrius had highlighted these intertextual lines in color, producing a glorious illuminated manuscript that could be both read and viewed: "the interwoven pigments of the colors delight the sensations of the eyes." Constantine concluded by announcing his seal of approval for both poem and poet: "this gift of your composition was therefore welcome to me."[6]

In his letter of reply Porfyrius profusely thanked Constantine for "the honor of your tireless clemency." Porfyrius knew that the emperor was very busy in the aftermath of his recent military campaigns with celebrating his "triumphs and laurel wreaths" and issuing "the declarations of laws and statutes." But he was also impressed and grateful that Constantine had nevertheless taken time to announce his support for literature and oratory: "you applaud the Muses as your friends." Porfyrius could hence claim that in contrast to other poets he had found the inspiration for his poem not at some sacred grove or through

---

[6] Constantine, *Epistula* 1, Homer and Virgil, 2, later age, reward, 6, "saeculo meo," 9, old and new, 11, pigments, 12, gift. In the salutation of his letter Constantine used "Maximus," the title voted to him by the senate soon after his victory over Maxentius; Porfyrius used the same title for the emperor in the salutation of his letter: see Chapter 6, with Barnes (1975a) 185, "the letter was written in November/December 312," and Corcoran (1996) 152. For the debate over the sequence of the two letters, see Kluge (1924) 347, suggesting that Porfyrius was replying to Constantine. Porfyrius may have recited the panegyrical poem to Constantine before sending him the manuscript, because in his letter the emperor mentioned "the goodwill for your work that you sought from my ears": see Constantine, *Epistula* 14. For the controversy over the authenticity of the letters, see Millar (1977) 472n.46, rejecting the suggestion of Polara (1973) 1:XXXI–XXXII, 2:19–20, that the letters were medieval forgeries.

Porfyrius' panegyrical poem of 312 is not extant. But a hint of its opinions about Constantine's victory at Rome and subsequent acquisition of North Africa might have been recycled in *Carm.* 16.13–21: "When the peaceful Roman citizens see a thousand triumphs over enemies, when they see all your regions filled with goodness, Constantine, they will believe that nothing is more precious to themselves than you, the splendor of the world. With you as lord, the people of Carthage rejoice that they have always been kept safe by your right hand of vengeance. In these tranquil times Africa is more precious to the city [Rome] and enjoys a safe peace. Because Carthage displays its ancient splendor, Africa properly thinks that now it is fortunate, that now it is protected within the citadel of a divinity." Polara (1973) 2:97, suggests that the comments about Africa referred to Constantine's victory over Maxentius; Seeck (1908) 268–70, concludes that Porfyrius was himself a native of North Africa, if not of Carthage.

some intoxicating potion but in "the eternal happiness of your name."
He also seemed to hint that he could repay the emperor's goodwill only
by composing more panegyrical poems.[7]

Porfyrius' sigh of relief is still apparent in the flattery of his letter to
the emperor. He had presumably been quite worried about Constantine's reaction on entering Rome. Even though he had sent his panegyrical poem with apprehension to the emperor's "victorious hands,"
he had hoped that Constantine would read it with "your gentle eyes."
The emperor's gracious letter had allayed his fears. In fact, Constantine was favorable also to other supporters of Maxentius, including
some top magistrates whom he reappointed as prefects of Rome and
who most likely subsequently helped supervise the construction of the
commemorative arch dedicated in 315. That arch would attempt to
define Constantine's emperorship in terms of the traditions of the old
Republic, the precedents of earlier emperors who had respected those
traditions, and the prestige of the senators who were the guardians of
those traditions.[8]

In contrast, in his letter of appreciation Porfyrius had not approached
Constantine by highlighting those senatorial and Republican traditions.
Instead, he had wanted to emphasize classical culture. Rulers had always
been expected to show their regard for culture, and in particular for
the orators and poets who could depict their exploits in the proper
literary genres and extol their accomplishments in public performances.
Constantine himself eventually acquired a reputation for "nurturing the
fine arts, in particular the composition of literature." Porfyrius hence
represented himself to the emperor not as an apologetic senator but as
a supportive poet. In addition, notably missing from this exchange of
letters was any interest in religion. Porfyrius did mention "the lyre of
Apollo" and the temples of the Muses but as cultural icons and not as

---

[7] Porfyrius, *Epistula* 1, clemency, 3, happiness, 6, triumphs, laws, Muses. In *Epistula* 3 Porfyrius
noted that another incentive for writing was "the multiform repetition of your name." This
comment might imply that he had repeated Constantine's name in the intertextual lines of
the poem, as he would do in later poems.
[8] Porfyrius, *Epistula* 2, hands, eyes, with Chapter 6, on the arch.

deities for religious veneration; Constantine mentioned no gods at all. The emperor in fact seemed to have been pleased instead to have the opportunity to demonstrate his own familiarity with classical allusions and his own facility for replying in purple prose. Despite any previous political disagreements or current religious differences, they could now bond over classical culture. A shared appreciation for culture would overcome the horrors of the recent battle outside Rome and the anxiety of the senators waiting inside for their new overlord.[9]

Porfyrius had hence survived the immediate aftermath of Constantine's victory, in part through a direct appeal for clemency that defined their relationship in the neutral terms of culture. Subsequently, however, Porfyrius went into exile. Even though he later claimed that he had been exiled by "a false accusation," he may have been disqualified from holding offices, and he may also have had to leave Rome. But he was not alone among Roman senators in being exiled. One senator, even after holding two consulships, was forced into exile by a "decree of the highest order," the senate. This senator may have been C. Ceionius Rufius Volusianus, who had served as prefect of Rome and consul under Maxentius and subsequently held the same offices again under Constantine. Volusianus erected a dedication and a statue of the new emperor, and he was serving as prefect of Rome when Constantine returned in July 315. Despite his rank and prestige, however, Volusianus seems somehow to have lost support, because he was replaced as prefect in late August while Constantine was still in Rome. His successor as prefect of Rome was C. Vettius Cossinius Rufinus, another former officeholder under Maxentius.[10]

---

[9] Porfyrius, *Epistula* 3, Apollo, 8, temples of Muses. Nurturing: *Epitome de Caesaribus* 41.14. Constantine subsequently revealed his appreciation of acrostics and allegories in an extended exegesis of a Sibylline oracle and one of Virgil's *Eclogues* in his *Oratio ad sanctorum coetum* 18–20. Although the date and location of this oration are disputed, Edwards (2003) xxix, argues that it was "delivered to former subjects of Maxentius in Rome" in 315; see also Van Dam (2007) 294n.14, for other suggestions about date and location, and Girardet (2006b) 76–80, proposing Trier in 314.

[10] False accusation: Porfyrius, *Carm.* 2.31, "falso de crimine." Firmicus Maternus, *Mathesis* 2.29.10, exiles of senator and his son, adultery, 13, decree. For Volusianus' dedication and the rehabilitation of Maxentius' supporters, see Chapter 6.

This abrupt replacement hints at the possibility of infighting among former supporters of Maxentius who were now "rivals" for Constantine's patronage, first during his visits in 312 and 315, then during his subsequent extended absence. Already in 312, only one month after he entered Rome, Constantine issued an edict imposing harsh penalties on "informers": "the tongue of envy is to be amputated at its roots and ripped out." He had this edict posted in the Forum of Trajan, which was becoming a central site for honorific statues of senators. Because the edict was instead an admonition, however, the emperor was presumably deeply dismayed by the rivalries. As he left the capital in January 313, he repeated these penalties on informers, and he encouraged the senate to readmit the senators whom Maxentius had compelled to serve as shipmasters. These former senators were petitioning to be restored to their birthrights, and Constantine hoped for reconciliation. Despite this advice and the warnings, the sniping continued. In 315 Volusianus may have been banished soon after losing his prefecture. The son of this exiled senator, after being accused of adultery and perhaps magic, also went into exile after a trial before the emperor. This other banished senator may have been Volusianus' son, Ceionius Rufius Albinus.[11]

Porfyrius' banishment may likewise have been a consequence of strife among aristocrats at Rome. But as in the past, as a poet Porfyrius could sidestep the political wrangling by appealing to Constantine's patronage for culture. Just as he had once earned the emperor's goodwill by presenting a panegyrical poem, so he could again hope for the emperor's favor through flattery. This time, however, he would make his case by

---

[11] Informers: *CTh* 10.10.2, dated December 1, 312, 10.10.1, dated January 18, 313; restoration: *CTh* 15.14.4, dated January 13, 313; with Corcoran (1996) 154–55, 188–89, for the years. Firmicus Maternus, *Mathesis* 2.29.12, rivals, 14, adultery, 17, adultery, 18, "familiar with secret texts," trial before emperor, with Barnes (1975b), supporting the identification of the anonymous senators as C. Ceionius Rufius Volusianus and his son Ceionius Rufius Albinus, and associating Albinus' exile with the execution of Constantine's son Crispus in 326 and his recall with the execution shortly afterward of Constantine's wife, Fausta. Chastagnol (1962) 65–68, identifies the exiled son as C. Vettius Cossinius Rufinus, prefect of Rome in 315–316 and consul in 316, and *PLRE* 1:1004, 1006–8, "Anonymus 1," "Anonymus 12," as Porfyrius himself.

offering not a single poem but rather a "remarkable volume" containing a series of poems.[12]

In the first poem of the collection Porfyrius contrasted his current plight with his earlier situation. One distressing deprivation was the loss of the services of his calligrapher. In the past the Muse who had "presented a poem to the hands of the Augustus" had been shiny and gleaming, "ornamented in a beautiful little book," "glittering with purple everywhere, written in letters that sparkled with silver and gold, highlighting words on a path of paint." That earlier poem was presumably Porfyrius' panegyric of 312. Because Porfyrius' Muse had been smiling when she offered that original poem as "a token of the writer's gratitude," she had been "attractive to the sacred gaze of the lord," the emperor. But now the poet's Muse was "pale, stained with black on the page, separating the poems with only an impoverished red mark." Now his Muse entered "the rooms of the venerable palace" with trepidation. Porfyrius hence hoped that the emperor would revive his Muse, who was arriving as a supplicant. "Once he has granted forgiveness in his clemency, once he has restored your birthplace and your household, you will proceed... shining in a purple garment." By implication, if the emperor was willing to restore Porfyrius' Muse to her full colorful splendor, then he would also recall the poet from exile. Porfyrius could then resume his life, "just as in the past."[13]

[12] Volume: Jerome, *Chronicon* s.a. 329, "Porphyrius misso ad Constantinum insigni volumine exilio liberatur." Almost all of the medieval manuscripts referred to Porfyrius' collection of poems as "Panegyricus dictus Constantino Augusto" *vel sim*: see Polara (1973) 1:VII–XVII. This collection included *Carm.* 1–12, 13a–13b, 14–16, 18–19, 20a–20b: see Smolak (1989) 240, "Die Gedichte ab carm. 21 beziehen sich nicht auf Konstantin, scheinen also nicht zum 'Panegyricus' gehört zu haben," although Kluge (1924) 347–48, suggests that perhaps Porfyrius had been sending poems to Constantine individually, not as an anthology. *Carm.* 13b was a mirror image of 13a, with the same words in each line but in reverse order; *Carm.* 20 consisted of two parts, 20a and 20b; *Carm.* 17 was a spurious composition of the Middle Ages, see Polara (1973) 1:XXIX, 2:100–103. For Porfyrius' contribution to the development of Latin poetry, see Levitan (1985).

[13] Porfyrius, *Carm.* 1.1, ornamented, 3–4, glittering, 5, calligrapher ("scriptoris bene compta manu"), 6, gratitude, attractive, 7–8, pale, 9, rooms, 15–17, forgiveness, 18, past; the poem was written as an address to the Muse Thalia.

In the second poem Porfyrius combined his appeal with admiration of Constantine's recent accomplishments. This poem established a shape that he used in several other poems, a square of thirty-five lines of verse with thirty-five letters in each line. In his tribute Porfyrius emphasized the prestige of his current hometown by praising the emperor as the "ornament of Rome" and a "great parent of Rome." He also acknowledged that the emperor had in fact spent most of his time fighting battles, in part as an "avenger in civil wars." The purpose of this adulation was reinforcement for his request for a pardon. To make his petition perfectly clear, he repeated the same line six times, as the first, middle, and last lines horizontally in the square, as well as in vertical lines formed from the first column of letters (an acrostic), the middle column, and the final column (a telestic): "divine Caesar, with gentleness have pity on your poet."[14]

In subsequent poems Porfyrius continued to applaud Constantine's recent successes. One important topic was military campaigns. Porfyrius highlighted the emperor's victories over the Sarmatians along the Danube frontier during the summer of 323. He also repeatedly celebrated Constantine's defeat of his rival Licinius during the summer of 324: "I sing about the courageous deeds of a leader who already now rules the entire world." The victory allowed the emperor to unite the Roman empire under his sole rule: "Constantine, victor, your golden age prevails beneath the entire sky." Having recently reconquered the eastern provinces, he had become "the emperor of the Nile."[15]

A second important topic was dynastic succession and the promotion of Constantine's sons. Porfyrius noted that Constantine's predecessors included two generations of emperors, his "ancestor" Claudius, who had defeated the Goths, and his father, Constantius, who had been distinguished for his piety, peace, and justice. In addition to Constantine

[14] Porfyrius, *Carm.* 2.19, ornament, 25, parent, avenger.
[15] Porfyrius, *Carm.* 3.12–13, golden age, 5.3, "iam Nili princeps . . . Oriente recepto," 6.14–28, battles against Sarmatians at Campona, Margum, and Bononia, 7.32, "victor Sarmatiae totiens," 11.1–2, I sing, 12.4–5, "solus . . . Augustus," 13a.12, "solus," 14.2, "te solo principe."

himself, the proper heirs were his sons: "by his divine command brave Claudius... gives an illustrious empire to him [Crispus]." The two oldest sons, the young man Crispus and the young boy Constantine II, had already become Caesars, junior emperors, in 317. According to Porfyrius, the sons were a guarantee of the future prosperity of the empire: "through you and your sons... the affairs of the people flourish." In addition, Crispus was already participating in campaigns against the Franks, and Constantine II could anticipate similar engagements: "throughout the entire world Victory prevails as a fortunate companion for your Caesars." The sons would continue Constantine's reign and his military successes: "the fortunate achievements of the offspring are worthy of association with their father's honorary titles." Porfyrius could hence look forward to celebrating the impending twentieth anniversary of Constantine's accession, as well as the tenth anniversary of the investment of his two sons, "Constantinian offspring," as Caesars. In fact, together the emperors might anticipate celebrating even the thirtieth anniversary of Constantine's accession.[16]

Porfyrius reiterated the themes of military victories and dynastic succession in the intertextual patterns embedded in the poems. In one poem the pattern outlined the formation of troops in a cavalry squadron. In another the pattern depicted a ship, complete with a mast and sails, a stern, oars, and a battering ram projecting from the prow. This ship was a tribute to Crispus, who had commanded Constantine's fleet in 324 and destroyed Licinius' navy. In another poem the pattern portrayed a palm leaf, commemorating both Constantine's victory over Licinius and his impending twentieth anniversary. And in another poem the intertextual pattern celebrated upcoming anniversaries:

[16] Porfyrius, *Carm.* 4.1, twentieth anniversary, 3, offspring, 5.35, thirtieth anniversary, 7.27–30, sons, Victory, 8.27–30, Claudius and Constantius, 10.25–28, Franks, 29–31, Claudius and Crispus, 16.35, "vicennia praecipe vota," 19.37–38, fortunate achievements. For Claudius as Constantine's fictional ancestor, see the introduction to this Chapter. In 321 the orator Nazarius had likewise praised Crispus and Constantine II in his panegyric at Rome and anticipated the upcoming anniversaries: *Panegyrici latini* 4(10).2.2–3, anniversaries, 3.4–7, Caesars, 36–38, Crispus and Constantine II, with Chapter 6. Porfyrius may still have been in Rome during the delivery of this panegyric.

"twentieth anniversary of the Augustus, tenth anniversary of the Caesars."[17]

In the final poem of the collection Porfyrius regretted that he was not able to join in the festivities at Rome. Senators in particular would be honoring the emperor. "The order [of senators], distinguished in their robes [decorated] with the purple [stripes] of their honors, invokes these [vows] with their auspicious lips, and they happily present gifts. Already Rome, the capital of the world, is bestowing gifts and crowns, presenting statues of Victory that glitter with gold for the triumphal processions. Already the vows are echoed in theaters and choruses." In this description Porfyrius seemed to be recalling an earlier celebration of a victory at Rome, such as the arrival of Constantine in 312. Porfyrius himself had most likely witnessed that earlier celebration. Now, however, his exile prevented him from attending the current festival. "An unjust situation has not allowed me to celebrate these events, and I am removed from the happy festivities."[18]

In these poems Porfyrius celebrated recent campaigns of Constantine and his sons during the early 320s, in particular the victories over Licinius; sometimes he seemed to anticipate events, such as the formal foundation of Constantinople, "second Rome," and the upcoming celebration of a triumph or an imperial anniversary. Most likely he presented his collection of poems to Constantine soon after the emperor's final victory over Licinius in September 324. Again the emperor was generous to the poet. In fact, after his return from exile Porfyrius served as prefect of Rome twice, for a month in 329 and for another month in 333. His amnesty paralleled the recall of Ceionius Rufius Albinus, the senator banished on charges of adultery and magic, who likewise returned from exile to become a consul and prefect of Rome in 335.[19]

---

[17] Intertextual patterns: Porfyrius, *Carm.* 5 intertextual, "Aug XX Caes X," 6.2, "per effigiem turmarum," 9.1, "virtutum . . . palmam," 19.25–26, "visam contexere navem | Musa sinit." For Crispus' naval command, see *Origo Constantini imperatoris* 5.23–27.

[18] Porfyrius, *Carm.* 20a.12–21, celebration at Rome, 22–24, unjust situation.

[19] References to Constantinople: Porfyrius, *Carm.* 4.6, "Ponti nobilitas, altera Roma," 18.33–34, "Ponti decus . . . , | Roma soror." Constantine founded Constantinople and proclaimed Constantius, his third son, as a Caesar on the same day, November 8, 324. But in his poems

In his correspondence with Constantine in 312, Porfyrius had hardly alluded to any deities. In this later collection of poems he had again used primarily literary references and allusions. Because the poet hoped to appeal once more to the emperor's shared love of classical culture, religion seems again to have been an afterthought. Occasionally Porfyrius noted divine support for the emperor's successes, by describing him as "the pleasing glory of the highest god" and by suggesting that he had been assisted by "the pious commands of the highest god." Sometimes he was more explicit. Once he promised that Sol, the sun god, would help; in another poem he addressed Constantine himself as Sol: "in the purple glow [of his robes] the commander must be venerated as Sol."[20]

Even more surprising was the inclusion of unmistakable references to Christianity. In one poem Porfyrius claimed that people thought themselves worthy of Constantine's support because they were "approved beneath the law of Christ." The intertextual pattern in that poem furthermore spelled out the name of Jesus. It also depicted the christogram, the symbol formed from the first two Greek letters of *Christ*. This christogram likewise appeared in the intertextual patterns of other poems, including the mast of the ship that commemorated Crispus' naval victory. One of the intertextual lines of verse used as a diagonal bar in one of the christograms again referred to "the highest god," but this time apparently in a Christian context: "through the permanent command and assistance of the highest God [you, Constantine, are] safe." In an intertextual line in another poem Porfyrius explicitly noted

---

Porfyrius referenced only two Caesars, Crispus and Constantine II: note in particular *Carm.* 14.36, "gemino Caesare." Barnes (1975a) 184, concludes that Porfyrius sent his collection of poems to Constantine in autumn of 324 and was recalled soon afterward, while Barnes (1981) 219, delays his recall until summer of 325. According to Polara (1978), the references to Constantinople were hence the earliest indications of Constantine's plan to found a new capital. Porfyrius' return from exile: Jerome, *Chronicon* s.a. 329, although the date was incorrect.

[20] Porfyrius, *Carm.* 2.26, "summi laus grata dei," 12.6, assistance from Sol, 16.30, "dei pia numina summi," 18.7, Constantine addressed as Sol, 25, "venerandus dux erit ut Sol."

Christ's support for Constantine and his dynasty: "Christ has allocated rulership to you and to your sons."[21]

In 312 Porfyrius had been carefully discreet when corresponding with Constantine, not referring to Christianity, hardly mentioning any deities at all. Back then the emperor's religious preferences were perhaps in flux, and it was more prudent to use literary culture rather than religion as the medium for petition and flattery. But by 324 even a pagan poet like Porfyrius could not avoid some references to Christianity. By then the christogram had appeared on Constantine's coins, and the emperor had publicly demonstrated his patronage for Christianity. But whether because of his own distaste or because of lingering uncertainty about the emperor's preferences, Porfyrius was still remarkably circumspect in his references to Christianity in the panegyrical poems. Excepting one oblique mention of Christ, he included all of the other references to Christian symbols and Christian names in the intertextual lines and patterns of the poems. He furthermore obscured his most explicit reference to Christ's assignment of rulership in a foreign language, using Latin letters to form a hexameter verse in Greek words. Although Porfyrius was asking the emperor for amnesty and a recall from exile, he was nevertheless quite reticent to insert references to Christianity in his poems.[22]

After the battle at the Milvian Bridge, Porfyrius had obtained Constantine's goodwill without mentioning Christianity at all. More than a decade later he apparently thought that the emperor would again be sympathetic to the use of cultural and literary references. As in 312, so

---

[21] Porfyrius, *Carm.* 8.5, "Christi sub lege probata," 14 intertextual, "summi dei auxilio nutuque perpetuo tutus," 16 intertextual, Νεῖμέν σοι βασιλεῦ Χριστὸς καὶ σοῖς τεκέεσσι. The christogram as an intertextual pattern: Porfyrius, *Carm.* 8, 14, 19.

[22] *Carm.* 24 was addressed to Christ and emphasized the importance of his incarnation and crucifixion for salvation, but Porfyrius was not the author: see Polara (1973) 1:xxx–xxxi, 2:153, 157–58. For Porfyrius as a pagan, note that Bede would decline to cite examples of rhythm from Porfyrius' poems after characterizing them as pagan: see Bede, *De arte metrica* (*PL* 90.173D).

again still in 324 a pagan senator could successfully petition the emperor without highlighting Christianity.

A Dispute in North Africa

By the early fourth century North Africa had become marginal to the military campaigns of emperors. In 297 Maximian had campaigned in Mauretania, and in the following year he resided in Carthage. The legends on coins minted at Carthage celebrated the emperor's "fortunate arrival." Then he left for Rome. Maximian was hence the last legitimate emperor ever to visit North Africa. But because the region remained vitally important as a major source of grain and olive oil for the large population of Rome, ruling the capital required control over North Africa. As an emperor who identified himself with the welfare of Rome, Maxentius had learned firsthand about the consequences of losing control of North Africa when the revolt of Domitius Alexander disrupted the supply of grain and caused a temporary food shortage. The hardship at the capital had been severe enough that Maxentius would be accused of having "murdered the Roman people through a famine."[23]

After his victory in 312 Constantine inherited the responsibility of ensuring the food supply of the capital. Because meeting that obligation presupposed establishing his authority over North Africa and its resources, a visit to Carthage would certainly have helped. Instead, Rome was as far south as Constantine ever traveled in his western empire. As a result, if he was to be a distant emperor, he would need to measure his authority in North Africa in other ways. One was demonstrations of support from the cities; another was the loyalty of his imperial magistrates.

During the initial years after the battle at the Milvian Bridge, cities in several African provinces set up dedications in honor of Constantine,

---

[23] Maximian in Mauretania: *Panegyrici latini* 8(5).5.2, 9(4).20.2, with the discussion of Nixon and Rodgers (1994) 174–75n.83. Coins: Sutherland (1967) 411–15. Return to Rome: *ILS* 1:148, no. 646. Famine: *Panegyrici latini* 12(9).4.4, with Chapter 9, for the revolt of Domitius Alexander, and Jaïdi (2003), for the importance of grain from North Africa for Rome during the fourth century.

either alone or sometimes in tandem with Licinius, emperor in the East. The dedications combined great honor with great relief. At Thamugadi in Numidia, for instance, the community hailed Constantine as "victor, always and everywhere," at Uccula in Africa Proconsularis as "best emperor, beyond the other emperors, unconquered," and at Uchi Maius in Africa Proconsularis as "our restorer." At Cillium in Africa Proconsularis a local notable rededicated an honorific arch. At Lambaesis in Numidia the people set up verses thanking Constantine for removing the "savage wars of the tyrant." Some dedications dropped a subtle hint of future expectations. At Muzuc in Byzacena the community hailed the emperor as "most generous." One city responded to imperial generosity by memorializing the emperor's name. After being "restored and embellished," Cirta in Numidia changed its name to Constantina. In 315, cities erected more dedications in honor of the tenth anniversary of Constantine's reign; the dedications began to include his sons after their promotions as junior emperors. With the establishment of "a priesthood for [Constantine's] Flavian dynasty," communities throughout Africa honored both the emperor and his descendants. Now the cities of North Africa acknowledged only Constantine's imperial rule. As a result, once Constantine attacked Licinius, some communities chiseled off the references to his rival.[24]

---

[24] Dedications: Grünewald (1990) 197, no. 107, Lambaesis, 198, no. 109, Thamugadi, 199, no. 118, Uccula, 200, no. 126, Uchi Maius, 203, no. 138 (+ *ILS* 2.1:388, no. 5570), Cillium, with Lepelley (1979–1981) 1:90–98, on the limits of Constantine's support for building activities in North Africa. Priesthood, Constantina: Aurelius Victor, *De Caesaribus* 40.28.

An inscription on a plaque from Iol Caesarea in Mauretania Caesariensis is sometimes cited as a commemoration of the battle at the Milvian Bridge. This marble plaque depicted a procession of men carrying a miniature model of a bridge and a placard with an inscription identifying the bridge: for photographs, see Mastino and Teatini (2001) 291, 299, and Corbier (2006) 59, Fig. 29. The text of this inscription is disputed, however. *ILS* 1:155, no. 686, and Grünewald (1990) 193, no. 84, print the text with an explicit reference to Constantine: "Pons Mulvi(us) | expeditio | imperatoris | [Co]n[stantini]." Mastino and Teatini (2001) 302, instead suggest a revised final line without Constantine's name: "in Ger[maniam]." This different final line is printed in *L'année épigraphique 2001* (2004) 730–31, no. 2138, and even already in *ILS* 2.2:CLXXI, no. 686. Mastino and Teatini (2001), survey imperial campaigns against Germans; Corbier (2006) 56, notes that such processions with models and placards were characteristic of triumphs or imperial funerals; Östenberg (2009) 199–215,

Imperial magistrates had also erected some of the dedications. At Constantina, for instance, the provincial governor and the financial officer set up matching dedications soon after 312 that praised Constantine as "the celebrator of triumphs over all peoples and the conqueror of all factions, who through his auspicious victory has illuminated with a new light the liberty that had been oppressed by the darkness of slavery." At Lepcis Magna in Tripolitania the provincial governor honored the emperor by erecting "a marble statue that sparkled with his divinity."[25]

Immediately after his victory Constantine had worked to ensure the loyalty of his imperial magistrates in North Africa. One of his first actions was to meet with some of them at Rome. There they could see the head of Maxentius, and they might have been the couriers who soon brought the head to North Africa. The governor of the province of Africa Proconsularis was Anullinus, who was perhaps a son of Gaius Annius Anullinus. Annius Anullinus had himself previously served as governor of Africa Proconsularis, and as prefect of Rome in 306 he had supported the proclamation of Maxentius as emperor. Maxentius had appointed him to serve again as prefect of Rome on the day before the battle of the Milvian Bridge. Maxentius may also have selected his son as governor. After his victory, Constantine retained Annius Anullinus as prefect of Rome for another month. As another sign of reconciliation with the senators of Rome, he appointed (or retained) Anullinus as governor.[26]

Soon afterward Constantine sent a letter to Anullinus in Africa Proconsularis, in which he instructed the governor to restore to the

---

surveys the use of models of conquered cities in triumphal processions. This plaque and its inscription hence referenced the bridge but not the battle, and should not be associated with Constantine.

[25] Dedications: Grünewald (1990) 195–96, nos. 97–98, Constantina, 204, no. 147, Lepcis Magna, with *PLRE* 1:685, "Val. Paulus 12," 771, "Laenatius Romulus 4."

[26] For the meeting with the magistrates of Africa, see Eusebius, *HE* 10.6.4, citing Constantine's letter to bishop Caecilianus of Carthage: "know that I have given orders to Anullinus the proconsul and to Patricius the vicar of the provinces when they were present"; with *PLRE* 1:78–79, "Anullinus 2," "C. Annius Anullinus 3," 673, "Patricius 1."

Christian church any confiscated possessions. In the letter Constantine seemed to be testing Anullinus' trustworthiness. The emperor wanted Anullinus to restore the possessions "as soon as you receive this letter." The quickness of his response would be an indication that "you have rendered the most attentive obedience to our command." Constantine subsequently sent another letter to Anullinus about privileges for clerics. This time when Anullinus replied in April 313, he noted that "the celestial document of your majesty," that is, the emperor's letter, had been both "received and adored." The governor had apparently performed a ceremony of reverence on receiving the emperor's letter. Constantine's initial concern was not Christianity in North Africa but the loyalty of his magistrates.[27]

The emperor's support for Christianity may nevertheless have been another aspect of his policy of ensuring the reliability of North Africa, in particular as he was preparing to leave Italy soon to return to the northern frontier in Gaul. At the same time as he was writing to the governor, he wrote to Caecilianus, bishop of Carthage. The typical protocol of interaction between imperial courts and provincials consisted of a "constant dialogue of petition and response." In this case presumably Caecilianus had written to the emperor first, and Constantine was responding to a request from a provincial notable who happened to be a bishop. In his letter Constantine offered to reimburse the expenses of some clerics serving "the most holy catholic religion." He also noted that he had already arranged for payment by issuing instructions to various magistrates, including the chief financial officer of Africa, the administrator of the imperial properties, the governor, and the vicar. In a subsequent decision in February 313, Constantine exempted the clerics who served "in the catholic church that Caecilianus administers" from having to perform municipal liturgies. This generosity helped fashion a distinctive image of the new emperor in North Africa. His imperial administration was there to serve the provincials. Rather than only

---

[27] Eusebius, *HE* 10.5.16–17, letter, obedience, 7.1–2, second letter. Augustine, *Ep.* 88.2, citing a copy of Anullinus' *relatio*: "scripta caelestia maiestatis vestrae accepta atque adorata," with Corcoran (1996) 156, on the adoration of imperial letters.

exporting resources from North Africa, Constantine was dispersing funds and granting privileges.[28]

These gifts publicized Constantine's munificence toward Christians, and more requests apparently arrived at his court. He continued his openhandedness, and later in the year he was instructing a governor in southern Italy to extend the same exemptions to clerics in his province. Now it had become worthwhile to acquire the emperor's patronage. As a result, in North Africa his largesse exacerbated an ongoing dispute.[29]

Constantine had decided to support "catholic" Christians in North Africa, whom he identified with the leadership of Caecilianus. In contrast, opponents who had not accepted Caecilianus' legitimacy as bishop of Carthage reacted by claiming to be the true representatives of the "catholic church" and therefore the proper recipients of the emperor's patronage. These opponents were subsequently known as "the faction of Donatus," that is, Donatist Christians, named after a rival bishop of Carthage. They requested that the governor Anullinus forward to the emperor a sealed package containing their charges against Caecilianus as well as an unsealed petition. In their petition they appealed to Constantine's "just pedigree" by noting that in the past his father, the emperor Constantius, had not enforced persecution of Christians. This recollection was presumably a hint that Constantine should demonstrate similar restraint. It is notable that the petitioners apparently did not describe the emperor as a fellow Christian but instead referenced

---

[28] Eusebius, *HE* 10.6.1–5, letter to Caecilianus, dated to winter of 312–313, 7.1–2, letter to Anullinus, dated February 313. Quotation about dialogue from Millar (1983) 80. Constantine planned to pay Caecilianus 3,000 *folles*: see Eusebius, *HE* 10.6.1. A *follis* was a sealed purse containing a standard number of low-value coins, typically for a total value in the early fourth century of 12,500 denarii: see Jones (1964) 440, and Hendy (1985) 338–40. Under Constantine a large gold coin (solidus) was worth a maximum of 1,000 denarii: see Hendy (1985) 466. In a period of rapid inflation these numbers are of dubious value. But simply as a heuristic exercise, combining them suggests that Constantine's gift to Caecilianus may have been worth about 37,500 solidi, or about 521 pounds of gold. This was about one-fifth the value of the emperor's concurrent gifts to the Church of St. John Lateran and the Church of St. Peter at Rome (see below in this Chapter).

[29] Governor of Lucania and Bruttium: *CTh* 16.2.2, dated October 21, 313.

his sense of justice. They furthermore asked for judges from Gaul to resolve their quarrel.[30]

According to a later historian, at the time Constantine was "still unfamiliar with these issues." The restrictions on imperial authority had always been practical rather than constitutional. Because so many communities and individuals submitted so many petitions and letters, emperors certainly needed the assistance of court officials and secretaries to write up responses. "Delegation was an inescapable corollary of imperial rule." So was ignorance about many current affairs, and often emperors depended on petitioners to supply the background information. In the bustle of dealing with issues at Rome and establishing a new regime in North Africa, Constantine would have had to rely on advisers. Even though in his earlier letter to Caecilianus the emperor had arranged the funding for the clerics, he had also referred the details of the payments to a separate list compiled by bishop Ossius of Corduba. Constantine had endorsed the administrative format but delegated the ecclesiastical details to a churchman. In his letter he (or a court secretary) may well have simply repeated back Caecilianus' own description of his catholic Christian community without being aware that "catholic" was a disputed characterization in North Africa. The petition of the Donatist faction, however, exposed the fault lines and involved the emperor directly in an overseas regional ecclesiastical dispute.[31]

By then Constantine had returned to northern Gaul and was campaigning again on the Rhine frontier. In June he sent a letter to Miltiades, bishop of Rome, to establish a tribunal to hear the accusations against Caecilianus. In his letter he informed Miltiades that he had already invited Caecilianus, ten of his supporters, and ten of his accusers to sail to Rome, and that three bishops from Gaul would be joining

---

[30] Augustine, *Ep.* 88.1, "pars Donati," 2, documents forwarded by Anullinus in April. Donatist petition: Optatus, *Contra Donatistas* 1.22.2.

[31] Optatus, *Contra Donatistas* 1.22.1, "imperatorem Constantinum harum rerum adhuc ignarum." Eusebius, *HE* 10.6.2, referring to Ossius' βρέουιον, his "brief." Quotation from the excellent account of the working of the imperial administration in Kelly (2004) 191.

Miltiades as judges. Constantine's primary concern was, again, not necessarily Christian affairs but maintaining peace in his new provinces
in North Africa. He worried about the disputes that splintered both
bishops and "the great majority of the people." His choice of bishops
as judges reflected his personal connections. He had presumably met
Miltiades during his visit to Rome, and the three bishops of Cologne,
Autun, and Arles represented cities he had visited in Gaul. Constantine forwarded to them copies of the documents he had received from
Anullinus.[32]

The council convened by Miltiades at Rome in early autumn of 313
vindicated Caecilianus. Donatus himself, in person, admitted that he
had rebaptized and reconsecrated bishops who had lapsed during the
persecutions under the Tetrarchs, and none of his supporters verified
any accusations against Caecilianus. Miltiades and the three bishops
from Gaul were joined by fifteen more bishops from Italy, and all voted
against Donatus. Miltiades concluded his own verdict by announcing
that Caecilianus remained in good standing with his ecclesiastical community. On hearing the decision, Constantine thought that "a proper
conclusion had been imposed on all troublemaking and quarrels."[33]

Donatus and his supporters disagreed and instead made accusations against Miltiades and his allegedly biased tribunal. Some of them
apparently visited the emperor's court in Gaul to complain again about
Caecilianus. Constantine brushed them off. "I replied that they were
talking about this issue to no avail, because the case had been concluded
at Rome by competent and most upright bishops." The Donatists
responded with more complaints about the inadequacy of the judicial
procedure and the honesty of the judges. The emperor then decided
to hold another hearing at a council of bishops in Arles. In spring
of 314 he began to invite bishops to attend, including the bishop of
Syracuse. He also wrote to the vicar of Africa to arrange transportation
for Caecilianus, his entourage, and some of his opponents. Again the

---

[32] Letter to Miltiades: Eusebius, *HE* 10.5.18–20.

[33] Description of council at Rome: Optatus, *Contra Donatistas* 1.23.1–24.2. Conclusion: Optatus, Appendix 3.29b.

emperor's primary apprehension was the potential for unrest in "our Africa." "As a result of these altercations the highest divinity could perhaps be moved not only against the human race, but also against me. Through his celestial nod he has entrusted to my oversight all earthly affairs for administration." Constantine's primary concern was his imperial authority in North Africa.[34]

In these letters Constantine repeatedly talked about Christianity. One striking characteristic, though, is the awkwardness of his terminology. He referred to the Christian God variously as "the divinity of the great God," "the deity," "omnipotent God," and "the highest divinity." He was apparently unfamiliar with the ecclesiastical hierarchy when he mentioned churchmen "whom they are accustomed to call clerics." In his letter to the vicar he claimed to have learned that "you too are a worshipper of the highest God." Even if Constantine was associating the vicar's religion with his own, this statement was not a firm indication of devotion to Christianity. The emperor's stilted language seemed to imply that he was only just beginning to learn details about Christianity.[35]

Constantine apparently attended the council at Arles in August 314, joining more than thirty bishops as well as two priests and two deacons sent by Silvester, the new bishop of Rome. The bishops and their attendant clerics formed a microcosm of the regions that now made up his empire, including Britain, Gaul, Spain, Italy, Sicily, Africa, and even Dalmatia on the eastern coast of the Adriatic Sea. In Constantine's new western Mediterranean empire Arles was the geographical center. Even if Arles did not become an important residence for Constantine, it still seemed to be a better situated hub for a western empire that emphasized both the northern frontier on the Rhine and now North Africa. The city soon acquired a special association with the Constantinian dynasty. Constantine himself quite likely imported the obelisk that was erected

---

[34] Letter to bishop Chrestus of Syracuse: Eusebius, *HE* 10.5.21–23. Letter to vicar Aelafius: Optatus, Appendix 3.29b, our Africa, 30a, I replied, 30b, altercations.

[35] Eusebius, *HE* 10.5.20, divinity of the great God, 6.5, divinity of the great God, 7.2, clerics, deity. Optatus, Appendix 3.30a, omnipotent God, 30b, worshiper.

in the circus, and in 316 his son Constantine II was born in Arles. Not surprisingly, Arles too, like other cities, eventually acquired a new name, "Constantina," derived from the emperor's name. As an occasional imperial residence, Arles would seem to have become an alternative western capital, a "miniature Rome in Gaul."[36]

Despite the gravity of the issues, the emperor apparently enjoyed the sessions at the council. "He was eager to attend their debates and to sit together with the bishops." Without his bodyguards, he was on his own, "one [participant] in the midst of many." Afterward the bishops wrote to bishop Silvester of Rome about their decisions. Their deliberations had included ecclesiastical issues, such as the celebration of Easter and the consecration of bishops, and the treatment of problematic converts, such as soldiers, chariot drivers in the circus races, theatrical performers, and magistrates. In addition, they again vindicated Caecilianus. Some opponents reconciled with Caecilianus on the spot. Others, "the most stubborn and the most litigious," appealed yet again to the emperor. In response, this time Constantine simply ended the proceedings. "He was weary and ordered everyone to return to their sees."[37]

Soon afterward Constantine sent a general letter to the "catholic bishops." This letter served several purposes. It was a compliment to the bishops for a decision rendered "through the very bright light of catholic law." It was a small, rambling sermon about "the eternal and incomprehensible religious piety of our God" and "the victorious providence of Christ the Savior." It was also a personal confession about the emperor's own religious journey. After noting that God offered

---

[36] Birth of Constantine II at Arles: *Epitome de Caesaribus* 41.4. Charron and Heijmans (2001), and Heijmans (2004) 243, assign the erection of the obelisk to early in Constantine's reign. Arles as Constantina: Leo I, *Ep.* 65.3 (*PL* 54.882A) = *Epistolae Arelatenses* 12, ed. Gundlach (1892) 19, with Grünewald (1990) 36–38, suggesting that Constantine may have resided at Arles during the early years of his reign, and Heijmans (2006), for a survey of the monuments at Arles. Miniature Rome: Ausonius, *Ordo urbium nobilium* 10.2, "Gallula Roma."

[37] Eager: Eusebius, *Vita Constantini* 1.44.2, on the assumption that this description of the emperor's attendance at a council refers to the council of Arles: so Barnes (1981) 58, but disputed by Cameron and Hall (1999) 221. Optatus, Appendix 4.31a, letter to Silvester, 31b, other decisions, 32a, weary. Most stubborn: Augustine, *Ep.* 88.3. For the complete lists of the twenty-two canons and of the bishops and clerics in attendance, see Munier (1963) 9–22.

"a way of salvation," Constantine admitted his dependency: "I have learned this from many examples, and I measure these same [gifts] by my own experiences." He then summarized the trajectory of his religious development. "Initially there were in me [characteristics] that seemed to lack justice, and I thought that a higher power did not see anything that I did within the secrets of my heart. . . . But omnipotent God, who resides in the heights of heaven, gave [me] what I did not deserve. Certainly what he bestowed through his celestial benevolence upon me, his servant, cannot be mentioned or enumerated."[38]

In this letter Constantine had mastered Christian terminology, and his confession seemed to use the language of a Christian conversion experience. Now the emperor was characterizing himself as God's servant. Now he was referring to Jesus. "For the first time we find the name of Christ in an imperial letter." The significant turning point in Constantine's awareness of his Christian beliefs was not a vision or his victory at the Milvian Bridge two years earlier, but instead his participation in the council at Arles.[39]

This council established precedents for Constantine's subsequent reign. He socialized with bishops and began to identify himself with these "most beloved brothers." He apparently relished talking about theology, he sent letters to bishops urging his doctrinal preferences, and he used Christian language to articulate his life's trajectory. He increasingly associated himself with the life of Jesus. He also failed in his hope for ecclesiastical harmony. Constantine thought that the verdict of bishops should end ecclesiastical disputes. "The judgment of bishops ought to be regarded as if the Lord himself was sitting in judgment." He was dismayed to discover that the Donatists instead considered this episcopal tribunal similar to a secular court, whose decisions could be appealed. "The furious audacity of madness! As is customary to happen in the cases of pagans, they have introduced an appeal." In addition, the disgruntled Donatists attacked the emperor personally. "They demand

---

[38] Optatus, Appendix 5.32a, piety, confession, 32b, catholic law, providence, with Chapter 6, on the possible influence of Lactantius' ideas.

[39] Quotation about name of Christ translated from Maier (1987–1989) 1:168n.5.

judgment for me; I myself anticipate the judgment of Christ." Despite this failure and this criticism, Constantine remained an optimist. Eleven years later he would again participate with the bishops at the council of Nicaea. Not surprisingly, the outcome was similarly inconclusive.[40]

As long as he remained in the West, Constantine continued his involvement in the ecclesiastical disputes in North Africa. His concern may have been more pragmatic than strictly religious, however. Because his empire now included Rome, his magistrates were responsible for supplying the capital with grain and olive oil from North Africa. Even after his return to Trier, he could not avoid issuing instructions about shipmasters in Africa and bread makers at Rome. He also wanted to prevent any feuding among churchmen that might grow into a challenge to his authority and disrupt the supply of food to Rome. Dealing with churchmen tested his patience, and over the years Constantine repeatedly complained about their "stubbornness" and "insanity." He ordered the competing factions to appear before him again during his visit to Rome in the summer of 315. After some of the antagonists failed to attend, he heard their case instead at Milan during the autumn and again pronounced Caecilianus "completely innocent." He issued an edict ordering the confiscation of Donatist properties. At one point he hoped to travel to Africa to demonstrate to both Caecilianus and his opponents the proper form of veneration for the "highest . . . divinity."[41]

Eventually Constantine began to disengage. He conceded his ineffectiveness: "the reasoning of our policy was not able to subdue the force of that innate wickedness." He was also thinking about other priorities. His victory over Maxentius in 312 had immediately involved him in the civil and religious affairs of North Africa; the outcome of a

---

[40] Optatus, Appendix 5.32a, brothers, 32b, judgment for me, judgment of bishops, 33a, audacity. Some of Constantine's quips were repeated in Optatus, *Contra Donatistas* 1.23.1, 25.1.

[41] Regulations from Trier: *CTh* 11.30.4, 13.5.2–3, apparently all excerpted from the same constitution issued in June 314; for the date, see Seeck (1919) 98. The recipient, Amabilianus, is apparently the first attested *praefectus annonae Africae*: see *PLRE* 1:49, "Amabilianus." Optatus, Appendix 6.33b, stubbornness, 7.34a, insanity, "when I arrive in Africa," 9.35a, reasoning. Augustine, *Ep.* 43.7.20, Rome and Milan, 88.3, edict.

subsequent civil war presented new concerns elsewhere in the empire, including the supply of a new capital city and participation in another controversy over ecclesiastical doctrines. After his victory over Licinius in 324, Constantine spent most of his time in the East. Now he was less involved with Rome and the Donatist controversy and more involved with Constantinople and the Arian controversy. Now he had to worry about his authority in Egypt, a flashpoint for theological disputes but also the primary source of grain for Constantinople. The common denominator was a concern over effective administration. First Rome and North Africa, then Constantinople and Egypt: again the supply of food for a capital city may have guided his involvement in religious affairs.[42]

In 330 Constantine replied once more to the African bishops. They had written to complain that Donatists had seized the church at Constantina that the emperor himself had once ordered to be constructed. As compensation they asked for an imperial estate. Constantine agreed, and he also ordered the construction of a new church at imperial expense. At the same time he wrote to the governor of Numidia with instructions to exempt the clerics whom the "injustice of the heretics" had compelled to serve on municipal councils. Almost twenty years earlier, at the beginning of his involvement with churchmen in North Africa, the emperor had used his beneficence as leverage. Now, because of his engagement in eastern affairs, because of his realistic assessment of the complexity of resolving this ecclesiastical dispute, generosity was all he had left to offer these African bishops.[43]

THE ARCH AT MALBORGHETTO

During the late summer and early autumn of 312 Constantine and his army had marched from northern Italy to Rome on the Flaminian Way. After crossing the western Alps into northern Italy earlier in the year, he

---

[42] Reasoning: Optatus, Appendix 9.35a.

[43] Church at Constantina, imperial estate, new church: Optatus, Appendix 10.36b; injustice: CTh 16.2.7. Both the letter to the bishops and the edict to the governor were sent from Serdica on February 5, 330.

CONSTANTINE'S INVASION OF ITALY

Cologne
Deutz
Trier
Rhine
Danube
RAETIA
ALPS
Aquileia
Milan
Brescia
Verona
Turin
Po
Susa
ADRIATIC SEA
Modena
AEMILIAN WAY
Ravenna
APENNINES
Rimini
Fanum Fortunae
Intercisa
Metaurus
FLAMINIAN WAY →
Tiber
Hispellum
Carsulae
Spoletium
Narnia
Interamna
Ocriculum
Aqua Viva
Malborghetto
Rome
APPIAN WAY

Miles   0   50   100
Kilometers 0   50   100   150

Map by Ian Mladjov

had advanced east across the Po River valley and seized the cities of Susa, Turin, Milan, and Brescia. After defeating Maxentius' troops stationed at Verona, he would have moved south to link up with the Flaminian Way at Rimini, still about 150 miles from Rome. From Rimini he would have marched along the coast to Fanum Fortunae (modern Fano) and then followed the highway into the interior almost due south across the Apennine Mountains. North of Rome the Flaminian Way crossed the Tiber on the Milvian Bridge and then followed the curve of the river for almost two miles before entering the capital through the Aurelian Wall by way of the Flaminian Gate.

The Flaminian Way had been constructed in the later third century B.C. to connect the capital with the cities of northeastern central Italy and new settlements on the north Adriatic coast, and to provide access to the Po valley. Originally this great highway had assisted the expansion of Roman hegemony into northern Italy; subsequently it also served as a site for celebrating emperors' overseas successes. After his decisive victory at the battle of Actium in 31 B.C., Augustus had decided to commemorate the end of the civil wars by enhancing the Flaminian Way. While his generals were to fund the repaving of the other roads in Italy with their booty, he himself paid for improvements to the entire length of the Flaminian Way. At Rome he erected a statue of himself on an honorific arch on the Milvian Bridge, that is, perhaps on a gateway arch at one end of the bridge or on a double arch in the center of the bridge. At Narnia (modern Narni) he built a bridge supported on famously high arches. At Rimini he erected another statue of himself on a commemorative arch. In return the senate and people of Rome had a dedication engraved on the arch at Rimini that complimented the emperor for rebuilding the Flaminian Way and "the other very famous roads of Italy with his foresight and his funds." Decades later Augustus was still maintaining this connection with central and northern Italy through his generosity. He paid for improvements to the Aemilian Way that led northwest from Rimini to the Po valley, and toward the end of his life he donated funds for the construction of a wall at Fanum Fortunae. A dedication in honor of Augustus' munificence was engraved on an arch at Fanum Fortunae. Immediately after his final victory in the civil wars, and then subsequently throughout his entire reign until his death in A.D. 14, Augustus had reasserted his patronage for the towns of central and northeastern Italy along the entire length of the Flaminian Way.[44]

When emperors returned to Rome from their campaigns on the northern frontiers, they followed the Flaminian Way south through central Italy, trailing "a long plume of dust." "All of Rome" would come out to greet them on the highway. Because the Flaminian Way was so vital to travelers between northern Italy and Rome, subsequent emperors maintained and improved the highway to leave monuments and dedications as public mementos of their accomplishments. Vespasian constructed a remarkable tunnel at Intercisa, and Trajan repaired a bridge over the Metaurus River. Almost two centuries later Diocletian and his fellow emperors again repaired apparently the same bridge. Maxentius appointed a superintendent to look after the Flaminian Way; his maintenance may ironically have paved the way for Constantine to advance on Rome. In addition, because many estates and tombs lined the road outside Rome, especially in the suburbs, private landowners may also have contributed to upkeep.[45]

About eight miles north of the Milvian Bridge a huge commemorative monument was constructed near the Flaminian Way at the modern

[44] Repaving of roads, Flaminian Way: Suetonius, *Augustus* 30.1. Augustus' improvements: Augustus, *Res gestae* 20.5, "during my seventh consulship [in 27 B.C.] I restored the Flaminian Way from the city [of Rome] to Rimini." Bridge at Narnia: Procopius, *Bella* 5.17.11. Statues and arches at Rome and Rimini: Dio, *Historiae Romanae* 53.22.1–2, with De Maria (1988) 260–62, no. 48, arch at Rimini, 269, no. 58, discussing coins minted in Spain that might have depicted the arch on the Milvian Bridge. Dedication at Rimini: *ILS* 1:24, no. 84. Milestone near Bologna on Aemilian Way: *ILS* 2.2:cxxvii, no. 9371, dated 2–1 B.C. Wall and arch at Fanum Fortunae: *ILS* 1:27, no. 104, dated A.D. 9–10, with De Maria (1988) 242–43.

[45] Dust, all of Rome: Martial, *Epigrammata* 10.6.5–6, describing the anticipation of Trajan's arrival in 99. Vespasian's tunnel: *Epitome de Caesaribus* 9.9–10. *ILS* 1:78, no. 299, Trajan's bridge, 267, no. 1217, dedication to C. Vettius Cossinius Rufinus, *curator viae Flaminiae*, 2.1:449, no. 5900, Diocletian's bridge, with *PLRE* 1:777, "C. Vettius Cossinius Rufinus 15." Tombs: Juvenal, *Saturae* 1.170–71, with Ashby and Fell (1921), surveying the monuments along the entire highway. For a large villa near Aqua Viva, about twenty-five miles north of Rome, that was owned by the family of Junius Bassus, consul in 331, see Evrard (1962).

site of Malborghetto. This monument was a *quadrifrons* arch, a bulky structure with an archway on each of its four sides. Although its footprint was more square than rectangular, in terms of its height and the area of its base the arch was comparable in size to the arch of Constantine inside Rome. The four-way arch was not quite square, almost fifty feet wide on the north and south faces, and almost forty feet wide on the faces parallel to the Flaminian Way. The four corner piers were each about fifteen feet by eleven feet at their bases; the front and back archways were each almost twenty feet wide, and the side archways a few feet narrower; each of the archways was more than thirty feet high. Over the archways a decorated ledge encircled the monument, topped by a massive attic. The entire monument was almost sixty feet high. The facades of the archways, including the faces of the piers and the attic, were covered most likely with a veneer of marble panels or blocks, some probably carved to depict scenes, and large statues most likely stood on top of the monument. But excepting a few fragments, all of this sheathing and the decorations have disappeared, and today only the brick core remains.[46]

This massive arch was constructed in the early fourth century, at about the same time as the gigantic Baths of Diocletian, located in a northern residential neighborhood of Rome between the Viminal and Quirinal Hills, and the large Basilica Nova (also known as the Basilica of Maxentius or the Constantinian Basilica), located on the northern edge of the Forum. Constantine was the one emperor of this period who had a specific personal interest in constructing a memorial arch at a location

---

[46] For the dimensions of the arch at Malborghetto, see Toebelmann (1915) 2–8; because of subsequent modifications, the height is uncertain. For a reconstruction, see Toebelmann (1915) Tafel XIII, reprinted in Messineo and Calci (1989) 71 fig. 62; but considered "largamente ipotetico" by De Maria (1988) 243. The arch at Malborghetto was hence larger even than the *quadrifrons* arch in the Forum Boarium west of the Palatine Hill, sometimes known as the "arch of Janus." The "arch of Janus" was constructed (or reconstructed) in the early fourth century and is usually identified with the "arch of the divine Constantine" mentioned in *Curiosum* and *Notitia*, ed. Nordh (1949) 91: see De Maria (1988) 319–20, and Richardson (1992) 208. Coarelli (2007) 321, suggests that Constantius II erected this arch in the Forum Boarium during his visit to Rome in 357.

on the Flaminian Way outside Rome. The obvious association would be a connection with his victory in the battle against Maxentius.[47]

One possibility is that the arch commemorated the spot where he and his army had witnessed the vision of the cross in the sky. In fact, this is a most improbable interpretation. The first known account of this vision was Constantine's own story, which he could have told to Eusebius and other bishops in the East only in 325 at the earliest, and perhaps not until much later. Even the emperor himself did not talk about his vision until later in his reign. In the West knowledge about the witnessing of the cross was even more tardy. It finally entered common circulation only in the early fifth century after Rufinus had included a story about the emperor's dream in his translation of Eusebius' *History*. The arch at Malborghetto was the wrong sort of monument to commemorate the witnessing of the cross, and it was constructed far too early.[48]

Another, much more likely possibility is that this arch memorialized not a moment of religious insight but a military success. For an army heading south toward Rome this section of the Flaminian Way in the southern foothills of the Apennines offered opportunities to rest and resupply. In 69, troops loyal to Vespasian had stopped at Carsulae, where

---

[47] Messineo and Calci (1989) 81–83, date the arch to the early fourth century on the basis of construction techniques, architectural details, and the bricks. A stamp on a brick used in the vault of the south archway implies a date during the reign of Tetrarchic emperors: see Messineo and Calci (1989) 52, 82 fig. 73, "OFF · CR · AVGG · ET · CAESS · NN" in a circle, i.e., "Off(icina) Cr(?) Augg(ustorum) et Caess(arum) nn(ostrorum)" (= "workshop of/at Cr(?) belonging to our two Augusti and two Caesars"), and "SR" in the center, i.e., "s(ummae) r(ei)" (= "belonging to the state treasury"). A brick with an identical stamp was found on the Esquiline Hill: see *CIL* 15.1:393, no. 1564.2, dated between 293 and 305 during the reign of Diocletian and his fellow Tetrarchs. Steinby (1986) 117, 152, suggests that "CR" referred to the name of the workshop or a magistrate, perhaps "Cr(escentis)." Frothingham (1915) 159, also found a brick from the arch with the fragmentary stamp "DD · NN," i.e., "dd(ominorum) nn(ostrorum)" (= "belonging to our two lords"). One block in the arch was a recycled gravestone engraved with a fragmentary dedication: see *CIL* 11.2.2:1360, no. 7774, with Messineo and Calci (1989) 87, 89 fig. 89, dating the dedication to the first century A.D.

[48] For the arch as a commemoration of the vision, see Toebelmann (1915) 31, with Chapters 3, on Rufinus' translation, and 4, on Constantine's later memory of his vision. Also unlikely is the suggestion of Girardet (2006b) 74, that the arch marked the spot where Constantine decided to use the chi-rho symbol as an emblem on his soldiers' shields.

their proximity to other "very prosperous cities" guaranteed "safe access to supplies." Subsequently those troops marched farther south along the Flaminian Way to Narnia, Ocriculum, and Saxa Rubra, before some of them crossed the Milvian Bridge to enter Rome. In 193 Septimius Severus had met a delegation of senators at Interamna. In 307 Galerius and his troops likewise had camped at Interamna on their way to Rome. In 312 Constantine and his troops may have advanced a bit farther before setting up camp. This arch at Malborghetto may have commemorated the site of his army's final encampment before the battle against Maxentius, perhaps even the exact spot of the commander's tent.[49]

If so, then the arch was similar in function to the monument that Augustus had erected at the site of his final encampment in western Greece before the battle of Actium in 31 B.C. Augustus' memorial was a large open terrace surrounded on three sides by a stoa. An altar and large statues stood in the middle of the terrace, bronze rams from captured

---

[49] Vespasian's troops: Tacitus, *Historiae* 3.60, 78–79, 82. Septimius Severus: SHA, *Severus* 6.2. Galerius' troops: *Origo Constantini imperatoris* 3.6. For the arch as a marker of the final encampment, see Kuhoff (1991) 157; of the emperor's tent, Coarelli (2007) 435, "precisely at the location of the *praetorium* in Constantine's camp." According to Zosimus, *Historia nova* 2.16.1, "Constantine advanced to Rome with his army and encamped in a field that was in front of the city, open, and suitable for his cavalry"; but Zosimus also implied that this field was the site of the final battle.

Aurelius Victor, *De Caesaribus* 40.23, located Maxentius' defeat at Saxa Rubra ("Red Rocks," near modern Grottarossa), on the Flaminian Way a few miles north of the Milvian Bridge, just south of Prima Porta, and several miles south of Malborghetto. Kuhoff (1991) 157, suggests that Saxa Rubra was the site of only an initial skirmish, but Barnes (1981) 305n.144, dismisses the battle by claiming that Aurelius Victor confused the invasion of 312 with Septimius Severus' invasion of 193 (see Aurelius Victor, *De Caesaribus* 19.4). As another contribution to revisionist history, note that in 1912 a dedication commemorating the 1600th anniversary of Constantine's victory was erected at Prima Porta under the auspices of pope Pius X. This dedication identified the site of the victory as Saxa Rubra: for the text, see Kuhoff (1991) 157n.80.

Another possibility, of course, is that the arch at Malborghetto had nothing to do with Constantine's victory. Frothingham (1915) 159–60, argues that this sort of four-way arch "was associated with topographical boundaries and not primarily with triumphs," and that "the arch marks the boundary of the jurisdiction of the urban magistrates in Diocletian's reorganization of Italy."

ships were displayed as trophies on the front facade, and a dedicatory inscription commemorated "the victory in the war he waged on behalf of the Republic." Nearby Augustus founded a new city whose name celebrated his victory, Nicopolis.[50]

If the arch at Malborghetto can be associated with Constantine, it was most likely constructed in time for him to celebrate its dedication during his visit to Rome in 315 or in 326. The arch inside Rome anticipated Constantine's transformation into a civilian emperor. In contrast, this arch in the suburbs most likely explicitly honored his military victory. Only his victory at the Milvian Bridge had made it possible for him to celebrate his tenth and his twentieth anniversaries at Rome, and Constantine knew that he had owed that victory to his troops. Malborghetto was perhaps Constantine's equivalent of a "city of victory."

The arch at Malborghetto was not the only monument on the Flaminian Way that commemorated Constantine. In early 313 the emperor left Rome to return to northern Italy, almost certainly by marching north on the Flaminian Way. During his subsequent visits to Rome he again traveled along the Flaminian Way. In 315 on his way to Rome he passed through Aqua Viva, a town north of Malborghetto; in 326 he passed through Spoletium (modern Spoleto) on his return trip. Various towns along the Flaminian Way set up dedications and monuments in his honor. In the mid-330s the people of Hispellum asked Constantine for permission to construct a new temple in honor of the emperor's Flavian dynasty and to establish a new festival that included theatrical shows and gladiator games. They also requested that he bestow on their city a new name derived from his dynastic name. Constantine agreed with their requests, and he allowed the city to be renamed as Flavia Constans, to commemorate both his family's dynastic Flavian name and the name of his youngest son, Constans. The people of Hispellum were presumably readying their city in anticipation

---

[50] Monument at Nicopolis: Strabo, *Geographia* 7.7.6, Suetonius, *Augustus* 18.2, Dio, *Historiae Romanae* 51.1.2–3, with Zachos (2003), for an excellent survey of the archaeology of the monument and a revised text of the dedication, and Lange (2009) 95–123.

of Constantine's expected return to Rome to celebrate the thirtieth anniversary of his accession. By reminding the emperor that their city was "adjacent and next to the Flaminian Way," perhaps they were hinting that the emperor might like to stop and visit the new temple. At Fanum Fortunae the dedication on the arch in honor of Augustus' generosity, then more than three centuries old, would be revised in honor of Constantine. Because this new dedication celebrated Constantine as "divine," it had been added after his death in 337. At some time Fanum Fortunae also added "Flavia" to its name. Previously it had been a "Julian" city, named after Augustus' imperial dynasty; now it too was renamed after Constantine's Flavian dynasty.[51]

The connection between the cities on the Flaminian Way and the Constantinian imperial dynasty lingered into the next generation. When Constantius visited Rome in 357, he of course traveled on the Flaminian Way. On his trip to the capital he stopped at Ocriculum, in the foothills of the Apennines, and he made a contribution, in the name of himself and his cousin Julian, his fellow emperor, to repair the bathhouse that had burned down at Spoletium. Monuments and dedications commemorated Constantine and his Flavian imperial dynasty along the entire length of the Flaminian Way, from Fanum Fortunae in the north to Malborghetto in the south.[52]

The original patron of the highway, Gaius Flaminius, had been a consul and a famous general in the later third century B.C. Augustus' patronage had promoted support for his Julian dynasty. But now, with

---

[51] Aqua Viva: *CTh* 8.18.1, with the emendation in Seeck (1919) 163. Spoletium: *CTh* 16.5.2. Favors for Hispellum: Van Dam (2007) 23–129, 363–67. New inscription at Fanum Fortunae: *ILS* 1:159, no. 706 = Grünewald (1990) 216, no. 234, with De Maria (1988) 215, on rededicating Augustus' arch. "Flavia Fanestri": *Consultatio veteris cuiusdam iurisconsulti* 9.4, in an edict issued in 365.

Note also a tombstone at Spoletium for a *protector*, a junior officer, from the Legio II Italica Divitiensis: see *ILS* 1:549, no. 2777. This legionary unit presumably took its name from Castellum Divitia (modern Deutz), a fortified camp established by Constantine on the east bank of the Rhine: see Chapter 10. Jones (1964) 1084n.43, suggests that this *protector* was serving at Constantine's court during the invasion of 312.

[52] Ocriculum: Ammianus Marcellinus, *Res gestae* 16.10.4. Baths at Spoletium: *ILS* 1:166, no. 739 = Conti (2004) 144–45, no. 124.

the construction of all of the Constantinian monuments during the fourth century, the entire Flaminian Way might well have been renamed after Constantine's imperial dynasty as the "Flavian Way."

A Dedication, a Statue, and a Hand

When Constantine entered Rome on October 29, the day after his victory over Maxentius, a crowd welcomed him as "redeemer, savior, and benefactor." Eusebius described this ceremonial arrival in the edition of his *Ecclesiastical History* published already in late 313 or 314. To compose this description so soon after the battle, he had clearly relied on an anonymous written source. His narrative continued by claiming that the emperor acknowledged the compliments from the crowd and soon ordered that "a commemoration of the Savior's suffering should be erected in the hand of a statue of himself." This statue was set up "at a site that was as public as any in Rome."[53]

After his entry into Rome many statues of Constantine were erected "in the most distinguished locations; most were of gold or silver." The statue that Constantine ordered to be erected is commonly identified with the colossal marble statue that was on display in the apse at the west end of the Basilica Nova. Maxentius had initiated construction of this huge basilica on the ridge between the Forum and the Colosseum. Because the basilica was not yet completed in 312, Constantine had an opportunity to supervise some remodeling. In fact, after he subsequently completed the basilica, it came to be known as Basilica Constantiniana, the "Constantinian Basilica." In addition, the senate sanctioned the rededication of this basilica "to the merits of Flavius," that is, to Constantine, whose official imperial name, as inscribed on the nearby commemorative arch, was Flavius Constantinus. By appropriating the name of this basilica and receiving credit for its construction, Constantine had stolen a centerpiece of Maxentius' monumental legacy.[54]

---

[53] Acclamations, site: Eusebius, *HE* 9.9.10, with Chapter 5, for discussion of Eusebius' source.
[54] Statues: Aurelius Victor, *De Caesaribus* 40.28, with La Rocca and Zanker (2007), discussing the large marble head of Constantine recently found in the Forum of Trajan. For the

He may also have stolen Maxentius' statue. Today all that survives of the colossal statue are several huge fragments, including most famously the head and the right hand, as well as the right upper arm and elbow, the right knee, the right shin and calf, the right foot, a piece of the lower left leg, and the left foot. The fragments were discovered in the ruins of the Basilica Nova in the later fifteenth century but subsequently moved to the Capitoline Hill, where they are on display in the courtyard of the Palazzo dei Conservatori. In the mid-twentieth century another fragment, a piece of the left chest and shoulder, was also discovered in the Basilica Nova, and other fragments might still be identified.[55]

This statue was huge, and the head alone, from crown to chin, was about six feet high. One possibility is that the statue was an original of Constantine, sculpted after his initial arrival at Rome and placed in the basilica. Another, much more likely possibility is that it had originally been a statue of a god such as Jupiter or Apollo or of an earlier emperor such as Domitian, Trajan, Hadrian, or Commodus, previously on display elsewhere in the capital but moved to the basilica and recut with the face of Constantine. Yet another possibility is that it had previously been a statue of Maxentius, itself recut from an earlier statue and already intended for display in his new basilica. Depictions of Maxentius' head and face, on statues and on coins, typically followed the blocklike style of the Tetrarchic emperors, with a stubble beard and staring eyes. Recutting his face into the leaner clean-shaven face of Constantine would have been straightforward.[56]

identification of the statue mentioned by Eusebius with the colossal statue, see L'Orange (1984) 75, Curran (2000) 82, "widely regarded as being the statue which Eusebius of Caesarea described," and Lenski (2008) 206–7. Basilica Constantiniana: *Curiosum* and *Notitia*, ed. Nordh (1949) 78, 100. Merits of Flavius: Aurelius Victor, *De Caesaribus* 40.26, with Van Dam (2007) 86–88.

[55] See Presicce (2007), for the discovery and early displays of the fragments.

[56] Modification of the head: see Presicce (2007) 128, "Das Gesicht zeigt unbestreitbare Anzeichen für eine Überarbeitung"; with Van Dam (2007) 89n.12, for various suggestions about the origin of the colossal statue. For the availability of huge statues in Rome, note that the emperor Severus Alexander was thought to have honored earlier "deified emperors" by erecting "colossal statues, some nude and on foot, others on horseback," in the Forum of

In his *History* Eusebius noted that Constantine furthermore gave directions for "the people who had erected [his statue] to engrave this very inscription in these words in the language of the Romans," that is, in Latin. Although he had most likely acquired this information about the inscription in Latin from his anonymous source, in his own narrative Eusebius nevertheless cited the dedication in a Greek version. Almost a century later in his translation of Eusebius' *History*, however, Rufinus cited a Latin version of the dedication that was not an exact translation of Eusebius' Greek version. Instead, his version was most likely copied from the actual dedication that was still on display in Rome. Because Rufinus had lived in Rome as a student during the 360s, and because he had certainly visited Rome again in the late fourth century before starting his translation, he could have seen the dedication. Elsewhere in his translation he occasionally updated Eusebius' comments about Rome with more contemporary information. In this case too, rather than merely translating Eusebius' Greek version of the dedication back into Latin, Rufinus had most likely cited the original.[57]

In the Latin version of the dedication Constantine proclaimed his recent success. "In this exceptional symbol, which is a token of true excellence, I restored the city of Rome, which has been rescued from the yoke of a tyrant's domination, as well as the senate and the Roman people to [their] original liberty and nobility." Two characteristics of the dedication are noteworthy. One is the use of the conventional terminology of earlier emperors like Augustus who had claimed to have restored the Republic. In this dedication Constantine mentioned the senate and people of Rome, their liberty and nobility, and his defeat

---

Nerva: see SHA, *Severus Alexander* 28.6. For the similarities between the emperors' heads, see Evers (1992) 17, "Mit ihrer Haartracht nehmen die Maxentius-Porträts diejenigen Konstantins und seiner Nachfolger vorweg," and R. R. R. Smith (1997) 185, on Maxentius, "a less aged, more vigorous tetrarchism," and Constantine from the early 310s, "a taller, more thin-faced profile, a clean-shaven, youthful, handsome face."

[57] Directions: Eusebius, *HE* 9.9.10, with Pietri and Pietri (1999–2000) 2:1925–40, for an overview of Rufinus' life. For the suggestion that Rufinus cited the original Latin text of this dedication, see Moreau (1954) 2:444, Christensen (1989) 300, Grünewald (1990) 71, and Heim (2001) 208, "La formule de Rufin n'est pas une rétroversion."

of a tyrant. Even though he had grown up with Tetrarchic notions of imperial rule, once he arrived at Rome he quickly adopted more traditional Republican terminology. A few years later in 315 the senate and people would use the inscriptions and the iconography on the arch as a medium to remind Constantine of how they hoped he would behave like a conventional emperor at Rome. In the primary dedication, for instance, they would praise him for having saved them from a tyrant and his faction. But as Constantine's own dedication already indicated, he did not need much reminding. Immediately after his arrival at the capital he was already presenting himself as a Republican emperor.[58]

A second notable characteristic of the Latin version of the dedication is the absence of any explicit allusion to Christianity. The referent of "this exceptional symbol" remains unclear. Even though Eusebius had clearly linked the dedication with a statue planned by Constantine, Rufinus did not mention any statue that the emperor initiated. His surrounding narrative was again not a direct translation of Eusebius' account. Rufinus noted instead that the senate had decided to erect "images in honor of him [Constantine] as he celebrated a triumph." Because Constantine had concluded that his success was due "not to his own excellence but to a divine gift," he suggested that "a standard of the Lord's cross be depicted in his right hand and that [the words of the dedication] be inscribed underneath." In Rufinus' telling, the senate took the initiative in setting up statues, and Constantine suggested only the addition of a dedication and a depiction of a cross. The "exceptional symbol" mentioned in the dedication was "a token of true excellence," that is, the excellence that he would not attribute to himself. Even if the emperor ordered the depiction of a cross in the hand of a statue, "this exceptional symbol" was not necessarily a reference to a cross. Instead, in the original Latin text of this dedication, as quoted by Rufinus, Constantine seemed more interested in establishing his credentials as

[58] Text of dedication in Rufinus, *HE* 9.9.11: "In hoc singulari signo, quod est verae virtutis insigne, urbem Romam senatumque et populum Romanum iugo tyrannicae dominationis ereptam pristinae libertati nobilitatique restitui," with Eder (2005) 17, on Augustus: "an abiding component of his actions: his respect of the power of republican traditions."

a traditional Republican emperor, not as an overtly Christian emperor. This dedication was designed for a local audience that included senators, not specifically for Christians at Rome or throughout the empire.[59]

Eusebius had interpreted the dedication differently, however. At the end of 312 Maximinus, the emperor in the East, had notified his prefect about a new policy of religious toleration. "If anyone, by his own choice, decides that the worship of the gods must be observed, it is appropriate to welcome such people; but if others wish to observe their own worship, you should leave [the decision] to their authority." Because his see of Caesarea was a provincial capital, Eusebius had apparently seen a copy of this letter that the prefect distributed to the provincial governors. At about the same time he learned from his anonymous source that after the battle at the Milvian Bridge, Constantine had communicated with Maximinus. Even though Constantine was perhaps only announcing his victory to a fellow emperor, Eusebius nevertheless concluded that Maximinus had adopted his new policy of toleration in response to pressure from Constantine. Because Maximinus had previously promoted a harsh persecution of Christians, Eusebius furthermore concluded that an opponent of Maximinus was not just a supporter of Christianity but a Christian himself. With this image of a Christian Constantine in mind, Eusebius hence interpreted the Latin text of this dedication as another example of Constantine's public announcement of his own Christianity.[60]

Eusebius seems to have known nothing about Constantine's reign as an emperor in the West until he read this anonymous source. Most likely the entire source was written in Latin. It certainly seems to have quoted Constantine's dedication in Latin. Eusebius provided two Greek

---

[59] Rufinus, *HE* 9.9.10–11. Grégoire (1932) 140–41, suggests that the statue was holding a *vexillum*, a military standard consisting of an upright spear and a crossbar, offered by the senate as a sign of triumph: "it n'était pas encore chrétien ni christianisant" (p. 143); Kuhoff (1991) 171, argues that in the political situation after the battle at the Milvian Bridge the erection of a statue and a dedication with the Christian symbols described by Eusebius would be "unthinkable."

[60] Eusebius, *HE* 9.9.12, correspondence of Constantine and Licinius with Maximinus, 9a.8, Maximinus' letter.

translations of the dedication, one published soon afterward in his *History*, and the other published decades later in his *Life of Constantine*. In the early version the emperor was construed to claim that he had rescued the city "from the yoke of the tyrant," in the later version "from the tyrannical yoke." Because the two Greek versions were not verbatim the same, presumably Eusebius or one of his secretaries had reread the original text and retranslated it for citation in *Life*. These small verbal discrepancies indicate that Eusebius did not have a fixed Greek text of the dedication available. Instead, the text of the dedication in the anonymous source that he or his secretary first translated for *History*, and then translated again for *Life*, had been in Latin. In the process of offering a Greek translation of that Latin dedication, however, Eusebius simultaneously provided an interpretation based on a string of inferences about Constantine's Christianity.[61]

In particular, the Greek translation (in both versions) rendered "this exceptional symbol" as "this symbol of salvation." This ingenious translation transformed the bland and indeterminate reference to an "exceptional symbol" in the original Latin dedication into a more specifically religious "symbol of salvation." Eusebius furthermore interpreted the "symbol of salvation" as a cross and then concluded that the dedication was referring to an actual cross in the hand of a statue of the emperor. He claimed that Constantine had ordered the people of Rome to erect a

[61] Text of dedication in Eusebius, *HE* 9.9.11: τούτῳ τῷ σωτηριώδει σημείῳ τῷ ἀληθεῖ ἐλέγχῳ τῆς ἀνδρείας τὴν πόλιν ὑμῶν ἀπὸ ζυγοῦ τοῦ τυράννου διασωθεῖσαν ἠλευθέρωσα, ἔτι μὴν καὶ τὴν σύγκλητον καὶ τὸν δῆμον Ῥωμαίων τῇ ἀρχαίᾳ ἐπιφανείᾳ καὶ λαμπρότητι ἐλευθερώσας ἀποκατέστησα. Text of dedication in Eusebius, *Vita Constantini* 1.40.2, same as the version in *HE* 9.9.11, with the exception of one phrase: . . . τὴν πόλιν ὑμῶν ζυγοῦ τυραννικοῦ διασωθεῖσαν . . . Hall (1993) 254, suggests that the later version in *Life* was more generic to allude to the victory over Licinius too: "Maxentius is not the only tyrant."

Two additional issues are relevant. One is Eusebius' knowledge of Latin, which was minimal at best. Most likely his secretaries provided the Greek translations of Latin documents in *History* and *Life*: see Van Dam (2007) 194–95. Another is his technique for reading and excerpting texts. Eusebius probably presided over a roomful of deacons, who acted as his secretaries. After they read and copied the texts, Eusebius offered his own comments, which were also recorded: for this model, see Mras (1954) LVII–LVIII, elaborated by Grafton and Williams (2006) 212–15.

statue of himself holding "a commemoration of the Savior's suffering." "Afterward they set him [the statue] up holding the symbol of salvation in his right hand." On the basis of a mistranslation of the dedication, a misunderstanding of its connection to a statue, and an inference about Constantine's Christianity, Eusebius equated the "symbol of salvation" mentioned in his translation of the dedication with a "symbol of salvation" in the statue's hand. Although Constantine had wanted to present himself in this dedication at Rome as a traditional Republican emperor, Eusebius concluded that he had represented himself as an overtly Christian emperor, and he adjusted his translation and narrative accordingly.[62]

Eusebius' misreading and Rufinus' subsequent lack of clarity raise the question whether Constantine had intended the dedication to accompany a statue at all. Perhaps he built a different sort of monument, or possibly erected only the dedication. Even if he did erect a statue of himself to accompany the dedication, it would more likely have been in the guise of a traditional emperor. The cross in its hand was most likely a figment of Eusebius' creative translation.[63]

ON THE OTHER HAND
Modern scholars have often reinforced (although perhaps unwittingly) Eusebius' distinctive interpretation of the dedication in their own interpretations of another colossal right hand. This other right hand was found during work on a wall below the Capitoline Hill and is almost identical in size and appearance to the right hand found with the other fragments of the colossal statue in the Basilica Nova. It too is on display in the same courtyard of the Palazzo dei Conservatori but set against

---

[62] Eusebius, *HE* 9.9.10, commemoration, τὸ σωτήριον σημεῖον, with Winkelmann (2004) 63–67, rejecting the addition of σταυροῦ or τοῦ σταυροῦ, "the symbol of salvation *of the cross*," in some Greek manuscripts as later glosses. Note that in the index of Greek words for their dual edition of Eusebius' *HE* and Rufinus' *HE*, Schwartz and Mommsen (1903–1909) 3:203, indicate that the Latin equivalent of Eusebius' σωτηριώδης was *salutaris*. Conversely, as the Greek equivalent of Rufinus' *singularis*, Grégoire (1932) 142, suggests ἐξαίρετος.

[63] For a suggestion that Constantine had responded to the acclamations with an order to erect only the dedication, see Christensen (1989) 290.

the opposite wall. One possibility is that this other hand had been the original right hand of the colossal statue and that it had been replaced when the statue had been recast as Constantine. According to one modern interpretation, because this original hand had been designed to hold "an object similar to a rod" that only pointed up, "perhaps like a traditional scepter," it had been discarded and replaced by another hand that could hold an object with a shaft that extended from the ground to the hand and then above the hand, "perhaps like a flagstaff." In this case, recycling the statue as Constantine had also required the replacement of the right hand to hold a cross.[64]

This theory of a replacement hand has furthermore encouraged speculation about the timing. The hand may have been replaced immediately when the statue was transformed into Constantine soon after his victory over Maxentius. Another interpretation suggests that the colossal statue originally depicted Constantine in the guise of a pagan god, Jupiter for instance, holding a scepter. Only after his victory in 324 over Licinius, his last imperial rival, did Constantine have the scepter replaced by a cross, a more obviously Christian symbol, in the grip of a new right hand. In both cases Eusebius' misreading of the dedication has provided modern scholars with a rationale for the replacement of the hand. Holding a cross required a new right hand.[65]

[64] The hand found with the head and other fragments in the Basilica Nova is the famous hand often depicted in books about Constantine. This hand was broken off at the wrist. The other right hand was broken off across the palm at the bottom of the ball of the thumb. For descriptions and photographs of the two hands, see L'Orange (1984) 71–74 with Tafeln 50–51, and Stuart Jones (1926) 11–12 with Plate 5. Quotations about scepter and flagstaff translated from L'Orange (1984) 73, who argues that the hand from the Basilica Nova was a replacement for the other, original hand.

[65] At some time a metal diadem might have been added to the head: see L'Orange (1984) 76–77. Portraits of Constantine wearing a diadem first appeared on his coins during his war with Licinius in 324: see Bruun (1966) 44–45, 147, 660, and Bastien (1992–1994) 1:143–66. For the suggestion that the original hand was likewise replaced after 324, see Kolb (2001) 206–8.

After examining various early drawings of the fragments, Presicce (2007) 119, concludes that the extended index finger on the right hand found in the Basilica Nova was a restoration apparently of the seventeenth century and claims that it did not correspond to the original pose. As a result, the beautiful reconstruction of the colossal statue in Demandt

Replacing the entire hand is nevertheless an implausible explanation, if only for practical considerations. If a sculptor could recut the head as Constantine, he could certainly also recut the hand to fit a new implement. In addition, a new staff, whether a cross or not, would presumably have been constructed from wood or metal, and it would have been much easier to make a new staff fit an existing hand than to carve an entirely new huge hand from a marble block.[66]

Another, more likely possibility is that originally there had been two similar colossal seated statues, one of which was recast as Constantine (or first as Maxentius and then as Constantine), while the other was eventually discarded. A model for such a pair of seated statues would be the life-size statues of Hadrian and Marcus Aurelius at each end of the Rostra, as depicted in a panel on the arch of Constantine. The statue of Hadrian in particular was holding a floor-length scepter in his left hand and a globe in his right hand. This statue of Hadrian was apparently a close mirror image of the colossal statue of Constantine. The other right hand should hence not be used to support the modern conjecture that the original colossal statue had been remodeled to hold a cross. Rather than having been the original hand of a single statue, it seems more likely that this other right hand had belonged to a second colossal statue. Only the hand has survived of this second statue.[67]

and Engemann (2007) 131, depicts all the fingers of Constantine's right hand curled around a floor-length staff (not a cross!). On the other hand, however, although the index finger and three other fingers had to be reattached, this original index finger was extended up. By analogy, perhaps the extended index finger on the hand from the Basilica Nova was indeed restored correctly.

[66] Fittschen and Zanker (1985) 148, dismiss L'Orange's interpretation of a replacement hand: "Leider ist diese geistreiche Kombination rein hypothetisch." Hannestad (2007) 101, also questions the need to replace the hand: "dann wäre es aber ein kleinerer Eingriff gewesen, einfach das Zepter durch ein Kreuz auf derselben Hand zu ersetzen."

[67] For the possibility of a second statue, see Stuart Jones (1926) 12, suggesting that the other right hand "appears to have belonged to a colossal statue similar to that of Constantine." An examination of the types of marble cannot resolve the connection between the head and the right hands; note Stuart Jones (1926) 13n.2, "it appears that different qualities of marble were used for different parts of the statue." Both hands were carved from marble from Luna in northern Italy, while the head was carved from Pentelic marble from Attica.

In the account of Constantine's dedication and monuments at Rome published in the first edition of his *History*, Eusebius had interpreted and translated the information in the anonymous Latin source in a distinctive way that reinforced his inferences about Constantine. In his later writings Eusebius referred to the monuments three more times, and he also supplied more details. The inclusion of the additional details does not imply that over the years Eusebius had acquired more information to corroborate his first account. Instead, as he became more certain about Constantine's Christianity, he also seems to have become more certain about the Christian character of the monuments at Rome. Eusebius reinforced his earlier interpretation with repetition and supposition, not more research.

Shortly after publishing the first edition of *History* Eusebius delivered an oration at Tyre, perhaps in 315, to celebrate the dedication of a rebuilt church. In this oration he praised the contemporary emperors who supported Christianity. These unnamed emperors were Constantine and Licinius, who both "recognize Christ, the Son of God, as the all-powerful Emperor of everything." Eusebius then praised their public acknowledgment of the Christian God. "On tablets they call him Savior, and in an imperishable record, in imperial letters in the middle of the city that rules over the cities throughout the world, they inscribe his successes and his victories over the impious." Even though Eusebius mentioned the initiative of both emperors, he was certainly alluding to Constantine's dedication and monuments at Rome. But now, within a year or two of publishing his initial description, he was much more explicit about their Christian character. In the version in the first edition of *History* Eusebius had noted that Constantine himself had been hailed as "savior" on entering Rome; in the version in this oration he claimed that Constantine (and, nominally, Licinius) had set up dedications in honor of Jesus Christ the Savior. Eusebius subsequently included this oration as part of a new final tenth book for the edition of *History* published before October 316.[68]

---

[68] Oration at Tyre: Eusebius, *HE* 10.4.16, with Barnes (1981) 162, for the date of the oration, and Chapter 5, for the editions of *History*.

Twenty years later Eusebius returned to this story. In a panegyric celebrating the thirtieth anniversary of Constantine's reign in July 336, he again mentioned the emperor's construction of a monument of commemoration and a series of dedications at Rome. This time there was no hint of participation by Licinius. "Through prudent reasoning he [Constantine] returned a prayer of gratitude to the cause of this victory. With a loud voice and on [inscribed] tablets he proclaimed to all men the symbol that brought victory. In the middle of the ruling city he erected this huge memorial against all enemies, this distinctly imperishable symbol of salvation for the Roman empire and this protection for the entire kingdom." In this account Eusebius did not mention a statue and provided no details about the large memorial, although its description as a "symbol of salvation" might imply that he thought it was a cross. He delivered this oration in the emperor's presence in the imperial palace at Constantinople. Perhaps by then he had already heard Constantine's memories about his vision, his dream, and the construction of his military standard. If so, then the emperor's stories about the importance of the cross in his military campaigns would certainly have strengthened Eusebius' original interpretation of the dedication at Rome.[69]

But it is also possible to think about the influence in the opposite direction. According to Eusebius, the emperor truly enjoyed the oration. "While he listened, the friend of God resembled a happy man." Afterward the emperor hosted a banquet and expressed his appreciation. "After listening, he said as much while he dined and talked with the bishops who were in attendance." This banquet might have been an appropriate occasion for Constantine finally to share his memories of his earlier campaigns. Perhaps it was hearing Eusebius' description of his behavior at Rome that revived his memories of the events so long before. If so, then Eusebius' recycled account of the events of 312 may have helped prompt and shape Constantine's own memories. In this case the emperor's memories about his vision, his dream, and the military standard were not a source for Eusebius' account but

---

[69] Eusebius, *De laudibus Constantini* 9.8, σωτήριον τουτὶ σημεῖον.

rather a consequence of hearing Eusebius' account of his monuments at Rome. Constantine may have finally decided to share his memories only after hearing Eusebius' account in the panegyric of the monuments at Rome.[70]

After Constantine's death in 337, Eusebius returned once more to the emperor's monuments at Rome. This final version in *Life* combined his first version in *History* (then more than twenty years old) with his most recent version in the anniversary panegyric. Eusebius first quoted from *History* his extended narrative of the battle and Constantine's victorious entry into Rome. He then inserted a description of the emperor's construction of a memorial that closely, but not exactly, repeated his account in the panegyric. "He immediately returned a prayer of gratitude to the cause of victory. In a great text and on [inscribed] tablets he proclaimed to all men the symbol of salvation. In the middle of the ruling city he erected this huge memorial against the enemies, and in distinctly imperishable letters he engraved this sign of salvation for the Roman empire and this protection for the entire kingdom." Eusebius followed that description with an account of the emperor's statue that closely, but not exactly, repeated his account in *History*. "At a site that was on the public properties at Rome they erected a tall shaft in the form of a cross in the hand of a statue of himself made in the appearance of a man. Immediately he ordered them to engrave this very inscription in these words in the language of the Romans." Eusebius concluded by quoting again a Greek version of the dedication.[71]

In *Life* this account of monuments and a dedication at Rome remained as the conclusion to Eusebius' narrative of Constantine's campaign against Maxentius in 312. Much of that narrative had been recycled from *History*. But the account of monuments could serve as a proper pendant, because in *Life* Eusebius had introduced his narrative

---

[70] Listened, dined: Eusebius, *Vita Constantini* 4.46.
[71] Eusebius, *Vita Constantini* 1.39.3–40.1, derived from *De laudibus Constantini* 9.8; 1.40.2, derived from *HE* 9.9.10–11. Note that the translation of *Vita Constantini* 1.40.2 in Cameron and Hall (1999) 85, overlooks the phrase about the site in Rome.

from *History* with new episodes based on Constantine's own stories about his vision, his dream, and the construction of his military standard. In *Life* the narrative of Constantine's expedition against Maxentius finally had a proper symmetry, neatly compressed between matching bookends: a prelude of stories about Constantine's vision of the cross and dream about Jesus Christ, based on the emperor's own belated memories, and a postlude of stories about a monument, a statue, and a dedication that honored the cross and the Savior, based on Eusebius' own early misunderstandings.

Eusebius had gradually accumulated a lifetime of inferences and elaborations about Constantine's monuments at Rome. Long ago he had acquired information about Constantine's activities at Rome in 312 from an anonymous Latin source. Initially in *History* he had interpreted the dedication and the monuments in terms of his own conjectures (and perhaps hopes) about Constantine as a Christian. Over the decades he had expanded his account, not on the basis of additional information but rather as a result of his increasing confidence in his initial deductions. "Eusebius' description develops from an assemblage of various imaginary artistic and literary components into a new, non-historical synthesis."[72]

In the account in *Life* his misinformation finally crowded out whatever trustworthy information still remained. By combining the elaborated account in the panegyric with his initial deductions in *History*, Eusebius identified the "huge memorial" with a statue of the emperor. He repeated his peculiar reading of the dedication and identified its purpose as announcing the role of "the sign of salvation," that is, the cross, in protecting the empire. In his initial account in *History* Eusebius had already misconstrued his anonymous source. His subsequent accounts of the monuments at Rome, including the final version in *Life*, are even more unreliable as starting points for the discussions of modern historians and art historians.

Modern scholars should instead rank Rufinus' account of the monuments at Rome more highly. In contrast to Eusebius, Rufinus had

---

[72] Quotation about Eusebius' description translated from Kuhoff (1991) 171.

visited Rome and seen the monuments and the dedication. Eusebius' initial account was derivative, based on a faulty reading of a Latin source; Rufinus' account was based on personal inspection. In particular, modern scholars should cite and analyze Constantine's dedication in Rufinus' Latin version rather than in Eusebius' Greek translations. Rufinus' Latin version quite probably corresponded to the actual dedication. In an odd reversal of expectations, with regard to the dedication Eusebius was the translator, not Rufinus.

CHURCHES AND RITUAL TOPOGRAPHY

During his long reign the emperor Augustus had accelerated the transformation of Republican Rome into imperial Rome. In the early empire the capital was already enormous, with a population of about one million residents. Emperors guaranteed the import of huge amounts of grain, olive oil, and wine, both for free distribution and for sale at reduced prices. They financed and administered the utilitarian infrastructure with the construction and maintenance of long aqueducts and vast underground drains. They transformed the monumental skyline with the construction of large plazas and buildings, including temples, forums, baths, and entertainment venues such as the Colosseum. They also contributed impressive memorials in honor of their own achievements, including statues, decorated columns, and commemorative arches. Emperors were competing against the reputations of their predecessors. The immense size and extravagance of the Baths of Caracalla, constructed in the early third century, misled medieval cartographers into thinking that the complex had been the imperial palace. A century later the Baths of Diocletian could accommodate almost twice as many bathers. By enhancing the capital and its amenities, emperors demonstrated their commitment to ancestral traditions, in particular the heritage of the Republic, even as they flaunted their own authority and wealth before large appreciative audiences. Rome became a giant stage set for the display and performance of Republican emperorship.[73]

[73] Cartographers: DeLaine (1997) 41. Baths of Diocletian: Olympiodorus, *Frag.* 41.1, ed. Block-ley (1981–1983) 2:204. For Rome and Republican emperorship, see Van Dam (2010) 18–22.

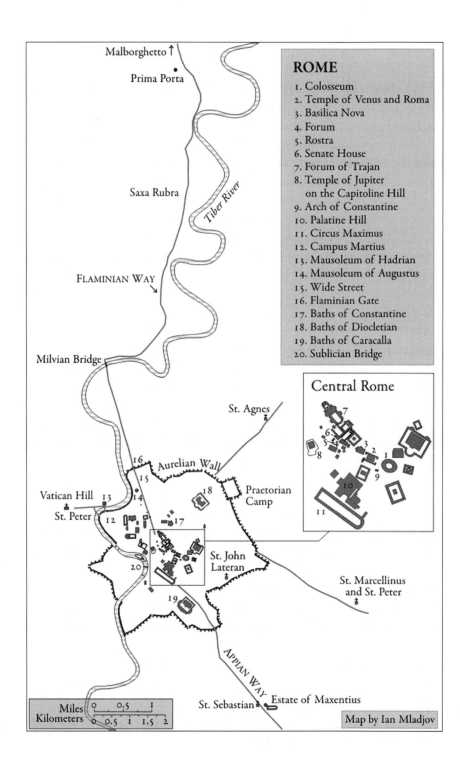

Malborghetto ↑

• Prima Porta

Saxa Rubra

Tiber River

FLAMINIAN WAY →

Milvian Bridge

St. Agnes

16
Aurelian Wall
15
Vatican Hill   13
14
St. Peter   12
17
18
Praetorian Camp

St. John Lateran

20

19

St. Marcellinus and St. Peter

APPIAN WAY

St. Sebastian •   Estate of Maxentius

Miles   0   0,5   1
Kilometers   0   0,5   1   1,5   2

Map by Ian Mladjov

ROME

1. Colosseum
2. Temple of Venus and Roma
3. Basilica Nova
4. Forum
5. Rostra
6. Senate House
7. Forum of Trajan
8. Temple of Jupiter on the Capitoline Hill
9. Arch of Constantine
10. Palatine Hill
11. Circus Maximus
12. Campus Martius
13. Mausoleum of Hadrian
14. Mausoleum of Augustus
15. Wide Street
16. Flaminian Gate
17. Baths of Constantine
18. Baths of Diocletian
19. Baths of Caracalla
20. Sublician Bridge

Central Rome

7
6
5   3   2   1
8
9
10
11

The great size and magnificence of Rome were also meant to remind provincials of their subordination to imperial rule. Most of the supplies for Rome were imported from overseas provinces through the process of tribute exaction as taxes and rents. The emperors' agents supervised the collection, transportation, storage, and distribution of grain from Egypt, Sicily, and North Africa, of olive oil from Spain and North Africa, and of wine from Gaul and Spain. They brought in colored marbles from quarries all over the empire, at great expense and effort. They arranged for the capture and transport of exotic animals from frontier regions and borderlands, as well as the magnificent display of horses from the provinces in the races in the circuses and the conspicuous slaughter of wild animals during staged hunts in amphitheaters. In 303 the emperors Diocletian and Maximian brought thirteen elephants with them to Rome, as well as six chariot drivers and 250 horses. Early imperial Rome was a consumer capital whose incessant demands ensured that the entire Mediterranean world was toiling to its rhythm.[74]

After his arrival at Rome, Constantine contributed more buildings and more monuments. He renovated the Circus Maximus, the premier arena for chariot racing and horse racing, with "lofty porticoes and red columns flecked with gold." He completed another bath complex north of the imperial forums and repaired an aqueduct. In return, the senate and people quickly accepted Constantine as the new patron of Rome, in part by overtly shifting their allegiance from his predecessor. Maxentius too had cultivated a special relationship with the capital. He had most likely rededicated the colossal bronze statue of the sun god Sol that stood next to the Colosseum in honor of his son. On a ridge overlooking Sacred Street, leading into the Forum, he had also rebuilt the Temple of Venus and Roma and constructed the Basilica Nova. After Constantine's victory at the Milvian Bridge, however, some of Maxentius' monuments were quickly dismantled or reassigned.[75]

<hr />

[74] Gifts: Chronographer of 354, *Chronica urbis Romae*, s.v. Diocletianus et Maximianus, ed. Mommsen (1892) 148. For Rome as a symbol of imperialism, see Van Dam (2010) 1–3, 22–24.

[75] Porticoes: *Panegyrici latini* 4(10).35.5. Circus Maximus, bath complex: Aurelius Victor, *De Caesaribus* 40.27–28, with Humphrey (1986) 129, suggesting that Constantine enlarged the seating area of the Circus. Aqueduct: *ILS* 1:158, no. 702 = Grünewald (1990) 219, no. 256. For Maxentius' monuments, see Chapter 9.

Because Constantine remodeled the Basilica Nova, the senate sanctioned the rededication of both it and the Temple of Venus and Roma "to the merits of Flavius," that is, to Flavius Constantine. Thereafter the regionary catalogs referred to the basilica as the "Constantinian Basilica." In addition, Maxentius' dedication of the colossal statue was removed, and the plaque was reused backward as just another marble block in the construction of the attic of the arch of Constantine. On that arch one of the new panels depicted Constantine observing the battle of the Milvian Bridge, with the goddess Roma at his side. The attendance of Roma may have been an allusion to the rededication of the Temple of Venus and Roma. Two other new panels on the arch depicted Constantine behaving like an ideal emperor by delivering a public speech on the Rostra in the Forum and distributing gifts to senators. The relationship between Constantine and the residents of Rome seemed thoroughly conventional. "Constantine by the Senate's decision took over the monumental center of Rome." The new emperor funded new building projects and remodeled existing structures; in return, the senate and people sanctioned his emplacement as a benefactor in the monumental landscape of downtown Rome. The city of Rome now supported Constantine.[76]

The urban topography of Rome was an incentive for emperors to perform traditional ceremonies. When Diocletian and Maximian had visited Rome in 303, they had met in the Temple of Jupiter on the Capitoline Hill. This great temple was a focus of Roman religious cults and a manifestation of the eternity of Rome. To commemorate the twentieth anniversary of their rule the emperors also erected a monument at the back of the Rostra in the old Forum. Their monument consisted of five columns, four displaying statues of the guardian spirits of the four current emperors, the middle one topped with a statue of Jupiter. On the one surviving pedestal of this Monument of Five

---

[76] Merits of Flavius: Aurelius Victor, *De Caesaribus* 40.26. Basilica Constantiniana: *Curiosum* and *Notitia*, ed. Nordh (1949) 78, 100; also known as the Basilica of Constantine in the mid-fifth century: see Polemius Silvius, *Laterculus* 4, s.v. "Basilicae XI," ed. Mommsen (1892) 545. Quotation about monumental center from Krautheimer (1983) 26.

Columns reliefs depicted an emperor and senators participating in a sacrifice. As professional soldiers who spent most of their reigns on or near the frontiers Diocletian and his fellow Tetrarchic emperors had little in common with Rome. But when they visited the capital, they presented themselves as proper Roman emperors, mindful of the traditions of the capital. Because they had already adopted Jupiter as a patron deity of the Tetrarchy, in Rome they could now show their respect for the Temple of Jupiter and participate in a communal festival of sacrifice.[77]

Constantine had most likely accompanied Diocletian and his court to Rome, and as a junior military officer he may have joined in these ceremonies with the emperors. When he later returned as an emperor himself, however, eventually he decided not to participate in an "ancestral festival" on the Capitoline Hill, presumably at the Temple of Jupiter. At first, perhaps during his initial visit in 312, he had joined his soldiers in celebrating these "customs," but during a subsequent visit, most likely his final visit in 326, he declined to attend the "holy rituals." His snub was deeply upsetting, and the senate and the people were said to have reacted with "hatred." Constantine's withdrawal from an ancestral festival suggests that he was already thinking about the capital in terms of a different ritual topography and a different ceremonial landscape. The traditional symbolic terrain of Rome was no longer adequate or necessary for representing his imperial rule.[78]

Rome eventually was known for its churches, and several were associated specifically with Constantine and his family. One was the Lateran Basilica, later known as the Church of St. John Lateran. Constantine may well have decided to initiate construction in early November 312, soon after his initial entry into Rome. This was a commodious church,

[77] Meeting: *Panegyrici latini* 6(7).15.6. Rome's eternity: Ammianus Marcellinus, *Res gestae* 22.16.12, with Grig (2009), on the abiding symbolic potency of the Capitoline Hill. For the Monument of Five Columns, see Chapter 6.

[78] For the likelihood of Constantine's visiting Rome in 303, see Barnes (1981) 25. Ancestral festival, hatred: Zosimus, *Historia nova* 2.29.5, with Chapters 3 and 6. Modern discussion of the date and significance of this withdrawal is extensive; for an overview, see Paschoud (1979–2000) 1:238–40.

almost as large as Maxentius' Basilica Nova, and it soon became the
official cathedral of the bishop of Rome. As an imperial foundation
this church too came to be known as a "Constantinian Basilica." A
second Constantinian foundation was the Church of St. Peter on the
Vatican Hill, which was even larger than the Church of St. John Lateran. Although construction did not begin until later in Constantine's
reign or perhaps soon afterward, the monumental complex eventually
included a porch and a large courtyard in front of the church. Inside the
church on the arch that separated the nave from the transept an inscription commemorated the emperor's victories and recorded his gratitude
for God's guidance: "under your leadership the world has raised itself
triumphant to the stars. As a result, Constantine the victor has built
this hall for you." Accompanying this dedication was a mosaic depicting the emperor as he presented a model of the church to Jesus Christ
and St. Peter. Two other churches became burial sites for members of
Constantine's family. His mother was buried in a mausoleum attached
to the Church of St. Marcellinus and St. Peter, and his two daughters
were buried in a mausoleum next to the Church of St. Agnes.[79]

Constantine and his family furthermore enriched the churches
with extensive endowments and lavish gifts. Constantine endowed the
Church of St. John Lateran and its adjacent baptistery with the revenues
from numerous estates in Italy, Sicily, and North Africa, the regions he
had recently acquired after his victory over Maxentius. He also presented the church and the baptistery with two near-life-size statues of
Jesus made of silver, four silver statues of angels, silver statues of the
apostles, numerous gold and silver chandeliers, liturgical goldware and

---

[79] For discussion of these churches, see Curran (2000) 93–115, Bowersock (2005), attributing
the construction of the Church of St. Peter to the emperor Constans, and Kinney (2005), on
the reuse of classical materials. Basilica Constantiniana: *Liber pontificalis* 34.9. Dedication in
Church of St. Peter: de Rossi (1857–1888) 2.1:20, no. 6 = Diehl (1925–1931) 1:340, no. 1752 =
Grünewald (1990) 221, no. 263. Mosaic: Frothingham (1883), and Krautheimer (1937–1980)
5:177. Two daughters: Ammianus Marcellinus, *Res gestae* 21.1.5. Other significant churches
that might be attributed to Constantine's initiative include the Church of St. Sebastian on
the Appian Way, the Church of St. Paul outside the Wall on the Ostiensian Way, and the
Church of St. Lawrence outside the Wall on the Tiburtinian Way: see Odahl (2004) 130–42,
MacMullen (2009) 135–40, and Chapter 9.

silverware, and silver candlesticks. According to later traditions, the gifts totaled more than 1,100 pounds of gold and more than 11,000 pounds of silver. To the Church of St. Peter, Constantine presented the revenues from estates in Syria and Egypt, among the regions he acquired after his final victory over Licinius in 324, as well as gold and silver chandeliers and candlesticks and liturgical goldware and silverware, totaling almost 300 pounds of gold and more than 1,600 pounds of silver. Later traditions would also claim that Constantine and his mother, Helena, had donated a large cross of gold to the Church of St. Peter. The gold and silver in the gifts to these two churches alone represented the equivalent of almost 2,400 pounds of gold, or about 172,000 large gold coins. Gifts to other churches in Rome, as well as to churches elsewhere in Italy, increased that total by about 40 percent.[80]

The gifts, even if amortized over several years, represented a considerable outlay, while the transfer of the revenues of the estates to the churches at Rome and in Italy reduced the emperor's annual income by the equivalent of about 470 pounds of gold. Emperors consistently supplemented the annual salaries of their soldiers with regular donatives of gold and silver coins to celebrate their accessions and anniversaries. It is not surprising that during the years following his victory at Rome, Constantine's donatives to his soldiers seem to have been a bit light. He was instead beginning to spend his resources on churches.[81]

All of these churches at Rome were in the outskirts, either just inside the Aurelian Wall or in outlying suburbs. Various factors had influenced the selection of the sites. After his victory at the Milvian Bridge, Constantine inherited imperial houses and estates throughout the capital, including property located in the residential Lateran neighborhood

---

[80] *Liber Pontificalis* 34.9–12, gifts and estates for Church of St. John Lateran, 13–15, gifts and estates for baptistery, 16–20, cross, gifts, and estates for Church of St. Peter, 21–33, gifts to other churches, with Davis (2000) xxix, suggesting that this information was derived from a "source document . . . compiled near the end of Constantius II's reign," and Bauer and Heinzelmann (1999), for the Church of the Apostle Peter, Paul, and John the Baptist at Ostia. The ratio of gold to silver was 1:14.4, and 72 solidi were minted from a pound of gold: see Hendy (1985) 465, 480–82.

[81] For the diminished donatives, see Abdy (2006), and Tomlin (2006).

on the Caelian Hill next to the wall. Fausta, his wife, already owned a house in this district. In this neighborhood the Church of St. John Lateran was built squarely on top of the barracks of the *equites singulares*, an elite cavalry unit that had supported the emperor Maxentius. In this case the foundation of the new church on the rubble of this military camp clearly demonstrated the demolition of Maxentius' military support. Two suburban churches likewise underscored the end of Maxentius' reign. The Church of St. Marcellinus and St. Peter, located about two miles east of the city's wall on the Labicanan Way, displaced a cemetery filled with graves of members of the *equites singulares*. The Church of St. Agnes, located about one mile northeast of the wall on the Nomentanan Way, displaced a cemetery used for members of the praetorian guard, another military unit that had supported Maxentius. The churches also honored saints' shrines. The Church of St. Agnes commemorated the tomb of an early martyr, "buried in sight of the towers." The Church of St. Peter commemorated the apostle's tomb on the Vatican Hill, west of the city. The availability of imperial property, the acknowledgment of earlier traditions about the location of saints' tombs, and the desire for revenge on Maxentius' military supporters had combined to influence the shaping of ecclesiastical topography.[82]

---

[82] Fausta's "house on the Lateran": Optatus, *Contra Donatistas* 1.23.2, with the overview of imperial Lateran properties in Fried (2007) 74–88; but Liverani (1995), suggests that this Fausta was a daughter of Anicius Faustus, a former consul and prefect of Rome: see *PLRE* 1:329, "Anicius Faustus 6." Destruction of praetorian camps: Zosimus, *Historia nova* 2.17.2, with Speidel (1986), on the support of the *equites singulares* for Maxentius. Buried: Prudentius, *Peristephanon* 14.3. Krautheimer (1983) 7–40, argues that Constantine deliberately built the Church of St. John Lateran in the outskirts of Rome to avoid offending the sensibilities of senators: "a policy of sparing pagan sentiment" (p. 29); Curran (2000) 70–90, sidesteps the issue of paganism by stressing the "single-mindedness of Constantine" (p. 90) in promoting himself in the traditional center of Rome; Bowes (2008) 589, emphasizes that the location of churches was contingent on "the vagaries of private donations."

Excavations in the Lateran neighborhood have uncovered a building with six frescoes and their accompanying painted inscriptions: see the extensive discussion and photographs in Scrinari (1991) 136–49, frescoes, 162–73, inscriptions. This building might be identified as Fausta's house. Although now faded and damaged, the frescoes apparently depicted members of Constantine's family, including Constantine himself; Fausta; his father, Constantius; and his mother, Helena (perhaps replacing an image of Theodora, Constantius' wife). The

In a Christian Rome this hinterland of new churches would become more important than the old Republican and early imperial downtown. As a result, the increasing importance of the churches turned the symbolic topography of Rome inside out. Senators publicized their priorities through their preferences for ancestral ceremonies and monuments or for new churches. In the mid-fourth century an arrogant pagan senator funded expensive traditional games but belittled the beggars who had gathered on the Vatican Hill. By the end of the century a humble Christian senator hosted a large banquet for poor people in the Church of St. Peter. Emperors faced the same options. After Constantine few emperors visited Rome during the fourth century. When they did, however, they had to choose how to represent themselves, as traditional Republican emperors who might participate in processions with senators through the old downtown or as Christian emperors who patronized bishops, their congregations, and their suburban churches.[83]

In 357 the emperor Constantius arrived with his troops and paraded directly to the Forum, where he addressed senators in the senate house and the people from the Rostra. During the remaining month of his visit he tried to accommodate different expectations. As a traditional emperor he toured "the streets of the eternal city" with senators as his guides, and he was impressed at the vastness of the Forum of Trajan. He viewed the Temple of Jupiter on the Capitoline Hill, and he read the names of the gods inscribed on the facades of ancient temples. He appointed senators to pagan priesthoods, and he retained

fragmentary inscriptions commemorated emperors and imperial women. Because the lines of the inscriptions were often superimposed, G. Alföldy, in *CIL* 6.8.2:4551–52, no. 40769, suggests that the inscriptions and frescoes, or perhaps only some of them, were first painted in 315 and subsequently revised until perhaps 350. An inscription that mentioned the fourth consulship of Licinius in 315 presumably coincided with Constantine's return to Rome to celebrate the tenth anniversary of his emperorship. One line in this inscription is especially suggestive: "[in] signo [h]oc est patris victoria," "in this symbol is the victory of the father." The ambiguity of this line invites speculation. Was "the father" Constantine or God the Father? Was "this symbol" a cross, the military standard in the shape of a cross, or something else?

[83] Games and contempt of C. Ceionius Rufius Volusianus: Ammianus Marcellinus, *Res gestae* 27.3.6. Banquet of Pammachius: Paulinus of Nola, *Ep.* 13.11–13, with Grig (2006).

the privileges of the Vestal Virgins. At the same time, as a Christian emperor he attempted to settle a dispute over the city's episcopacy between two rivals, one now in exile, the other quite unpopular. This dispute involved the use of churches, because the supporters of one bishop would "not enter a house of prayer when the other was inside." Constantius decided that both bishops would jointly administer this particular church.[84]

But when he announced this compromise in the Circus Maximus, the crowd mocked his decision. The equivocation was bad enough. In addition, the Circus was considered a "temple" for ancestral cere-monies. Various monuments and buildings in Rome were apparently still reserved for specific expectations about emperors, and the cel-ebration of games was the wrong venue for a serious proclamation about ecclesiastical affairs. Perhaps to repair the damage to his image, the emperor subsequently presented a huge obelisk from Egypt to be erected in the Circus Maximus. His model as benefactor for such a gift was Augustus. In the Circus, Constantius was still expected to appear like a traditional Republican emperor, not a Christian emperor.[85]

According to one observer of Constantius' visit, even though the emperor had preferred "other religious ceremonies," he had neverthe-less supported the established priesthoods and rituals "for the sake of the empire." Subsequent emperors who visited Rome were less will-ing to balance these old traditions and their own religion, and they increasingly tended to prioritize their images as Christian rulers. In 403 the emperor Honorius visited Rome to celebrate a triumph and to assume a consulship for the next year. He had previously established his

---

[84] Parade, tour: Ammianus Marcellinus, *Res gestae* 16.10. Streets, temples, priesthoods, virgins: Symmachus, *Relationes* 3.7. Dispute between Liberius and Felix: Theodoret, *HE* 2.17.4, house of prayer. This feud continued into the next generation, when the supporters of the rivals Damasus and Ursinus fought over the Church of St. John Lateran and the Church of St. Agnes: see *Collectio Avellana* 1.6, 12, with Curran (2000) 129–42, on the dispute, and Sághy (2000), for Damasus' poems that redefined the churches and the martyrs.

[85] Ammianus Marcellinus, *Res gestae* 17.4.1, erection of Constantius' obelisk, 12, comparison with Augustus, 28.4.29, temple. Theodoret, *HE* 2.17.5, circus, 6, mockery. Dedication of obelisk: *ILS* 1:165, no. 736.

court in northern Italy, initially at Milan, then at Ravenna, and a few years earlier he had ignored an invitation from the senate to celebrate a consulship at Rome. When he did finally arrive, meeting the senate and viewing the old monuments in central Rome were not his top concerns. Instead, he passed by the grand mausoleum of Hadrian in favor of visiting the Church of St. Peter, where "he removed his diadem and beat his breast [at the tomb] where the body of the fisherman is buried." "In order to pray for salvation from the Lord that pious and Christian emperor hurried not to the grandiose temple of an emperor but to the tomb of the fisherman." In 450 on the day after his arrival at Rome the emperor Valentinian III likewise went directly to the Church of St. Peter to celebrate a festival in honor of the apostle. Honorius and Valentinian were more interested in presenting themselves as Christian emperors paying their respects to St. Peter at a suburban church, than as traditional emperors presiding over ancestral ceremonies in downtown Rome.[86]

Even after emperors no longer resided in the West, the new priorities remained influential for visiting rulers. Gelasius, the bishop of Rome, once reminded king Theoderic of the Ostrogoths about the appropriate relationship between rulership and Christianity. Although the king certainly wanted to preserve "the laws of the Roman emperors," for "the enhancement of his good fortune" he also had to show "reverence for the blessed apostle Peter." In 500 Theoderic demonstrated that he did indeed understand how to behave like a proper Christian ruler at Rome. Upon his arrival he first visited the Church of St. Peter, where

---

[86] Ceremonies, empire: Symmachus, *Relationes* 3.7. Invitation to Honorius in 397: Symmachus, *Ep.* 6.52. Honorius' visit in 403: Augustine, *Serm. Mayence* 61 = *Serm. Dolbeau* 25.26, ed. Dolbeau (1996) 266, mausoleum, diadem, *Serm. Mayence* 55 = *Serm. Dolbeau* 22.4, ed. Dolbeau (1996) 557, pray, with Liverani (2008) 13–16, on the routes of emperors through late antique Rome, and Chapter 10. After his death in 423 Honorius was buried in a rotunda attached to the south end of the transept of the Church of St. Peter: see Paul the Deacon, *Historia Romana* 13.7, with Koethe (1931). Festival of St. Peter on February 22: Valentinian III, *Ep. ad Theodosium Augustum* = [bishop Leo of Rome], *Ep.* 55 (*PL* 54.857A–860B). In 467 the Gallic aristocrat Sidonius arrived at Rome on the Flaminian Way and likewise first visited the Church of St. Peter: see Sidonius, *Ep.* 1.5.9, "before I reached the [city's] boundary, I knelt at the triumphal thresholds of the apostles."

he "met with the blessed Peter." At this suburban church "outside the city" the king also met with the senate and the people, who were being led by the bishop of Rome. Only then did Theoderic enter the city to perform conventional imperial duties, such as visiting the senate house, greeting the senate "with remarkable courtesy," appointing new magistrates, addressing the people in the Forum, entering the palace in triumph, presiding over games in the Circus Maximus, distributing grain, and restoring buildings.[87]

A Byzantine emperor from Constantinople likewise paid his respects to the apostle in 663. After Constans II was greeted by the bishop of Rome, clergymen, and other citizens outside the city, he first went to the Church of St. Peter to pray. On two subsequent Sundays Constans returned to "the doors of the blessed Peter" to celebrate mass, and he presented a cloak woven with gold threads to the church. In 774 Charlemagne, king of the Franks, interrupted his campaign against the Lombards in Italy to visit Rome. He arrived on Easter Saturday and walked directly to the Church of St. Peter. There he kissed each of the front steps before greeting bishop Hadrian, who was standing at the doors of the church with his clerics and the people of Rome. Over the following three days Charlemagne celebrated mass at various churches in and near Rome. During late antiquity the performance of Christian rulership at Rome typically started at the Church of St. Peter in the suburbs and then expanded to include traditional imperial activities and additional liturgical services in the city.[88]

This realignment of imperial ceremonial and symbolic topography was an extended consequence of Constantine's actions at Rome after his victory at the Milvian Bridge. He had begun to fund the construction

---

[87] Fragment of Gelasius' letter, dated to 496: *Epistulae Theodericianae variae* 6, and ed. Thiel (1868) 489–90. Theoderic at Rome: *Anonymus Valesianus*, Pars posterior 12.65–68, with Heres (1982) 143–46, on Theoderic's building projects, Vitiello (2004), for an excellent commentary on Theoderic's "patina di 'principato'" (p. 102), Vitiello (2005) 13–38, on the increasing importance of the Church of St. Peter for visiting rulers, and Arnold (2008), on Theoderic as a Roman emperor. Courtesy: Cassiodorus, *Chronica* s.a. 500.

[88] Constans II at Rome: *Liber pontificalis* 78.2–3. Doors: Paul the Deacon, *Historia Langobardorum* 5.11. Charlemagne's visit: *Liber pontificalis* 97.35–40.

of suburban churches, most likely immediately after his arrival, and sooner or later he had declined to visit the Temple of Jupiter on the Capitoline Hill. As a result, Constantine initiated a shift of priorities at Rome, in ceremonies from Republican emperorship to Christian emperorship, in values from traditional munificence to Christian generosity, in topography from the old imperial center to the ecclesiastical hinterland.

Historians quickly noticed. In the past the monumental layout of Rome had virtually compelled emperors to show their respect for Republican traditions in traditional ceremonies. With the construction of more churches and shrines, however, it became much easier to act like Christian emperors. In a section of his *Ecclesiastical History* composed before Constantine's reign, Eusebius noted that St. Peter and St. Paul had been commemorated in cemeteries. A century later, however, in his translation of Eusebius' *History* Rufinus omitted the reference to mere cemeteries. After the extensive construction and the enrichment of many churches through imperial patronage, he could emphasize instead "the most splendid monuments" dedicated to the saints.[89]

Constantine had hence used the city of Rome as a "text," like his letters and edicts, for publicizing his preferences. After his reign Rome had a different look and a different identity, and "Rome," the idea of Rome, a different meaning. He, and subsequent Christian rulers, had already started to rewrite imperial Rome into ecclesiastical Rome.

VICTORY

Constantine's victory at the battle of the Milvian Bridge posed an uncomfortable dilemma. Because he had invaded Italy, because his opponent had been another Roman emperor, his campaign seemed upside down. Lactantius' tart comment about Galerius' earlier invasion

---

[89] From cemeteries to monuments: Eusebius and Rufinus, *HE* 2.25.5, with the excellent survey of Humphries (2007): "there was an increased tendency to use the spaces of the church for such displays by secular rulers" (p. 49).

of Italy was again applicable: "Roman soldiers were attacking Rome." After the battle the emperor's new subjects had an interest in softening this inconvenient truth. Even though the people of Rome and the residents of Italy and North Africa were ready to celebrate, they wanted to affirm that the battle had marked a victory at Rome, not over Rome, and that it had signaled liberation, not conquest.[90]

For Constantine too this was an awkward victory. In his guise as a military commander he may have initiated construction of a commemorative arch at Malborghetto to honor his soldiers and their final encampment. But in Rome an emperor was not expected to celebrate a formal triumph for a victory "over Roman blood" in a civil war. Instead, Constantine had to represent himself as more of a civilian ruler, committed to the heritage of the capital. He erected a statue with a dedication that announced his acceptance of ancestral traditions, and he calmed the anxieties of aristocrats like Porfyrius with his display of reconciliation. He met with imperial magistrates from his newly acquired provinces, and he responded to petitions from provincial leaders, including the bishop of Carthage. Through his patronage for the construction of new churches he modified the symbolic topography of the capital. Even as Constantine reinvented himself as an emperor at Rome, he was reinventing Rome.[91]

Commemorating the battle at the Milvian Bridge was apparently not to be included in this makeover, however. Long ago after defeating his final rival Augustus claimed to have restored the Republic. His victory at the battle at Actium in 31 B.C. became "the birth-legend in the mythology of the Principate." During that campaign he had presented himself as the guardian of the interests of "the whole of Italy" as well as the provinces in the West against the armies of Egypt and the East, whose success, it was rumored, would have guaranteed the transfer of the capital to Alexandria. After the battle Augustus returned to Rome and decorated new buildings in the Forum with his trophies. He also

---

[90] Roman soldiers: Lactantius, *De mortibus persecutorum* 27.3.

[91] Roman blood: Ammianus Marcellinus, *Res gestae* 16.10.1, commenting on Constantius' visit to Rome in 357 after his victory over Magnentius.

instituted an "Actian Festival" to be celebrated at Rome every four years, and the day of his victory became an annual public holiday.[92]

After his victory Constantine had a similar opportunity at Rome. During the procession marking his triumphant entry the people surged to mock the decapitated head of Maxentius and to see the new emperor. During his residence the crowds were able to watch the emperor when he joined in celebrating "the days of entertainments and the eternal games": "everyone was happy with the duration of the spectacles." But after the initial celebrations there were no subsequent festivals in honor of the battle at the Milvian Bridge.[93]

In the mid-fourth century the people of Rome still celebrated the Constantinian dynasty of emperors in a series of annual games and festivals on state holidays. The celebrations commemorated military victories over barbarians, the birthdays of emperors, and the dates of their accessions to imperial rule. The celebration of Constantine's victory over Maxentius was rather oblique, with festivals commemorating "the expulsion of the tyrant" on October 28 and "the arrival of the divine [Constantine]" on October 29. In these festivals the people were celebrating not the battle but the ouster of a tyrant and the formal entry of an emperor. Only one of Constantine's imperial rivals was mentioned by name at a commemorative festival. After his initial victory over Licinius at Hadrianople in early summer of 324, Constantine had defeated him again, this time conclusively, two months later at Chrysopolis. Thereafter the people of Rome celebrated on July 3 the anniversary of "Licinius, who was put to flight," and on September 18 extensive triumphal games. Because the triumphal games coincided with the anniversary of the accession of the emperor Trajan, they were celebrated with forty-eight races in the circus, twice the usual number.[94]

[92] Quotation about birth legend from Syme (1939) 297. Italy: Augustus, *Res gestae* 25.2. Dio, *Historiae Romanae* 50.4.1, Alexandria, 53.1.4–5, Actian Festival, with Lange (2009) 132–34, for the public holiday. For the Forum, see Zanker (1988) 79–100, "Actium was Augustus's triumph over the so-called eastern barbarian" (p. 84), and Lange (2009) 160–66.

[93] *Panegyrici latini* 12(9).18.3, mockery, 19.6, days.

[94] *Fasti Furii Filocali*, July 3, "Fugato Licinio," September 18, "N(atalis) Traiani, Triumphales," ed. Degrassi (1963) 251, 255. For the festivals of October 28 and 29, see Chapter 1.

Augustus could properly claim to have fought overseas on behalf of Rome and Italy. But because Constantine had invaded Italy and marched against a rival who was posing as the protector of Rome, his victory seemed to contradict Augustus' claim, and the Milvian Bridge could not become the symbol of triumph that Actium had been for Augustus. With his victory over Licinius, however, Constantine had seemingly imitated Augustus by again connecting West and East and reunifying the empire. In 312 Constantine had attacked Rome; in 324 he had defended Rome. As a result, at Rome the victory over Licinius would seem more consequential and more worthy of remembrance than the victory over Maxentius.

BACKWARD AND FORWARD

CHAPTER EIGHT

A FTER ANALYSIS AND INTERPRETATION, A NEW NARRATIVE. So far, however, this critique of ancient accounts of the battle at the Milvian Bridge has challenged the expectation of a new master narrative of the battle and its consequences in two related ways.

One is the emphasis on the constructed nature of the early accounts of the battle and its aftermath. The anonymous orator of 313, the designers and sculptors of the arch at Rome, the rhetorician Lactantius, the bishop Eusebius, the poet Porfyrius, the panegyrist Nazarius, and Constantine himself all had their own agendas, which they could promote through the medium of discussing the battle or the emperor's vision. For modern historians one important implication of this focus on the construction of ancient texts should not be simply a reverse emphasis on deconstruction, as if it were possible, through careful scrutiny, to find true details or an accurate basic framework behind the ancient authors' agendas. Too often positivism is hypercritical and hypercredulous at the same time. Instead, the lesson should be the realization that our modern narratives are likewise constructed. We historians need to acknowledge that we are both scholars, reading and interpreting ancient texts, and authors, writing and constructing new texts.

The second challenge to writing a new narrative is chronology, or rather, the direction of the chronology. So far the discussion in this book has proceeded essentially backward, starting with modern scholarship, withdrawing to medieval and Byzantine perspectives and then to historical accounts derived from some of the earlier accounts, retreating to very early accounts, and finally examining some of the immediate reactions. Such a backward discussion is stimulating to write but also advantageous to think with. It still has a linear chronology but in reverse. Rather than adding deposits of nuance, it brushes away layers of speculation and misdirection. Rather than gathering and accruing, it excavates and disperses. Best of all, a reverse narrative is not infected with the hidden assumptions about inevitable outcomes that weaken so many discussions of the development of Christianity and the rise of a Christian emperor in the Roman world. In a reverse narrative there can be no teleology.

The arrow of time should be as much of an issue for historians as it is for physicists. A forward narrative does not match up with the thinking of ancient people, who were aware of the weight of the past and had hopes for the future but certainly could not anticipate the long-term outcomes of their actions. A forward narrative furthermore does not match up with the way modern historians typically think about topics in their fields, zooming backward and forward simultaneously. Like archaeologists, historians often excavate the past in reverse but then write up their findings from the bottom layer to the top, going forward. A forward narrative is hence another rhetorical tactic used by modern historians to confer authority on their analyses by leaving the impression that they alone have been able to see the proper flow of past events. A forward narrative of events appears to be more convincing because its plot seems to replicate the original experience of those events. A forward narrative can be compelling because it implies an implicit inevitability, an embedded intelligent design, an unspoken preordained outcome. But in fact, a narrative that moves forward chronologically is no less artificial than a reverse narrative. Even a forward narrative is an interpretive representation of past events, not an accurate portrayal. It is simply our familiarity with forward narratives that makes them appear to be less affected.

Constantine is a wonderful topic for thinking forward and backward about Roman history. Ancient Roman historians were already classifying his reign as both an end and a beginning. Eusebius made the emperor's victory over Licinius the culmination of his narrative of early Christianity; subsequent ecclesiastical historians made Constantine the first of an extended sequence of Christian emperors. Pagan historians made him responsible for future misfortunes by blaming him for initiatives that they thought had undermined the empire, such as the promotion of barbarians as consuls and the withdrawal of troops from the frontiers. In contrast, one historian implied that Constantine's behavior had degenerated by suggesting that during his reign he had aged backward. "For [the first] ten years he was truly extraordinary. For the next twelve years he was a bandit. For the last ten years he was a little boy, because of his unrestrained generosity." In this historian's perspective, during his emperorship Constantine had regressed from mature adulthood to rebellious adolescence to innocent childhood. Already in antiquity historians were using Constantine's reign to look both backward and forward.[1]

We modern historians likewise need to invent narrative techniques that better reflect the contingencies and uncertainties of living in the ancient world. To do so we might look sideways at contemporary popular culture. Pop culture offers movies whose stories begin at the end, go backward, and end at the beginning, or whose hero is born as an old man and dies as a baby. The imagination of a novelist can conjure up "a topsy-turvy world in which, so to speak, time's arrow moves the other way." "One thing led to another – actually it was more like the other way round." Contemporary television shows and novels include both flashbacks and flash-forwards. On television some of the "reality" shows are scripted, while some of the fictional dramas

---

[1] Barbarians: Ammianus Marcellinus, *Res gestae* 21.10.8. Frontiers: Zosimus, *Historia nova* 2.34. Regression: *Epitome de Caesaribus* 41.16.

are based on "true" events. To correspond to *cinéma vérité* perhaps there should be *histoire vérité*, veristic history, which would narrate the battle of the Milvian Bridge as a movie, a television show, or a graphic novel. Academics may indulge in highly technical postmodern analysis, but pop culture is often so much more creative at using the rhetorical strategies of postmodern society as effective narrative media.[2]

For us historians one way forward is to celebrate and profit from the constructedness of our modern discussions. Rather than simply analyzing the rhetorical strategies in ancient texts, we should embrace those strategies in our own narratives. For ancient texts narratology offers a framework for analysis and interpretation, but for our modern texts it can offer techniques for composition and presentation. Whether consciously or not, as both scholars of the past and authors in the present we historians are all narratologists.[3]

A backward narrative can now segue into a forward narrative. Even in a conventional forward narrative it is possible to tell the story of the battle of the Milvian Bridge in a different way. The most important requirement is to discard the obsession with Christianity. Over the past few decades the field of early Christian studies has flourished along with the blossoming of late antique studies. But the lingering weakness of early Christian studies remains its single-minded focus on Christianity. In early Christian studies all events and ideas from antiquity are typically seen as somehow improving or obstructing the success of Christianity. In fact, most events and ideas acquired their significance for Christianity only in retrospect. One such event was the battle at the Milvian Bridge.

To imagine a different narrative we need to extract the battle from the religious context that tends to dominate modern scholarship about the age of Constantine. Already at the time the battle did have larger implications. But the future of Christianity in the Roman world was not

---

[2] Quotations from Amis (1991) 56, one thing, 95, world.

[3] For history and narrative, see Prince (1995) 130: "narratology has underlined the extent to which narrative inhabits not only literary texts and ordinary language but also scholarly or technical discourse."

necessarily the most consequential outcome. Instead, the battle at the Milvian Bridge influenced the development of imperial authority and the dynamics of the relationship between Rome and the frontiers. To tell that story about emperorship and empire, however, we furthermore need to look away from Constantine and remember another emperor.

REMEMBERING
MAXENTIUS

CHAPTER NINE

Y EARS AFTERWARD CONSTANTINE REMEMBERED THE BATTLE at the Milvian Bridge as the moment when he had first used a military standard constructed in the shape of a cross. Before the battle, he claimed, both he and his army had witnessed a vision of the cross in the sky, and Jesus Christ himself had appeared in a dream to explain the vision and direct him to build a battle standard. In his *Life of Constantine* Eusebius subsequently embedded those memories in a religious context and transformed the vision and the battle into moments of conversion to Christianity, of the emperor personally and of the empire in general. In this process of remembering and recording, however, both emperor and bishop had furthermore tried to forget someone else. During the battle outside Rome another emperor had also been present. But when Maxentius had fallen into the Tiber River, he had at the same time slipped into oblivion.

Constantine's memories and Eusebius' reinterpretation of those memories have set the tone for modern scholarship too, and overlooking Maxentius has reinforced the notion that the battle was all about Constantine and Christianity. In contrast, focusing on Maxentius offers an opportunity to avoid highlighting Christianity. The confrontation between these two emperors instead emphasized other consequential trends. One concerned the orientation of the Roman empire. Maxentius symbolized the conventional importance of Rome as the capital, while Constantine represented the increasing significance of frontier zones, in particular in the north along the Rhine and the Danube. A second trend concerned the nature of Roman emperorship. At the time Maxentius seemed to be reviving an older, traditional Republican image of emperors, while Constantine seemed to continue the newer Tetrarchic model of divine emperors, but within Christianity rather than in opposition.

In the early fourth century both the contours of empire and the nature of imperial rule were contested, and Maxentius and Constantine represented alternative possibilities. One was a civilian emperor residing at Rome, and the other was a military emperor campaigning on the frontiers. To evaluate these contrasting notions of empire and emperorship, it is necessary to remember Maxentius at the Milvian Bridge.

EMPIRE

In 306 Maxentius was living in a "public villa" a few miles east of Rome. He was then in his early twenties and already married to Valeria Maximilla, the daughter of Galerius and most likely the granddaughter of Diocletian. Because her father was a ruling emperor, Valeria Maximilla would be acclaimed in a dedication as a "most noble woman." Maxentius too was the offspring of an emperor. But his father, Maximian, had recently retired, and Maxentius had been passed over for promotion as a new junior emperor. Once, when he had been hailed as the "divine and immortal offspring of Maximian," he had appeared to be the heir apparent to membership as a new emperor in the Tetrarchy. Now he was simply a private citizen. As a result, Maxentius seems to have identified himself with the senate at Rome. Another dedication would hail him with a traditional title of senatorial rank as a "most distinguished man." The nominal dedicator of both inscriptions was Valerius Romulus, his infant son. By giving his son the name of the legendary founder of Rome, Maxentius was presumably advertising another link to the ancient traditions of the capital.[1]

Rome had long been a privileged city in the empire. The enormous population of the capital was supported at the expense of provinces throughout the Mediterranean through the requisition and delivery of grain and other supplies. The residents of Italy likewise enjoyed exceptional privileges, including freedom from the stationing of troops and immunity from the payment of direct taxes. For centuries Italy had been a civilian region, mostly outside the framework of the imperial administration: "Italy was not treated like a province." At the end of the third century, however, Diocletian and his fellow emperors in the Tetrarchy initiated an administrative reorganization. One notable innovation was the division of the current provinces into smaller provinces. By approximately doubling the number of provinces, Diocletian doubled the number of provincial magistrates who were responsible for the assessment and collection of taxes. In Italy he furthermore completed the reorganization of the current regions into districts that were the equivalents of provinces. He also extended the "oppressive evil of taxes" to "a part of Italy," that is, northern Italy, where Maximian and his court took up residence in Milan and Aquileia during the mid-290s. "A new law was imposed for the payment of taxes, so that the army and the emperor, who are always or usually there, could be supplied." Under the Tetrarchs the districts of northern Italy were being treated like outlying provinces and were expected to pay taxes.[2]

Diocletian retired in 305, and in the following year Galerius, one of the new senior emperors, decided to impose taxes on peninsular Italy and to register even the people of Rome. Galerius was a native of the province of Dacia, and one observer claimed that he still nursed a

---

[1] Villa: Eutropius, *Breviarium* 10.2.3, and *Epitome de Caesaribus* 40.2, with Barnes (1982) 38, on Valeria's mother. Offspring: *Panegyrici latini* 10(2).14.1. Dedications on Labicanan Way, outside Praeneste: *ILS* 1:152, nos. 666–67. Maxentius as a *privatus*: Lactantius, *De mortibus persecutorum* 18.11.

[2] Quotation about Italy from Millar (1986) 296, with Van Dam (2007) 23–27, 70–78, (2010) 5–33, on Rome's privileged standing in the empire. Oppressive evil, new law: Aurelius Victor, *De Caesaribus* 39.31.

grudge for the defeat of the Dacian kingdom north of the Danube by the emperor Trajan – almost two centuries earlier! Galerius was thought to have dreamed about promoting the centrality of his native region in the Balkans by replacing the Roman empire with a "Dacian empire." He hence hoped to reverse the relationship of priority between capital and provinces: "the [burdens] that Romans had long ago imposed on the defeated by right of war, that man dared to impose on Romans and their subjects." To implement his directive he sent census-takers to the capital. Not surprisingly, the people of Rome revolted. Because Galerius also tried to eliminate the camp of the praetorian guards, the solders killed some of the magistrates. On October 28, 306, the people and the soldiers at Rome invested Maxentius as their emperor.[3]

Maxentius was certainly not a passive participant in this coup. He had already enlisted the support of the three tribunes of the urban cohorts, he was prepared to kill the vicar of Rome who opposed him, and he promised to reward his supporters with "substantial gifts." The slight of being overlooked when new emperors had been selected in the previous year was perhaps one motivation. Another may have been envy on seeing the portrait of one particular new emperor. Constantine was another son of an emperor in the original Tetrarchy, but he too had been sidelined in the selection of new emperors in the previous year. In July 306, however, after the death of his father, Constantius, the troops in Britain had readily hailed him as emperor. Constantine had immediately sent a portrait of himself to Galerius, who had reluctantly acknowledged him as a new Caesar. In anticipation of imposing his new regulations on peninsular Italy, Galerius may in turn have sent portraits of the revamped Tetrarchy for display at Rome, "in accordance with custom."[4]

---

[3] Lactantius, *De mortibus persecutorum* 23.5, right of war, 26.2–3, census takers, revolt, 27.8, Dacian empire. Aurelius Victor, *De Caesaribus* 40.5, proclamation by "vulgus turmaeque praetoriae," with Speidel (1986) 256–57, interpreting *turmae praetoriae* as the *equites singulares*, an elite cavalry unit.

[4] Portrait to Galerius: Lactantius, *De mortibus persecutorum* 25.1–3. Envy and portrait at Rome, custom, tribunes, gifts: Zosimus, *Historia nova* 2.9.2–3, with Paschoud (1979–2000) 1:207–8, on the tribunes.

A display of imperial portraits that included Constantine would have been hard for Maxentius to tolerate. Constantine may have been about a decade older than Maxentius, and a year later he would become Maxentius' brother-in-law. But at the time of their respective coups, Maxentius likely still thought of his rival as a lesser relative. Although Constantine's father, Constantius, may have been an emperor, his mother, Helena, had a suspect background. Supposedly Maxentius dismissed Constantine as "the son of an ignoble woman." In addition, because Constantius had subsequently married Theodora, Maxentius' half sister, Maxentius had previously become something like a stepuncle to Constantine. Now, however, the nephew had surpassed the uncle. Maxentius responded by destroying statues of Constantine and defacing his portraits.[5]

The proclamations of first Constantine and then Maxentius as local emperors had challenged the disregard for hereditary succession that characterized the Tetrarchic system. In 305 these two sons of emperors had been passed over in the selection of new emperors to replace the retiring Diocletian and Maximian. In the next year, however, Constantine had muscled his way into the Tetrarchy by intimidating Galerius into accepting him as a replacement for his father with the title of Caesar. Initiative and priority had its rewards, because three months later Galerius would not do the same for Maxentius. The symmetry of the Tetrarchy implied that "he could not appoint three Caesars." Galerius was even thought to have said that Maxentius, his own son-in-law, was simply not worthy of becoming an emperor.[6]

Instead, Maxentius adopted a different tactic that posed yet another challenge to Tetrarchic emperorship. In contrast to the Tetrarchic

---

[5] Woman: Zosimus, *Historia nova* 2.9.2. Statues and portraits: *Panegyrici latini* 4(10).12.2. For the relationships and ages, see Barnes (1982) 34–37, arguing that Theodora was the daughter, not stepdaughter, of Maximian and that Maxentius had been born in circa 283, 39–42, that Constantine had been born in 272 or 273. Perhaps Maxentius also objected to Constantine to protect the succession rights of his nephews, that is, Constantius' sons with Theodora: see Van Dam (2007) 109, 302, for Constantine's half brothers.

[6] Lactantius, *De mortibus persecutorum* 18.11, not worthy, 26.4, three Caesars, with Van Dam (2007) 103–4, for the Tetrarchic disregard of hereditary succession, and Leadbetter (2009) 177–205, on Galerius' politicking with Maxentius and Constantine between 306 and 308.

emperors, who had demoted the significance of Rome and Italy by imposing taxes, Maxentius presented himself as the guardian of Rome, its traditions, and its prerogatives. The other emperors, predictably, did not share his aggrandizement of himself or of Rome. Early in 307 Galerius sent Severus, the other senior emperor, to invade Italy. In anticipation of this attack initiated by his father-in-law, Maxentius had quickly summoned Maximian, his father, back from retirement by hailing him as "Augustus for a second time." When Severus appeared at the wall of Rome, his troops defected to Maximian, their former commander, and Severus was forced to retreat to Ravenna. In late summer Galerius himself invaded Italy and marched on Rome, with the expectation of "extinguishing the senate and slaughtering the people." His invasion was another attempt to demonstrate that Rome and central Italy were no longer the hub of the empire. During his march on Rome he treated Italy like a war zone and its residents like non-Romans. Along the Flaminian Way his troops pillaged livestock from the Italians, "as if from barbarians." By behaving like a "destroyer of Italy," Galerius seemed to have forfeited his title of Roman emperor.[7]

Soon, however, Galerius too was forced to retreat back north to the Balkans, defeated by his own ignorance. Because he had never seen Rome before, "he thought it was not much larger than the cities he already knew," and he did not bring enough troops to conduct a proper siege. In addition, Rome had become an enormous fortified garrison. During the early 270s the emperor Aurelian had initiated construction of a massive new wall, which eventually extended twelve miles in circumference and enclosed more than five square miles. Perhaps as a response to the invasions of Severus and Galerius, Maxentius began the digging of a ditch, and he partially reconstructed the wall. In a significant reversal, central Italy had become a battle zone, and the wall of Rome now seemed to define a frontier boundary, similar to

---

[7] Invasion of Severus: Lactantius, *De mortibus persecutorum* 26, Zosimus, *Historia nova* 2.10.1; of Galerius: Lactantius, *De mortibus persecutorum* 27. Plundering of Flaminian Way: *Origo Constantini imperatoris* 3.7.

Hadrian's Wall in northern Britain. In fact, because Maxentius did not go out to fight Severus or Galerius, his entire empire seemed to consist only of Rome: he was "an emperor inside the security of the wall."[8]

Maxentius' imperial rule did include more than Rome and central Italy, since he also controlled northern and southern Italy, Sardinia, Corsica, Sicily, and much of North Africa. In North Africa the legends on coins minted at Carthage hailed him as the "defender of his Africa" and the "defender of his Carthage." In 308, however, local troops revolted and proclaimed the vicar Domitius Alexander as emperor in Africa. Alexander may have already been serving as vicar for a few years before Maxentius' accession. As a result, because he had not been appointed by Maxentius, as emperor he seems to have considered himself to be a colleague of Constantine, not of Maxentius. The legends on his coins minted at Carthage furthermore suggested that he was offering himself as a protector of "the senate and people of Rome." From his base in Africa, Alexander seems to have implied that he would save Rome from Maxentius.[9]

Alexander's revolt certainly led to a disruption in the supply of grain to Rome, and Maxentius was even compelled to levy a tax on the people of Rome, in particular on senators. Imposing this new tax was

[8] Cities: Lactantius, *De mortibus persecutorum* 27.2. Moat: Chronographer of 354, *Chronica urbis Romae*, ed. Mommsen (1892) 148, "fossatum aperuit, sed non perfecit," with Coarelli (2007) 18–27, on the Aurelian Wall. The extensive renovation of the wall attributed to Maxentius by Richmond (1930) 251–56, was instead completed during the reign of Honorius in the early fifth century: see Heres (1982) 103–5, 131, 203–11. Security: *Panegyrici latini* 12(9).14.4.

[9] For the extent of Maxentius' empire, note *Panegyrici latini* 12(9).25.2–3: by defeating Maxentius, Constantine was credited with conquering Italy, Rome, Africa, and "the islands of the Sea of Africa." Maxentius' coins at Carthage: Sutherland (1967) 417–19, and Cullhed (1994) 46. Alexander's revolt: Aurelius Victor, *De Caesaribus* 40.17–18, *Epitome de Caesaribus* 40.2, 6, Zosimus, *Historia nova* 2.12, 14, with *PLRE* 1:43, "L. Domitius Alexander 17," and Barnes (1982) 14–15, for the chronology. Alexander had been serving as vicar since 303 if he can be identified with Valerius Alexander: see *PLRE* 1:44, "Val. Alexander 20." Dedication to Alexander and Constantine, found perhaps near Sicca Veneria: *ILS* 2.2:XXIII, no. 8936 = Grünewald (1990) 44, 211, no. 197. Alexander's coins: Sutherland (1967) 420, "this bold claim to represent the central will and favour of Rome," 434, no. 72, "S P Q R OPTIMO PRINCIPI."

an ironical necessity, because it was precisely opposition to taxes that had led to his proclamation as emperor. But in the following year Maxentius' troops were able to regain control in North Africa. He still ruled a mini-Mediterranean empire with its capital at Rome.[10]

Maxentius did not behave like a Mediterranean emperor, however, or even a western Mediterranean emperor. His only trips outside Rome were to his large estate on the Appian Way, less than two miles south of the city's wall. This complex included an expansive villa, a dynastic mausoleum, and a circus for racing. Maxentius remodeled the villa to incorporate a large hall in the shape of a basilica, including an apse. Such a great hall was common for hosting audiences in imperial palaces. Maxentius also added the circus. This circus was sizable, more than 1,600 feet long, and quite commodious, with seating for about ten thousand spectators. It was also elaborately decorated. The barrier down the center of the racetrack displayed a series of monuments, including an obelisk in the middle as well as statues of Victory and various deities.[11]

A palace and a circus were the characteristic buildings of cities that served as imperial residences, such as Rome itself. The Tetrarchic emperors and their successors had constructed palaces and circuses at their favorite residences, including Nicomedia, Sirmium, and Trier. Eventually these new imperial cities would come to supersede Rome. Maxentius' estate on the Appian Way was his equivalent of the new imperial residences, his alternative to the old capital, but with one significant difference. Those other residences were typically near the frontiers, far away on the periphery of the empire; Maxentius' replacement capital, his "New Rome," was on the periphery only of Rome itself. In

[10] Disruption of grain supply: *Panegyrici latini* 12(9).4.4. Famine and tax of gold: Chronographer of 354, *Chronica urbis Romae*, ed. Mommsen (1892) 148. Levy on senators: Aurelius Victor, *De Caesaribus* 40.24, with Chapter 7, discussing the involvement of Porfyrius.

[11] For recent excavations of Maxentius' villa, see Conlin, Haeckl, and Ponti (2006/2007); Frazer (1966), emphasizes the associations with Hercules. Mausoleum: see Johnson (2009) 86–93, "a copy of the Pantheon in its general plan and form" (p. 90). Circus: see Humphrey (1986) 282–87, decorations on barrier, 582–602, evaluation of remains.

Maxentius' empire the "frontier zone" was effectively just outside the wall of Rome, and his new "frontier capital" was merely in the suburbs.[12]

In contrast, Constantine was a true frontier emperor. During a campaign with his father in Scotland he had even seen the "Ocean" that was thought to encircle the outer rim of the known world. After his father's death in 306 Constantine was acclaimed as emperor at York, about seventy-five miles south of Hadrian's Wall and far from the Mediterranean core of the Roman world. Proclamation in northern Britain was such an obvious stigma that one orator had to resort to an ingenious assertion. He argued that Constantine's acclamation in "the regions that are next to the sky" had been a blessing in disguise, because it had been easier for the gods to send an emperor "from the end of the world."[13]

Constantine soon relocated to the Rhine frontier, and during his early years he campaigned primarily in northern Gaul, with an occasional visit or two back to Britain. Even though he repeatedly fought against Franks and other barbarians, he also formed various alliances with the inhabitants of "the farthest edge of barbarian regions." Some of his first supporters included a king of the Alamans along the upper Danube frontier and a king of the Franks in northern Gaul. One encampment was at Noviomagus (modern Nijmegen), near the mouth of the Rhine, which generations later was still remembered as "the famous camp of the divine Constantine." His preferred residence was Trier, where he constructed or completed buildings that were characteristic of an imperial capital, including an enormous basilica to host receptions and a circus that was compared to the Circus Maximus at Rome. Constantine's early power base was in the North, and his new imperial residence was in an actual frontier zone in northern Europe.[14]

---

[12] Note Humphrey (1986) 601: "we should see the whole complex – palace, circus and mausoleum – as the equivalent of imperial residences at the tetrarchic capitals"; also Coleman (2000) 218: "the association of palace and circus which developed for the Circus Maximus is replicated by . . . Maxentius."

[13] *Panegyrici latini* 6(7).7.2, Ocean, 9.5, world and sky.

[14] *Panegyrici latini* 6(7).22.5, buildings at Trier, 12(9).25.2, farthest edge. King Crocus and Alamans: *Epitome de Caesaribus* 41.3, with Drinkwater (2007) 146. King Bonitus and Franks: Ammianus Marcellinus, *Res gestae* 15.5.33. Noviomagus: Ausonius, *Mosella* 11.

The invasion of Italy was hence a diversion from Constantine's campaigns on the Rhine frontier. In the maneuvering among the emperors after Galerius' death in 311, Maximinus seized Asia Minor and threatened Licinius, then ruling in the Balkans. Maxentius declared war on Constantine. His ostensible justification was revenge for the death of his father, which he blamed on his rival. Perhaps Maxentius had also concluded that Constantine, because he was so far away, was a safe opponent whom he would never need to confront in battle. As a result, he stationed his troops at Verona in expectation of an attack from Licinius, but perhaps also with the intention of marching north toward the Danube or of invading the Balkans himself. Despite his declaration of war against Constantine, Maxentius seems to have been concerned more about the boundary between Italy and the Balkans and less about the boundary between Gaul and Italy. He was apparently not anticipating an invasion from Gaul.[15]

For Maxentius and his supporters Constantine's invasion was therefore not only unexpected. It also revived alarming memories for the people of central Italy and Rome. Long ago Celtic peoples from Gaul had expanded into Italy and threatened Roman interests. In 390 B.C. they had even captured Rome itself. This moment of humiliation lingered as a powerfully unsettling myth about the potential for attacks from the north. According to Livy's history of early Rome, "the Gauls generated a huge terror because of the memory of this earlier disaster." This collective myth in turn branded the people of Gaul, especially of central and northern "Long-Haired" Gaul, with disparaging prejudices. As "barbarians" they deserved to be attacked and defeated by Roman generals such as Julius Caesar, who campaigned in Gaul, crossed the Rhine into Germany, and sailed to Britain during the 50s B.C.[16]

After their incorporation under Roman rule the people of Gaul might still be considered with suspicion as potential rebels. In the confusion

---

[15] Maxentius' declaration of war: Lactantius, *De mortibus persecutorum* 43.4. For the suggestion that Maxentius wanted to invade Raetia or the Balkans, see Zosimus, *Historia nova* 2.14.1.

[16] Terror: Livy, *Ab urbe condita* 6.42.7, with Drinkwater (1983) 48, on "the deep-seated Roman fear of Gauls which was always lurking under the surface ready to bedevil Gallo-Roman relations."

234 OF MEMBERING CONSTANTINE AT THE MILVIAN BRIDGE

of the civil war of A.D. 69, Gallic and Germanic peoples along the lower Rhine revolted against imperial rule and briefly established an independent "Gallic empire" in northern Gaul. During the 260s and early 270s local rulers established another temporary "Gallic empire" that was centered in northern and central Gaul and acquired support also in Britain and Spain. At the time the frontiers were under pressure, and the Gallic emperors were seemingly trying to sustain the illusion of Roman rule by characterizing themselves as "defenders of the Roman name." They represented their Gallic empire as an attempt to remain Roman, not to secede from Roman rule. But from the perspective of the emperors in the center, these Gallic emperors had been merely breakaway usurpers.[17]

Constantine's invasion of Italy revitalized those entrenched fears about a threat from northern Europe. His objective in invading Italy may have been simply to forestall Licinius' advance from the Balkans rather than to confront Maxentius. Whatever his intentions, his invasion nevertheless appeared to pose another threat to Italy from Gaul. Barbarians from the North were again threatening the classical civilization of the South. According to a later historian, although Maxentius hoped to defend Italy with a Mediterranean army that included "Romans," "Italians," "Sicilians," and "Carthaginians," Constantine's army had been enlisted from "barbarians, including Germans, other Celtic peoples, and recruits from Britain," and he appeared to be the renegade commander of "an army of Gauls." The "Gallic terror" had reappeared, and another barbarian army of Gauls and Germans was marching against Rome.[18]

The battle at the Milvian Bridge underscored the tension about the long-standing uneasiness between northern Europe and Mediterranean Europe, and more generally about the changing dynamics between core and periphery in the empire. The reign of Maxentius had represented

---

[17] "Gallic empire" of first century: Tacitus, *Historiae* 4.58; of third century: Eutropius, *Breviarium* 9.9.3. Defenders: SHA, *Tyranni triginta* 5.5.

[18] Armies of Maxentius and Constantine: Zosimus, *Historia nova* 2.15. Army of Gauls: Libanius, *Orat.* 30.6.

an empire that was still focused on Rome. In his perspective the other emperors "were fighting battles on the frontiers on his behalf." Perhaps he thought of Constantine as one of those subordinate emperors who would campaign on the remote northern frontier in the name of the old capital and its emperor. One dedication to Maxentius in North Africa in fact hailed him as a senior emperor, "unconquered, pious, fortunate Augustus," but Constantine as only a junior emperor, "most noble Caesar." As an emperor who resided at Rome, Maxentius seemed to think that he could claim priority over the other emperors: "Maxentius benefited from the majesty of his city."[19]

In contrast, even after 312 Constantine's empire was still not focused on Rome. After his victory over Maxentius he did not take up residence in Rome, or even in a city in northern Italy. During his entire reign of thirty-one years he spent a total of about five months in Rome, divided among three separate visits. After each short visit he soon returned to "the Celts and the Gauls" or to the Balkans. Constantine spent almost all of his long reign on the extended northern frontier that stretched from Britain along the Rhine through northern Italy and the Balkans along the Danube to Constantinople. He resided for more than ten years at Trier and other cities near the Rhine, more than seven years in Sirmium and Serdica in the Balkans, and about seven years in Constantinople. Constantine was a distinctly frontier emperor. His reign was the logical extension of the separatist "Gallic empire" of the late third century and Galerius' fantasy of a "Dacian empire" in the Balkans, combined with his own later ambition of establishing an "eastern empire" centered at Constantinople.[20]

In Constantine's Roman empire the imperial capital had changed its address to a northern frontier zone. According to a third-century

---

[19] *Panegyrici latini* 12(9).3.7, majesty, 14.6, battles. Dedication: Grünewald (1990) 213, no. 208, found in Africa Proconsularis. Unless Constantine's title was a deliberate slight, it can help date this dedication to 307. Maxentius started using the title of Augustus probably in early 307, while Constantine regained his title of Augustus only later in 307: see Barnes (1982) 5, 13.

[20] Celts and Gauls: Zosimus, *Historia nova* 2.17.2, with Van Dam (2007) 35–78, discussing the orientation of Constantine's empire.

historian, "Rome is wherever the emperor is." Not surprisingly, Constantine thought of Constantinople as "New Rome," he called Serdica "my Rome," and Trier would be known as "Belgian Rome." In addition, during his reign Constantine never visited any of the provinces in the great arc around the southern Mediterranean that extended from Aquitania in southwestern Gaul through Spain, North Africa, and Egypt to Palestine and southern Syria, including southern Italy, the Greek peninsula, and western Asia Minor. As a result, his empire was the opposite of Maxentius' empire. Maxentius' empire had consisted almost exclusively of Rome alone, with some authority also in the rest of Italy, western Mediterranean islands, and North Africa; Constantine's Roman empire seemed not to include Rome at all. In his empire of the North, the Mediterranean had become a frontier zone and Rome was a peripheral city.[21]

During the early fourth century the favored status of Rome and central Italy was fading while frontier regions were becoming more prominent. Through his dream of a Dacian empire the emperor Galerius had reaffirmed the increasing significance of the Balkan regions along the Danube frontier. Alexander's revolt in North Africa against Maxentius might have conjured up memories of the ancient prominence of Carthage and its bygone wars with Rome. The reign of Constantine raised questions initially about the autonomy of northern Gaul and the Rhine frontier regions, and subsequently about the possibility of a distinct eastern empire with its capital at Constantinople.

In the long perspective of Roman history this folding of space seemed to be accompanied by a reversal in the flow of time. The kinetic interactions of the later Roman empire were reverting far back to the older dynamics of the Mediterranean and its neighbors before Roman imperial expansion. The overseas expansion of Italian armies during the

---

[21] Rome and emperor: Herodian, *Historiae* 1.6.5. New Rome: Sozomen, *HE* 2.3.5. My Rome: Anonymus post Dionem (= Dio Continuatus), *Fragmenta* 15.1, ed. Müller (1851) 199. Belgian Rome: Vollmer and Rubenbauer (1926). After his visit to Rome in 326 Constantine may have initiated repairs for roads across northern Italy, perhaps in anticipation of his trip from the Balkans to Trier in 328: see Herzig (1989), for milestones.

third, second, and first centuries B.C. that had led to the political unification of the Mediterranean, the formation of the Roman empire, and the centrality of Rome was being challenged. Outlying regions such as northern Europe, the Balkans, North Africa, and the Greek East seemed to be spinning away to become separate, even replacement, empires. Whatever his success at defending frontiers, Constantine's victory at Rome marked another reversal of Roman imperialism. The Mediterranean was no longer central to Roman imperial rule.[22]

Constantine's reign would reshape the political and cultural dynamics of the Mediterranean world in general and of Europe in particular. The battle at the Milvian Bridge heralded the interaction between North and South that would dominate the history of medieval Europe. Maxentius' empire seemed to look back to an early narrative of Roman imperial history that was still focused on Rome, Italy, and the Mediterranean, while Constantine's empire looked forward to the trends of medieval European history. His victory was a preview of the eventual dominance of northern continental Europe over southern Mediterranean Europe.

EMPERORSHIP

Over the centuries, Rome had become the largest heritage site in the ancient world. In late antiquity its hills and forums were so crowded with dedications and commemorative buildings that the number of statues was thought to match the size of the population of residents. The capital had become a stable for "vast herds of equestrian monuments." Looking after all the historical relics would have been a full-time job for the municipal magistrate with the indecorous, but utilitarian, title of "tribune in charge of the shiny stuff."[23]

This shiny stuff recalled over a millennium of heroes and their epic deeds. At the western end of the old Forum, near the senate house,

---

[22] Note Whittaker (1994) 241: "In the fourth and fifth centuries we witness the reverse process of the conquests that had begun with Julius Caesar and Augustus"; and Miles (2003) 139–40, for reviving memories of the Punic Wars.

[23] Cassiodorus, *Variae* 7.13.1, herds, 15.3, number of statues. "Tribunus rerum nitentium": *Notitia Dignitatum in partibus Occidentis* 4.17.

was the Lapis Niger, the "Black Stone" that was thought to mark the grave of Romulus, the legendary founder of the city during the eighth century B.C. On the Capitoline Hill was the Temple of Jupiter, whose looming presence guaranteed the eternity of Rome. In 303 Diocletian and Maximian had met in this temple when they visited the capital to celebrate a triumph. In honor of the twentieth anniversary of their reign they erected a new Monument of Five Columns on the back edge of the Rostra, the speakers' platform located in the Forum at the foot of the Capitoline Hill. The reliefs on the one surviving pedestal depicted an emperor and senators participating together in a sacrifice. Jupiter was already the most important of the patron deities of the Tetrarchic emperors; but highlighting the veneration of Jupiter on this monument furthermore honored the expectation of cooperation between emperors and senators that had long characterized imperial rule at Rome.[24]

In fact, Tetrarchic rule was antithetical to the expectations of learned senators concerning traditional emperorship at Rome. Diocletian and Maximian had instituted the Tetrarchy in 293 to accommodate four concurrent emperors and to define an order of succession as senior emperors were replaced by junior emperors. In their legislation the Tetrarchic emperors seemingly tried to disguise the novelty of their collegiate rule by presenting themselves as guardians of "old laws and the public discipline of the Romans." One of them, Galerius, even celebrated an illustrious victory by lauding himself as a "second Romulus," the new founder of Rome. In reality, however, the emperors were all career soldiers, and they had not received an extensive education in classical culture and ancient history. Lactantius, the same rhetorician who recorded these emperors' attempts at presenting themselves as champions of ancient traditions, also mocked Galerius for his total lack of refinement: "the barbarity in this beast was innate, and his

---

[24] Temple of Jupiter and eternity of Rome: Ammianus Marcellinus, *Res gestae* 22.16.12. For the Monument of Five Columns, see Chapter 6. For the contribution of Diocletian and Maximian to the reconstruction of the Forum and the area around the senate house, see Chronographer of 354, *Chronica urbis Romae*, s.v. Diocletianus et Maximianus, ed. Mommsen (1892) 148, with the overview of Machado (2006) 161–68.

savagery was foreign to Roman blood." At least one of the emperors returned the slight. Licinius was thought to have been outright hostile to learning and rhetoric, which he considered "a poison and a public pestilence."[25]

Their absence from Rome was another indication of their disregard of conventional expectations. Of the Tetrarchic emperors, Diocletian visited Rome once, perhaps twice, and Maximian at least twice. Constantius, Maximinus, and Licinius never visited; Galerius and Severus showed up outside the wall only to besiege the city. Despite its traditions and its reputation, despite its monumental grandeur and scenic attractions, Rome was not important to Tetrarchic emperors.

Tetrarchic emperorship also disregarded the ideology of equality between emperors and senators. Diocletian was subsequently credited with modifying the appearance and image of emperors. He had his robes and his shoes decorated with gemstones. He had people greet him as "Lord" in public, and he "allowed himself to be worshipped and addressed as god." He also introduced the practice of "adoration," a public display of obeisance to emperors by their subjects. When he and Maximian met at Milan in late 290, the entourage of dignitaries admitted to greet them in the palace, including perhaps the leading senators who had come from Rome, was expected to "adore their sacred faces."[26]

Traditionalists were predictably upset at the novelties of Tetrarchic emperorship. In the mid-fourth century the senator Eutropius, for instance, was quite miffed, and in his overview of Roman history he did not disguise his dismay. In his opinion the rule of Tetrarchic emperors had promoted the wrong political model by reviving aspects of the original kings at Rome and undermining the improvements of the Republic. Not only were Tetrarchic innovations characteristic of "the custom of kings." They also contradicted the notion of "Roman liberty"

---

[25] Lactantius, *De mortibus persecutorum* 9.1, barbarity, 9, second Romulus, 34.1, old laws. Poison: *Epitome de Caesaribus* 41.8.

[26] Gemstones: Eutropius, *Breviarium* 9.26. Lord, god: Aurelius Victor, *De Caesaribus* 39.4. Meeting at Milan: *Panegyrici latini* 11(3).11.1, adore, 3, dignitaries, 12.2, senators.

that Eutropius identified as the essence of the Republic. In this sort of "Republican" narrative, when Julius Caesar had ignored "the custom of Roman liberty" and humiliated the senate, Eutropius characterized his actions as "those of a king, almost a tyrant." Diocletian likewise had not tolerated the "liberty of the Roman people" during his visit to Rome. Eutropius preferred instead to highlight the importance of the senate for safeguarding these traditions and expectations. In his estimation, the reputation of emperors was contingent on their attitudes toward senators. Bad emperors treated senators badly, while good emperors treated them fairly. The early emperors who had acquired reputations for having treated senators with respect included Augustus and Trajan. In the later empire the highest praise senators could bestow on an emperor was to proclaim him "more fortunate than Augustus, better than Trajan."[27]

Maxentius had shared this traditionalist perspective by pointedly snubbing high Tetrarchic ceremonial. In particular, he declined to adore Maximian or Galerius, perhaps in part because one was his father and the other his father-in-law. After his accession as emperor in 306 he did not seek entrance into the Tetrarchy or recognition from Galerius, the more influential of the senior emperors. Even after Galerius had invaded Italy, Maxentius seems to have declined an overture to reach a peaceful settlement. Likewise the legends on coins minted in regions he controlled did not mention Galerius' reign. Instead, on his coins Maxentius associated himself with the emperors Maximian, Galerius, and Constantius only after they had died. The legends on the coins emphasized not his connections with them as Tetrarchic emperors but rather his dynastic relationships with his father, father-in-law, and brother-in-law. In various ways Maxentius rejected Tetrarchic emperors and Tetrarchic emperorship.[28]

---

[27] Eutropius, *Breviarium* 6.25, Julius Caesar, 8.5.3, acclamation, 9.26, kings, liberty. Roman people: Lactantius, *De mortibus persecutorum* 17.2, with Rees (2004) 50: "Long gone is Augustus' Republican charade of 'first among equals.'"

[28] No adoration: Lactantius, *De mortibus persecutorum* 18.9. Overture from Galerius: *Origo Constantini imperatoris* 3.7. For the coins commemorating Maximian, Galerius, and Constantius, see Cullhed (1994) 76–79.

From the beginning of his reign Maxentius represented himself instead as an heir to Augustus, who claimed to have revived the institutions and traditions of the Republic. The legends on Maxentius' coins immediately styled him as *princeps invictus*, "unconquered first man." Although *princeps* was typically not part of the official titulature of emperors, it was commonly applied to emperors, primarily because it had been the title preferred by Augustus. Even though Maxentius subsequently assumed the common title of Augustus, "senior emperor," the legends on his gold coins nevertheless continued to style him *princeps imperii Romani*. Maxentius' standing as "first man of the Roman empire" was an affront not only to the other emperors but also to the underlying Tetrarchic expectations of harmony and cooperation. Ruling as *princeps* implied that there could be no other emperors of similar authority and status. A "first man" seemed to rank over all other emperors.[29]

The legends on his coins also presented Maxentius as *conservator urbis suae*, the "defender of his city." His piety toward ancient customs at Rome was apparent in different formats. One was his appointment of senators from distinguished families at Rome as prefects of the capital. Gaius Annius Anullinus was already serving as prefect of Rome when he supported Maxentius' proclamation as emperor in October 306. He had previously served as a consul and as governor of Africa Proconsularis. His successor as prefect of Rome was Attius Insteius Tertullus, who had previously held a suffect consulship and perhaps served as governor of Africa Proconsularis. Aurelius Hermogenes, another of Maxentius' prefects of Rome, had previously served as governor of the province of Asia. Gaius Ceionius Rufius Volusianus had already served as governor of Africa Proconsularis when Maxentius sent him as praetorian prefect to deal with a revolt in North Africa. After his successful

---

[29] See Sutherland (1967) 49–52, for the legends on Maxentius' coins, and Cullhed (1994) 36–44, for an excellent discussion of the policies implicit in the legends, with Hekster (1999) 724, "a constant return to traditional Roman values in Maxentius' policies." For the possibility that renovation of the friezes on Augustus' Altar of Peace might be dated to Maxentius' reign, see Hannestad (1994) 66–67.

campaign he served as prefect of Rome and held a consulship. His fellow consul, Aradius Rufinus, subsequently served as prefect of Rome. Because senators still dominated the political and social life of Rome, Maxentius needed their support. By promoting them, he could also show his support for ancestral customs.[30]

A second strategy of traditionalism was his patronage for construction projects that enhanced the Forum and the area next to the Colosseum. Toward the west end of the Forum, Maxentius rebuilt the Basilica Aemilia, first constructed in the second century B.C. More of his construction was concentrated toward the east end of the Forum. He rebuilt the Temple of Venus and Roma, which had been damaged recently in a fire. He initiated construction of the vast Basilica Nova, which may have served the juridical and administrative duties of the prefects of Rome. The location of this basilica on the Velian ridge was perhaps an attempt to recall the tomb of Publius Valerius Publicola, a legendary founding father of the Republic. Near Sacred Street leading to the Forum, Maxentius may have rededicated the ancient circular Temple of Jupiter Stator in honor of his son Romulus. He apparently rededicated the colossal bronze statue that stood next to the Colosseum in honor of his son, perhaps with the intention that it would become "the architectural pivot" of a new imperial forum. Not surprisingly, he also appointed a "curator of sacred sanctuaries" to look after the shrines of Rome.[31]

---

[30] For the details of the careers of Maxentius' prefects of Rome, see Chastagnol (1962) 45–62, and *PLRE* 1:79, "C. Annius Anullinus 3," 424, "Aurelius Hermogenes 8," 775, "Aradius Rufinus 10," 883–84, "Attius Insteius Tertullus 6," 976–78, "C. Ceionius Rufius Volusianus 4."

[31] For Maxentius' projects, see Cullhed (1994) 49–57, Curran (2000) 54–63, Van Dam (2007) 81–82, and Leppin and Ziemssen (2007) 52–105. Basilica Nova: Coarelli (1986) 20, connection with P. Valerius Publicola, 22–31, judicial hall, and Giavarini (2005), a comprehensive survey of the impressive construction techniques. The identification of the rotunda on Sacred Street as the "Temple of Romulus" is contested: see Coarelli (2007) 89–91, associating it with the Temple of Jupiter Stator; Richardson (1992) 333–34, and Papi (1999), for alternative identifications; and the excellent survey of Dumser (2006), suggesting that the rotunda was an audience hall. Quotation about pivot from Ensoli (2000) 87. Curator: *ILS* 2.2:XXIII, no. 8935, with *PLRE* 1:638, "Furius Octavianus 4."

Yet another strategy was apparent in the images and legends on Maxentius' coins. One common image depicted the goddess Roma, the personification of the city, seated in a temple (perhaps the Temple of Venus and Roma that he was rebuilding). Another image depicted the wolf that had suckled the twins Romulus and Remus. With these images Maxentius was honoring the deified personification of the city and some very old traditions. In return, some images depicted Roma handing the emperor a globe, the symbol of universal rule. One legend described "eternal Roma" as the "promoter of our Augustus." Another proclaimed Mars, the father of Romulus and Remus, as the "propagator of our Augustus." On his coins Maxentius was claiming to be the heir of traditions that went all the way back to the founding of Rome.[32]

During his reign Maxentius set up a dedication in honor of Mars and his sons, Romulus and Remus, precisely on April 21, the anniversary of the city's foundation. The statue base with this dedication was found at the west end of the Forum, near the senate house and the Black Stone marking the legendary site of Romulus' grave. The dedication commemorated Mars as "unconquered father" and his sons as "the founders of their eternal city." Nearby in the Forum one of Maxentius' praetorian prefects set up two dedications, and perhaps also statues, in honor of the emperor. Another dedication honored Maxentius for his display of "old-fashioned oversight and exceptional piety." Maxentius made a point of identifying himself as a conventional Republican emperor associated with Rome and its traditions.[33]

Maxentius' monuments might also have included an initial version of what became the arch of Constantine. For the debate over whether the arch was new for Constantine, new for Maxentius, or a remodeled version of an earlier Flavian or Hadrianic arch, see Van Dam (2007) 89n.12. Marlowe (2006), highlights the visual and ideological associations between the arch and the nearby colossal statue of the sun god Sol, which Maxentius had apparently rededicated to his son.

[32] For the images and legends on the coins, see Cullhed (1994) 46–49, with the excellent photographs in Leppin and Ziemssen (2007): "Kein Kaiser hat so wie er auf die stadtrömische Tradition gesetzt" (p. 32).

[33] Dedication to Mars: *ILS* 2.2:XXIII, no. 8935. Dedications to Maxentius by Manlius Rusticianus: *ILS* 2.2:XXIII, no. 8934, and *CIL* 6.8.2:4538, no. 40726, with *PLRE* 1:787, "Manlius

After his victory at the Milvian Bridge, Constantine likewise briefly assumed characteristics of a Republican emperor. His initial celebratory dedication used traditional terminology, and he appointed senators (including some of Maxentius' former supporters) to high offices. He banned weapons and military uniforms from the city. While at Rome, Constantine too apparently tried to follow the paradigm of Augustus. But this was also the paradigm of Maxentius. As a result, to enhance his new credentials as a Republican emperor, Constantine had to redefine Maxentius and his emperorship. Once his rival, now Maxentius had to become his opposite.[34]

Constantine's propaganda hence highlighted Maxentius' similarity to Romulus not as a founder but as a murderer who had killed his brother to become the legendary first king of Rome. Maxentius too had been the "murderer of the city." Another perspective favorable to Constantine condemned Maximian, Maxentius' father, as Tarquin the Proud, the last hated king of Rome whose overthrow had marked the establishment of the Republic. By classifying his rival as a "king," Constantine could pose as the new founder of the Republic. The establishment of his rule now marked another transition from monarchy to Republic at Rome. Not surprisingly, the legends on Constantine's coins hailed him as the "liberator of his city" and the "restorer of his city."[35]

But overall Constantine never fully identified with Rome and its traditions. Instead, the legacy of the Tetrarchy remained more important. Tetrarchic emperors had defined their political legitimacy and power in terms of a religious idiom. Diocletian and Maximian had soon identified themselves with Jupiter (or Zeus), the lord of the gods, and his

---

Rusticianus 3." Dedication to Maxentius: *CIL* 6.4.2:3477, no. 33857; the reference to *censura vetus* in this fragmentary dedication might be a compliment for reinstating an "old assessment," that is, restoring the exemption from taxation at Rome.

[34] Weapons and uniforms: Aurelius Victor, *De Caesaribus* 40.25, with Chapter 6.

[35] Murderer: *Panegyrici latini* 12(9).18.1. Tarquin: Lactantius, *De mortibus persecutorum* 28.4. Coins: Sutherland (1967) 387–88, nos. 303–4, 312. Note that at Volsinii in Tuscia the head on a statue of Augustus was recut as Constantine: see Giuliano (1991), dating the transformation between 312 and 315, and Van Dam (2007) 27–34, on Constantine's support for a pagan festival at Volsinii.

assistant Hercules by adding "Jovius" and "Herculius" to their official imperial names; in 305 Diocletian retired from emperorship in the presence of a statue of Jupiter perched on a column outside Nicomedia. Their successors likewise added the names of Jovius and Herculius. Even Constantine, during the years when he was allied with Maximian, added the name of Herculius. Tetrarchic emperors articulated their rulership not through their reverence for the ancestral traditions of the Republic but through a symbolic identification with powerful gods.[36]

Constantine of course eventually discarded the affiliations with pagan gods. But he seems to have retained the underlying religious framework of Tetrarchic emperorship. Even as an emperor who supported Christianity he relied on an association with, even an identification with, a deity to legitimate his imperial power. For this sort of ideology Old Rome was not the best venue, as Diocletian had already discovered. When Diocletian had no longer been able to tolerate the people of Rome, he had immediately left for Ravenna. For his own new religious imperial ideology Constantine likewise preferred a new capital that was isolated from the traditions of the old Republic. The past history of Old Rome was an obstacle; in contrast, Constantinople, New Rome, could be a capital without the constraints of ancestral traditions.[37]

At Constantinople, Constantine highlighted his intimacy with Jesus Christ. In the center of a new forum he erected a giant statue of himself on top of a tall column, in which he was thought to have placed a relic of the True Cross, the cross on which Jesus had been crucified. Over an entrance to the palace he hung a portrait of himself and his sons, with a cross overhead and a serpent underfoot, that recalled his victory over Licinius and hinted at his role as a savior who had defeated evil. His mausoleum contained a niche for his sarcophagus surrounded by twelve cenotaphs that represented the twelve apostles. This shrine

---

[36] For Constantine at Rome, see Chapters 6–7. Jovius and Herculius: see Van Dam (2007) 84–85, Constantine, 230–51, Tetrarchs.

[37] Diocletian's departure: Lactantius, *De mortibus persecutorum* 17.2–3. For the rewriting of the histories of Rome and Constantinople in late antiquity, see Van Dam (2010) 33–41, 62–71.

evoked the site of Jesus' tomb at Jerusalem, located next to the Church of the Holy Sepulcher in which the twelve columns encircling the apse commemorated the twelve apostles. The monuments at the new capital highlighted Constantine's standing as the equivalent of Jesus Christ. Not surprisingly, some residents of Constantinople offered prayers to the statue of Constantine "as if to a god."[38]

Churchmen likewise contributed to the making of this image of Constantine as an analogue of Jesus Christ. In his panegyrics and his *Life of Constantine* Eusebius in particular had emphasized the affiliation between the emperor and Jesus Christ. One of his goals, of course, was to use an image of "Constantine" as a medium for promoting his own theology. To fulfill this theological objective he emphasized the similarity between the emperor and Jesus Christ. In the confession of faith at the beginning of *Ecclesiastical History* Eusebius had described Jesus Christ as "the angel of great guidance." In *Life* he described the emperor as "a heavenly angel of God." His recollection of the anniversary banquet that Constantine had hosted for churchmen after the council of Nicaea was especially ecstatic: "one might think that an image of Christ's kingdom was becoming apparent." At the ceremony of dedication for the Church of the Holy Sepulcher in 335, one of the bishops in attendance announced that Constantine, because he had been worthy of imperial rule in this life, would in the future reign with the Son of God.[39]

By then both Eusebius and Constantine were far from thinking about imperial rule in terms of the traditional expectations about acting like a Republican emperor. Eusebius and other churchmen had survived the persecutions of the Tetrarchic emperors to see the appearance of a Christian emperor. But their ideas about emperorship had obviously been shaped by Tetrarchic ideas. Tetrarchic emperors had been identified

---

[38] Statue and relic: Socrates, *HE* 1.17. Eusebius, *Vita Constantini* 3.3, portrait, 4.58–60, mausoleum, with Van Dam (2007) 297–300, on the Church of the Holy Sepulcher. Prayers: Philostorgius, *HE* 2.17.

[39] Eusebius, *HE* 1.2.3, angel, *Vita Constantini* 3.10.3, heavenly angel, 15.2, Christ's kingdom, 4.48, reign with Son, with Chapter 4, for the theological implications.

with pagan gods; a Christian emperor was now identified with Jesus Christ. Even though the association of imperial rule with pagan cults was moribund, the identification of emperors with a divinity lingered in these early ideas about Christian emperorship. Maxentius' emperorship emphasized Rome and its senatorial and Republican traditions; Constantine's emperorship continued Tetrarchic notions about divine rule but in a Christian guise.

Their relationships with the army provided one more distinctive contrast between Constantine and Maxentius. Constantine was a lifetime soldier. Long before they married, Fausta had once presented Constantine with "a helmet that glistened with gold and jewels and that was decorated with the feathers of a beautiful bird." Fausta had already realized that the way to her future husband's heart was through the toys of war. As a young man Constantine had served in the army as a junior officer. He had accompanied Galerius during an invasion of the Persian empire, and he had fought in the cavalry against the Sarmatians on the Danube frontier. As an emperor he led many of his campaigns in person. At the end of his life, when he was in his sixties, he was still preparing for another campaign against the Persian empire. Even after demonstrating his support for Christianity, Constantine's first priority remained the army and military campaigns. From his youthful military service to his final plans for one more grand campaign, Constantine had always been a warrior.[40]

In contrast, Maxentius had no military experience either before or during his imperial rule. Once, it was thought, he had intended to march into Raetia, a frontier zone along the upper Danube. Once he had planned to cross to North Africa to deal with a potential revolt. Instead, he relied on substitute commanders. When he had faced an actual revolt by a usurper in North Africa, he sent his troops under the command of his praetorian prefect. In Italy he had declined to engage the armies of Severus or Galerius, trusting instead to shelter behind the wall of Rome. A rhetorician criticized Maxentius for failing to attack

---

[40] *Panegyrici latini* 6(7).3.3, soldier, 7(6).5.3, tribunates, 6.2, helmet. Sarmatians: *Origo Constantini imperatoris* 2.3.

as Galerius had retreated from Italy, and a historian simply dismissed him as a "coward, not inclined to war."[41]

Maxentius' reign instead seemed to personify the ideals of an emperor as subsequently recommended by some of the panels in the frieze on the arch of Constantine. He was a civilian emperor who wore a toga, not a military emperor dressed in armor or a general's cloak. Not only did he not go out on campaigns, but inside Rome he did not even train as a soldier. "He did not pant in the Campus [Martius], and he did not practice with weapons." Maxentius' notion of a "military expedition" was to visit the luxurious Gardens of Sallust in a northern district of Rome, but still well inside the city's wall.[42]

Constantine's invasion hence exposed the inadequacy of Maxentius as a military commander and his limitations as an emperor at Rome. When Constantine entered northern Italy, Maxentius was still in Rome. His troops at Verona were being commanded instead by "very brave generals and a very tenacious prefect." As Constantine approached Rome, Maxentius' army at first prepared to fight "without an emperor." When Maxentius still remained inside the wall, the people mocked him as a "deserter." Constantine's invasion also forced Maxentius to choose his true capital, either Old Rome or his "New Rome" at his villa in the suburbs. A few days before the final battle Maxentius sent his family to safety "in a private residence." Because Constantine was approaching from the north, it would have been sensible to seek shelter in the emperor's villa south of the city. But as a result, "by leaving the palace" in Rome, Maxentius was thought to have "abdicated his imperial rule."[43]

Like most other emperors of late antiquity, in the end Maxentius too seemed to have abandoned Rome for an alternative imperial residence.

---

[41] Zosimus, *Historia nova* 2.12.2, North Africa, 14.1, Raetia, 2, prefect Rufius Volusianus. Aurelius Victor, *De Caesaribus* 40.18, prefect Rufius Volusianus, 20, "pavidus et imbellis." Galerius' retreat: Lactantius, *De mortibus persecutorum* 27.4.

[42] Campus, military expedition: *Panegyrici latini* 12(9).14.4.

[43] *Panegyrici latini* 12(9).8.1, generals, prefect, 16.5, private residence, abdicated rule, with *PLRE* 1:713, "Ruricius Pompeianus 8." Lactantius, *De mortibus persecutorum* 44.6, without, 7, deserter; also 44.1: initially Maxentius' troops against Constantine were commanded by "capable generals."

His attempt to make amends by facing his rival was no compensation. Finally he decided to emerge from behind the city's wall: "he marched out to battle dressed in armor." The Tiber now seemed to mark the northern boundary of his empire, and by crossing the river he was seemingly initiating his own campaign beyond a frontier. The only military battle Maxentius ever commanded in person was against Constantine in 312. That battle ended in disaster.[44]

FORGETTING MAXENTIUS

The Tiber was a river of oblivion. The bodies of executed criminals were dumped in the Tiber; so might be the bodies of disgraced or unpopular emperors. When the news of Tiberius' death was announced in 37, some witty residents of Rome shouted, "Tiberius to the Tiber!" Vitellius was executed in 69 and his corpse dragged into the Tiber; in 222, soldiers decapitated Elagabalus and dunked his body in sewers before throwing it in the Tiber. After the battle at the Milvian Bridge, Constantine's soldiers retrieved Maxentius' body from the river and paraded into Rome carrying his "wicked head" on a spear.[45]

Constantine himself was guilty of identity theft. With the approval of the senate he commandeered Maxentius' buildings and monuments at Rome. He may have confiscated his rival's estate in the suburbs to erect a statue of Claudius Gothicus, an earlier emperor whom he was advertising as an ancestor, on the center barrier of the circus. He also appropriated Maxentius' family. Fausta, Maxentius' sister and Constantine's wife, was blended into Constantine's dynasty of Flavian emperors with the official name of Flavia Maxima Fausta. After Eutropia, Maxentius' mother and Constantine's mother-in-law, supposedly announced

---

[44] In armor: *Panegyrici latini* 12(9).8.6. For the Tiber as a "frontier," note Procopius, *Bella* 5.19.2–3: during their siege of Rome in 537 the Ostrogoths worried that destruction of the Milvian Bridge would separate their encampments on the left bank "inside the river" from access to the right bank "outside the river as far as the [Mediterranean] sea."

[45] Suetonius, *Tiberius* 75.1, *Vitellius* 17.2. Elagabalus: Dio, *Historiae Romanae* 80.20.2, Herodian, *Historia* 5.8.8–9, SHA, *Antoninus Elagabalus* 33.7. Head and procession: *Panegyrici latini* 12(9).18.3, and Zosimus, *Historia nova* 2.17.1. In the panel on the arch of Constantine depicting the battle at the Milvian Bridge, Speidel (1986) 258, suggests that the soldier shown drowning in the river at the feet of Constantine was Maxentius himself.

that Maximian had not been Maxentius' father, Constantine rehabili-
tated Maximian, his father-in-law, as his own ancestor. Eutropia subsequently visited Palestine and recommended that Constantine construct
a church at an important biblical site. Maxentius had become emperor
with the support of his family's reputation; now his father, his mother,
and his sister had become props for Constantine's imperial rule. As a
son and a brother Maxentius had been disinherited.[46]

As an emperor he was also discarded. Once Maxentius had tried
to suppress a revolt in North Africa by sending a portrait of himself to Carthage; after the battle Constantine soon sent Maxentius'
head to Africa as proof that his rival's reign was over. According to a
panegyrist, people happily preferred this new image: "mighty Africa,
how you exulted!" A portrait marked the beginning of imperial rule;
the emperor's head marked the end. When he fell into the Tiber,
Maxentius lost his empire, his monuments, and his family. Now he
had been forgotten.[47]

In its own anonymous way Maxentius' reign nevertheless previewed
and contributed to some future trends at both Rome and Constantinople. At Rome his reign accelerated the increasing importance of the
suburbs. Long before Maxentius began to expand his villa complex,
Christians had been developing the same area along and near the
Appian Way. From the late second or early third century they had established new cemeteries and catacombs. Eventually they added shrines
and churches dedicated to martyrs and bishops. Even as Maxentius was
developing his estate as an alternative imperial residence, it was already
being surrounded by Christian sites. In fact, across from his estate on
the other side of the Appian Way a large church was constructed over
the catacombs, later known as the Church of St. Sebastian. The layout
of this church suggests that it was built in the first half of the fourth

---

[46] Statue in circus: Humphrey (1986) 286–87, 601, with Chapter 7, for Claudius as an ancestor
of Constantine. Denial of Maximian's paternity: *Panegyrici latini* 12(9).3.4, 4.3–4, *Epitome
de Caesaribus* 40.13, *Origo Constantini imperatoris* 4.12. Eutropia in Palestine: Eusebius, *Vita
Constantini* 3.52, with Van Dam (2007) 301–2.

[47] Portrait: Zosimus, *Historia nova* 2.12.1. Head in Africa: *Panegyrici latini* 4(10).32.6–8.

century and that it might be attributed to the initiative of Constantine himself. Maxentius' development of his suburban estate had previewed the support of Constantine and subsequent Christian emperors for suburban churches. In this perspective the unintended heirs of Maxentius' reign were the Christian community and the bishops of Rome.[48]

Maxentius' reign also marked the limits, even the end, of Republican emperorship. Subsequent emperors defined themselves instead as Christian emperors. The one conspicuous exception was, of course, Julian, who did appeal to the traditions of Rome during his civil war against Constantius. In a letter to the senate in 361 he censured his uncle Constantine as "an innovator and a disturber of ancient laws and traditional custom," and to restore "ancient law" he subsequently abolished some of Constantine's edicts. Like earlier emperors, he furthermore showed his respect for Rome by providing grain from his own resources, by making concessions to senators, and perhaps by aligning himself with the ancient cults of the capital. He even had Helena, his wife and Constantine's daughter, buried in Rome. One historian thought that Julian himself should subsequently have been buried in "the eternal city" next to "the monuments of earlier deified [emperors]." For a brief moment Julian was posing as a Republican emperor.[49]

On the other hand, Julian too never visited Rome. He seems to have promoted the traditions of the old capital simply as another way of annoying his Christian opponents. The guiding principles of his reign were instead his support for pagan cults and his devotion to Greek culture. After emerging as sole emperor, he visited Constantinople. As the new eastern capital, New Rome superficially resembled Old Rome, with its customary buildings and its own senate. One important

---

[48] See Spera (2003), for the development of "a new, Christianized panorama" along the Appian Way (p. 39). For the uncertainty over the dating of the Church of St. Sebastian, see Curran (2000) 97–99, with Nieddu (2009) 140–48, suggesting Constantine's reign.

[49] Ammianus Marcellinus, *Res gestae* 21.1.5, burial of Helena, 10.7–8, Julian's letter, 12.24–25, concessions, 25.10.5, Julian's fantasy burial. Ancient law: *CTh* 2.5.2, 3.1.3. Grain: *Panegyrici latini* 3(11).14.1–2. For cults, see Ehling (2001) 295: "In höherem Grade als seine unmittelbaren Vorgänger und Nachfolger hat sich Kaiser Julian um die römische Senatsaristokratie und die Stadt Rom bemüht."

difference, however, was its historical backstory. The new capital had no burdensome traditions inherited from Roman history or unrealistic expectations about the Republic to complicate or restrain emperors' behavior. New Rome could instead develop into a Christian capital, following the lead of Constantine, and a Greek capital, following the lead of Julian. At Constantinople eastern emperors could eventually act like Greek Christian emperors without even having to pretend to behave like Republican emperors.[50]

As an attempt to revive a traditional Republican emperorship and an earlier perspective on the centrality of Rome in the empire, Maxentius' reign was a dead end. But as a preview of various aspects of the future, his reign can claim some significance. The oddity, of course, is that his reign became prescient precisely because he was defeated. Without Constantine's victory at the Milvian Bridge, Maxentius' reign might not be so memorable.

[50] For Julian's preferences, see Van Dam (2002) 163–80, 195–202, (2007) 200–8; for the development of Greek Christian emperorship at Constantinople, see Van Dam (2010) 57–62.

BACK WORD:
THE BRIDGE

CHAPTER TEN

BEFORE THE BATTLE IN 312 THE MILVIAN BRIDGE HAD ALREADY been in use for more than five hundred years. The bridge was first attested in 207 B.C. when a crowd went out from Rome to greet messengers bringing news of a victory over a Carthaginian army in Italy. The recent construction of the Flaminian Way had no doubt increased traffic between Rome and northern Italy. This new highway was named after Gaius Flaminius, who had instigated its construction during his censorship in 220 B.C.; the "Mulvian" namesake behind the construction of the bridge is unknown. Over the centuries renovations were sometimes necessary for the bridge, organized under the Republic by magistrates such as the censors and subsequently by emperors such as Augustus.[1]

Two features distinguished the neighborhoods in this northern suburb around the bridge. One was the presence of large villas on both

[1] Victory over Hasdrubal: Livy, *Ab urbe condita* 27.51.2, with Messineo (2006), for a historical summary of the Milvian Bridge. Repairs of Marcus Aemilius Scaurus, censor in 109 B.C.: *De viris illustribus* 72.8, and Ammianus Marcellinus, *Res gestae* 27.3.9; for Augustus, see Chapter 7.

sides of the river. The other was a reputation for scandal and debauchery. Marcus Antonius once stopped to drink in a tavern at Saxa Rubra, north of the bridge. Nero enjoyed the nightlife in the vicinity of the bridge, where "he might indulge in lewd behavior more easily outside the city." From the bridge Wide Street ran in a straight line into the center of Rome. On this "Broadway" young men liked to show off by spinning the wheels of their chariots.[2]

The construction of the Aurelian Wall in the late third century left this district around the Milvian Bridge as a reception area on the outskirts of the city. The bridge marked a convenient staging point where delegations could greet dignitaries arriving from the north and escort them to the city center. After his victory Constantine entered Rome in the company of a "retinue of senators" who led his chariot through the "dense crowds of people." In 403 the emperor Honorius traveled from Ravenna on the Flaminian Way to visit Rome. When he reached the Tiber, presumably at the Milvian Bridge, he performed a libation of greeting. As he entered the capital, people stood on rooftops along the streets from the Milvian Bridge to the Palatine Hill. In 799, long after emperors had vanished in Italy, bishop Leo III returned after a trip to appeal for the assistance of the Frankish king Charlemagne in northern Gaul. Clerics, aristocrats, soldiers, and the people of Rome welcomed their bishop at the bridge with "spiritual hymns." Then they accompanied him, not downtown as in the past, but to a focal point of Christian Rome, the Church of St. Peter in the western suburbs.[3]

REMEMBERING THE BRIDGE

Before his invasion of Italy, Constantine had fought against the Franks and other peoples in northern Gaul. During his campaign he constructed a bridge across the Rhine linking Cologne with Deutz, a fort on the "barbarian" east bank. The construction of bridges had long

---

[2] Villas: Cicero, *Orat. in Catilinam* 3.2.5. Marcus Antonius: Cicero, *Orat. Philippicae* 2.31.77. Nero: Tacitus, *Annales* 13.47. Chariots: Juvenal, *Saturae* 1.58–62.
[3] Constantine's arrival: *Panegyrici latini* 12(9).19.1. Honorius: Claudian, *De sexto consulatu Honorii* 520, libation, 543–45, arrival. Leo III: *Liber pontificalis* 98.19.

been publicized as an important achievement of military operations along the Rhine and Danube frontiers. During his campaigns in Gaul during the mid-first century B.C., Julius Caesar had constructed two bridges across the Rhine "to terrorize the Germans." For his campaigns against the Dacians in the early second century, the emperor Trajan had built a lengthy stone bridge across the Danube, whose massive foundations were a permanent reminder that "human creativity could build anything." Bridges defined emperors. One of Trajan's contemporaries thought that an epic poem about the emperor's triumphs in his Dacian campaigns should certainly mention "the new bridges constructed over the rivers." In his later discussion of Christian emperors and the traditional priesthoods of Rome the historian Zosimus would revive an ancient etymology that associated *pontifex*, "priest," with *pons*, "bridge." As *pontifex maximus*, "highest priest," each emperor, including Christian emperors, could be imagined not only as the head of the priestly colleges but also as the "greatest bridge-builder." Bridging rivers had become a sign of success for both emperors and the Roman state.[4]

According to the dedicatory inscription at the fort in Deutz, Constantine himself had crossed the Rhine to supervise construction. In addition to its strategic utility, this garrison staked a symbolic claim to these territories across the Rhine, "as if they had already been appropriated for Roman rule." The bridge likewise was meant to confirm the permanence of Roman rule, with its "foundations of impressive bulk" providing a "reliable, stable footing." "By constructing this bridge at Cologne," an orator announced to Constantine, "you taunt the remnants of a damaged tribe." According to this panegyrist, Constantine's sturdy bridge was much more impressive than the temporary pontoon

---

[4] Barbarian: *Panegyrici latini* 6(7).13.2. Terrorize: Julius Caesar, *Bellum Gallicum* 4.19. Trajan's bridge: Dio, *Historiae Romanae* 68.13.5. Epic poem: Pliny the Younger, *Ep.* 8.4.2. Constantine was also credited with the construction of a stone bridge across the Danube: Aurelius Victor, *De Caesaribus* 41.18, and *Chronicon Paschale* s.a. 328. Etymology of *pontifex*: Zosimus, *Historia nova* 4.36, with Hallett (1970), for the transition in meaning from "bridge-builder" to "priest," and the discussion in Rüpke (2008) 61–65, including the evidence for Constantine as *pontifex maximus*.

bridges constructed by a Persian king long ago across the Hellespont and by the emperor Gaius across the bay of Baiae.[5]

In anticipation of Constantine's invasion Maxentius had constructed just such a pontoon bridge across the Tiber. His new bridge was presumably a tactical replacement for the Milvian Bridge. Denying access across the Milvian Bridge, perhaps by destroying a span, would have been too time consuming in the frenzy of battle, whereas a pontoon bridge could be easily cut loose. This stratagem backfired, however, as Maxentius was caught in his own trap. His pontoon bridge was most likely swept away too.

Why did Maxentius engage Constantine and his army in direct combat? Another strategy was available, and it had already proved its value. In previous years Maxentius had prevailed over invasions by rival emperors simply by remaining inside the massive wall of Rome. In 307 the emperor Severus had advanced "to the wall of the city." Then his troops defected, and he had to flee back to Ravenna. Later in 307 the emperor Galerius marched into Italy. He approached Rome supposedly with the intention of slaughtering the senate and people. But once he saw the enormity of the capital, he realized that his army was not large enough to enforce a siege. Because the soldiers were also upset about having to assault fellow Romans, Galerius soon retreated before his entire army could defect. As Constantine approached Rome in 312, Maxentius had already stockpiled supplies for a long siege. He could again have stayed safely inside the city's wall.[6]

Instead, he eventually emerged. Because Maxentius' decision to join his troops seems to have been unexpected, contemporaries were a bit puzzled about his motives. One orator concluded that a god had turned against him. Lactantius emphasized the discontent at Rome. The people were mocking Maxentius as a "deserter," and they seemed to be

---

[5] Dedication: *ILS* 2.1:xxiv, no. 8937 = Grünewald (1990) 183, no. 15, with Grünewald (1989) 174, discussing the survival of the dedication. As if: Ammianus Marcellinus, *Res gestae* 29.6.2, commenting on Valentinian's garrison across the Danube. *Panegyrici latini* 6(7).13.1, constructing, 3, foundations, 4, other bridges.

[6] Lactantius, *De mortibus persecutorum* 26.8–11, Severus, 27.2–8, Galerius. Preparation for siege: *Panegyrici latini* 12(9).16.1.

shifting their support to his rival: "in unison the people shouted that Constantine could not be conquered." In addition, the senators who inspected the Sibylline books offered what Maxentius understood to be a favorable oracle. So he marched out to the battle. After he crossed the Tiber, "the bridge was severed behind him."[7]

A famous episode in Roman historical mythology may also have influenced Maxentius. Long ago at the end of the sixth century B.C. an ally of the last king of Rome had been prevented from entering the city by the stubborn defiance of a single Roman soldier. According to legend, first with a few companions, then single-handedly, Horatius Cocles had defended the Sublician Bridge. Once his comrades had destroyed the bridge behind him, Horatius jumped into the Tiber and swam to safety. Through his heroism he had saved the new Republic. In his honor the people erected a statue, located adjacent to the Forum. This statue of Horatius remained on view for centuries.[8]

During the late Republic and the early empire the valor of Horatius was a standard archetype. In one of his philosophical treatises Cicero hailed Horatius as an exemplar of courage. In his great epic poem about the founding of the Roman state, Virgil included the moment when "[Horatius] Cocles dared to cut the bridge" as one important episode in a short summary of "Italian affairs and the triumphs of Romans." The poet Propertius cited Horatius' defense of the bridge to reassure the people of Rome about their security: "the gods built these walls, and the gods are also defending them."[9]

The legend of Horatius lived on in late antiquity. In 313 an orator referenced Horatius in a panegyric before Constantine. A fourth-century compilation of biographies of great heroes from the Republic and empire summarized the story and mentioned the statue. In the early

[7] God: *Panegyrici latini* 4(10).28.1. Lactantius, *De mortibus persecutorum* 44.7, deserter, in unison, 9, bridge.

[8] Horatius at the bridge, statue in Comitium: Livy, *Ab urbe condita* 2.10. Statue: Pliny the Elder, *Historia naturalis* 34.11.22.

[9] Cicero, *De officiis* 1.18.61. Virgil, *Aeneis* 8.626, Italian affairs, 650, bridge. Propertius, *Elegi* 3.11.63, bridge, 65, walls, with Roller (2004) 10–28, on Horatius as a model for imitation during the late Republic and early empire.

fifth century a poet compared a recent victory over a Visigothic army in northern Italy to Horatius' defense of Rome: "he crossed the Tiber [while carrying] the shield with which he had protected the city."[10]

During his reign Maxentius had represented himself as the defender of Rome, "his city." Perhaps it is possible to imagine that at a moment of crisis he had looked for inspiration to the legends about the foundation of the city and the establishment of the Republic. Because he and Constantine were brothers-in-law, their imminent confrontation would be a replay of the quarrel between the brothers Romulus and Remus over the foundation of Rome. By defeating Constantine, Maxentius would confirm his reputation as the new founder of the city. In the process, he could in addition become the new savior of the Republic. He would be the new Horatius defending another bridge. Remembering history may have contributed to Maxentius' defeat at the battle of the Milvian Bridge.

---

[10] Reference: *Panegyrici latini* 12(9).18.2. Summary: *De viris illustribus* 11, with Schmidt (1989a), for the date of the treatise. Shield: Claudian, *De sexto consulatu Honorii* 486.

EDITIONS AND TRANSLATIONS

※ ※ ※

In this book all translations from Greek and Latin texts are by the author. In this list of editions and translations, full references for books already cited in the notes are in the Bibliography.

Ambrose, *De obitu Theodosii*: ed. O. Faller, *Sancti Ambrosii opera: Pars septima*. CSEL 73 (1955), pp. 371–401 – tr. J. H. W. G. Liebeschuetz and C. Hill, *Ambrose of Milan: Political Letters and Speeches*. TTH 43 (2005), pp. 177–203.

Ambrosiaster, *Quaestiones veteris et novi testamenti*: ed. A. Souter, *Pseudo-Augustini Quaestiones veteris et novi testamenti cxxvii. Accedit appendix continens alterius editionis quaestiones selectas*. CSEL 50 (1908).

Ammianus Marcellinus, *Res gestae*: ed. and tr. J. C. Rolfe, *Ammianus Marcellinus*, 3 vols. LCL (1935–1940).

Anonymus post Dionem (= Dio Continuatus), *Fragmenta*: ed. and tr. [Latin] Müller (1851), pp. 192–99.

Anonymus Valesianus, Pars posterior: ed. and tr. J. C. Rolfe, *Ammianus Marcellinus*, Vol. 3. LCL (1939), pp. 530–69.

Anthologia graeca: ed. and tr. W. R. Paton, *The Greek Anthology*, 5 vols. LCL (1916–1918).

Athanasius, *Apologia contra Arianos, De decretis Nicaenae synodi, De synodis Arimini in Italia et Seleuciae in Isauria*: ed. H.-G. Opitz, *Athanasius Werke 2.1: Die Apologien* (Berlin and Leipzig, 1935–1941), pp. 1–45, 87–168, 231–78 – tr. A. Robertson, *Select Writings and Letters of Athanasius, Bishop of Alexandria*. NPNF, Second series 4 (1892; reprinted 1991).

Augustine –

De civitate Dei: ed. B. Dombart and A. Kalb, *Sancti Aurelii Augustini De civitate Dei*, 2 vols. CChr., Series latina 47–48 (1955) – tr. H. Bettenson, *Augustine: Concerning the City of God against the Pagans* (Harmondsworth, 1967).

Epistulae: ed. A. Goldbacher, *S. Aureli Augustini Hipponiensis episcopi epistulae*. CSEL 34.1–2, 44, 57–58 (1895–1923) – tr. J. G. Cunningham, in *The Confessions and Letters of St. Augustin, with a Sketch of His Life and Works*, ed. P. Schaff. NPNF 1 (1892), pp. 219–593.

Augustus, *Res gestae*: ed. and tr. Cooley (2009), pp. 58–101.

Aurelius Victor, *De Caesaribus*: ed. F. Pichlmayr and R. Gruendel, *Sexti Aurelii Victoris Liber de Caesaribus*. Teubner (1970), pp. 77–129 – tr. H. W. Bird, *Liber de Caesaribus of Sextus Aurelius Victor*. TTH 17 (1994).

Ausonius, *Gratiarum actio, Mosella*: ed. and tr. H. G. Evelyn White, *Ausonius*, 2 vols. LCL (1919–1921).

Cassiodorus –

Chronica: ed. T. Mommsen, *Chronica minora saec. IV. V. VI. VII*, Vol. 2. MGH, Auctores antiquissimi 11 (1894), pp. 120–61.

Variae: ed. T. Mommsen, *Cassiodori Senatoris Variae*. MGH, Auctores antiquissimi 12 (1894), pp. 1–385 – selection tr. S. J. B. Barnish, *The* Variae *of Magnus Aurelius Cassiodorus Senator*. TTH 12 (1992).

Chronicon Paschale: ed. L. Dindorf, *Chronicon Paschale ad exemplar Vaticanum*, Vol. 1. Corpus Scriptorum Historiae Byzantinae (Bonn, 1832) – tr. Mi. Whitby and Ma. Whitby, *Chronicon Paschale 284–628 AD*. TTH 7 (1989).

Chronographer of 354, *Chronica urbis Romae*: ed. Mommsen (1892), pp. 143–48.

Cicero –

De officiis: ed. and tr. W. Miller, *Cicero, De officiis*. LCL (1913).

Orationes in Catilinam: ed. A. C. Clark, tr. C. Macdonald, *Cicero, In Catilinam I–IV, Pro Murena, Pro Sulla, Pro Flacco*. LCL (1977), pp. 32–165.

Orationes Philippicae: ed. and tr. D. R. Shackleton Bailey, rev. J. T. Ramsey and G. Manuwald, *Cicero, Philippics*, 2 vols. LCL (2009).

Claudian, *De sexto consulatu Honorii*: ed. and tr. M. Platnauer, *Claudian*, Vol. 2. LCL (1922), pp. 70–123.

Collectio Avellana: ed. O. Guenther, *Epistulae imperatorum pontificum aliorum inde ab a.CCCLXVI usque ad a.DLIII datae Avellana quae dicitur collectio*, 2 vols. CSEL 35.1–2 (1895–1898).

Constantine –

Epistula [ad Porfyrium]: ed. Polara (1973), Vol. 1, pp. 4–6.

Oratio ad sanctorum coetum: ed. I. A. Heikel, *Eusebius Werke 1: Über das Leben Constantins. Constantins Rede an die heilige Versammlung. Tricennatsrede an Constantin*. GCS 7 (1902), pp. 154–92 – tr. Edwards (2003), pp. 1–62.

Constitutum Constantini: ed. Fuhrmann (1968), pp. 55–98 – tr. Edwards (2003), pp. 92–115.

Consultatio veteris cuiusdam iurisconsulti: ed. J. Baviera, *Fontes iuris Romani antejustiniani, Pars altera: Auctores* (Florence, 1940), pp. 594–613.

Corippus, *In laudem Iustini*: ed. and tr. Av. Cameron, *Flavius Cresconius Corippus, In laudem Iustini Augusti minoris libri IV* (London, 1976).

CTh = Codex Theodosianus: ed. T. Mommsen, *Codex Theodosianus 1.2: Theodosiani libri XVI cum Constitutionibus Sirmondianis* (Berlin, 1905) – tr. C. Pharr et al., *The Theodosian Code and Novels and the Sirmondian Constitutions* (1952; reprinted Westport, Conn., 1969), pp. 3–486.

Cyril of Jerusalem, *Epistula ad Constantium*: ed. E. Bihain, "L'épître de Cyrille de Jérusalem à Constance sur la vision de la Croix (BHG³ 413): Tradition manuscrite et édition critique." *Byzantion* 43 (1973), pp. 286–91.

De viris illustribus: ed. F. Pichlmayr and R. Gruendel, *Sexti Aurelii Victoris Liber de Caesaribus*. Teubner (1970), pp. 25–74.

Dio, *Historiae Romanae*: ed. and tr. E. Cary, *Dio's Roman History*, 9 vols. LCL (1914– 1927).

Epistulae Theodericianae variae: ed. T. Mommsen, *Cassiodori Senatoris Variae*. MGH, Auctores antiquissimi 12 (1894), pp. 389–92.

Epitome de Caesaribus: ed. F. Pichlmayr and R. Gruendel, *Sexti Aurelii Victoris Liber de Caesaribus*. Teubner (1970), pp. 133–76.

Eunapius –

Fragmenta historica: ed. and tr. Blockley (1981–1983), Vol. 2, pp. 6–127.

Vitae sophistarum: ed. and tr. W. C. Wright, *Philostratus and Eunapius: The Lives of the Sophists*. LCL (1921), pp. 342–565.

Eusebius of Caesarea –

De laudibus Constantini: ed. I. A. Heikel, *Eusebius Werke 1: Über das Leben Constantins. Constantins Rede an die heilige Versammlung. Tricennatsrede an Constantin*. GCS 7 (1902), pp. 195–259 – tr. Drake (1976), pp. 83–127.

HE = Historia ecclesiastica: ed. E. Schwartz, in Schwartz and Mommsen (1903– 1909), Vols. 1–2 – tr. K. Lake, J. E. L. Oulton, and H. J. Lawlor, *Eusebius: The Ecclesiastical History*, 2 vols. LCL (1926–1932).

Vita Constantini: ed. Winkelmann (1991) – tr. Cameron and Hall (1999).

Eutropius, *Breviarium*: ed. H. Droysen, *Eutropi Breviarium ab urbe condita cum versionibus graecis et Pauli Landolfique additamentis*. MGH, Auctores antiquissimi 2 (1879) – tr. H. W. Bird, *Eutropius: Breviarium*. TTH 14 (1993).

Evagrius, *HE = Historia ecclesiastica*: ed. J. Bidez and L. Parmentier, *The Ecclesiastical History of Evagrius with the Scholia* (London, 1898) – tr. Whitby (2000).

Fasti Furii Filocali: ed. Degrassi (1963), pp. 238–61.

Firmicus Maternus, *Mathesis*: ed. W. Kroll and F. Skutsch, *Iulii Firmici Materni Matheseos libri VIII*, 2 vols. Teubner (1897–1913) – ed. and tr. [French] P. Monat, *Firmicus Maternus, Mathesis*, 3 vols. Budé (2nd ed. 2002–2003).

[Gelasius of Cyzicus,] *HE = Historia ecclesiastica*: ed. G. C. Hansen, *Anonyme Kirchengeschichte (Gelasius Cyzicenus, CPG 6034)*. GCS, Neue Folge 9 (2002).

Gregory of Nyssa, *Vita Macrinae*: ed. V. W. Callahan, in *Gregorii Nysseni opera ascetica*. Gregorii Nysseni opera 8.1 (Leiden, 1952), pp. 370–414 – tr. V. W. Callahan, *Saint Gregory of Nyssa: Ascetical Works*. FC 58 (1967), pp. 163–91 – ed. and tr. [French] P. Maraval, *Grégoire de Nysse: Vie de sainte Macrine*. SChr. 178 (1971).

Gregory of Tours, *Historiae*: ed. B. Krusch and W. Levison, *Gregorii episcopi Turonensis libri historiarum X*. MGH, Scriptores rerum Merovingicarum 1.1, 2nd ed. (1937– 1951) – tr. O. M. Dalton, *The History of the Franks by Gregory of Tours* (Oxford, 1927), Vol. 2.

Herodian, *Historiae*: ed. and tr. C. R. Whittaker, *Herodian*, 2 vols. LCL (1969–1970).
Jerome –
  Chronicon: ed. R. Helm, *Eusebius Werke 7: Die Chronik des Hieronymus: Hieronymi Chronicon*, 2nd ed. GCS 47 (1956) – *Chron.* s.a. 327 to end: tr. M. D. Donalson, *A Translation of Jerome's* Chronicon *with Historical Commentary* (Lewiston, 1996), pp. 39–57.
  De viris illustribus: ed. E. C. Richardson, *Hieronymus, Liber de viris inlustribus. Gennadius, Liber de viris inlustribus.* Texte und Untersuchungen zur Geschichte der altchristlichen Literatur 14.1 (Leipzig, 1896), pp. 1–56 – tr. T. P. Halton, *Saint Jerome, On Illustrious Men.* FC 100 (1999).
  Epistulae: ed. I. Hilberg, *Sancti Eusebii Hieronymi epistulae*, 3 vols. CSEL 54–56 (1910–1918) – ed. and tr. [French] J. Labourt, *Jérôme: Correspondance*, 8 vols. Budé (1949–1963) – selection tr. W. H. Fremantle, *St. Jerome: Letters and Select Works.* NPNF, Second series 6 (1892; reprinted 1954), pp. 1–295.
John Malalas, *Chronographia*: ed. J. Thurn, *Ioannis Malalae Chronographia.* Corpus Fontium Historiae Byzantinae 35, Series Berolinensis (Berlin, 2000) – tr. Jeffreys, Jeffreys, and Scott (1986).
Julian, *Caesares, Contra Galilaeos, Epistula ad Athenienses, Epistulae*: ed. and tr. W. C. Wright, *The Works of the Emperor Julian*, 3 vols. LCL (1913–1923).
Julius Caesar, *Bellum Gallicum*: ed. and tr. H. J. Edwards, *Caesar, The Gallic War.* LCL (1917).
Juvenal, *Saturae*: ed. and tr. G. G. Ramsay, *Juvenal and Persius.* LCL (1918), pp. 2–307.
Lactantius –
  De mortibus persecutorum: ed. and tr. Creed (1984).
  De opificio Dei: ed. S. Brandt, *L. Caeli Firmiani Lactanti opera omnia, Partis II Fasciculus I: Libri de opificio Dei et de ira Dei, Carmina fragmenta, Vetera de Lactantio testimonia.* CSEL 27.1 (1893), pp. 3–64 – ed. and tr. [French] M. Perrin, *Lactance, L'ouvrage du Dieu créateur*, 2 vols. SChr. 213–214 (1974).
  Epitome divinarum institutionum: ed. S. Brandt, *L. Caeli Firmiani Lactanti opera omnia, Pars I: Divinae Institutiones et Epitome divinarum institutionum.* CSEL 19 (1890), pp. 675–761 – ed. and tr. [French] M. Perrin, *Lactance, Épitomé des institutions divines.* SChr. 335 (1987).
  Institutiones divinae: ed. S. Brandt, *L. Caeli Firmiani Lactanti opera omnia, Pars I: Divinae Institutiones et Epitome divinarum institutionum.* CSEL 19 (1890), pp. 1–672 – *Institutiones divinae* 1–2, 4–5: ed. and tr. [French] P. Monat, *Lactance, Institutions Divines.* SChr. 204–205, 326, 337, 377 (1973–1992) – tr. A. Bowen and P. Garnsey, *Lactantius: Divine Institutes.* TTH 40 (2003).
Libanius, *Orationes*: ed. R. Foerster, *Libanii opera*, Vols. 1–4. Teubner (1903–1908) – *Orat.* 1: ed. and tr. A. F. Norman, *Libanius: Autobiography and Selected Letters*,

Vol. 1. LCL (1992), pp. 52–337 – selection ed. and tr. A. F. Norman, *Libanius: Selected Works*, 2 vols. LCL (1969–1977) – selection tr. A. F. Norman, *Antioch as a Centre of Hellenic Culture as Observed by Libanius.* TTH 34 (2000) – *Orat.* 59: tr. M. H. Dodgeon, in Lieu and Montserrat (1996), pp. 164–205.

Liber pontificalis: ed. L. Duchesne, *Le Liber Pontificalis: Texte, introduction et commentaire*, Vol. 1. Bibliothèque des Ecoles françaises d'Athènes et de Rome, 2ᵉ série (Paris, 1886) – tr. Davis (2000).

Livy, *Ab urbe condita*: ed. and tr. B. O. Foster et al., *Livy*, 14 vols. LCL (1919–1959).

Martial, *Epigrammata*: ed. and tr. D. R. Shackleton Bailey, *Martial: Epigrams*, 3 vols. LCL (1993).

Nicholas Mesarites, *Ecphrasis*: ed. and tr. G. Downey, "Nikolaos Mesarites, Description of the Church of the Holy Apostles at Constantinople: Greek Text Edited with Translation, Commentary and Introduction." *Transactions of the American Philosophical Society* n.s. 47, no. 6 (1957), pp. 861–918.

Notitia Dignitatum: ed. O. Seeck, *Notitia Dignitatum accedunt Notitia urbis Constantinopolitanae et Laterculi provinciarum* (Berlin, 1876), pp. 1–225.

Optatus –
  Appendix: ed. C. Ziwsa, *S. Optati Milevitani libri VII.* CSEL 26 (1893), pp. 185–216 – tr. M. Edwards, *Optatus: Against the Donatists.* TTH 27 (1997), pp. 150–201.
  Contra Donatistas: ed. C. Ziwsa, *S. Optati Milevitani libri VII.* CSEL 26 (1893), pp. 1–182 – ed. and tr. [French] M. Labrousse, *Optat de Milève, Traité contre les Donatistes*, 2 vols. SChr. 412–413 (1995–1996) – tr. M. Edwards, *Optatus: Against the Donatists.* TTH 27 (1997), pp. 1–149.

Origo Constantini imperatoris (= *Anonymus Valesianus*, Pars prior): ed. and tr. J. C. Rolfe, *Ammianus Marcellinus*, Vol. 3. LCL (1939), pp. 508–31 – tr. J. Stevenson, in Lieu and Montserrat (1996), pp. 43–48.

Panegyrici latini: ed. and tr. [French] E. Galletier, *Panégyriques latins*, 3 vols. Budé (1949–1955) – ed. R. A. B. Mynors, *XII Panegyrici latini.* OCT (1964) – tr. Nixon and Rodgers (1994), pp. 41–516.

Parastaseis syntomoi chronikai: ed. T. Preger, *Scriptores originum Constantinopolitanarum*, Vol. 1. Teubner (1901), pp. 19–73 – tr. Cameron and Herrin (1984), pp. 56–165.

Paul the Deacon –
  Historia Langobardorum: ed. L. Bethmann and G. Waitz, "Pauli Historia Langobardorum." MGH, Scriptores rerum Langobardicarum et Italicarum saec. VI–IX (1878), pp. 45–187 – tr. W. D. Foulke, *Paul the Deacon, History of the Lombards* (1907; reprinted Philadelphia, 1974).
  Historia Romana: ed. H. Droysen, *Eutropi Breviarium ab urbe condita cum versionibus graecis et Pauli Landolfique additamentis.* MGH, Auctores antiquissimi 2 (1879), pp. 183–224.

Paulinus of Nola, *Epistulae*: ed. G. de Hartel, *Sancti Pontii Meropii Paulini Nolani epistulae*. CSEL 29 (1894) – tr. P. G. Walsh, *Letters of St. Paulinus of Nola*, 2 vols. ACW 35–36 (1966–1967).

Peter the Patrician, *Fragmenta*: ed. and tr. [Latin] Müller (1851), pp. 184–91.

Philostorgius, *HE*: ed. J. Bidez, *Philostorgius Kirchengeschichte: Mit dem Leben des Lucian von Antiochien und den Fragmenten eines arianischen Historiographen*. GCS 21 (1913); Second edition rev. F. Winkelmann. GCS (1972), Third edition (1981) – tr. P. R. Amidon, *Philostorgius, Church History*. Society of Biblical Literature, Writings from the Greco-Roman World 23 (Atlanta, 2007).

Photius, *Bibliotheca*: ed. and tr. [French] R. Henry, *Photius: Bibliothèque*, 8 vols., and Index, ed. J. Schamp. Budé (1959–1991).

Pliny the Elder, *Historia naturalis*: ed. and tr. H. Rackham, W. H. S. Jones, and D. E. Eichholz, *Pliny: Natural History*, 10 vols. LCL (1938–1963).

Pliny the Younger, *Epistulae*: ed. and tr. B. Radice, *Pliny: Letters and Panegyricus*, 2 vols. LCL (1969).

Polemius Silvius, *Laterculus*: ed. Mommsen (1892), pp. 518–23, 535–51.

Porfyrius –
   Carmina: ed. Polara (1973), Vol. 1, pp. 7–121.
   Epistula [ad Constantinum]: ed. Polara (1973), Vol. 1, pp. 1–3.

Procopius, *Bella*: ed. and tr. H. B. Dewing, *Procopius*, Vols. 1–5. LCL (1914–1928).

Propertius, *Elegi*: ed. and tr. G. P. Goold, *Propertius, Elegies*. LCL (1990).

Prudentius, *Contra orationem Symmachi, Peristephanon*: ed. and tr. H. J. Thomson, *Prudentius*, 2 vols. LCL (1949–1953).

Rufinus, *HE = Historia ecclesiastica*: ed. T. Mommsen, in Schwartz and Mommsen (1903–1909), Vols. 1–2 – *HE* 10–11: tr. P. Amidon, The Church History *of Rufinus of Aquileia: Books 10 and 11* (New York, 1997).

SHA = Scriptores Historiae Augustae, *Antoninus Elagabalus, Divus Claudius, Severus, Severus Alexander, Tyranni triginta*: ed. and tr. D. Magie, *The Scriptores Historiae Augustae*, 3 vols. LCL (1921–1932).

Sidonius, *Epistulae*: ed. and tr. W. B. Anderson, *Sidonius: Poems and Letters*, 2 vols. LCL (1936–1965).

Socrates, *HE = Historia ecclesiastica*: ed. G. C. Hansen, with M. Sirinian, *Sokrates: Kirchengeschichte*. GCS, Neue Folge 1 (1995) – tr. A. C. Zenos, in *Socrates, Sozomenus: Church Histories*. NPNF, Second series 2 (1890; reprinted 1973), pp. 1–178.

Sozomen, *HE = Historia ecclesiastica*: ed. J. Bidez, *Sozomenus: Kirchengeschichte*. GCS 50 (1960); rev. G. C. Hansen. GCS, Neue Folge 4 (2nd ed. 1995) – tr. C. D. Hartranft, in *Socrates, Sozomenus: Church Histories*. NPNF, Second series 2 (1890; reprinted 1973), pp. 236–427.

Strabo, *Geographia*: ed. and tr. H. L. Jones, *The Geography of Strabo*, 8 vols. LCL (1917–1932).

Suda: ed. A. Adler, *Suidae Lexicon*, 5 vols. Lexicographi Graeci 1. Teubner (1928–1938).

Suetonius, *Augustus, Tiberius, Vitellius*: ed. and tr. J. C. Rolfe, *Suetonius*, 2 vols. LCL (1914).

Symmachus –
   Epistulae: ed. O. Seeck, *Aurelii Symmachi quae supersunt*. MGH, Auctores antiquissimi 6.1 (1883), pp. 1–278 – *Ep.* 1–10: ed. and tr. [French] J. P. Callu, *Symmaque: Lettres*, 4 vols. Budé (1972–2002).
   Relationes: ed. O. Seeck, *Aurelii Symmachi quae supersunt*. MGH, Auctores antiquissimi 6.1 (1883), pp. 279–317 – ed. and tr. R. H. Barrow, *Prefect and Emperor: The Relationes of Symmachus A.D. 384* (Oxford, 1973).

Tacitus –
   Annales: ed. C. D. Fisher, *Cornelii Taciti Annalium ab excessu divi Augusti libri*. OCT (1906) – tr. M. Grant, *Tacitus: The Annals of Imperial Rome* (Harmondsworth, rev. ed. 1977).
   Historiae: ed. C. D. Fisher, *Cornelii Taciti Historiarum libri*. OCT (1911) – tr. K. Wellesley, *Tacitus: The Histories* (Harmondsworth, 1964).

Themistius, *Orationes*: ed. G. Downey and A. F. Norman, *Themistii orationes quae supersunt*, 2 vols. Teubner (1965–1971) – selection tr. P. Heather and D. Moncur, *Politics, Philosophy, and Empire in the Fourth Century: Select Orations of Themistius*. TTH 36 (2001).

Theodoret, *HE = Historia ecclesiastica*: ed. L. Parmentier, *Theodoret: Kirchengeschichte*. GCS 19 (1911); Second edition rev. F. Scheidweiler. GCS 44 (1954); Third edition rev. G. C. Hansen. GCS, Neue Folge 5 (1998) – tr. B. Jackson, in *Theodoret, Jerome, Gennadius, Rufinus: Historical Writings, Etc.* NPNF, Second series 3 (1892; reprinted 1989), pp. 33–159 – ed. J. Bouffartique, A. Martin, L. Pietri, and F. Thelamon, tr. [French] P. Canivet, *Théodoret de Cyr, Histoire ecclésiastique*, 2 vols. SChr. 501, 530 (2006–2009).

Theophanes, *Chronographia*: ed. C. de Boor, *Theophanis Chronographia*, Vol. 1 (Leipzig, 1883) – tr. C. Mango and R. Scott, with G. Greatrex, *The Chronicle of Theophanes Confessor: Byzantine and Near Eastern History A.D. 284–813* (Oxford, 1997).

Urkunde(n): ed. H.-G. Opitz, *Athanasius Werke 3.1: Urkunden zur Geschichte des arianischen Streites 318–328* (Berlin and Leipzig, 1934–1935).

Virgil, *Aeneis*: ed. and tr. H. R. Fairclough, rev. G. P. Goold, *Virgil, Eclogues, Georgics, Aeneid, Appendix Vergiliana*, 2 vols. LCL (1999–2000).

Zonaras, *Annales*: ed. L. Dindorf, *Ioannis Zonarae Epitome historiarum*, 6 vols. Teubner (1868–1875) – selection tr. T. M. Banchich and E. N. Lane, *The History of Zonaras*

from Alexander Severus to the Death of Theodosius the Great. Routledge Classical
Translations (London, 2009).
Zosimus, *Historia nova*: ed. L. Mendelssohn, *Zosimi comitis et exadvocati fisci historia
nova.* Teubner (1887) – ed. and tr. [French] Paschoud (1979–2000) – tr. R. T. Ridley,
Zosimus, New History: A Translation with Commentary. Byzantina Australiensia 2
(Canberra, 1982).

BIBLIOGRAPHY

✤ ✤ ✤

Abdy, R. (2006). "In the Pay of the Emperor: Coins from the Beaurains (Arras) Treasure." In *Constantine the Great: York's Roman Emperor*, ed. E. Hartley, J. Hawkes, and M. Henig, with F. Mee, pp. 52–58. York.

Adler, W. (2008). "Early Christian Historians and Historiography." In *The Oxford Handbook of Early Christian Studies*, ed. S. A. Harvey and D. G. Hunter, pp. 584–602. Oxford.

Alcock, S. E. (2001). "The Reconfiguration of Memory in the Eastern Roman Empire." In *Empires: Perspectives from Archaeology and History*, ed. S. E. Alcock, T. N. D'Altroy, K. D. Morrison, and C. M. Sinopoli, pp. 323–50. Cambridge.

Alföldi, A. (1932). "The Helmet of Constantine with the Christian Monogram." *Journal of Roman Studies* 22:9–23.

———. (1947). "On the Foundation of Constantinople: A Few Notes." *Journal of Roman Studies* 37:10–16.

———. (1948). *The Conversion of Constantine and Pagan Rome*, tr. H. Mattingly. Oxford.

Amerise, M. (2008). "Das Bild Konstantins des Großen in der *Bibliothéke* des Photios." In *Konstantin der Grosse: Das Bild des Kaisers im Wandel der Zeiten*, ed. A. Goltz and H. Schlange-Schöningen, pp. 23–34. Beihefte zum Archiv für Kulturgeschichte 66. Cologne.

Amici, A. (2000). "*Divus Constantinus*: Le testimonianze epigrafiche." *Rivista storica dell'antichità* 30:187–216.

Amis, M. (1991). *Time's Arrow, or The Nature of the Offence*. London.

Arnold, J. J. (2008). "Theoderic, the Goths, and the Restoration of the Roman Empire." Ph.D. Dissertation, Department of History, University of Michigan.

Ashby, T., and R. A. L. Fell (1921). "The Via Flaminia." *Journal of Roman Studies* 11:125–90.

Athanassiadi, P. (1981). *Julian and Hellenism: An Intellectual Biography*. Oxford.

Barnes, T. D. (1973). "Lactantius and Constantine." *Journal of Roman Studies* 63:29–46. Reprinted in T. D. Barnes, *Early Christianity and the Roman Empire*, Chapter 6. London, 1984.

———. (1975a). "Publilius Optatianus Porfyrius." *American Journal of Philology* 96:173–86. Reprinted in T. D. Barnes, *Early Christianity and the Roman Empire*, Chapter 10. London, 1984.

———. (1975b). "Two Senators under Constantine." *Journal of Roman Studies* 64:40–49. Reprinted in T. D. Barnes, *Early Christianity and the Roman Empire*, Chapter 9. London, 1984.

————. (1980). "The Editions of Eusebius' *Ecclesiastical History.*" *Greek, Roman and Byzantine Studies* 21:191–201. Reprinted in T. D. Barnes, *Early Christianity and the Roman Empire*, Chapter 20. London, 1984.

————. (1981). *Constantine and Eusebius.* Cambridge, Mass.

————. (1982). *The New Empire of Diocletian and Constantine.* Cambridge, Mass.

Bastien, P. (1992–1994). *Le buste monétaire des empereurs romains*, 3 vols. Numismatique romaine, Essais, recherches et documents 19. Wetteren.

Bauer, F. A., and M. Heinzelmann (1999). "The Constantinian Bishop's Church at Ostia: Preliminary Report on the 1998 Season." *Journal of Roman Archaeology* 12:342–53.

Baynes, N. H. (1931). *Constantine the Great and the Christian Church.* The British Academy: The Raleigh Lecture on History 1929. London.

Beacham, R. C. (1999). *Spectacle Entertainments of Early Imperial Rome.* New Haven, Conn.

————. (2005). "The Emperor as Impresario: Producing the Pageantry of Power." In *The Cambridge Companion to the Age of Augustus*, ed. K. Galinsky, pp. 151–74. Cambridge.

Beard, M., J. North, and S. Price (1998). *Religions of Rome*, 2 vols. Cambridge.

Berger, A. (2008). "Legitimation und Legenden: Konstantin der Große und sein Bild in Byzanz." In *Konstantin der Grosse: Das Bild des Kaisers im Wandel der Zeiten*, ed. A. Goltz and H. Schlange-Schöningen, pp. 5–21. Beihefte zum Archiv für Kulturgeschichte 66. Cologne.

Bleckmann, B. (1992). "Pagane Visionen Konstantins in der Chronik des Johannes Zonaras." In *Costantino il Grande dall'antichità all'umanesimo: Colloquio sul Cristianesimo nel mondo antico. Macerata 18–20 Dicembre 1990*, ed. G. Bonamente and F. Fusco, Vol. 1:151–70. Macerata.

————. (2004). "Bemerkungen zum Scheitern des Mehrherrschaftssystems: Reichsteilung und Territorialanspruche." In *Diokletian und die Tetrarchie: Aspekte einer Zeitenwende*, ed. A. Demandt, A. Goltz, and H. Schlange-Schöningen, pp. 74–94. Millennium-Studien zu Kultur und Geschichte des ersten Jahrtausends n. Chr. 1. Berlin.

————. (2006). "Späte historiographische Quellen zu Konstantin dem Grossen: Überblick und Fragestellungen." In *Konstantin der Grosse: Geschichte-Archäologie-Rezeption*, ed. A. Demandt and J. Engemann, pp. 21–30. Schriftenreihe des Rheinischen Landesmuseums Trier 32. Trier.

————. (2007). "Einleitung." In H. Schneider (tr.), *Eusebius von Caesarea, De vita Constantini: Über das Leben Konstantins*, pp. 7–106. Fontes Christiani 83. Turnhout.

Blockley, R. C. (1981–1983). *The Fragmentary Classicising Historians of the Later Roman Empire: Eunapius, Olympiodorus, Priscus and Malchus*, 2 vols. ARCA Classical and Medieval Texts, Papers and Monographs 6, 10. Liverpool.

de Boor, C., ed. (1978). *Georgii Monachi Chronicon*, 2 vols. Corrected edition edited by P. Wirth. Teubner. Stuttgart.

Bowersock, G. W. (2005). "Peter and Constantine." In *St. Peter's in the Vatican*, ed. W. Tronzo, pp. 5–15. Cambridge.

Bowes, K. (2008). *Private Worship, Public Values, and Religious Change in Late Antiquity.* Cambridge.

Brown, T. S. (1995). "Byzantine Italy, *c.* 680-*c.* 876." In *The New Cambridge Medieval History, Volume II c. 700–c. 900*, ed. R. McKitterick, pp. 320–48. Cambridge.

Brubaker, L. (1994). "To Legitimize an Emperor: Constantine and Visual Authority in the Eighth and Ninth Centuries." In *New Constantines: The Rhythm of Imperial Renewal in Byzantium, 4th–13th Centuries. Papers from the Twenty-Sixth Spring Symposium of Byzantine Studies, St Andrews, March 1992*, ed. P. Magdalino, pp. 139–58. Society for the Promotion of Byzantine Studies, Publications 2. Aldershot.

Bruggisser, P. (2002). "Constantin aux Rostres." In *Historiae Augustae Colloquium Perusinum*, ed. G. Bonamente and F. Paschoud, pp. 73–91. Historiae Augustae Colloquia, n.s. 8 = Munera 18. Bari.

Bruun, C. (1995). "The Thick Neck of the Emperor Constantine: Slimy Snails and 'Quellenforschung.'" *Historia* 44:459–80.

Bruun, P. M. (1954). "The Consecration Coins of Constantine the Great." In *Commentationes in honorem Edwin Linkomies sexagenarii* A.D. *MCMLIV editae*, ed. H. Zilliacus and K.-E. Henriksson = *Arctos* n.s. 1:19–31.

———. (1958). "The Disappearance of Sol from the Coins of Constantine." *Arctos* n.s. 2:15–37. Reprinted in P. Bruun, *Studies in Constantinian Numismatics: Papers from 1954 to 1988*, pp. 37–48. Acta Instituti Romani Finlandiae 12. Rome, 1991.

———. (1962). "The Christian Signs on the Coins of Constantine." *Arctos* n.s. 3:5–35. Reprinted in P. Bruun, *Studies in Constantinian Numismatics: Papers from 1954 to 1988*, pp. 53–69. Acta Instituti Romani Finlandiae 12. Rome, 1991.

———. (1966). *The Roman Imperial Coinage, VII: Constantine and Licinius* A.D. *313–337*. London.

———. (1997). "The Victorious Signs of Constantine: A Reappraisal." *Numismatic Chronicle* 157:41–59.

Burckhardt, J. (1949). *The Age of Constantine the Great*, tr. M. Hadas. Reprinted Berkeley, 1983.

Burgess, R. W., ed. (1993). *The* Chronicle *of Hydatius and the* Consularia Constantinopolitana*: Two Contemporary Accounts of the Final Years of the Roman Empire.* Oxford Classical Monographs. Oxford.

———. (1997). "The Dates and Editions of Eusebius' *Chronici canones* and *Historia ecclesiastica*." *Journal of Theological Studies* n.s. 48:471–504.

———, with W. Witakowski. (1999a). *Studies in Eusebian and Post-Eusebian Chronography.* Historia, Einzelschriften 135. Stuttgart.

————. (1999b). "ΑΧΥΡΩΝ or ΠΡΟΑΣΤΕΙΟΝ? The Location and Circumstances of Constantine's Death." *Journal of Theological Studies n.s.* 50:153–161.

————. (2008). "The Summer of Blood: The 'Great Massacre' of 337 and the Promotion of the Sons of Constantine." *Dumbarton Oaks Papers* 62: 5–51.

Busch, A. W. (2007). "'*Militia in urbe*': The Military Presence in Rome." In *The Impact of the Roman Army (200 B.C.–A.D. 476): Economic, Social, Political, Religious and Cultural Aspects. Proceedings of the Sixth Workshop of the International Network Impact of Empire (Roman Empire, 200 B.C.–A.D. 476), Capri, March 29–April 2, 2005*, ed. L. de Blois and E. Lo Cascio, with O. Hekster and G. de Kleijn, pp. 315–41. Impact of Empire 6. Leiden.

Cameron, Av. (1983). "Constantinus Christianus." *Journal of Roman Studies* 73:184–90.

————. (1997). "Eusebius' *Vita Constantini* and the Construction of Constantine." In *Portraits: Biographical Representation in the Greek and Latin Literature of the Roman Empire*, ed. M. J. Edwards and S. Swain, pp. 145–74. Oxford.

————. (2005). "The Reign of Constantine, A.D. 306–337." In *The Cambridge Ancient History, Second Edition, Volume XII: The Crisis of Empire, A.D. 193–337*, ed. A. K. Bowman, P. Garnsey, and Av. Cameron, pp. 90–109. Cambridge.

Cameron, Av., and S. G. Hall, tr. (1999). *Eusebius, Life of Constantine: Introduction, Translation, and Commentary.* Oxford.

Cameron, Av., and J. Herrin, with Al. Cameron, R. Cormack, and C. Roueché (1984). *Constantinople in the Early Eighth Century: The* Parastaseis Syntomoi Chronikai. Columbia Studies in the Classical Tradition 10. Leiden.

Carriker, A. (2003). *The Library of Eusebius of Caesarea.* Supplements to Vigiliae Christianae 67. Leiden.

Charron, A., and M. Heijmans (2001). "L'obélisque du cirque d'Arles." *Journal of Roman Archaeology* 14:373–80.

Chastagnol, A. (1962). *Les fastes de la préfecture de Rome au Bas-Empire.* Études prosopographiques 2. Paris.

Chausson, F. (2002a). "La famille du préfet Ablabius." *Pallas* 60:205–29.

————. (2002b). "Une soeur de Constantin: Anastasia." In *"Humana sapit": Études d'antiquité tardive offertes à Lellia Cracco Ruggini*, ed. J.-M. Carrié and R. L. Testa, pp. 131–55. Bibliothèque de l'Antiquité tardive 3. Turnhout.

————. (2007). *Stemmata aurea: Constantine, Justine, Theodose. Revendications généalogiques et idéologie impériale au IVᵉ siècle ap. J.-C.* Centro ricerche e documentazione sull'antichità classica, Monografie 26. Rome.

Chenault, R. R. (2008). "Rome without Emperors: The Revival of a Senatorial City in the Fourth Century CE." Ph.D. Dissertation, Interdepartmental Program in Greek and Roman History, University of Michigan.

Christensen, A. S. (1980). *Lactantius the Historian: An Analysis of the* De mortibus persecutorum. Opuscula Graecolatina 21. Copenhagen.

Christensen, T. (1983). "The So-Called *Appendix* to Eusebius' *Historia Ecclesiastica* VIII." *Classica et Mediaevalia* 34:177–209.

———. (1989). *Rufinus of Aquileia and the* Historia Ecclesiastica, *Lib. VIII–IX, of Eusebius.* Det Kongelige Danske Videnskabernes Selskab, Historisk-filosofiske Meddelelser 58. Copenhagen.

Christie, N. (2006). *From Constantine to Charlemagne: An Archaeology of Italy,* A.D. *300–800.* Aldershot.

Clarke, G. (2005). "Third-Century Christianity." In *The Cambridge Ancient History, Second Edition, Volume XII: The Crisis of Empire,* A.D. *193–337,* ed. A. K. Bowman, P. Garnsey, and Av. Cameron, pp. 589–671. Cambridge.

Clauss, M. (2006). "Die alten Kulte in konstantinischer Zeit." In *Konstantin der Grosse: Geschichte-Archäologie-Rezeption,* ed. A. Demandt and J. Engemann, pp. 39–47. Schriftenreihe des Rheinischen Landesmuseums Trier 32. Trier.

Coarelli, F. (1986). "L'urbs e il suburbio." In *Società romana e imperio tardoantico 2, Roma: Politica, economia, paesaggio urbano,* ed. A. Giardina, pp. 1–58, 395–412. Rome.

———. (2007). *Rome and Environs: An Archaeological Guide,* tr. J. J. Clauss and D. P. Harmon. Berkeley, Calif.

Coates-Stephens, R. (2001). "*Muri dei bassi secoli* in Rome: Observations on the Re-Use of Statuary in Walls Found on the Esquiline and Caelian after 1870." *Journal of Roman Archaeology* 14:217–38.

Coleman, K. (2000). "Entertaining Rome." In *Ancient Rome: The Archaeology of the Eternal City,* ed. J. Coulston and H. Dodge, pp. 210–58. Oxford University School of Archaeology, Monograph 54. Oxford.

Conlin, D. A., A. E. Haeckl, and G. Ponti (2006/2007). "The Villa of Maxentius on the Via Appia: Report on the 2005 Excavations." *Memoirs of the American Academy in Rome* 51–52, pp. 347–70.

Conti, S., ed. (2004). *Die Inschriften Kaiser Julians.* Altertumswissenschaftliches Kolloquium, Interdisziplinäre Studien zur Antike und zu ihrem Nachleben 10. Stuttgart.

Cooley, A. E. (2009). *Res Gestae Divi Augusti: Text, Translation, and Commentary.* Cambridge.

Corbier, M. (2006). "L'écriture dans l'espace public romain." In M. Corbier, *Donner à voir, donner à lire: Mémoire et communication dans la Rome ancienne,* pp. 53–75. Paris.

Corcoran, S. (1996). *The Empire of the Tetrarchs: Imperial Pronouncements and Government AD 284–324.* Oxford.

Creed, J. L., ed. and tr. (1984). *Lactantius, De mortibus persecutorum.* Oxford Early Christian Texts. Oxford.

Cullhed, M. (1994). *Conservator urbis suae: Studies in the Politics and Propaganda of the Emperor Maxentius.* Skrifter Utgivna av Svenska Institutet I Rom, 8°, 20. Stockholm.

Curran, J. (2000). *Pagan City and Christian Capital: Rome in the Fourth Century.* Oxford.

Dagron, G. (1984). *Constantinople imaginaire: Études sur le recueil des "Patria."* Bibliothèque byzantine, Études 8. Paris.

Davies, P. S. (1989). "The Origin and Purpose of the Persecution of AD 303." *Journal of Theological Studies* n.s. 40:66–94.

Davis, R., tr. (2000). *The Book of Pontiffs* (Liber Pontificalis): *The Ancient Biographies of the First Ninety Roman Bishops to* A.D. *715,* 2nd ed. TTH 6. Liverpool.

Dearn, A. (2003). "The Coinage of Vetranio: Imperial Representation and the Memory of Constantine the Great." *Numismatic Chronicle* 163:169–91.

De Decker, D. (1968). "La politique religieuse de Maxence." *Byzantion* 38:472–562.

———. (1978). "Le «Discours à l'Assemblée des Saints» attribué à Constantin et l'oeuvre de Lactance." In *Lactance et son temps: Recherches actuelles. Actes du IVᵉ Colloque d'études historiques et patristiques, Chantilly 21–23 septembre 1976,* ed. J. Fontaine and M. Perrin, pp. 75–87. Théologie historique 48. Paris.

Degrassi, A., ed. (1963). *Inscriptiones Italiae, Volumen XIII: Fasti et Elogia. Fasciculus II: Fasti anni Numani et Iuliani, accedunt Ferialia, Menologia rustica, Parapegmata.* Rome.

DeLaine, J. (1997). *The Baths of Caracalla: A Study in the Design, Construction, and Economics of Large-Scale Building Projects in Imperial Rome.* Journal of Roman Archaeology, Supplementary Series 25. Portsmouth.

Demandt, A. (2006). "Wenn Kaiser träumen . . . Die Visionen Konstantins des Grossen." In *Konstantin der Grosse: Geschichte-Archäologie-Rezeption,* ed. A. Demandt and J. Engemann, pp. 49–59. Schriftenreihe des Rheinischen Landesmuseums Trier 32. Trier.

Demandt, A., and J. Engemann, ed. (2007). *Imperator Caesar Flavius Constantinus: Konstantin der Grosse. Ausstellungskatalog.* Mainz.

De Maria, S. (1988). *Gli archi onorari di Roma e dell'Italia romana.* Bibliotheca archaeologica 7. Rome.

Devos, P. (1982). "Une recension nouvelle de la Passion grecque *BHG* 639 de saint Eusignios." *Analecta Bollandiana* 100:209–28.

Diehl, E., ed. (1925–1931). *Inscriptiones latinae Christianae veteres,* 3 vols. Berlin.

Digeser, E. D. (1994). "Lactantius and Constantine's Letter to Arles: Dating the *Divine Institutes." Journal of Early Christian Studies* 2:33–52.

———. (1997). "Lactantius and the Edict of Milan: Does It Determine His Venue?" In *Studia Patristica Vol. XXXI: Papers Presented at the Twelfth International Conference on Patristic Studies Held in Oxford 1995. Preaching, Second Century,*

Tertullian to Arnobius, Egypt before Nicaea, ed. E. A. Livingstone, pp. 287–95. Leuven.

———. (1998). "Lactantius, Porphyry, and the Debate over Religious Toleration." *Journal of Roman Studies* 88:129–46.

———. (2000). *The Making of a Christian Empire: Lactantius and Rome*. Ithaca, N.Y.

———. (2002). "Porphyry, Julian, or Hierokles? The Anonymous Hellene in Makarios Magnes' *Apokritikos*." *Journal of Theological Studies* n.s. 53:466–502.

Dindorf, G., ed. (1829). *Georgius Syncellus et Nicephorus Cp.*, Vol. 1. Corpus Scriptorum Historiae Byzantinae. Bonn.

Dolbeau, F., ed. (1996). *Augustin d'Hippone, Vingt-six sermons au peuple d'Afrique*. Collection des Études augustiniennes, Série antiquité 147. Paris.

Drake, H. A. (1988). "What Eusebius Knew: The Genesis of the *Vita Constantini*." *Classical Philology* 83:20–38.

———. (2000). *Constantine and the Bishops: The Politics of Intolerance*. Baltimore.

———. (2009). "Solar Power in Late Antiquity." In *The Power of Religion in Late Antiquity*, ed. A. Cain and N. Lenski, pp. 215–26. Farnham.

Drijvers, J. W. (1992). *Helena Augusta: The Mother of Constantine the Great and the Legend of Her Finding of the True Cross*. Brill's Studies in Intellectual History 27. Leiden.

———. (2004). *Cyril of Jerusalem: Bishop and City*. Supplements to Vigiliae Christianae 72. Leiden.

———. (2007). "Eusebius' *Vita Constantini* and the Construction of the Image of Maxentius." In *From Rome to Constantinople: Studies in Honour of Averil Cameron*, ed. H. Amirav and B. ter Haar Romeny, pp. 11–27. Late Antique History and Religion. Leuven.

———. (2009). "The Power of the Cross: Celestial Cross Appearances in the Fourth Century." In *The Power of Religion in Late Antiquity*, ed. A. Cain and N. Lenski, pp. 237–48. Farnham.

Drinkwater, J. F. (1983). *Roman Gaul: The Three Provinces, 58 BC–AD 260*. Ithaca, N.Y.

———. (2000). "The Revolt and Ethnic Origin of the Usurper Magnentius (350–353), and the Rebellion of Vetranio (350)." *Chiron* 30:131–59.

———. (2007). *The Alamanni and Rome 213–496 (Caracalla to Clovis)*. Oxford.

Dumser, E. A. (2006). "The AETERNAE MEMORIAE Coinage of Maxentius: An Issue of Symbolic Intent." In *Imaging Ancient Rome: Documentation – Visualization – Imagination*, ed. L. Haselberger and J. Humphrey, pp. 107–18. *Journal of Roman Archaeology*, Supplementary Series 61. Portsmouth.

Eder, W. (2005). "Augustus and the Power of Tradition." In *The Cambridge Companion to the Age of Augustus*, ed. K. Galinsky, pp. 13–32. Cambridge.

Edwards, M., tr. (2003). *Constantine and Christendom: The Oration to the Saints, the Greek and Latin Accounts of the Discovery of the Cross, the Edict of Constantine to Pope Silvester*. TTH 39. Liverpool.

Ehling, K. (2001). "Kaiser Julian, der Senat, und die Stadt Rom." *Zeitschrift für Papyrologie und Epigraphik* 137:292–96.

Elliott, T. G. (1987). "Constantine's Conversion: Do We Really Need It?" *Phoenix* 41:420–38.

Ensoli, S. (2000). "I colossi de bronzo a Roma in età tardoantica: Dal Colosso di Nerone al Colosso di Costantino. A proposito dei tre frammenti bronzei dei Musei Capitolini." In *Aurea Roma: Dalla città pagana alla città cristiana*, ed. S. Ensoli and E. La Rocca, pp. 66–90. Rome.

Evers, C. (1991). "Remarques sur l'iconographie de Constantin: A propos du remploi de portraits des «bons empereurs»." *Mélanges de l'École française de Rome*, Antiquité 103:785–806.

———. (1992). "Betrachtungen zur Ikonographie des Maxentius: Zu einer neuen Portrat-Replik im Kestner-Museum Hannover." *Niederdeutsche Beiträge zur Kunstgeschichte* 31:9–22.

Evrard, G. (1962). "Une inscription inédite d'Aqua Viva et la carrière des Iunii Bassi." *Mélanges de l'École française de Rome*, Antiquité 74:607–47.

Ewig, E. (1956). "Der Bild Constantins des Grossen in den ersten Jahrhunderten des abendländischen Mittelalters." *Historisches Jahrbuch* 75:1–46. Reprinted in E. Ewig, *Spätantikes und frankisches Gallien: Gesammelte Schriften (1952–1973)*, ed. H. Atsma (Munich, 1976–1979), 1:72–113.

Favro, D. (2005). "Making Rome a World City." In *The Cambridge Companion to the Age of Augustus*, ed. K. Galinsky, pp. 234–63. Cambridge.

Feeney, D. (2007). *Caesar's Calendar: Ancient Time and the Beginnings of History*. Sather Classical Lectures 65. Berkeley, Calif.

Fehl, P. P. (1993). "Raphael as a Historian: Poetry and Historical Accuracy in the Sala di Costantino." *Artibus et historiae* 14, no. 28:9–76.

Feissel, D. (1985). "Inscriptions du IVe au VIe siècle." In D. Feissel and A. Philippidis-Braat, "Inventaires en vue d'un recueil des inscriptions historiques de Byzance, III: Inscriptions du Péloponnèse (à l'exception de Mistra)," *Travaux et Mémoires* 9:267–395.

Ferguson, T. C. (2005). *The Past Is Prologue: The Revolution of Nicene Historiography*. Supplements to Vigiliae Christianae 75. Leiden.

Fittschen, K., and P. Zanker (1985). *Katalog der römischen Portrats in den Capitolinischen Museen und den anderen kommunalen Sammlungen der Stadt Rom, I: Kaiser- und Prinzenbildnisse*. Beiträge zur Erschließung hellenistischer und kaiserzeitlicher Skulptur und Architektur 3. Mainz.

Flower, H. I. (2006). *The Art of Forgetting: Disgrace and Oblivion in Roman Political Culture*. Studies in the History of Greece and Rome. Chapel Hill, N.C.

Foss, C. (1995). "Nicomedia and Constantinople." In *Constantinople and Its Hinterland: Papers from the Twenty-Seventh Spring Symposium of Byzantine Studies,*

Oxford, April 1993, ed. C. Mango and G. Dagron, with G. Greatrex, pp. 181–90. Society for the Promotion of Byzantine Studies, Publications 3. Aldershot.

Fowden, G. (1994a). "Constantine, Silvester and the Church of S. Polyeuctus in Constantinople." *Journal of Roman Archaeology* 7:274–84.

———. (1994b). "The Last Days of Constantine: Oppositional Versions and Their Influence." *Journal of Roman Studies* 84:146–70.

Frazer, A. (1966). "The Iconography of the Emperor Maxentius' Buildings in Via Appia." *Art Bulletin* 48:385–92.

Fried, J. (2007). Donation of Constantine *and* Constitutum Constantini: *The Misinterpretation of a Fiction and its Original Meaning*. Millennium-Studien zu Kultur und Geschichte des ersten Jahrtausends n. Chr. 3. Berlin.

Frothingham, A. L., Jr. (1883). "Une mosaique constantinienne inconnue à Saint-Pierre de Rome." *Revue archéologique*, série 3, 1:68–72.

———. (1915). "The Roman Territorial Arch." *American Journal of Archaeology* 19: 155–74.

Fuhrmann, H., ed. (1968). *Das Constitutum Constantini (Konstantinische Schenkung): Text*. Fontes iuris Germanici antiqui in usum scholarum ex Monumentis Germaniae Historicis separatim editi 10. Hannover.

Gascou, J. (1967). "Le rescrit d'Hispellum." *Mélanges d'archéologie et d'histoire* 79: 609–59.

Giavarini, C., ed. (2005). *The Basilica of Maxentius: The Monument, Its Materials, Construction, and Stability*. Studia Archaeologica 140. Rome.

Gibbon, E. (1932). *The Decline and Fall of the Roman Empire*, 3 vols. The Modern Library. New York.

Girardet, K. M. (2006a). *Die Konstantinische Wende: Voraussetzungen und geistige Grundlagen der Religionspolitik Konstantins des Großen*. Darmstadt.

———. (2006b). "Konstantin und das Christentum: Die Jahre der Entscheidung 310 bis 314." In *Konstantin der Grosse: Geschichte-Archäologie-Rezeption*, ed. A. Demandt and J. Engemann, pp. 69–80. Schriftenreihe des Rheinischen Landesmuseums Trier 32. Trier.

Giuliano, A. (1955). *Arco di Costantino*. Milan.

———. (1991). "Augustus-Constantinus." *Bollettino d'arte* 68–69:3–10.

Gradel, I. (2002). *Emperor Worship and Roman Religion*. Oxford Classical Monographs. Oxford.

Grafton, A., and M. Williams (2006). *Christianity and the Transformation of the Book: Origen, Eusebius, and the Library of Caesarea*. Cambridge, Mass.

Grant, R. M. (1980). *Eusebius as Church Historian*. Oxford.

Grégoire, H., ed. (1922). *Recueil des inscriptions grecques chrétiennes d'Asie Mineure*. Paris.

————. (1932). "La statue de Constantin et le signe de la croix." *L'antiquité classique* 1:135–43.

Grig, L. (2006). "Throwing Parties for the Poor: Poverty and Splendour in the Late Antique Church." In *Poverty in the Roman World*, ed. M. Atkins and R. Osborne, pp. 145–61. Cambridge.

————. (2009). "Imagining the Capitolium in Late Antiquity." In *The Power of Religion in Late Antiquity*, ed. A. Cain and N. Lenski, pp. 279–91. Farnham.

Grigg, R. (1977). "Constantine the Great and the Cult without Images." *Viator* 8:1–32.

Grillet, B. (1983). "Introduction: Chapitre I, La vie et l'oeuvre." In B. Grillet, G. Sabbah, and A.-J. Festugière, *Sozomène, Histoire ecclésiastique, Livres I-II: Texte grec de l'édition J. Bidez*, pp. 9–31. SChr. 306. Paris.

Groag, E. (1926). "Der Dichter Porfyrius in einer stadtrömischer Inschrift." *Wiener Studien* 45:102–9.

Grünewald, T. (1989). "Ein epigraphisches Zeugnis zur Germanenpolitik Konstantins des Grossen: Die Bauinschrift des Deutzer Kastells (CIL XIII 8502)." In *Labor omnibus unus: Gerold Walser zum 70. Geburtstag dargebracht von Freunden, Kollegen und Schülern*, ed. H. E. Herzig and R. Frei-Stolba, pp. 171–85. Historia, Einzelschriften 60. Stuttgart.

————. (1990). *Constantinus Maximus Augustus: Herrschaftspropaganda in der zeitgenössischen Überlieferung*. Historia, Einzelschriften 64. Stuttgart.

Guidi, M. (1907). "Un ΒΙΟΣ di Constantino." *Rendiconti della Reale Accademia dei Lincei, Classe di scienze morali, storiche e filologiche*, Serie quinta, 16:304–40, 637–62.

Guillaumin, M.-L. (1978). "L'exploitation des «Oracles Sibyllins» par Lactance et par le «Discours à l'Assemblée des Saints»." In *Lactance et son temps: Recherches actuelles. Actes du IVᵉ Colloque d'études historiques et patristiques, Chantilly 21–23 septembre 1976*, ed. J. Fontaine and M. Perrin, pp. 185–200. Théologie historique 48. Paris.

Gundlach, W., ed. (1892). *Epistolae Merowingici et Karolini aevi*. MGH, Epistolae 3. Berlin.

Haldon, J. F. (1994). "Constantine or Justinian? Crisis and Identity in Imperial Propaganda in the Seventh Century." In *New Constantines: The Rhythm of Imperial Renewal in Byzantium, 4th–13th Centuries. Papers from the Twenty-Sixth Spring Symposium of Byzantine Studies, St Andrews, March 1992*, ed. P. Magdalino, pp. 95–107. Society for the Promotion of Byzantine Studies, Publications 2. Aldershot.

Hall, L. J. (1998). "Cicero's *instinctu divino* and Constantine's *instinctu divinitatis*: The Evidence of the Arch of Constantine for the Senatorial View of the 'Vision' of Constantine." *Journal of Early Christian Studies* 6:647–71.

Hall, S. G. (1993). "Eusebian and Other Sources in Vita Constantini I." In *Logos: Festschrift für Luise Abramowski zum 8. Juli 1993*, ed. H. C. Brennecke, E. L. Grasmück, and C. Markschies, pp. 239–63. Beihefte zur Zeitschrift für die neutestamentliche Wissenschaft und die Kunde der älteren Kirche 67. Berlin.

Hallett, J. P. (1970). "'Over Troubled Waters': The Meaning of the Title *Pontifex.*" *Transactions and Proceedings of the American Philological Association* 101:219–27.

Hamilton, F. J., and E. W. Brooks, tr. (1899). *The Syriac Chronicle Known as That of Zachariah of Mitylene.* London.

Hannestad, N. (1994). *Tradition in Late Antique Sculpture: Conservation – Modernization – Production.* Acta Jutlandica 69.2, Humanities Series 69. Aarhus.

————. (2007). "Die Portratskulptur zur Zeit Konstantins des Grossen." In *Imperator Caesar Flavius Constantinus: Konstantin der Grosse. Ausstellungskatalog*, ed. A. Demandt and J. Engemann, pp. 96–112. Mainz.

Harris, W. V. (2005). "Constantine's Dream." *Klio* 87:488–94.

Hartley, E., J. Hawkes, and M. Henig, with F. Mees, ed. (2006). *Constantine the Great: York's Roman Emperor.* York.

Heck, E. (1972). *Die dualistischen Zusätze und die Kaiseranreden bei Lactantius: Untersuchungen zur Textgeschichte der* Divinae Institutiones *und der Schrift* De opificio Dei. Abhandlungen der Heidelberger Akademie der Wissenschaften, Philosophisch-historische Klasse 1972, 2. Heidelberg.

Hedrick, C. W., Jr. (2000). *History and Silence: Purge and Rehabilitation of Memory in Late Antiquity.* Austin, Tex.

Heijmans, M. (2004). *Arles durant l'antiquité tardive: De la* Duplex Arelas *à l'*Urbs Genesii. Collection de l'École française de Rome 324. Rome.

————. (2006). "Constantina urbs. Arles durant le IVe siècle: une autre résidence impériale?" In *Konstantin der Grosse: Geschichte-Archäologie-Rezeption*, ed. A. Demandt and J. Engemann, pp. 209–19. Schriftenreihe des Rheinischen Landesmuseums Trier 32. Trier.

Heim, F. (2001). "Constantin dans l'«Histoire ecclésiastique» de Rufin: fidélités et infidélités à Eusebe." *Euphrosyne* 29:201–10.

Hekster, O. (1999). "The City of Rome in Late Imperial Ideology: The Tetrarchs, Maxentius, and Constantine." *Mediterraneo Antico* 2:717–48.

Hendy, M. F. (1985). *Studies in the Byzantine Monetary Economy c. 300–1450.* Cambridge.

Heres, T. L. (1982). *Paries: A Proposal for a Dating System of Late-Antique Masonry Structures in Rome and Ostia.* Studies in Classical Antiquity 5. Amsterdam.

Herzig, H. E. (1989). "Regio XI Italiae: Auf den Spuren Konstantins des Grossen." In *Labor omnibus unus: Gerold Walser zum 70. Geburtstag dargebracht von Freunden, Kollegen und Schülern*, ed. H. E. Herzig and R. Frei-Stolba, pp. 59–69. Historia, Einzelschriften 60. Stuttgart.

Humphrey, J. H. (1986). *Roman Circuses: Arenas for Chariot Racing.* Berkeley, Calif.

Humphries, M. (1997). "*In nomine patris*: Constantine the Great and Constantius II in Christological Polemic." *Historia* 46:448–64.

————. (2007). "From Emperor to Pope? Ceremonial, Space, and Authority at Rome from Constantine to Gregory the Great." In *Religion, Dynasty, and*

Patronage in Early Christian Rome, 300–900, ed. K. Cooper and J. Hillner, pp. 21–58. Cambridge.

———. (2008a). "From Usurper to Emperor: The Politics of Legitimation in the Age of Constantine." *Journal of Late Antiquity* 1:82–100.

———. (2008b). "Rufinus's Eusebius: Translation, Continuation, and Edition in the Latin *Ecclesiastical History*." *Journal of Early Christian Studies* 16:143–64.

———. (2009). "The Mind of the Persecutors: 'By the Gracious Favour of the Gods.'" In *The Great Persecution: The Proceedings of the Fifth Patristic Conference, Maynooth, 2003*, ed. D. V. Twomey and M. Humphries, pp. 11–32. Irish Theological Quarterly Monograph Series 4. Dublin.

Jaïdi, H. (2003). "L'annone de Rome au Bas-Empire: difficultés structurelles, contraintes nouvelles et volonté impériale." In *Nourrir les cités de Méditerranée: Antiquité – Temps modernes*, ed. B. Marin and C. Virlouvet, pp. 83–102. L'Atelier Méditerranéen. Paris.

Jeffreys, E., M. Jeffreys, and R. Scott, tr. (1986). *The Chronicle of John Malalas: A Translation*. Byzantina Australiensia 4. Melbourne.

Johnson, M. J. (2009). *The Roman Imperial Mausoleum in Late Antiquity*. Cambridge.

Jones, A. H. M. (1954). "Notes on the Genuineness of the Constantinian Documents in Eusebius's Life of Constantine." *Journal of Ecclesiastical History* 5:196–200. Reprinted in A. H. M. Jones, *The Roman Economy: Studies in Ancient Economic and Administrative History*, ed. P. A. Brunt, pp. 257–62. Oxford, 1974.

———. (1964). *The Later Roman Empire*. Oxford.

———. (1972). *Constantine and the Conversion of Europe*. Harmondsworth. First published in 1949.

Kaegi, W. E., Jr. (1968). *Byzantium and the Decline of Rome*. Princeton, N.J.

Kazhdan, A. (1987). "'Constantin imaginaire': Byzantine Legends of the Ninth Century about Constantine the Great." *Byzantion* 57:196–250.

Kelly, C. (2004). *Ruling the Later Roman Empire*. Revealing Antiquity 15. Cambridge, Mass.

Kent, J. P. C. (1981). *The Roman Imperial Coinage, VIII: The Family of Constantine I, A.D. 337–364*. London.

Kinney, D. (2005). "Spolia." In *St. Peter's in the Vatican*, ed. W. Tronzo, pp. 16–47. Cambridge.

Kluge, E. (1924). "Studien zu Publilius Optatianus Porfyrius." *Münchener Museum* 4:323–48.

Koeppel, G. M. (1986). "Die historischen Reliefs der römischen Kaiserzeit IV: Stadtrömische Denkmäler unbekannter Bauzugehörigkeit aus hadrianischer bis konstantinischer Zeit." *Bonner Jahrbücher* 186:1–90.

Koethe, H. (1931). "Zum Mausoleum der weströmischen Dynastie bei Alt-Sankt-Peter." *Mitteilungen des deutschen archäologischen Instituts*, Römische Abteilung 46:9–26.

Kolb, F. (2001). *Herrscherideologie in der Spätantike*. Berlin.

Krautheimer, R., with W. Frankl, S. Corbett, and A. K. Frazer (1937–1980). *Corpus Basilicarum Christianarum Romae: The Early Christian Basilicas of Rome (IV–IX Cent.)*, 5 vols. Vatican City.

_____. (1983). *Three Christian Capitals: Topography and Politics*. Berkeley, Calif.

Kuhoff, W. (1991). "Ein Mythos in der römischen Geschichte: Der Sieg Konstantins des Großen über Maxentius vor den Toren Roms am 28. Oktober 312 n. Chr." *Chiron* 21:127–74.

Lane Fox, R. (1986). *Pagans and Christians*. New York.

Lange, C. H. (2009). *Res publica constituta: Actium, Apollo and the Accomplishment of the Triumviral Assignment*. Impact of Empire 10. Leiden.

Laqueur, R. (1929). *Eusebius als Historiker seiner Zeit*. Arbeiten zur Kirchengeschichte 11. Berlin.

La Rocca, E., and P. Zanker (2007). "Il ritratto colossale di Costantino dal Foro di Traiano." In *Res bene gestae: Ricerche di storia urbana su Roma antica in onore di Eva Margareta Steinby*, ed. A. Leone, D. Palombi, and S. Walker, pp. 145–68. Lexicon Topographicum Urbis Romae, Supplementum 4. Rome.

Lavin, I. (2005). "Bernini at St. Peter's: Singularis in singulis, in omnibus unicus." In *St. Peter's in the Vatican*, ed. W. Tronzo, pp. 111–243. Cambridge.

Leadbetter, B. (2009). *Galerius and the Will of Diocletian*. London.

Lemerle, P. (1971). *Le premier humanisme byzantin: Notes et remarques sur enseignement et culture à Byzance des origines au Xe siècle*. Bibliothèque byzantine, Études 6. Paris.

Lenski, N. (2002). *Failure of Empire: Valens and the Roman State in the Fourth Century A.D.* The Transformation of the Classical Heritage 34. Berkeley, Calif.

_____. (2006). "Introduction." In *The Cambridge Companion to the Age of Constantine*, ed. N. Lenski, pp. 1–13. Cambridge.

_____. (2008). "Evoking the Pagan Past: *Instinctu divinitatis* and Constantine's Capture of Rome." *Journal of Late Antiquity* 1:204–57.

Lepelley, C. (1979–1981). *Les cités de l'Afrique romaine au Bas-Empire*, 2 vols. Paris.

Leppin, H. (1996). *Von Constantin dem Großen zu Theodosius II.: Das christliche Kaisertum bei den Kirchenhistorikern Socrates, Sozomenus und Theodoret*. Hypomnemata 110. Göttingen.

_____. (2007). "Jacob Burckhardt and Paganism in the Roman Empire." In *Wolf Liebeschuetz Reflected: Essays Presented by Colleagues, Friends, & Pupils*, ed. J. Drinkwater and B. Salway, pp. 17–26. Bulletin of the Institute of Classical Studies, Supplement 91. London.

Leppin, H., and H. Ziemssen (2007). *Maxentius: Der letzte Kaiser in Rom*. Zaberns Bildbände zur Archäologie. Mainz.

Levitan, W. (1985). "Dancing at the End of the Rope: Optatian Porfyry and the Field of Roman Verse." *Transactions of the American Philological Association* 115:245–69.

Lieu, S. N. C. (1998). "From History to Legend and Legend to History: The Medieval and Byzantine Transformation of Constantine's *Vita*." In *Constantine: History, Hagiography and Legend*, ed. S. N. C. Lieu and D. Montserrat, pp. 136–76. London.

Lieu, S. N. C., and D. Montserrat (1996). *From Constantine to Julian: Pagan and Byzantine Views. A Source History*. London.

Lim, R. (1999). "People as Power: Games, Munificence, and Contested Topography." In *The Transformations of Urbs Roma in Late Antiquity*, ed. W. V. Harris, pp. 265–81. Journal of Roman Archaeology, Supplementary Series 33. Portsmouth.

Liverani, P. (1995). "Domus Faustae." In *Lexicon Topographicum Urbis Romae*, Vol. 2, ed. E. M. Steinby, pp. 97–99. Rome.

———. (2008). "Interventi urbani a Roma tra il IV e il VI secolo." *Cristianesimo nella storia* 29:1–31.

L'Orange, H. P., with R. Unger. (1984). *Das spätantike Herrscherbild von Diokletian bis zu den Konstantin-Söhnen 284–361 n. Chr.* Das römischen Herrscherbild 3, Vol. 4. Berlin.

L'Orange, H. P., and A. von Gerkan (1939). *Der spätantike Bildschmuck des Konstantinsbogens*. Studien zur spätantiken Kunstgeschichte 10. Berlin.

Louth, A. (1990). "The Date of Eusebius' *Historia ecclesiastica*." *Journal of Theological Studies* 41:111–23.

Machado, C. (2006). "Building the Past: Monuments and Memory in the *Forum Romanum*." In *Social and Political Life in Late Antiquity*, ed. W. Bowden, A. Gutteridge and C. Machado, pp. 157–92. Late Antique Archaeology 3.1. Leiden.

MacMullen, R. (1969). *Constantine*. New York.

———. (1984). *Christianizing the Roman Empire (A.D. 100–400)*. New Haven, Conn.

———. (2009). *The Second Church: Popular Christianity A.D. 200–400*. Writings from the Greco-Roman World, Supplement Series 1. Atlanta, Ga.

Magdalino, P. (1994). "Introduction." In *New Constantines: The Rhythm of Imperial Renewal in Byzantium, 4th–13th Centuries. Papers from the Twenty-Sixth Spring Symposium of Byzantine Studies, St Andrews, March 1992*, ed. P. Magdalino, pp. 1–9. Society for the Promotion of Byzantine Studies, Publications 2. Aldershot.

Maier, J.-L. (1987–1989). *Le dossier du Donatisme*, 2 vols. Texte und Untersuchungen 134–135. Berlin.

Malosse, P.-L. (1997). "Libanius on Constantine Again." *Classical Quarterly* 47:519–24.

———. (2000). "Libanios, ses «temoins oculaires», Eusèbe et Praxagoras: Le travail préparatoire du sophiste et la question des sources dans l'*Eloge de Constance et de Constant*." *Revue des études grecques* 113:172–87.

Markopoulos, A. (1994). "Constantine the Great in Macedonian Historiography: Models and Approaches." In *New Constantines: The Rhythm of Imperial Renewal in Byzantium, 4th–13th Centuries. Papers from the Twenty-Sixth Spring Symposium of Byzantine Studies, St Andrews, March 1992*, ed. P. Magdalino, pp. 159–70. Society for the Promotion of Byzantine Studies, Publications 2. Aldershot.

Marlowe, E. (2006). "Framing the Sun: The Arch of Constantine and the Roman Cityscape." *Art Bulletin* 88:223–42.

Martin, A. (2006). "Introduction." In *Théodoret de Cyr, Histoire ecclésiastique: Tome I (Livres I–II)*, ed. J. Bouffartique, A. Martin, L. Pietri, and F. Thelamon, pp. 9–92. SChr. 501. Paris.

Mastino, A., and A. Teatini (2001). "Ancora sul discusso «trionfo» di Costantino dopo la battaglia del Ponte Milvio: Nota a proposito di *CIL*, VIII, 9356 = 20941 (Caesarea)." In *Varia epigraphica: Atti del Colloquio internazionale di epigrafia, Bertinoro, 8–10 giugno 2000*, ed. G. Angeli Bertinelli and A. Donati, pp. 273–327. Epigrafia e antichità 17. Faenza.

Maxwell, J. L. (2006). *Christianization and Communication in Late Antiquity: John Chrysostom and His Congregation in Antioch*. Cambridge.

Mennella, G. (2004). "La campagna di Costantino nell'Italia nord-occidentale: la documentazione epigrafica." In *L'armée romaine de Dioclétien à Valentinien Ier: Actes du Congrès de Lyon (12–14 septembre 2002)*, ed. Y. Le Bohec and C. Wolff, pp. 359–69. Université Jean Moulin-Lyon 3, Collection du Centre d'Études Romaines et Gallo-Romaines n.s. 26. Lyon.

Messineo, G. (2006). "Mulvius Pons." In *Lexicon Topographicum Urbis Romae – Suburbium*, ed. A. La Regina. Vol. 4, ed. V. F. Nicolai, M. G. G. Cecere, and Z. Mari, pp. 76–77. Rome.

Messineo, G., and C. Calci (1989). *Malborghetto*. Lavori e Studi di Archeologia 15. Rome.

Miethke, J. (2008). "Die 'Konstantinische Schenkung' in der mittelalterlichen Diskussion: Ausgewählte Kapitel einer verschlungenen Rezeptionsgeschichte." In *Konstantin der Grosse: Das Bild des Kaisers im Wandel der Zeiten*, ed. A. Goltz and H. Schlange-Schöningen, pp. 35–108. Beihefte zum Archiv für Kulturgeschichte 66. Cologne.

Miles, R. (2003). "Rivaling Rome: Carthage." In *Rome the Cosmopolis*, ed. C. Edwards and G. Woolf, pp. 123–46. Cambridge.

Millar, F. (1969). "P. Herennius Dexippus: The Greek World and the Third-Century Invasions." *Journal of Roman Studies* 59:12–29.

———. (1977). *The Emperor in the Roman World (31 B.C.–A.D. 337)*. London.

———. (1983). "Empire and City, Augustus to Julian: Obligations, Excuses and Status." *Journal of Roman Studies* 73:76–96.

———. (1986). "Italy and the Roman Empire: Augustus to Constantine." *Phoenix* 40:295–318.

Miller, P. C. (1994). *Dreams in Late Antiquity: Studies in the Imagination of a Culture*. Princeton, N.J.

Milner, C. (1994). "The Image of the Rightful Ruler: Anicia Juliana's Constantine Mosaic in the Church of Hagios Polyeuktos." In *New Constantines: The Rhythm of Imperial Renewal in Byzantium, 4th–13th Centuries. Papers from the Twenty-Sixth*

Spring Symposium of Byzantine Studies, St Andrews, March 1992, ed. P. Magdalino, pp. 73–81. Society for the Promotion of Byzantine Studies, Publications 2. Aldershot.

Momigliano, A. (1963). "Pagan and Christian Historiography in the Fourth Century A.D." In *The Conflict between Paganism and Christianity in the Fourth Century*, ed. A. Momigliano, pp. 79–99. Oxford.

Mommsen, T., ed. (1892). *Chronica minora saec. IV. V. VI. VII*, Vol. 1. MGH, Auctores antiquissimi 9. Berlin.

Moreau, J., ed. and tr. (1954). *Lactance, De la mort des persécuteurs*, 2 vols. SChr. 39. Paris.

Mras, K. (1954). "Einleitung." In K. Mras, ed., *Eusebius Werke 8: Die Praeparatio Evangelica. Erster Teil: Einleitung, Die Bücher I bis X*, pp. xiii–lviii. GCS 43.1. Berlin.

Müller, C., ed. (1851). *Fragmenta historicorum graecorum*, Vol. 4. Paris.

Munier, C., ed. (1963). *Concilia Galliae a. 314–a. 506*. CChr., Series latina 148. Turnhout.

Nicholson, O. (1989). "Flight from Persecution as Imitation of Christ: Lactantius' Divine Institutes IV.18, 1–2." *Journal of Theological Studies* n.s. 40:48–65.

———. (1999). "*Civitas quae adhuc sustentat omnia*: Lactantius and the City of Rome." In *The Limits of Ancient Christianity: Essays on Late Antique Thought and Culture in Honor of R. A. Markus*, ed. W. E. Klingshirn and M. Vessey, pp. 7–25. Ann Arbor, Mich.

———. (2000). "Constantine's Vision of the Cross." *Vigiliae Christianae* 54:309–23.

Nieddu, A. M. (2009). *La Basilica Apostolorum sulla Via Appia e l'area cimiteriale circostante*. Monumenti di antichità cristiana pubblicati a cura del Pontificio Istituto de archeologia cristiana, II serie, 19. Vatican City.

Nixon, C. E. V., and B. S. Rodgers, tr. (1994). *In Praise of Later Roman Emperors: The Panegyrici Latini. Introduction, Translation, and Historical Commentary with the Latin Text of R. A. B. Mynors*. The Transformation of the Classical Heritage 21. Berkeley, Calif.

Noble, T. F. X. (1984). *The Republic of St. Peter: The Birth of the Papal State, 680–825*. Philadelphia.

Nora, P. (1989). "Between Memory and History: *Les lieux de mémoire*." *Representations* 26:7–24.

Nordh, A., ed. (1949). *Libellus de regionibus urbis Romae*. Skrifter Utgivna av Svenska Institutet i Rom 3. Lund.

Odahl, C. M. (2004). *Constantine and the Christian Empire*. London.

Östenberg, I. (2009). *Staging the World: Spoils, Captives, and Representations in the Roman Triumphal Procession*. Oxford Studies in Ancient Culture and Representation. Oxford.

Opitz, H.-G. (1934). "Die Vita Constantini des Codex Angelicus 22." *Byzantion* 9:535–93.

Painter, B. W. (2005). *Mussolini's Rome: Rebuilding the Eternal City*. New York.

Papi, E. (1999). "Romulus, Divus, Templum." In *Lexicon Topographicum Urbis Romae*, Vol. 4, ed. E. M. Steinby, pp. 210–12. Rome.

Parmentier, L., and F. Scheidweiler, ed. (1954). *Theodoret, Kirchengeschichte*, 2nd ed. GCS 44. Berlin.

Paschoud, F., ed. and tr. (1979–2000). *Zosime, Histoire nouvelle*, 3 vols. Budé. Paris.

Pelling, C. (2009). "Seeing through Caesar's Eyes: Focalisation and Interpretation." In *Narratology and Interpretation: The Content of Narrative Form in Ancient Literature*, ed. J. Grethlein and A. Rengakos, pp. 507–26. Trends in Classics – Supplementary Volumes 4. Berlin.

Pietri, C. (1983). "Constantin en 324: Propagande et théologie imperiales d'après les documents de la *Vita Constantini*." In *Crise et redressement dans les provinces européennes de l'empire (milieu du IIIe au IVe siècle ap. J.C.). Actes du Colloque de Strasbourg (décembre 1981)*, pp. 63–90. Strasburg. Reprinted in C. Pietri, *Christiana respublica: Eléments d'une enquête sur le christianisme antique* 1:253–80. Collection de l'École française de Rome 234. Paris, 1997.

Pietri, C., and L. Pietri (1999–2000). *Prosopographie chrétienne du Bas-Empire 2: Prosopographie de l'Italie chrétienne (313–604)*, 2 vols. Rome.

Pohlkamp, W. (2007). "Konstantin der Große und die Stadt Rom im Spiegel der römischen Silvester-Akten (*Actus Silvestri*)." In *Kaiser Konstantin der Grosse: Historische Leistung und Rezeption in Europa*, ed. K. M. Girardet, pp. 87–111. Bonn.

Polara, G., ed. (1973). *Publilii Optatiani Porfyrii carmina*, 2 vols. Corpus scriptorum latinorum Paravianum. Turin.

———. (1978). "La fondazione di Costantinopoli e la cronologia dei carmi di Optaziano." *Koinonia* 2:333–38.

Presicce, C. P. (2007). "Konstantin als Iuppiter: Die Kolossalstatue des Kaisers aus der Basilika an der Via Sacra." In *Imperator Caesar Flavius Constantinus: Konstantin der Grosse. Ausstellungskatalog*, ed. A. Demandt and J. Engemann, pp. 117–31. Mainz.

Price, R. M. (2005). "*In hoc signo vinces*: The Original Context of the Vision of Constantine." In *Signs, Wonders, Miracles: Representations of Divine Power in the Life of the Church. Papers Read at the 2003 Summer Meeting and the 2004 Winter Meeting of the Ecclesiastical History Society*, ed. K. Cooper and J. Gregory, pp. 1–10. Studies in Church History 41. Woodbridge.

Price, S. R. F. (1987). "From Noble Funerals to Divine Cult: The Consecration of Roman Emperors." In *Rituals of Royalty: Power and Ceremonial in Traditional Societies*, ed. D. Cannadine and S. Price, pp. 56–105. Cambridge.

Prince, G. (1995). "Narratology." In *The Cambridge History of Literary Criticism, Volume 8: From Formalism to Poststructuralism*, pp. 110–30. Cambridge.

Quednau, R. (2006). "Zum Wandel des Konstantin-Bildes in der Kunst: Raphael und Rubens/Pietro da Cortona." In *Konstantin der Grosse: Geschichte-Archäologie-Rezeption*, ed. A. Demandt and J. Engemann, pp. 273–84. Schriftenreihe des Rheinischen Landesmuseums Trier 32. Trier.

Rapp, C. (2005). *Holy Bishops in Late Antiquity: The Nature of Christian Leadership in an Age of Transition*. The Transformation of the Classical Heritage 37. Berkeley, Calif.

Rees, R. (2004). *Diocletian and the Tetrarchy*. Debates and Documents in Ancient History. Edinburgh.

Richardson, L., Jr. (1992). *A New Topographical Dictionary of Ancient Rome*. Baltimore.

Richmond, I. A. (1930). *The City Wall of Imperial Rome: An Account of Its Architectural Development from Aurelian to Narses*. Oxford.

Roller, M. B. (2004). "Exemplarity in Roman Culture: The Cases of Horatius Cocles and Cloelia." *Classical Philology* 99:1–56.

de Rossi, J. B., ed. (1857–1888). *Inscriptiones Christianae urbis Romae septimo saeculo antiquiores*, 2 vols. Rome.

Rougé, J. (1978). "A propos du manuscrit du «De mortibus persecutorum»." In *Lactance et son temps: Recherches actuelles. Actes du IVᵉ Colloque d'études historiques et patristiques, Chantilly 21–23 septembre 1976*, ed. J. Fontaine and M. Perrin, pp. 13–22. Théologie historique 48. Paris.

Rüpke, J. (2008). *Fasti sacerdotum: A Prosopography of Pagan, Jewish, and Christian Religious Officials in the City of Rome, 300 BC to AD 499*, tr. D. M. B. Richardson. Oxford.

Ruysschaert, J. (1962–1963). "Essai d'interprétation synthétique de l'Arc de Constantin." *Atti della Pontificia Accademia Romana di Archeologia* (série III), Rendiconti 35:79–100.

Sághy, M. (2000). "*Scinditur in partes populus*: Pope Damasus and the Martyrs of Rome." *Early Medieval Europe* 9:273–87.

Scheidel, W. (2009). "Sex and Empire: A Darwinian Perspective." In *The Dynamics of Ancient Empires: State Power from Assyria to Byzantium*, ed. I. Morris and W. Scheidel, pp. 255–324. Oxford Studies in Early Empires. Oxford.

Schlange-Schöningen, H. (2006). "Das Bild Konstantins in der Neuzeit." In *Konstantin der Grosse: Geschichte-Archäologie-Rezeption*, ed. A. Demandt and J. Engemann, pp. 285–96. Schriftenreihe des Rheinischen Landesmuseums Trier 32. Trier.

Schmidt, P. L. (1989a). "De viris illustribus." In *Restauration und Erneuerung: Die lateinische Literatur von 284 bis 374 n. Chr.*, ed. R. Herzog, pp. 187–90. Handbuch der Altertumswissenschaft, Abteilung 8: Handbuch der lateinischen Literatur der Antike 5. Munich.

―――. (1989b). "Die sogenannte Enmannsche Kaisergeschichte (= EKG)." In *Restauration und Erneuerung: Die lateinische Literatur von 284 bis 374 n. Chr.*, ed. R. Herzog, pp. 196–98. Handbuch der Altertumswissenschaft, Abteilung 8: Handbuch der lateinischen Literatur der Antike 5. Munich.

Schott, J. M. (2008). *Christianity, Empire, and the Making of Religion in Late Antiquity*. Divinations: Rereading Late Ancient Religion. Philadelphia.

Schwartz, E. (1909). "Einleitung zum griechischen Text." In E. Schwartz and T. Mommsen, ed., *Eusebius Werke 2.3: Die Kirchengeschichte*, pp. xv–ccxlviii. Second edition by F. Winkelmann. GCS 9, Neue Folge 6.3. Reprinted Berlin, 1999.

———, ed. (1933–1935). *Acta conciliorum oecumenicorum, Tomus alter, Volumen primum*, 3 vols. Berlin.

Schwartz, E., and T. Mommsen, ed. (1903–1909). *Eusebius Werke 2: Die Kirchengeschichte*, 3 vols. Second edition by F. Winkelmann. GCS 9, Neue Folge 6.1–3. Reprinted Berlin, 1999.

Scott, R. (1994). "The Image of Constantine in Malalas and Theophanes." In *New Constantines: The Rhythm of Imperial Renewal in Byzantium, 4th–13th Centuries. Papers from the Twenty-Sixth Spring Symposium of Byzantine Studies, St Andrews, March 1992*, ed. P. Magdalino, pp. 57–71. Society for the Promotion of Byzantine Studies, Publications 2. Aldershot.

Scrinari, V. S. M. (1991). *Il Laterano imperiale, Vol. I: Dalle «aedes Laterani» alla «Domus Faustae»*. Monumenti di Antichità cristiana, II serie, 11. Vatican City.

Seeck, O. (1908). "Das Leben des Dichters Porphyrius." *Rheinisches Museum* 63:267–82.

———. (1919). *Regesten der Kaiser und Päpste für die Jahre 311 bis 476 n. Chr.: Vorarbeit zu einer Prosopographie der christlichen Kaiserzeit*. Stuttgart.

Singor, H. (2003). "The Labarum, Shield Blazons, and Constantine's Caeleste Signum." In *The Representation and Perception of Roman Imperial Power. Proceedings of the Third Workshop of the International Network Impact of Empire (Roman Empire, c. 200 B.C.–A.D. 476), Netherlands Institute in Rome, March 20–23, 2002*, ed. L. de Blois, P. Erdkamp, O. Hekster, G. de Kleijn, and S. Mols, pp. 481–500. Impact of Empire 3. Amsterdam.

Slater, C. (1986). *Trail of Miracles: Stories from a Pilgrimage in Northeast Brazil*. Berkeley.

Smith, M. D. (1997). "The Religion of Constantius I." *Greek, Roman and Byzantine Studies* 38:187–208.

———. (2000). "The Religious Coinage of Constantius I." *Byzantion* 70:474–90.

Smith, R. R. R. (1997). "The Public Image of Licinius I: Portrait Sculpture and Imperial Ideology in the Early Fourth Century." *Journal of Roman Studies* 87:170–202.

Smolak, K. (1989). "Publilius Optatianus Porfyrius." In *Restauration und Erneuerung: Die lateinische Literatur von 284 bis 374 n. Chr.*, ed. R. Herzog, pp. 237–43. Handbuch der Altertumswissenschaft, Abteilung 8: Handbuch der lateinischen Literatur der Antike 5. Munich.

Speidel, M. P. (1986). "Maxentius and His *Equites Singulares* in the Battle at the Milvian Bridge." *Classical Antiquity* 5:253–62.

Spera, L. (2003). "The Christianization of Space along the Via Appia: Changing Landscape in the Suburbs of Rome." *American Journal of Archaeology* 107:23–43.

Steinby, M. (1986). "L'industria laterizia di Roma nel tardo imperio." In *Società romana e impero tardoantico 2, Roma: Politica, economia, paesaggio urbano*, ed. A. Giardina, pp. 99–164, 438–446. Rome.

Stuart Jones, H. (1926). *A Catalogue of the Ancient Sculptures Preserved in the Municipal Collections of Rome: The Sculptures of the Palazzo dei Conservatori*. Oxford.

Sutherland, C. H. V. (1967). *The Roman Imperial Coinage, VI: From Diocletian's Reform (A.D. 294) to the Death of Maximinus (A.D. 313)*. London.

Syme, R. (1939). *The Roman Revolution*. Oxford.

Tabbernee, W. (1997). "Eusebius' 'Theology of Persecution': As Seen in the Various Editions of His Church History." *Journal of Early Christian Studies* 5:319–34.

Thiel, A., ed. (1868). *Epistolae Romanorum pontificum genuinae et quae ad eos scriptae sunt a S. Hilaro usque ad Pelagium II*, Vol. 1. Braunsberg.

Thomas, R. (1992). *Literacy and Orality in Ancient Greece*. Key Themes in Ancient History. Cambridge.

Toebelmann, F. (1915). *Der Bogen von Malborghetto*. Abhandlungen der Heidelberger Akademie der Wissenschaften, Stiftung Heinrich Lanz, Philosophisch-historische Klasse 2. Heidelberg.

Tomlin, R. (2006). "The Owners of the Beaurains (Arras) Treasure." In *Constantine the Great: York's Roman Emperor*, ed. E. Hartley, J. Hawkes, and M. Henig, with F. Mee, pp. 59–64. York.

Trombley, F. R., and J. W. Watt, tr. (2000). *The Chronicle of Pseudo-Joshua the Stylite*. TTH 32. Liverpool.

Trout, D. E. (2003). "Damasus and the Invention of Early Christian Rome." *Journal of Medieval and Early Modern Studies* 33:517–36. Reprinted in *The Cultural Turn in Late Ancient Studies: Gender, Asceticism, and Historiography*, ed. D. B. Martin and P. C. Miller, pp. 298–315. Durham, N.C., 2005.

Tsitsiou-Chelidoni, C. (2009). "History beyond Literature: Interpreting the 'Internally Focalized' Narrative in Livy's *Ab urbe condita*." In *Narratology and Interpretation: The Content of Narrative Form in Ancient Literature*, ed. J. Grethlein and A. Rengakos, pp. 527–54. Trends in Classics – Supplementary Volumes 4. Berlin.

Van Dam, R. (1982). "Hagiography and History: The Life of Gregory Thaumaturgus." *Classical Antiquity* 1:272–308.

———. (1988). "Images of Saint Martin in Late Roman and Early Merovingian Gaul." *Viator* 19:1–27.

———. (2002). *Kingdom of Snow: Roman Rule and Greek Culture in Cappadocia*. Philadelphia.

———. (2003a). *Families and Friends in Late Roman Cappadocia*. Philadelphia.

———. (2003b). *Becoming Christian: The Conversion of Roman Cappadocia*. Philadelphia.

———. (2003c). "The Many Conversions of the Emperor Constantine." In *Conversion in Late Antiquity and the Early Middle Ages: Seeing and Believing*, ed. K. Mills and A. Grafton, pp. 127–51. Rochester, N.Y.

———. (2007). *The Roman Revolution of Constantine*. Cambridge.

———. (2008). "Imagining an Eastern Roman Empire: A Riot at Antioch in 387 C.E." In *The Sculptural Environment of the Roman Near East: Reflections on Culture, Ideology, and Power*, ed. Y. Z. Eliav, E. A. Friedland, and S. Herbert, pp. 451–81. Interdisciplinary Studies in Ancient Culture and Religion 9. Leiden.

———. (2010). *Rome and Constantinople: Rewriting Roman History during Late Antiquity*. Edmondson Historical Lectures 30. Waco, Tex.

Van Nuffelen, P. (2004). *Un héritage de paix et de piété: Étude sur les Histoires ecclésiastiques de Socrate et de Sozomène*. Orientalia Lovaniensia Analecta 142. Leuven.

Verduchi, P. (1995). "Equus: Constantinus." In *Lexicon Topographicum Urbis Romae*, Vol. 2, ed. E. M. Steinby, pp. 226–27. Rome.

Vitiello, M. (2004). "Teoderico a Roma: politica, amministrazione e propaganda nell'*adventus* dell'anno 500 (Considerazioni sull'*Anonimo Valesiano II*')." *Historia* 53:73–120.

———. (2005). *Momenti di Roma ostrogota: adventus, feste, politica*. Historia, Einzelschriften 188 (2005).

Vollmer, F. and H. Rubenbauer (1926). "Ein verschollenes Grabgedicht aus Trier." *Trierer Zeitschrift* 1:26–30.

Weiss, P. (2003). "The Vision of Constantine," tr. A. R. Birley. *Journal of Roman Archaeology* 16:237–59. Revised version of "Die Vision Constantins." In *Colloquium aus Anlaß des 80. Geburtstages von Alfred Heuß*, ed. J. Bleicken, pp. 143–69. Frankfurter althistorische Studien 13. Kallmünz, 1993.

Whitby, Mi. (1994). "Images for Emperors in Late Antiquity: A Search for New Constantine." In *New Constantines: The Rhythm of Imperial Renewal in Byzantium, 4th–13th Centuries. Papers from the Twenty-Sixth Spring Symposium of Byzantine Studies, St Andrews, March 1992*, ed. P. Magdalino, pp. 83–93. Society for the Promotion of Byzantine Studies, Publications 2. Aldershot.

———, tr. (2000). *The Ecclesiastical History of Evagrius Scholasticus*. TTH 33. Liverpool.

Whitehead, A. (2009). *Memory*. The New Critical Idiom. London.

Whittaker, C. R. (1994). *Frontiers of the Roman Empire: A Social and Economic Study*. Baltimore.

Wiemer, H.-U. (1994a). "Libanius on Constantine." *Classical Quarterly* 44:511–24.

————. (1994b). "Libanios und Zosimos über den Rom-Besuch Konstantins I. im Jahre 326." *Historia* 43:469–94.

Williams, M. S. (2008). *Authorised Lives in Early Christian Biography between Eusebius and Augustine*. Cambridge Classical Studies. Cambridge.

Wilson, A. (1998). "Biographical Models: The Constantinian Period and Beyond." In *Constantine: History, Hagiography and Legend*, ed. S. N. C. Lieu and D. Montserrat, pp. 107–35. London.

Winkelmann, F., ed. (1991). *Eusebius Werke 1.1: Über das Leben des Kaisers Konstantin*, 2nd ed. GCS. Berlin.

————. (2004). "Eduard Schwartz, Eusebius Werke: Die Kirchengeschichte (GCS IX/1–3, Leipzig 1903–1909). Eine vorbildliche Edition." *Zeitschrift für antikes Christentum* 8:59–78.

Wlosok, A. (1989). "L. Caecilius Firmianus Lactantius." In *Restauration und Erneuerung: Die lateinische Literatur von 284 bis 374 n. Chr.*, ed. R. Herzog, pp. 375–404. Handbuch der Altertumswissenschaft, Abteilung 8: Handbuch der lateinischen Literatur der Antike 5. Munich.

Woods, D. (2004). "The Constantinian Origin of Justina (Themistius, *Or.* 3.43b)." *Classical Quarterly* 54:325–27.

Woolf, G. (2003). "Seeing Apollo in Roman Gaul and Germany." In *Roman Imperialism and Provincial Art*, ed. S. Scott and J. Webster, pp. 139–52. Cambridge.

Wortley, J. (2009). "The 'Sacred Remains' of Constantine and Helena." In J. Wortley, *Studies on the Cult of Relics in Byzantium up to 1204*, Chapter 5. Farnham. Reprinted from *Byzantine Narrative: Papers in Honour of Roger Scott*, ed. J. Burke, pp. 351–67. Byzantina Australiensia 16. Melbourne, 2006.

Zachos, K. L. (2003). "The *Tropaeum* of the Sea-Battle of Actium at Nikopolis: Interim Report." *Journal of Roman Archaeology* 16:64–92.

Zanker, P. (1988). *The Power of Images in the Age of Augustus*, tr. A. Shapiro. Jerome Lectures 16. Ann Arbor, Mich.

INDEX

✿ ✿ ✿